S0-DGG-214

Microsoft Word for Windows 95 Made Easy
The Basics and Beyond!

Alan R. Neibauer

Osborne **McGraw-Hill**

Berkeley New York St. Louis San Francisco
Auckland Bogotá Hamburg London Madrid
Mexico City Milan Montreal New Delhi
Panama City Paris São Paulo Singapore
Sydney Tokyo Toronto

Osborne **McGraw-Hill**
2600 Tenth Street
Berkeley, California 94710
U.S.A.

For information on translations or book distributors outside the U.S.A., or to arrange bulk purchase discounts for sales promotions, premiums, or fundraisers, please contact Osborne **McGraw-Hill** at the above address.

Microsoft Word for Windows 95 Made Easy
The Basics and Beyond!

1234567890 DOC 998765

Publisher	**Indexer**
Lawrence Levitsky	David Heiret
Acquisitions Editor	**Computer Designer**
Joanne Cuthbertson	Jani Beckwith
Project Editor	**Designer**
Nancy McLaughlin	Roberta Steele
Copy Editor	**Illustrator**
Judith Brown	Rhys Elliot
Proofreader	**Quality Control Specialist**
Stefany Otis	Joe Scuderi

ISBN 0-07-882152-5

Microsoft Word for Windows 95 Made Easy

The Basics and Beyond!

About the Author...

Alan R. Neibauer has been writing popular books on word processing since 1985. He has published over 20 books on computer hardware and software. A graduate of the Wharton School, University of Pennsylvania, Neibauer has spent 12 years teaching computer science at the high school, college, and corporate levels.

Contents
at a Glance

Contents

Acknowledgments

Completing a book like this—on a major upgrade to a program that also requires a new operating system—takes teamwork. I'd like to thank the Osborne McGraw-Hill staff, especially Scott Rogers, Joanne Cuthbertson, Nancy McLaughlin, Heidi Poulin, and Kelly Vogel. Osborne's Production department merits special recognition as well, for their elegant arrangement of the text and art in this book.

I'd also like to thank the Microsoft Beta support team—particularly Sloan Crayton, Susan Fetter, and Garrison McCully—for their much appreciated help on the CompuServe forum.

Finally, thanks to Barbara, my bride of almost 30 years, for putting up with the long and irregular hours, the regular frustrations, and the unpredictable moods of a writer.

Introduction

Prepare to be impressed with Word for Windows 95. If you are new to Word, or to word processing in general, you'll be amazed at the power and versatility of Word, but quite pleased at how easy it is to learn and to use. If you are familiar with previous versions of Word, or with other word processing programs, then you also have a few treats waiting.

Don't like waiting to spell check until your entire document is complete? Word now checks your spelling as you type. Don't like searching through a dialog box to insert a special symbol or draw a line across the page? Word now does these for you as well. In fact, Word is designed to give you word processing power that is not only easy to use, but that can be performed automatically—yet you are still in complete control, and can turn on and off every automatic feature to suit your own tastes and work habits.

This book is a perfect companion to Word. It shows you how to use all the power of Word, but easily and quickly, without wasting your time. Your word processing skills are developed in a logical order from the very first chapter, which shows you how to create, save, and print your first Word document. As your skills increase, you'll learn more advanced features of this remarkable program. Once you've learned the basics, however, you can skip ahead to more advanced chapters and learn how to perform the specific tasks you need. If you are already familiar with Word, then this book will perfect your upgrade to the new version and its special features.

What's New!

Word for Windows 95, version 7, has some powerful and impressive improvements over previous editions. If you are familiar with another version of Word, however, you will still feel at home with this new release. Here's a summary of some of the new features:

◆ A *highlighter* tool that lets you highlight text in color on the screen.

◆ *Find All Word Forms* lets you locate and replace all forms of a root word.

◆ The *Address Book* stores names and addresses that you can quickly access to add to documents, e-mail messages, and form letters.

◆ *Automatic Spelling Check* now checks your spelling as you type, marking unknown words and letting you correct them using a convenient shortcut menu.

◆ AutoFormat As You Type formats your text, and inserts symbols and borders while you are typing.

◆ The *Answer Wizard,* which lets you request help by typing a question, such as "How do I create a table?"

There are also new features inherited from the Windows 95 operating system, such as:

◆ Send *e-mail* directly from Word, even add routine slips.

◆ Enhanced *Open* and *New* dialog boxes.

◆ New *Help system* dialog boxes and options.

How This Book Is Organized

This book is divided into five parts so you can learn even the most sophisticated features of Word gradually, but completely. In the five chapters in Part 1, you'll learn all about Word's basic features—how to enter commands as well as how to type, edit, print, and save documents.

In Chapter 1, you will learn how to interact with Word using toolbars, menus, dialog boxes, and the Help system. These features are the basic building blocks of all Windows 95 applications. You will also learn how to type and insert text and how to save and print documents, and you'll find out about the new Automatic Spelling Check that checks your spelling as you type! In Chapter 2, you will learn how to open existing documents and how to start a new one when you're already working in Word. Here you will learn the basics of editing—scroll through documents, selecting text, undoing mistakes, and changing the way Word displays documents on the screen. Editing is the entire focus of Chapter 3. In this chapter you'll discover how to move and copy text, and how to have Word insert text for you using special features call AutoText, AutoCorrect, and AutoFormat As You Type, a new feature in Word for Windows 95. Searching for and replacing text automatically is covered in Chapter 4, while Chapter 5 concentrates on using windows to edit more than one document at a time.

Part 2 of the book is all about formatting—making your documents easy and fun to read. In Chapter 6 you'll learn how to format characters, in Chapter 7 how to format lines and paragraphs, and in Chapter 8 how to format pages and sections of your documents. Then Chapter 9 will show you how to enhance the appearance of pages using headers and footers, page numbers, lines and boxes, and how to format an entire document with a click of the mouse using AutoFormat.

You move beyond the basics in the six chapters of Part 3. Chapter 10 shows you how to proof your documents with the spelling checker, the thesaurus, and the grammar checker. In Chapter 11 you'll learn how to easily create completely formatted documents using Word's templates and Wizards, and how to create your own templates to streamline your work. Chapter 12 is all about styles, a very powerful Word feature for formatting your documents easily and consistently. In Chapter 13 you'll learn how to type bulleted and numbered lists, and how to create eye-catching tables—even including formulas for spreadsheet-like capabilities.

Chapter 14 shows you how to use pictures and other graphics in your documents. For example, you'll learn how to use clip art, how to create special effects with WordArt, how to draw your own pictures right on the screen, and how to create charts and graphs. You'll then learn about desktop publishing in Chapter 15—including how to use columns, drop caps, scientific equations, and captions.

Creating special documents is covered in Part 4. In Chapter 16, for example, you'll learn how to create form letters, envelopes, labels, and catalogs. Chapter 17 shows you how to create a table of contents, a table of figures, a table of authorities, and an index for those really long documents. You'll learn how to create footnotes, endnotes, and annotations in Chapter 18, and even record a voice annotation that you can listen to while reading your document. In Chapter 19 you'll learn how to work with outlines and master documents, and in Chapter 20 you'll find out how to share information between applications—using Excel worksheets in Word tables, for example, and using Access databases in tables or for merging form letters.

Part V summarizes special Word features. In Chapter 21, for instance, you'll learn how to personalize the way Word looks and works to suit your own tastes and habits. Chapter 22 concentrates on helping you manage your documents so that you can find them on your disk and find out about them.

In Chapter 23 you'll learn about fields, forms, cross-references, bookmarks, and revisions. And in Chapter 24 you'll learn how to create time saving macros and how to customize the keyboard, menus, and toolbars.

Special Features

Throughout this book we've added special features to make learning Word easier. Look for these elements:

Note: Look here for a little extra information about the subject covered in the text.

Tip: Here you'll generally find a special or faster way to perform the Word task being discussed.

Remember: These are points you'll want to keep in mind as you work with the program.

Caution: These tell when you need to be extra careful.

Upgrader: Look here for information on how Word for Windows 95 differs from previous versions.

Conventions Used in This Book

We've done all we can to make it easy to learn about Word. Just read the text, following the step-by-step instructions and explanations given, and looking at the figures and illustrations. In a few instances, you'll see a numbered list of steps to follow—perform them exactly as shown to complete the task. Text that you should actually type will appear in boldface, like this: Type **Word makes it easy**. The names of menu commands and dialog box options will be shown capitalized, most often as they appear on the screen, as in the instruction to "Select Print from the File menu." (This means to pull down the File menu in the menu bar and then click on the Print option. You'll learn all about working with menus and dialog boxes in Chapter 1.)

Keystrokes that you press to perform a task are shown in small capital letters, such as ALT, CTRL, and F1. When you have to press several keys at the same time, they are shown separated with hyphens, as in CTRL-F9, which means that you should hold down the CTRL key, press and release F9, and then release CTRL.

In some instances you will be shown several ways to perform the same task. There may be instructions showing how to perform a task using the mouse and the toolbar, for example, followed by separate instructions for using the menu bar, a dialog box, or a combination of keys. Read all of the instructions and then perform the task in the way you feel is best or most convenient.

PART 1

Word Fundamentals

Getting Started with Word

1

Word for Windows is a powerful program but one that is remarkably easy and even fun to use. As you will soon discover, in Word you'll be able to create professional-looking documents with ease. If you have previously used any version of this extraordinary program, you'll be up and running with Word 7 in no time, and you can just scan through the first chapters. But don't worry if you are a new user, or even if this is your first foray into word processing in general. Once you learn how Word operates, you'll be word processing with the best of us!

Starting Word

Starting Word for Windows is as easy as pointing and clicking the mouse. Turn on your computer and monitor, and then wait until the Windows 95 desktop appears. The Welcome to Windows dialog box may appear, showing a useful tip or shortcut. Read the tip and then click on Close to clear it from the screen. Now click on the Start button at the lower-left corner of the taskbar to see a menu of options, as shown in Figure 1-1.

Tip: If you have not yet installed Word for Windows, see Appendix A.

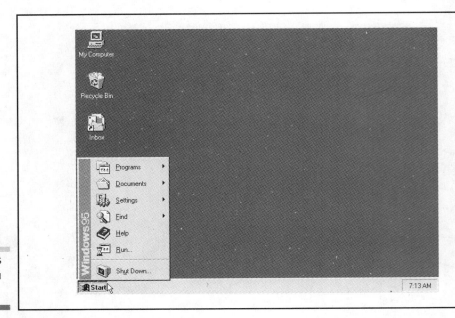

The Windows 95 Start menu
Figure 1-1.

Point to the Programs option at the top of the list. A menu will appear
listing programs, groups of programs, and some Windows 95 functions.
There should be an item with the Word icon and the name Microsoft Word,
as you can see.

Upgrader: With Windows 95, you only have to point at the items in
the Start list; you do not have to click. When you point to an item, Windows
automatically expands it to display the next level of options. If you have
been using earlier versions of Windows in which you've had to click or
double-click to open a group window, this new development may take some
time to get used to. At first, you may even find it annoying that Windows
expands items as you pass the mouse over them. However, after you use
Windows 95 for a little while, you'll probably be happy that it saves your
clicking finger some work.

Click on Microsoft Word to start the program. You must click on the
program name to execute it, but there is no need to double-click. You should
now be looking at the Word for Windows screen, shown in Figure 1-2. If a
window first appears describing new Word features, click on its Close
button, which is the tiny box containing an X located in the upper-right
corner of the window.

Note: If there is no item for Microsoft Word in the Programs list, then
look for a folder called Microsoft Office or Office95. Point to it to display its
contents, and then click on Microsoft Word. If you cannot find Word, the
program has not yet been installed on your computer. In some cases, you
might see two programs called Microsoft Word. One icon may represent an
older version of Word left over from your Windows 3.1 installation. In
Chapter 22, you will learn how to locate programs and documents using the
Find command, a new feature of Windows 95.

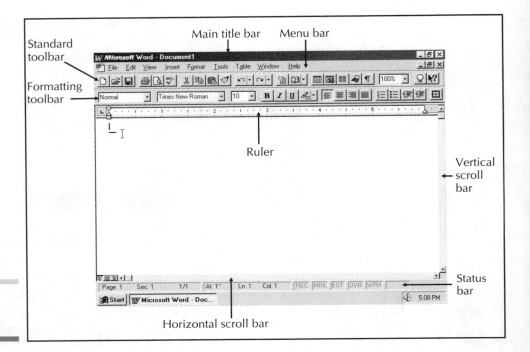

Standard toolbar

Formatting toolbar

Main title bar   Menu bar

Ruler

Vertical scroll bar

Status bar

Horizontal scroll bar

The Word screen
Figure 1-2.

Understanding the Word Window

Before going any further, take a moment to examine the Word for Windows screen. At the very top of the screen is the main *title bar*. On the left side of the title bar is the program *control menu* icon. The stylized letter *W* indicates that this menu controls the entire Word program. For example, you can use it to exit Word or to change the size and position of the Word screen.

Next to the control menu icon is the name of the program, followed by the name of the document. When you first start Word, it opens a new, blank window called Document1. When you write and save a document, the label Document1 will be replaced by the document name you assign. If you start a new blank document, Word will label it Document2 until you assign it a new title.

On the right side of the title bar are three buttons. From left to right, they are the Minimize button, the Restore button, and the Close button.

Thanks

Thanks

1

 The *Minimize button* reduces Word to an icon on the taskbar.

 The *Restore button* changes Word into a window. When Word does not fill the entire screen, this button becomes the Maximize button (explained shortly). Clicking on it will enlarge Word to fill the screen.

 The *Close button* closes Word.

 Upgrader: Old habits die hard. I can't tell you the number of times I've closed a window while thinking I was maximizing or restoring it. In Windows 95, the Close button is located where Windows 3.1 placed the Restore and Maximize buttons. Don't worry—you'll get used to the new arrangement in no time. But as you are learning Windows 95, make sure you click on the proper button, or you'll find yourself restarting applications time and again.

 Below the title bar is the *menu bar*. On the left-hand side of the menu bar is the *document* control menu icon. Notice that this icon consists of a stylized letter *W* over a picture of a document, which indicates that it controls the document window. You can use the document control menu to close a document, for instance, but not to exit Word itself.

You use the other commands on the menu bar to access the powers of Word, as you will soon learn. On the right of the menu bar are another set of Minimize, Restore, and Close buttons.

Why two control menus and two seemingly identical sets of buttons on the right? The two sets of buttons indicate that you are actually looking at two windows—the Word window and the document window. The Word window contains the entire Word program. Everything you see in this window has to do with Word. Part of the Word window, however, is the document window. This window contains the document that you are working on and some other objects, such as the ruler, that relate just to that document.

The buttons on the right of the menu bar control only the document window, not the Word program window. Clicking on the Minimize button shrinks your document to a small title bar, as shown here.

Clicking the Restore button returns the document window to its previous size and position. Clicking the Close button closes only the document, not Word itself. To exit Word, you would click on the close box on the title bar. The best way to understand this is to restore the document window. Do that now by clicking on the menu bar's Restore button.

Now look at your window, which should resemble Figure 1-3. The document window is a separate window with its own title bar, showing the name of the document. It is restored, in that it no longer fills the space available in the Word window. The document title bar now contains the document control menu and the Minimize, Maximize, and Close buttons, which makes it more obvious that these elements control only the document window.

 Click on the *Maximize button* that now appears on the document title bar. The document window maximizes—it enlarges to fill all of the available space in the Word program window.

 Note: Why all this time devoted to windows? Word achieves much of its power and flexibility through its ability to have more than one document open and displayed at the same time. You can have several documents open in their own windows, for example, to move or copy text among them. You'll learn more about this powerful feature in Chapter 5.

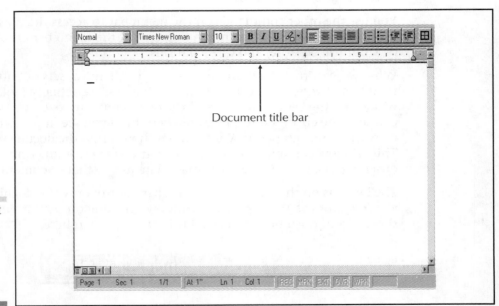

Document title bar

The document window, now restored to standard window size

Figure 1-3.

Below the menu bar are two toolbars and a ruler. When you first start Word, you'll see the Standard toolbar and below it the Formatting toolbar. You use the toolbars to give commands to Word, bypassing menus and dialog boxes.

Under the Formatting toolbar is the ruler. You use the ruler to change indentations, set tabs, and otherwise format lines and paragraphs. You will learn about the toolbars later in this chapter, and about the ruler in Chapter 7.

Under the ruler is the area where your document appears as you type. Think of the typing area as a sheet of paper inserted into the typewriter. You will see three objects in this area—the insertion point, the endmark, and the mouse pointer.

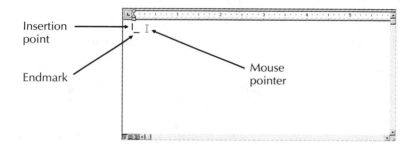

Insertion point

Endmark

Mouse pointer

♦ The blinking vertical line is the *insertion point*. This indicates where the next character typed will appear. As you type, the insertion point will always move to indicate the position of the next character.

♦ The small horizontal line is the endmark. The *endmark* indicates the end of your document, and it moves down as you insert text and up as you delete text.

♦ The *mouse pointer* indicates the position of the mouse. The shape of the pointer depends on its location. When the pointer is in the typing area, it appears as a large letter *I*. This is sometimes called the *text select point* or the *I-beam*.

At the bottom of the screen are the horizontal scroll bar and the status bar. There is also a vertical scroll bar along the right edge of the screen. You use the *scroll bars* to bring text into view that does not fit on the window.

The *status bar* gives you information about your document, the location of the insertion point, and the status of the Word program. The first section tells you about the page you are viewing.

♦ *Page* shows you the number of the page displayed on the screen.

♦ *Sec* reports the section of the document displayed. Sections let you have more than one page size, margin, or other format in the same document, such as a letter and its envelope.

♦ *1/1* indicates the number of the current page (the first number) and the total number of pages in the document.

The next section of the status bar tells you about the location of the insertion point.

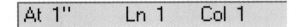

♦ *At* reports the distance from the current line to the top of the page.

♦ *Ln* is the line number where the insertion point is located, counting from the top of the page, not the start of the document.

♦ *Col* shows the character position from the left margin.

Next on the status bar, you'll see the mode display. Dimmed characters—those appearing gray rather than black—indicate that a mode is currently turned off. When you turn on a mode, its characters become darker.

♦ *REC* reports that the record macro function is on or off.

♦ *MRK* reports that the revision markings function is on or off.

♦ *EXT* indicates whether text selection is on or off.

♦ *OVR* shows whether Overtype mode is on or off.

♦ *WPH* indicates whether WordPerfect help is on or off.

To turn a mode on or off, double-click on the characters in the status bar. Double-clicking on REC, MRK, or WPH displays a dialog box. Double-clicking on EXT or OVR simply turns on or turns off the function.

At the very bottom of the screen is the Windows 95 *taskbar*. This is not part of the Word window, but it is a feature on the Windows desktop. You'll see the Start button, then the name of any open applications, followed by the current time.

Typing in Word

Typing in Word for Windows is not unlike typing with a typewriter. To get an uppercase letter, you hold down the SHIFT key and press the letter. To indent the start of a paragraph, or to create columns of numbers, you press the TAB key.

That is where the similarities end and the real fun of word processing begins. With Word, for example, you type until you reach the end of the paragraph, not just the end of the line. Instead of pressing the ENTER key at the right margin, Word does it for you. Word will even check your spelling as you type! Try Word now by typing the following sentence without pressing ENTER when the insertion point reaches the right margin: **Sliding Billy Watson was a vaudeville star and producer who gave W. C. Fields his first job and who started Fanny Brice in her career.**

Word senses when the word you are typing will not fit in the line, and it moves the word to the next line automatically, as shown here:

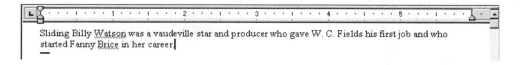

As you type, the insertion point moves over until it gets to the right margin, and then it moves down to the next line. With each new line, the Ln indicator in the status line changes.

But what are those wavy lines under the words "Watson" and "Brice"? As you started to type, you should have seen the icon shown here appear on the righthand side of the status bar.

The icon means that Word is checking your spelling as you type, and the wavy lines mean that those words were not in the dictionary. Proper names, and many technical terms, won't be in Word's dictionary, even though they

For clarity, most figures in this book will not show the lines that Word displays under words that aren't found in the dictionary.

are spelled correctly. Since these two words are correct, you can just ignore the wavy lines for now. If you do type a word that is spelled incorrectly, you can press BACKSPACE to delete it, and then type the word correctly.

Now press ENTER to end the paragraph and to move the insertion point down to the next line. You should press ENTER only to end a paragraph or to insert a blank line between paragraphs. Not only will this save you time, but it also allows you to easily change the appearance of entire paragraphs with just a click of the mouse. If you were to press ENTER at the end of each line, Word would consider each line a separate paragraph!

What about mistakes? If you make a mistake as you type, press the BACKSPACE key. Each time you press the BACKSPACE key, Word deletes one character to the left of the insertion point. You can also delete characters by pressing the DELETE key. Each time you press DELETE, Word deletes one character to the right of the insertion point.

Now press ENTER one more time to insert a blank line after the paragraph, and then type **Sliding Billy gained his name from his trademark slide across the stage, a precursor to Michael Jackson's Moon Walk.** Press ENTER when you are done typing.

Not only will Word move to the next line as you type, you don't have to worry when you reach the bottom of the screen or the end of the page. As you pass the last line on the screen, the lines at the top *scroll* up out of view into the computer's memory. You can use the scroll bars to bring text back into view, as explained in Chapter 2.

When you reach the end of a page, just keep on typing. Word will automatically start a new page. A dotted line will appear across the screen, and the Page indicator in the status bar increases by one. You will learn how to end pages when you want them to end in Chapter 3.

Tip: If you can't wait until Chapter 3, you can end a page manually by pressing CTRL-ENTER.

Inserting Text

The insertion point indicates where the next character you type will appear. So by moving the insertion point, you can insert characters within text already on the screen. To move the insertion point, place the mouse pointer where you want the insertion point to appear and click the left mouse button. The blinking insertion point will appear where you clicked. You cannot place the insertion point below the endmark or in the margins.

Note: It is important to remember that you must click the mouse after placing the pointer where you want to insert text. I frequently see beginning users make the mistake of pointing with the mouse and then typing. They are surprised that their text does not appear where the mouse is pointing. Clicking the mouse actually positions the insertion point.

Before trying to insert text, however, look at the status bar at the bottom of the screen. You should see that the OVR appears dimmed, as shown here.

The dimmed characters indicate that you are in *Insert mode*. As you type, characters to the right of the insertion point shift over, and even down to the next line if necessary, to make room. If you press the INS key on your keyboard, the letters *OVR* in the status bar will appear bold. This means that you are now in *Overtype mode*. Now characters that you type will replace those already on the screen, instead of pushing them to the right.

Tip: If you move the insertion point somewhere in existing text, take a quick look at the status bar to ensure you are in the correct mode. If you are in Overtype mode when you do not want to be, you'll be deleting characters as you type new ones!

Make certain that the letters *OVR* are dimmed. If they are bold, press the INS key. Now, place the mouse pointer just before the letter *M* in *Moon Walk* in the second paragraph, like this:

> Sliding Billy gained his name from his trademark slide across the stage, a precursor to Michael Jackson's
> Moon Walk.

When you have the point in that location, click the left mouse button to position the insertion point:

> Sliding Billy gained his name from his trademark slide across the stage, a precursor to Michael Jackson's Moon Walk.

Type **now famous**, and then press the SPACEBAR. Word inserts your new words into the paragraph, shifting the text over to the right and down as necessary:

> Sliding Billy gained his name from his trademark slide across the stage, a precursor to Michael Jackson's now famous Moon Walk.

Now, move the mouse so the pointer is in front of the first sentence. Click the left mouse button to place the insertion point at that position, and then press the TAB key. Word inserts the tab into the paragraph. In the same way, insert a tab in front of the second paragraph. Your document should look like this:

> Sliding Billy Watson was a vaudeville star and producer who gave W. C. Fields his first job and who started Fanny Brice in her career.
>
> Sliding Billy gained his name from his trademark slide across the stage, a precursor to Michael Jackson's now famous Moon Walk.

You can also move the insertion point with the arrow keys on the keyboard. Pressing the RIGHT, LEFT, UP, or DOWN ARROW moves the insertion point in that direction. Your keyboard may have two sets of arrow keys—one set on the numeric keypad and another set to the keypad's left. The functions of the *keypad* keys are controlled by the NUM LOCK key. When the Num Lock function is turned on, you'll probably see a light on your computer marked Num Lock. In some cases, there might be a light in the NUM LOCK key itself.

When Num Lock is on—when the light is lit—pressing an arrow on the keypad will insert numbers at the position of the insertion point. Pressing the UP ARROW will insert 8, the RIGHT ARROW will insert 6, the DOWN ARROW will insert 2, and the LEFT ARROW will insert 4—as indicated on the keycap. To use these arrow keys for moving the insertion point, press NUM LOCK to turn off the light.

Note: The NUM LOCK key does not affect the other set of arrows on the keyboard. These always move the cursor no matter how Num Lock is set.

Giving Commands to Word

Typing in Word, and using all of its powerful features, is really very easy. Word makes it effortless by providing you with a number of ways to give commands and to select options.

If you are at all familiar with any version of Windows, or with any Windows application, you already know the basics of working with Word. But don't worry if you are a new Windows user, you'll feel right at home in no time.

Using the Menu Bar

To start learning how to work with Word, look at the menu bar near the top of the screen.

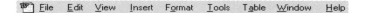

To select a menu bar option, you click on it with the mouse or hold down the ALT key and press the underlined letter of the menu item, such as ALT-F to select the File menu or ALT-A for the Table menu.

Caution: The underlined letter is not always the first character in the word.

When you select an item on the menu bar, Word displays a drop-down menu. A *drop-down menu* lists the operations that you can perform. For example, selecting File from the menu bar displays the drop-down menu shown in Figure 1-4.

If you want to display another menu instead of the one pulled down, just point to the other menu bar option with the mouse, or press the RIGHT ARROW or LEFT ARROW key.

Upgrader: Once a drop-down menu is displayed, you can drop down another by just dragging over a menu item with the mouse. You do not have to click on the other menu item.

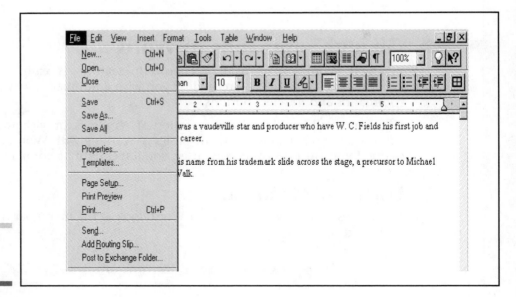

A drop-down
menu
Figure 1-4.

To select a command from the drop-down menu option, use any of
these techniques:

♦ Click on the option with the mouse.

♦ Press the underlined letter of the option.

♦ Press the UP ARROW or DOWN ARROW key to highlight the option and then
press ENTER.

To cancel a menu, click elsewhere on the window or press the ESC key.

Word's drop-down menus contain several types of commands. A dimmed
item on a menu cannot be selected—you must activate it by first performing
some other function. Some items are shown listed with an alternate shortcut
key, such as CTRL-N next to the New option. This means that you can
perform that same command by pressing CTRL-N without pulling down the
menu. An ellipsis (...) next to an item means that selecting it will display a
dialog box containing additional choices. A check mark indicates that the
option is turned on or selected.

*The alternate
shortcut keys
will not wor if
the drop-down
menu is
displayed*

Using Toolbars

To make it even easier to use Word, many functions that you perform using
menus have also been assigned to the toolbars. To use a toolbar, simply click
on the button for the task you want to perform. The picture on the button
indicates its function. So clicking the button with the picture of a printer, for

example, will print your document. Clicking on the button with an open folder will open a document.

Note: Word automatically displays a specialized toolbar when you perform some functions, such as drawing and outlining.

1

Don't worry, though, if some of the pictures are not self-explanatory. When you point to a button with the mouse, Word displays the *ToolTip*—a small box with the button's name, as shown here.

Word will also display a brief description of the button's function in the status bar:

Prints the active document using the current defaults

So if you are not sure what a button does, point to it with the mouse and read the ToolTip status bar description before you click.

Some objects in the toolbars contain text boxes with drop-down lists. A *text box* is where you type a choice or setting that you want to apply to your text. A *drop-down list* is indicated by a down-pointing arrow above a horizontal line. The list contains choices that you can select to insert into the box. Click on the down arrow to display the choices, as illustrated here.

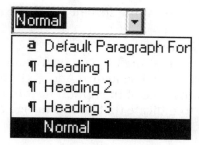

You have two ways to enter your desired choice into the text box:

♦   Click on the arrow to display the list box and make your selection from suggested options. When the list appears, select an item by clicking on it with the mouse or by highlighting it with the UP or DOWN keys. If a list box is not large enough to display all of the options, it will have a scroll bar on the right. You use the scroll bars to display additional choices. You'll learn how to use scroll bars in Chapter 2.

♦ Click in the box with the mouse, type the setting you want, and then press ENTER. For example, the Formatting toolbar has a list box for changing the size of your characters. The list has the most common sizes, but it does not list all of the sizes that are available. To select one of the sizes not listed, you have to type it in the text box.

Working with Dialog Boxes

Word displays a warning message if you type a setting into a text box that it cannot apply to the

Selecting some menu items and toolbar tools will display a dialog box. A *dialog box* contains one or more options you can choose from to tell Word how to perform the function.

Every dialog box has a title bar that gives the name of the box. Many Word dialog boxes look like a series of different pages. At the top of each page is a tab naming the category of options that the page contains. Clicking on a tab brings its page into the foreground. For example, in Figure 1-5 the Labels tab is selected, so the page containing options for creating labels is in the foreground. If you click on the Envelopes tab, options for creating envelopes will be displayed.

Click on the items that you want to select, or where you need to type your settings, or press TAB to move forward from item to item (or SHIFT-TAB to move backward). You can also move to an item by holding down the ALT key and pressing the underlined letter of the option you want to select.

Now let's look at the specific types of items that you'll find in dialog boxes.

Check Boxes

A *check box* is a small square next to an option. In Figure 1-5, there is a check box next to the Use Return Address option. When you click on the check box or the name of the option next to the box, Word places a check mark in the box to indicate that you've turned on the option.

Clicking on a box that already has a check mark will turn off the option, removing the check mark. With the keyboard, turn a check box off or on by pressing ALT and the underlined letter of

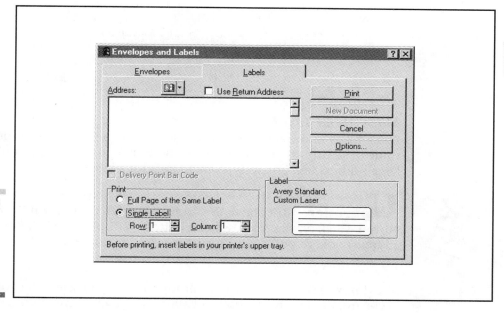

The Envelopes
and Labels
dialog box
contains
two pages
Figure 1-5.

the command. You can also move to the box with the TAB key and then press the SPACEBAR.

Sometimes, a number of check boxes are grouped together in one section of the dialog box. In most cases, the boxes within a group are nonexclusive. This means that you can turn on more than one box in the group at the same time. However, some combinations of boxes are exclusive; turning one on will turn another off. For example, you can only format characters as subscript or superscript, but not both. Clicking on the Subscript option will remove a check mark from the Superscript box:

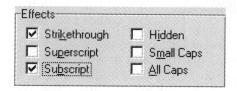

Option Buttons

An *option button* is a circle next to an option. Option buttons in a group are almost always exclusive—clicking on one button automatically turns off another in the group that is already selected. When you select an option button, Word places a small black circle inside of it. So in Figure 1-5, clicking on Full Page of the Same Label will turn off the Single Label option.

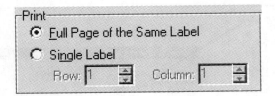

More About Text Boxes

You already know about text boxes. Move into a text box and then type the value or setting you want for that option. In Figure 1-5, you would use the large Address text box to type an address for a label.

Upgrader: Just above the Address box is a drop-down list next to a button. Click on the Address Book button to display the Windows Exchange address book, or pull down the list to select an address.

A text box may already contain information. If you select the box with the keyboard, the text in the box will automatically become highlighted and it will be erased when you start typing. If you click in a box to select it, however, the existing text will not become highlighted. You need to delete the existing text using the DELETE or BACKSPACE key. To select a box and highlight the text in one step, double-click on it.

Other dialog boxes contain text boxes with lists that are already displayed, such as the list shown here from the Font dialog box.

You do not have to click on an arrow to drop down this type of list. Notice that you can either type your setting in the text box or select it from the list. The scroll bar on the right of the list indicates that there are additional options that you can display.

In the lower-left corner of Figure 1-5, you can see two text boxes—Row and Column—with up and down arrows to the right. As with other text boxes, you can just enter your desired setting. You can also increase or decrease the setting in the box by clicking on the up or down arrow.

Preview Panels

Many Word dialog boxes affect the appearance of text or the format of pages. These boxes will include a *preview panel* that shows the effects of your selections, such as this panel from the Paragraph dialog box:

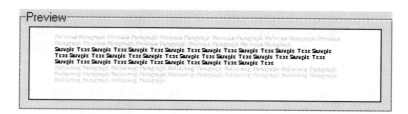

The graphic displayed in the panel will change as you select settings from the box. In Figure 1-5, the Label box is a preview panel. The description and graphic of the label will change after you choose settings by clicking on the Options button.

Command Buttons

Dialog boxes also contain command buttons. Clicking on a *command button* performs some action immediately. Most boxes have a command button labeled Cancel. Clicking on Cancel removes the dialog box from the screen and ignores any changes you made to the box. Clicking on OK or Close removes the box from the screen and accepts your changes to it, applying the settings to your document. With the keyboard, press ESC to choose Cancel. To choose other command buttons, move to the command button, then press ENTER.

Using Shortcut Menus

Word recognizes that when you are busy typing, you might not want to take the time to move the mouse all the way to the menu bar or toolbars. To save your hand the traveling distance, Word offers *shortcut menus*, which appear when you press the *right* mouse button. The options listed on shortcut menus depend on where you are pointing when you click the mouse button.

To look at a shortcut menu now, place the I-beam in the typing area and click the right mouse button. The shortcut menu that you see here will appear.

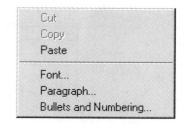

Point away from the menu and click the mouse to remove the menu from the screen. Now point anywhere in one of Word's toolbars and click the right mouse button. A different shortcut menu appears. Press the ESC key. This also clears a shortcut menu from the screen.

To select an option from a shortcut menu, point to it with the mouse and click the left mouse button.

To practice using a shortcut menu, let's correct the reported spelling errors indicated by the wavy lines. Point the mouse on the word "Watson" in the first sentence, and then click on the right mouse button. Word will display the shortcut menu you see here.

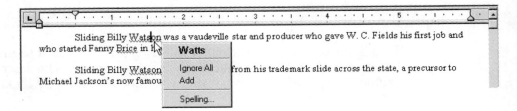

Word is suggesting that you may have meant to type "Watts" instead of "Watson". If you did make that mistake, just click on the word "Watts" to insert it in the text in place of "Watson". Since the word is indeed spelled correctly, click on Ignore All. This tells Word to assume that "Watson" is a correctly spelled word until you next exit Word for Windows. The wavy line is removed from "Watson" in both sentences.

 T ip: The Add command adds the word to the dictionary so it is no longer reported as misspelled. The Spelling command begins Word's interactive spelling checker. You'll learn more about these options in Chapter 10.

Now in the same way, remove the wavy line from the word "Brice". Point to the word and click the right mouse button to display a menu of choices:

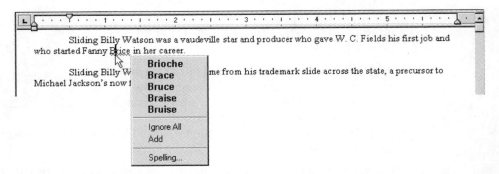

Notice that there are quite a few suggested spellings. Click on Ignore All, however, to accept the word as spelled correctly.

Getting Help from Word

No one, even a Word guru, can remember every Word feature and technique. That's why Word includes a comprehensive online help system. The help system contains information on every command, function, and technique that Word can perform. So if you need help, or forget exactly how something works, just ask Word for help.

Upgrader: Take some time to review this section on help even if you are familiar with earlier versions of Word. Help has been changed in Windows 95, with new dialog boxes, a hierarchical contents window, and new menu options for the help window .

To begin using help, click on Help in the menu bar to display the drop-down menu shown here.

Then click on Microsoft Word Help Topics to display the dialog box shown in Figure 1-6.

The four dialog box tabs offer you different ways to find information. The Contents tab displays a list of general topics. Next to each topic is an icon of a book. To find information,

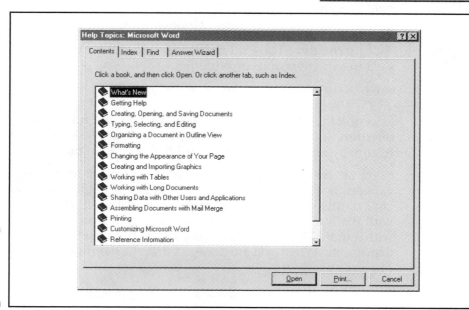

Word's Help Topics dialog box
Figure 1-6.

double-click on a topic to display subtopics, which may be additional books or icons representing specific information, as shown here.

Continue "opening books" until you see the information icon for the subject you want help on, and then double-click on the icon.

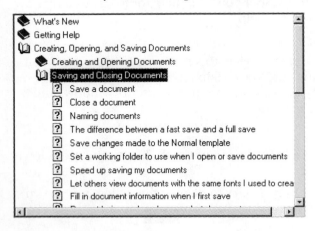

Clicking on the Index tab in the Help Topics window displays an alphabetical list of topics. Type the first several characters of the topic you want help with to scroll the list. Double-click on the exact topic to display the help window.

Selecting the Find tab in the Help Topics window lets you search all of Word's help screens for a specific word or phrase. The first time you select Find, Word may take several minutes as it creates a database of help words. It will then display the options that you see in Figure 1-7.

In the text box, type a word or phrase that describes the topic you need help on. As you type, Word will scroll the list of topics to display help words or phrases that match your entry. When you select an item from that list, Word displays in the second list box all of the help windows containing that word or phrase. Double-click on an item in the second list to display the help window.

Upgrader: The Find function works similarly to the Search feature used in earlier versions of Windows.

Selecting the Answer Wizard tab will let you find information by typing a question, such as "How do I change line spacing?". You can also access this feature by selecting Answer Wizard from the Help menu on the menu bar.

There are two types of help windows. One type, shown in Figure 1-8, explains how to perform a function. Read the help information and then click on the close box in the help window title bar (the box on the right with the X in it) to return to the document. A word or phrase underlined with a dotted line is called a *defined term*. Click on the term to display its definitions. When you are done reading the definition, click the mouse or press ESC.

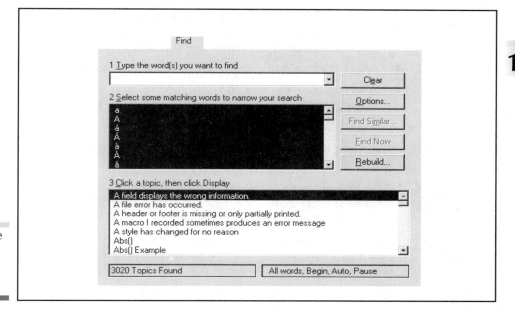

The Find page
in Word's
help system
Figure 1-7.

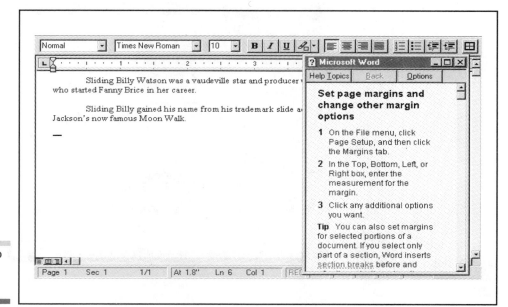

A typical help
window
Figure 1-8.

The help window contains a toolbar with three options:

You will learn about the clipboard in Chapter 3.

♦ Select *Help Topics* to return to the Contents window.

♦ Select *Back* to move to the previous help window in the sequence, if any.

♦ Select *Options* to print the help information, type an annotation, copy the information to the Clipboard, or change the way help windows are displayed.

Other help windows graphically illustrate a number of topics, as shown in Figure 1-9.

When you point to a topic in a graphical help window, the mouse pointer will appear as a small hand. Click on the term to display a window giving specific information about the topic.

If you do not like navigating through the help system, there is a faster way to get assistance. Use the F1 key or the Help button on the toolbar to get context-sensitive help.

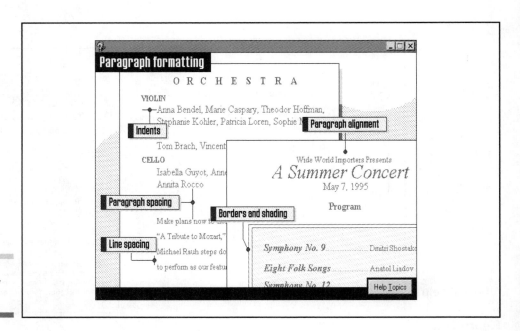

A graphical help window
Figure 1-9.

Context-sensitive help gives you information about the dialog box displayed at the time, or the toolbar or about the menu item that you select next. When you click the Help button on the toolbar, the mouse pointer changes to the shape that you see here.

Now click on the button or menu option you need help with. Word will display the specific help information. For example, to learn how any toolbar button works, click on the Help button and then click on the toolbar button. For help on a menu item, click on the Help button, drop down the menu, and then click on the item. With the keyboard, highlight a menu item or open a dialog box and then press F1.

Help for WordPerfect Users

If you are moving to Word from WordPerfect, choose WordPerfect Help from the Help menu or double-click on the dimmed letters *WPH* in the status bar. Figure 1-10 shows the Help for WordPerfect Users dialog box. To learn how to perform a familiar WordPerfect command in Word, click on it in the Command Keys list. A description of the Word equivalent will appear in the information panel to the right of the list. For more information about the command, click on the Help Text button. Click on Demo to see an animated sequence illustrating the function.

To customize the WordPerfect help system, click on Options to display the dialog box shown in Figure 1-11. Clicking on Help for WordPerfect Users in this dialog box will turn on the WordPerfect help function. With the function turned on, pressing a WordPerfect function key will explain how to

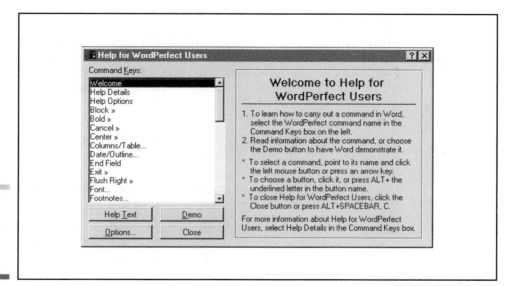

The help for WordPerfect Users dialog box

Figure 1-10.

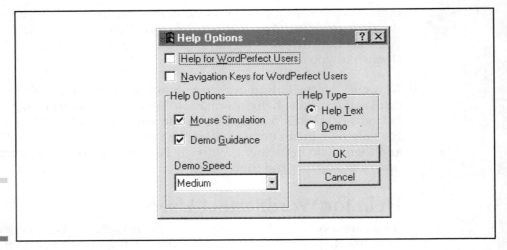

WordPerfect
Help Options
Figure 1-11.

perform the same task in Word. For example, if you press F8, the WordPerfect command to underline, a dialog box will appear explaining how to underline in Word. Choose from the other options in the dialog box to set up help the way you like it.

Finally, select About Microsoft Word from the Help drop-down menu to get information about your version of Word and details about your hardware and Windows environment. You can also find out how to get help directly from Microsoft.

Tip Wizard

Word's designers have tried to make the program as easy as possible to use. So you shouldn't be surprised that the help system can be interactive, responding to your actions automatically with handy tips or reminders. To turn on interactive help, click on the Tip Wizard button in the Standard toolbar. Word will display the Tip Wizard box just above the ruler:

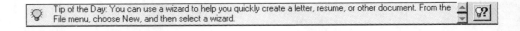

When you first turn on Tip Wizard, it will display the Tip of the Day, a handy tip taken at random from Word's list of tips.

If Word detects that you are doing something that can be done more easily, differently, or better, it will tell you about it in the Tip Wizard box. Word numbers the tips as it displays them. Use the up and down arrows on the right side of the box to scroll through the list of recently displayed tips. For more detailed information on a tip, display it in the Tip Wizard box and then click on the Show Me button.

Once you turn on the Tip Wizard, it will stay on until you turn it off. If you exit Word while the Tip Wizard is on, it will appear automatically the next time you start Word.

To turn off the Tip Wizard, click on the Tip Wizard button in the Standard toolbar once more.

T ip: Word contains a number of other interactive Wizards that take you step-by-step through creating even the most complex documents, such as resumes, faxes, legal pleadings, calendars, and tables. You will learn about these Wizards throughout this book.

Saving a Document

When you are finished working on your document, you'll want to print it out or save the document on your disk. By saving a document, you can complete or print it at some other time. To save the document now on your screen, click on the Save button in the toolbar, or select Save or Save As from the File menu.

Word will display the Save As dialog box shown in Figure 1-12.

U pgrader: Windows 95 uses newly designed Save and Open dialog boxes. You'll learn more about these boxes in Chapter 2 when we discuss opening a document.

Word will suggest a document name using the first sentence (up to 255 characters) of your document and adding the extension DOC. To use a different name, type it in the File Name text box. Now enter a name for the document you just created. Type the name you want to give the document, for example, **Biography of Sliding Billy Watson**, and then click on OK. The document's name will appear in the title bar.

T ip: When you display the Save As dialog box, the suggested name in the File Name text box will be highlighted. To enter your own document name, just start typing—the highlighted text will be deleted. If you first click elsewhere in the dialog box, the highlight will be removed from the name.

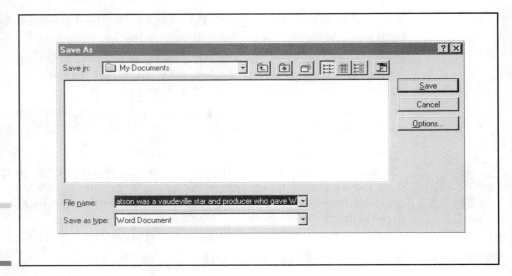

The Save As
dialog box
Figure 1-12.

To enter your document name, double-click in the File Name box to highlight the name, or select the box, delete the suggested name, and type in your own.

If you make any changes to the document after you save it, you'll need to save it again. Just click on the Save button or select Save from the File menu. You will learn more about saving edited documents in Chapter 2.

Upgrader: Long file names are one great feature of Windows 95. But don't worry if you still occasionally use DOS. Windows will automatically maintain an 8-character name for each file in addition to its long name.

By default, Word stores your documents in the My Documents directory. If you want to save the document on another disk or directory, type a full path and file name, as in **D:\Letters\Home**. You can also select a disk or a directory by pulling down the Save in list. Click on the list's drop-down arrow to display a list of the drives on your system. Click on the drive where you want to save the file to display a list of directories in the drive. Double-click on a directory where you want to save the document, and then enter a document name.

You can also quickly save documents in a Favorites folder—a subdirectory under your Windows 95 directory. To access this folder, click on the Look in Favorites button. You'll learn more about the Favorites folder in Chapter 2.

Note: Saving a document does not clear it from the screen, so you can save a document and then continue working on it. In Chapter 2 you will learn how to clear a document and then start on another.

Printing Documents

To print a document quickly and easily, use the toolbar. When you are ready to print your document, make sure your printer is turned on and ready. Then click on the Print button in the toolbar. Word prepares the document to be printed and transfers it to the Windows Print Manager.

Printing occurs in the background. This means Windows will print your document while you continue working in Word. You can even exit Word and return to the desktop. However, you cannot exit Windows until the entire document has been printed or transferred to your printer's memory.

Upgrader: Printing speed has been greatly improved in Windows 95 through the 32-bit architecture and new printer drivers.

You can also choose to select printing options before you print your document. To set printing options, select Print from the File menu or press CTRL-P to display the dialog box shown in Figure 1-13.

If you want to print the document using all of the default settings, just click on OK. But take a moment to notice the other options in the dialog box. You can select what parts of your document you want to print and the number of copies. You can also choose to print every page in the document (the default setting), only the page on which the insertion point is located, only text that is already selected, or a range of specific pages.

To print specific pages, click on the Pages option button and then enter a range such as **3-6** to print pages 3 through 6. Use a hyphen to specify consecutive pages. You can also use the hyphen to print from the start or to the end of the document. For instance, enter **-5** to print the first five pages, or enter **6-** to print from page six to the last page of the document. Use a

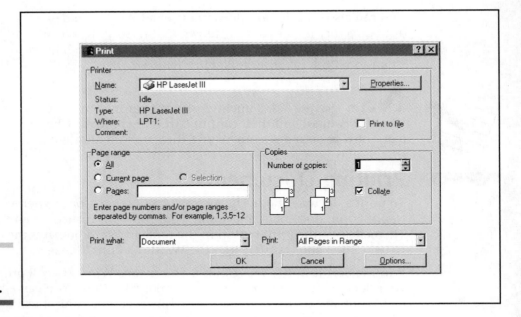

The Print
dialog box
Figure 1-13.

comma to indicate nonconsecutive pages. If you want to print just pages 3
and 6, for instance, enter **3,6**.

You can also select to print only odd or even pages by pulling down the
Print list box, and you can choose to save the printed output to a file and to
collate sets of multipage documents.

T ip: While you do not have to save a document before you print it, it is
a safe practice. It is possible to close a document before it has completed
printing. If you do not save the document, and then discover some
typographical or other error, you'll have to write it all over again.

Printing Problems

When you install Windows, or anytime after, you can tell it what printers
are connected to your computer. One printer is set as the default. This
means that Windows knows how to communicate with it to print your
documents correctly. If your printout does not look correct, then Windows
may be set up for the wrong printer. The printer actually connected to your
computer may not be the same one that Windows thinks is connected—or it
may be set up differently than expected.

Note: You may need to check the printer setup if you or someone who shares your computer has changed printers for a special task. A colleague may have used your computer to send a fax, for example, without then readjusting Windows for your printer.

1

To select the correct printer, choose Print from the File menu to display the Print dialog box. Look at the name of the printer in the Name list box. If the printer is incorrect, pull down the list connected to the box, as shown here.

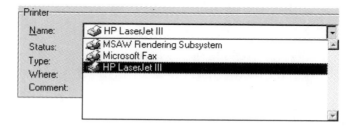

Click on the name of the printer you want to use. If you still have trouble printing, click on the Properties box and make certain your printer is set up correctly.

Tip: If your printer is not listed in the Name list, then it has not been added to the Windows environment. You'll need to add the printer using the Control Panel application. You'll find the Control Panel on the desktop in the My Computer folder, as well as in the Settings menu from the taskbar's Start button.

Exiting Word

When you are finished using Word, you should exit the program to return to the Windows desktop. Don't worry if you try to exit Word before saving your document—Word will give you a chance to save it.

To exit Word, select Exit from the File menu or press ALT-F4. If you've made any changes to your document since you last saved it, a dialog box will appear asking if you want to save the document before you leave Word. Select Yes to save the document, select No not to save it, or select Cancel to remain in Word.

Remember: You can also exit Word by double-clicking on the Word window control box, which is the stylized letter W on the left of the title bar.

Working with Documents

2

The magic of Word means that you can change a document as much as you want before you print it or distribute it. You can print draft copies to review the document. You can add or delete text. You can make sweeping changes time and again. Changing a document is called *editing*, and you can edit a document as you type it or after you've saved it on your disk.

Opening Existing Documents

To edit an existing document that is not already on the screen, you must first *open* it, or recall it from the disk. When you open a document, Word recalls it from the disk and displays it in a document window. Opening a document does not remove it from the disk, it just places a copy of it in your computer's memory.

Note: If you already have a document on the screen when you open another, Word opens another window for the new document. The window will appear in the foreground, showing the document you just opened. The other document window will move into the background. See Chapter 5 for more information on working with multiple documents.

Because you often work on a document in more than one session, Word makes it easy to reopen the last four documents that you worked on. Pull down the File menu. At the bottom of the menu, Word lists up to the last four documents that you've opened or saved. Because you saved a document in Chapter 1, you'll see that document's name, Biography of Sliding Billy Watson, listed just above the Exit command in the File menu, as shown in Figure 2-1. Click on the document name now to open it.

Once a document is open, you can edit it, print it, or just read it. Position the insertion point where you want to edit or insert text, and then type. With the document now on your screen, move the insertion point after the second paragraph, and then press ENTER to insert a blank line. Now complete the document so it appears as in Figure 2-2.

Using File Open

To open a document not listed in the File menu, you can either click on the Open tool in the Standard toolbar or select Open from the File menu. The Open dialog box will appear, as shown in Figure 2-3.

Word lists document files that have the DOC extension in the My Documents directory. Double-click on the document you want to open, or highlight its name and then click on Open.

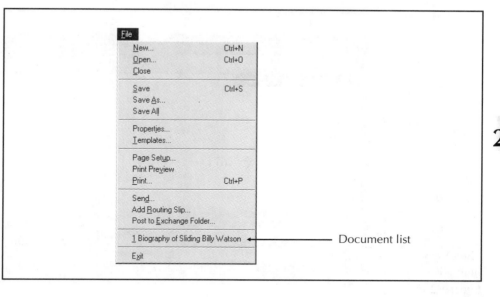

Word lists up
to your
last four
documents in
the File menu
Figure 2-1.

Document list

Don't panic if the document you want to open is not listed. You may have stored the document in another disk or directory, or with an extension other than DOC. To list all files in the current directory, click on the arrow next to the Files of Type box and then select All Files. If you still do not see the document name, select another directory using the Look In drop-down list.

Sliding Billy Watson was a vaudeville star and producer who gave W. C. Fields his first job and who started Fanny Brice in her career.

Sliding Billy gained his name from his trademark slide across the stage, a precursor to Michael Jackson's now famous Moon Walk.

Billy was born as Wolf Shapiro on October 12, 1876. His family moved from New York to Philadelphia, where Billy tried to settle down into a quiet family life. However, the call of the stage was too difficult for him to resist. He abandoned his wife and two children for the limelight and fame of vaudeville.

As a comedian, Billy worked his way up from a bit player to the lead role, but he gained most fame as both actor and producer in many popular vaudeville and burlesque shows. One of his most popular shows was Girls From Happyland, which Billy wrote with lyricist Albert Bagley.

In 1907, Billy married his second wife, Nellie Pfleger, who starred with him in many shows. However, life was to take some strange twists. Nellie was murdered in 1926 by a disgruntled employee of her club, the Three Hundred Club in Freeport, Long Island. Throughout the 1930s, Billy's first wife pursued him for failure to pay her $25 per week alimony. Billy was arrested a number of times, appeared in court in several states, and was even accused of bigamy.

The
completed
document
Figure 2-2.

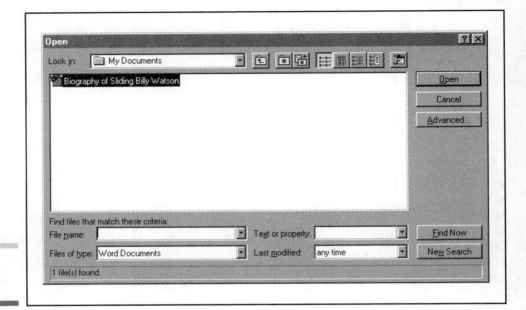

The Open
dialog box
Figure 2-3.

Open Dialog Options

Windows 95 has new and improved Open and Save dialog boxes that Word and other applications use. You can change the way the document list is displayed using the tools in the Dialog Box toolbar, which are listed in the following table.

Button	Name	Function
	Up One Level	Displays the next highest directory level.
	Look in Favorites	Displays the contents of the Favorites folder where you can store frequently used documents.
	Add To Favorites	Lets you insert documents and new folders into the Favorites directory.
	List	Displays just the document names.
	Details	Lists the document names, size, type, and date.

Button	Name	Function
	Properties	Displays specific details about the selected file, including the author, revision date, and statistics, such as the number of words and characters.
	Preview	Displays the selected document in a preview window. You can scroll the window to look through the document before you open it.
	Commands and Settings	Displays options to print the selected document without opening it, to display or change the document's properties, to sort the document list, and to search through subfolders.

The Save dialog box does not contain the Add to Favorites or Preview buttons, but it does include the Create New Folder button, which you can use to create a new subdirectory.

The Advanced and Find Now command buttons in the Open dialog box let you search for files no matter where they are in your computer. You use these buttons in conjunction with the text boxes at the bottom of the dialog box. You'll learn more about this dialog box, and the search feature, in Chapter 22.

Opening Documents from the Taskbar

Windows 95 maintains a list of the documents that you've most recently worked with. Because you access the list from the taskbar, you can open one of the documents from Word or any other Windows program.

Click on the Start button on the toolbar and then point to the Documents option. A list of the documents will appear, as shown in Figure 2-4. Click on the document you wish to open. If Word is not open when you select a Word document from the taskbar, Windows 95 will start Word automatically.

Saving Edited Documents

Once you edit a document, you must save it again to record your changes onto the disk. Because you made changes to the Biography of Sliding Billy Watson document, you must save it again. Click on the Save button in the Standard toolbar or select Save from the File menu.

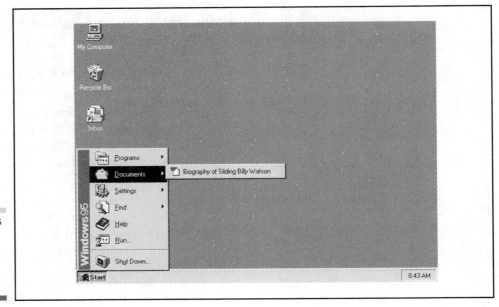

The Documents
list in the
Windows 95
taskbar
Figure 2-4.

Because the document already has a name—it's been saved once already—
Word saves the document without displaying the Save As dialog box. When
you save a document that you've already named, however, the previous
version of the document will be erased. For example, the version
of Biography of Sliding Billy Watson that had only two paragraphs is now
erased. The document now on your disk contains the completed document
that you just typed.

If you want to retain the original two-paragraph version, select Save As
from the File menu. Type a new name for the revised document, and then
click on OK.

Preventing Mistakes When Saving

Because it is all too easy to click on the Save button by mistake, instead of
selecting Save As, Word gives you several ways to avoid accidentally
overwriting a document. One way to prevent this from happening is to open
the document as *read-only*. To open a document as read-only, display the
Open dialog box. Click on the document name you want to open, then click
on the Commands and Settings button.

From the menu that appears, select Open Read Only to open the document.
If you now edit the document, you will not be able to save it with the same
name. When you click on the Save button, or select Save from the File

menu, the Save As dialog box will appear. To save your changes, you must save the edited document under a new name.

You can also tell Word to automatically save a backup copy of the original file. When you save a document, Word will give the original copy the extension BAK and then save the new version.

Saving backup copies, however, will not help if your computer goes haywire while you are working. Any changes that you've made to the document before saving it will be lost. As a safeguard against this, Word automatically saves a temporary copy of your document every ten minutes. If your machine locks up, or you have to reboot due to some system error, you will be able to restore your work the next time you start Word.

To set or change these backup features, select Options from the Tools menu, and then click on the Save tab to see the options shown in Figure 2-5.

Choose Always Create Backup Copy to have Word make a backup copy when you save a document. Click on Automatic Save Every to turn off or on the automatic save feature, and use the text box to change the time period for saving your work.

Closing Your Document

Saving a document does not clear it from the screen, so you can save your document and then print it or continue working on it. However, once you

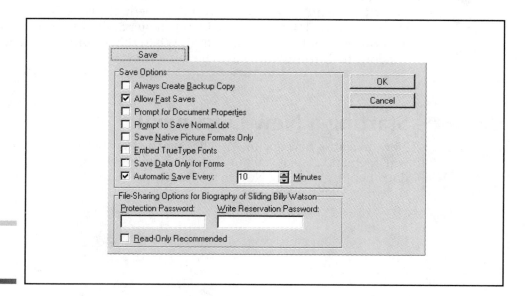

The Save
options
Figure 2-5.

save a document, you may want to start or open another. You might also change your mind about what you've typed and want to erase it all and start over. The Close command clears the current document from the screen, closing its document window.

To close the document now on your screen, Biography of Sliding Billy Watson, click once on the document's Close button, select Close from the File menu, or double-click on the document's control button. Remember, when the document window is maximized, its control button is on the left side of the menu bar.

Note: If you've changed the document since you last saved it, a dialog box will appear asking if you want to save the document now, before exiting. Select Yes to save the document, select No to discard your changes, or select Cancel to leave the document on the screen.

When you close all of the document windows in Word, the menu bar will display only the File and Help options; the ruler and scroll bars no longer appear. There is no document window, so you cannot type a document in this state. You can either close Word, open a document, or start a new document.

Note: Technically, there is a difference between closing the window with the Close button and closing the document with the Close command in the File menu. When you have a document displayed in more than one window, as you'll learn how to do in Chapter 5, the Close button closes the window but not the document itself. When the document is in just one window, both techniques have the same effect.

Starting a New Document

Now, to start a new document, click on the New button in the toolbar. Word will open and display a blank document window. You can also start a new document by selecting New from the File menu to display the dialog box shown in Figure 2-6.

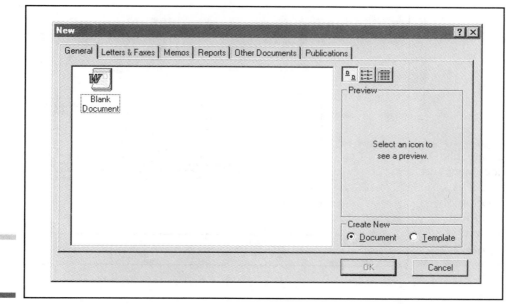

The New
dialog box
Figure 2-6.

Click on OK to open a blank document window. You will learn about the
other options in this dialog box in Chapter 11.

Tip: The first time you use the New option from the File menu, you
might see a message reporting that the "User Templates" could not be found.
User Templates are special documents that you create to streamline your
work. Just select OK. You'll learn about templates in Chapter 11.

Now, in a new document, type the letter shown in Figure 2-7. The letter will
be longer than your screen, so some lines of text will scroll off the top of the
screen as you type. When you are done, save the document with the name
Letter to Historical Society.

Scrolling in Your Document

You already know how to move the insertion point by clicking the mouse.
You also know that as you enter text at the bottom of the window, text at
the top will scroll up and out of view. So how do you move the insertion
point to a place in the document that you cannot see? The answer is
scrolling. Scrolling means to bring into view text that has disappeared off
the top or bottom, or the left or right, of the document window.

November 16, 1996

Dr. Wilma Stone
Theater Department
Smithsonian Historical Society
Washington, DC

Dear Dr. Stone:

Thank you for your interest in the burlesque project of the Historical Society of Philadelphia. During the past three years, we have been developing a display and program featuring our city's famous burlesque stars of the turn-of-the-century.

While Philadelphia was never the center of the burlesque industry, many of the most popular performers of the time started their careers in local clubs and theaters. In fact, burlesque was so popular in Philadelphia that it continued to thrive here even when the industry faded from the national scene.

Our program will feature over twenty Philadelphia performers who gained regional or national attention across the burlesque circuit known as the Columbia Wheel. Local artists will re-enact highlights from the popular shows so audience members can experience the thrill of this now lost theater art.

We are pleased that you are considering adding our program to the Institute's schedule for next year. We are looking forward to your visit to Philadelphia, and to sharing with you the exciting story of Philadelphia burlesque.

Sincerely,

Jane W. Wilcox
President

Create this document and save it as Letter to Historical Society **Figure 2-7.**

The simplest way to scroll the window is to use the arrow keys. When the insertion point is at the top line of the document window, pressing the UP ARROW will scroll a new line into view—if there are any. When the insertion point is on the last line in the window, pressing the DOWN ARROW will scroll a new line into view—again, if there are any. Try it now. Press the UP ARROW until the insertion point is at the first line of the screen, and then press the UP ARROW one more time. Now continue pressing the UP ARROW until the beginning of the document is displayed.

If you have to move a great distance through a long document, however, using the arrow keys is certainly not very efficient. That's why Word has *scroll bars*. You use the scroll bar on the left of the screen—the vertical scroll bar—to scroll up and down. You use the scroll bar at the bottom of the window—the horizontal scroll bar—to scroll left and right.

To scroll through your document line by line, just as you would by pressing the arrow key, click on the up or down triangles on the ends of the vertical scroll bar. To scroll screen by screen, click above or below the scroll box—the box within the bar.

Each time you click, Word scrolls the window about the same number of

lines that you can see. For example, if your Word window is set so you can see about 18 lines, clicking anywhere below the scroll box, but not on the down arrow, will display the next 18 lines.

You can also drag the scroll box to scroll to a relative position in the document. If you drag the box to the middle of the scroll bar, Word will display page 5 of a 9-page document, for example. As you drag the box, Word will display a small box, next to the scroll box, showing you the number of the current page.

2

Upgrader: The page number display when you drag the scroll box is a great new feature. No need to stop dragging just to see what page you're on!

There is one very important point to keep in mind when scrolling with the scroll bar: it does not move the insertion point. The insertion point actually remains where it is. Scrolling only changes the portion of the document being displayed on the screen. You'll notice that the page and section indicators in the status bar show the number of the page being displayed, but the At, Ln, and Col indicators will be blank.

If you want to edit or insert text in the area displayed, you must first click where you want to type. If you do not click the mouse, the screen will scroll back to its previous location when you begin typing or press an arrow key. As an example, drag the scroll box now to the very bottom of the scroll bar. You will see the end of the document. Press any character key. The screen scrolls back up, and the character you pressed appears at the start of the document. Press BACKSPACE to delete the character that you just inserted.

Caution: Beginners often make the mistake of scrolling the screen to where they want to enter text and then starting to type. The screen jumps back to its original location, and the characters appear there instead.

To go to the start of a specific page, use the Go To command. Select Go To from the Edit menu, or press CTRL-G, or double-click on the section of the status bar that shows the page number information. The Go To dialog box will appear.

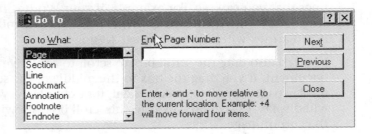

As soon as you type a page number in the Enter Page Number box, the Next command button will change to Go To. Type the page number you wish to move to and then select Go To or press ENTER. Word will scroll the screen so the start of the page is at the top of the document window, but it will not clear the Go To dialog box from the screen. Click on the box's Close button to clear it from the screen.

Tip: Rather than enter an exact number, you can use the plus (+) or (–) signs to move to a page relative to the current location. For example, entering +2 will move down two pages. Entering –2 will move two pages toward the start of the document.

Notice the other options in the Go To box. Rather than type the number of the page you want to go to, you can select Next to move down one page, or select Previous to move up one page. You can also go to a specific section, line, footnote, endnote, annotation, bookmark, graphic, table, equation, field, or object.

If you prefer to scroll using the keyboard instead of the mouse, you're in luck. Word provides a number of special key combinations for scrolling, as shown in Table 2-1. These commands actually move the insertion point as they scroll the screen.

Tip: Press SHIFT-F5 to quickly return to the previous position of the insertion point.

Key Combination	Movement of Insertion Point
RIGHT ARROW, LEFT ARROW, UP ARROW, DOWN ARROW	In the direction of the arrow
CTRL-RIGHT ARROW	To the beginning of the next word
CTRL-LEFT ARROW	To the beginning of the current word, then to the previous word
CTRL-DOWN ARROW	To the beginning of the next paragraph
CTRL-UP ARROW	To the beginning of the current paragraph
HOME	To the beginning of the line
END	To the end of the line
CTRL-PGUP	To the top of the screen
CTRL-PGDN	To the bottom of the screen
CTRL-HOME	To the start of the document
CTRL-END	To the end of the document
PGUP	Up one screen
PGDN	Down one screen
ALT-CTRL-PGUP	To the top of the previous page
ALT-CTRL-PGDN	To the top of the next page

Use These Key Combinations to Scroll the Document
Table 2-1.

Tip: Don't feel that you have to choose between using either the key combinations or the mouse to scroll. Use any combination that you feel comfortable with.

Selecting Text

When you want to perform some Word magic on one or more characters, you need to *select* them. Think of this as a two-step process:

1. Tell Word what characters you want to work with.
2. Tell Word what action to perform on those characters.

You can select text using either the mouse or the keyboard. Selected text appears highlighted—that is, light letters over a dark background.

It is easy to select text with the mouse by dragging. Move the I-beam so it is at one end of the text that you want to select. It can be at either end, in front of the first character or following the last character. For example, you can see here that I'm preparing to select the word "computer".

Using Word on a personal computer is really easy!

Now press and hold down the left mouse button. Keep the button down as you drag the mouse, until the pointer is at the other end of the text. When you reach the end of the text, release the mouse button. The selected text will appear highlighted.

Tip: Drag straight across the line, not up or down, unless you want to select more than one line of text.

Word uses an intelligent selection system. If you start dragging in the center of a word, the program will select the entire word when you get to the next one. To see how this works, move your mouse so the I-beam is before the letter *e* in the word "Society" in the first paragraph of the letter on your screen.

Now press and hold down the mouse button, and drag the mouse slowly toward the right. When you move the pointer past the space after the word, the space becomes selected. But as you select the first letter of the next word, that word and the entire previous word automatically become selected, not just the characters you originally highlighted, as shown here.

Thank you for your interest in the burlesque project of the Historical Society of Philadelphia. During the past three years, we have been developing a display and program featuring our city's famous burlesque stars of the turn-of-the-century.

Click the mouse to deselect the text, removing the highlighting.

If you drag to select the space before a word, Word automatically selects the whole word to the right as you drag onto its first characters. Similarly, when you select the space after a word, Word selects the whole word to the left as you drag onto its last character.

Note: Word calls this intelligent selection because it assumes you want to select the entire word. But there are times when intelligent selection can be downright annoying. For example, suppose you really do want to select just a few characters of one word and a few characters of the following word—not the entire words? The best way to do this is to drag the mouse so both words are selected, and then without releasing the mouse button, drag back toward the starting position. At one point the second word will become unhighlighted. Without releasing the mouse button, move the mouse back over the characters that you want to select.

2

Something similar occurs when you drag the mouse up or down. When you drag to the line above, Word automatically selects everything to the left of the original line and to the right of the new line, as shown here.

> During the past three years, we have been developing a display and program featuring our city's famous burlesque stars of the turn-of-the-century.
>   While Philadelphia was never the center of the burlesque industry, many of the most popular performers of the time started their careers in local clubs and theaters. In fact, burlesque was so popular in Philadelphia that it continued to thrive here even when the industry faded from the national scene.

If you drag down to the next line, Word selects everything to the right of the original and to the left of the next line.

As long as you do not release the mouse button, you can drag as much or as little text as you want. If you drag too far to the right, for example, just keep the mouse button down and drag back toward the left.

Tip: If you want to delete text quickly, select it with the mouse and then press the DEL or BACKSPACE key.

What if you select some text and then change your mind after you release the mouse button? Just move the mouse pointer so it is no longer on the selection and click the mouse. This removes all of the highlighting from the text so you can try it again.

Caution: Selected text will be deleted if you press any number, letter, or punctuation key, the SPACEBAR, or the ENTER key. Word uses this technique to make it easy for you to replace characters with something else. If you do not want to replace text, make certain that no text is selected before you start typing.

More Ways to Select Text

Just as there are many ways to scroll the screen and move the insertion point, there are many ways to select text. To quickly select an entire word, point to it with the mouse and then double-click. This not only selects the word but also the space following the word. Why? Because Word figures if you want to delete the word, then you do not want to leave an extra space between the words that remain there.

Clicking three times selects the entire paragraph. Remember that to Word, a paragraph is not a grammatical structure. It is the text between two locations where you pressed the ENTER key. To select a sentence, hold down the CTRL key when you click the mouse.

If you want to select a portion of text without dragging, use the SHIFT key. Place the insertion point at one end of the text, hold down the SHIFT key, and then click at the other end of the text.

Finally, you can also select text by clicking on the left margin. When you place the mouse pointer in the left margin, the pointer will be shaped like an arrow. Click the mouse once to select the line of text to the right of the pointer. Click twice to select the entire paragraph, and click three times to select the entire document. If you hold down the mouse button and drag in the left margin you will select multiple lines.

Tip: To select the entire document, choose Select All from the Edit menu or press CTRL-A.

If you want to select text using the keyboard, remember these two important keys: F8 and SHIFT. To simulate dragging, press the F8 key. The dimmed letters EXT in the status bar will become bold, indicating that you are in the Extend mode. Now text becomes selected as you move the insertion point using the arrow keys, other key combinations, and even by clicking the mouse. For example, if you press F8 and then the RIGHT ARROW, text becomes selected as the insertion point passes over it. To get out of Extend mode, press ESC.

Try using the Extend mode now. Move the insertion point to the start of the document on your screen, and then press F8. Now press the DOWN ARROW three times. As you press the DOWN ARROW, the text becomes selected just as if you were dragging the mouse. Now point the mouse somewhere in the second paragraph of the letter and click. Because you are still in Extend mode, the selected text is extended to where you clicked. Press ESC to exit Extend mode, and then click the mouse to deselect the text.

2

To simulate clicking, press the F8 key more than once. Press F8 twice to select a word, three times for the sentence, or four times to select the entire document.

You can also select text using SHIFT. When you hold down SHIFT, all of the insertion point movement keystrokes shown in Table 2-1 also select text. For instance, hold down SHIFT and press HOME to select text from the insertion point to the start of the line. Pressing HOME by itself simply moves the insertion point to the start of the document.

Selecting Rectangular Areas

You can also select a rectangular area of text, such as when you want to select one column in a table. With the mouse, hold down ALT, and then drag over the area you want to select, as shown here.

> Thank you for your interest in the burlesque project of the Historical Society of Philadelphia. During the past three years, we have been developing a display and program featuring our city's famous burlesque stars of the turn-of-the-century.
> While Philadelphia was never the center of the burlesque industry, many of the most popular performers of the time started their careers in local clubs and theaters. In fact, burlesque was so popular in Philadelphia that it continued to thrive here even when the industry faded from the national scene.
> Our program will feature over twenty Philadelphia performers who gained regional or national attention across the burlesque circuit known as the Columbia Wheel. Local artists will re-enact highlights from the popular shows so audience members can experience the thrill of this now lost theater art.

With the keyboard, select a rectangular area by pressing CTRL-SHIFT-F8, then use the arrow keys to select the area. Press ESC to deselect the area.

Using Undo and Redo

It would be nice if we never made mistakes, but unfortunately, life just isn't that perfect. It is all too easy to delete characters you really want, or type characters and then change your mind about them. Because Word knows we are not always perfect, it gives us a quick and easy way to correct our mistakes.

The Undo command reverses changes that you make in your document. Delete a paragraph by mistake? Use Undo to return it to the document. Type a sentence and then change your mind? Use Undo to remove it from the document.

There are two ways to use Undo—from the Edit menu or from the Standard toolbar. Let's look at the Edit menu first.

To reverse the change you just made to the document, pull down the Edit menu. The first item in the Edit menu is the Undo command. The full name of the command will depend on your last action. If you just typed something, the command will be Undo Typing. If you just deleted text, the command will be Undo Clear. Select the Undo command to cancel your last action.

T ip: You can also press CTRL-Z to perform the Undo operation.

Let's make some changes to the document on your screen to illustrate how Undo works. Move the insertion point directly after the word Philadelphia in the first paragraph of the letter.

Press the comma key and the SPACEBAR, and then type **Pennsylvania**. Now double-click on the word "famous" in that same paragraph and then press DELETE. Select Undo Clear from the Edit menu. Word replaces the word that you just deleted.

Word "remembers" all of your actions, not just the last one. Once you undo the very last action, Word will be prepared to undo the one before that. If you pull down the Edit menu again, the Undo command will be set for the second-to-last action that you performed. Pull down the Edit menu. The Undo command now appears as Undo Typing because you typed something just before you deleted the word "famous." Click on Undo Typing. The text you inserted is deleted.

T ip: If this is confusing, picture the Undo command as a stack of dishes. After you clean a dish, you place it on top of the stack. That's how Word treats your actions. When you undo a command, Word takes the action on top of the stack, the topmost dish, and reverses it. The action you performed just before the one you reversed is now on top of the stack and the next in line to be undone.

You can also undo actions by clicking on the Undo button in the Standard toolbar. Each time you click on the button, another action is reversed, just like selecting Undo from the Edit menu. Let's see how this works.

Move the insertion point to the very end of the document on the screen. Type the number **1**, point the mouse after the number and click. Press ENTER to move to a new line, type the number **2**, and click the mouse after it. Press ENTER and then type the number **3**. The mouse clicks after the numbers 1 and 2 force Word to treat your typing as three separate actions.

Tip: If you simply typed the three numbers, pressing ENTER after each, Word would treat all of the keystrokes as one "action." When you click the mouse in the text, select a toolbar button or menu item, or use a key combination to format text, Word separates one action from the next. Clicking the mouse after typing the number separates the action of typing that number from the action of pressing ENTER and typing the next.

Now click on the Undo button. The number 3 is deleted. Click again on the Undo button—the number 2 is deleted. Click again on the Undo button to delete the number 1.

Clicking on the down arrow next to the Undo button displays the Undo List—a list of your actions with the most recent on top. You can use the list to undo more than one action at a time. To see how this works, type the numbers **1**, **2**, and **3** again as you did before, clicking and pressing ENTER after numbers 1 and 2. Now click on the down arrow to display the Undo list.

Clicking on the item at the top of the list will undo the last action you performed. But clicking on any other item will not just reverse that action. If you select an item somewhere else on the list, Word undoes *every* action from there to the top of the list.

Each "Typing" represents another action. The first Typing represents the number 3, the second represents the number 2, and the third represents the number 1. If you click on the first Typing in the list, only the number 3 will be undone. But click now on the second Typing in the center of the list. Word deletes both the numbers 3 and 2—all of the actions from there to the top of the list. Now click on the Typing at the top of the list. The number 1 is deleted.

Caution: Not every action that you perform can be undone. For example, you cannot undo saving or printing your document. In such cases, the command in the Edit menu will appear as Can't Undo.

Redo

Word not only remembers the action that you took, it also remembers the actions that you undo. So if you undo something and then change your mind, you can *redo* it. After you undo something, pull down the Edit menu. The second option in the menu will be Redo. Like Undo, the name of the command will vary with the action, such as Redo Typing or Redo Clear.

Click on the Redo option to undo your last undo! Select Redo Typing from the Edit menu now. The number 1 that you just undid reappears. Click on the Undo button to remove it again. You can also click on the Redo button on the toolbar or select from the Redo list.

Repeating Actions

When you have not used the Undo command, the second command in the Edit menu will be Repeat. As with Undo and Redo, the full name of the command will depend on the last action you took. If you just typed text, for instance, the command will be Repeat Typing. If you just deleted text, the command will be Repeat Clear.

Use the Repeat command to repeat an action more than one time, such as entering the text you just typed in another location. To repeat text, for example, type it in one location, move the insertion point where you want to insert the same text, and then select Repeat from the Edit menu. If your last action cannot be repeated, the command will appear dimmed as Can't Repeat.

Tip: Press F4 to repeat your last action.

Documents with a View

Not every document you create will use the same format or overall design. Because documents can vary, Word gives you four different *views*, or ways to display documents on the screen. You can select the best view for each document. The views are Normal, Outline, Page Layout, and Master Document. When you first start Word, it will be in Normal view. When you want to see everything that's on a page, change to Page Layout view. Figure 2-8 shows your letter in Page Layout view.

You can change modes by selecting options from the View menu or by using the buttons listed here, which are located above the Page indicator.

Button	View	Function
≣	Normal	Displays your text in the typefaces and sizes in which they will appear when printed, but does not show headers, footers, page numbers, footnotes, columns, or other formats or elements that are not part of the body of your text. You will also see graphics, although they will appear at the left margin of the page instead of at their exact placement.
▣	Page Layout	Displays graphics exactly where they belong; also shows headers, footers, page numbers, footnotes, columns, and everything else. There will also be a ruler down the left side of the screen.
≣	Outline	Used for creating and organizing outlines. In Outline view, the ruler is replaced by the Outline toolbar.
No button	Master Document	This view is useful when you are working with a large document that is divided into sections. Select Master Document from the View menu—there is no Master Document button.

2

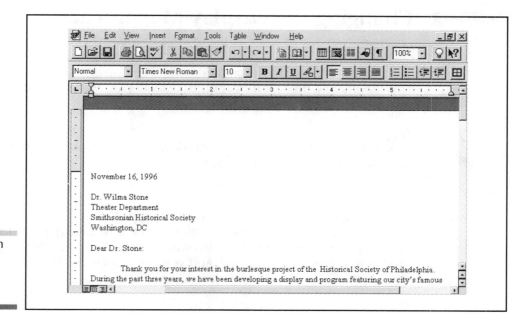

Your letter in Page Layout view
Figure 2-8.

Tip: I use Normal view for everyday typing and editing, when I'm not desktop publishing or working with sophisticated layouts, because it lets me see the maximum number of lines on the screen.

Two very useful features of Page Layout view are the Next Page and Previous Page buttons at the bottom of the vertical scroll bar. You can click on the Next Page button—the down-pointing arrow—to move down one page. Click on the Previous Page button—the up-pointing arrow—to move up one page.

The important point to remember is that you can type, edit, and format a document in all four views. Switching views changes how the document appears on the screen; it does not limit your capabilities.

Changing views does not affect the basic screen elements. The title bar, menu bars, scroll bars, and status bar, for example, still appear on the screen. To quickly remove these elements from the screen to show the maximum number of lines, change to Full Screen view by selecting Full Screen from the View menu. Word will remove the title and menu bars, toolbars, ruler, status bar, and scroll bars so the text window fills more of the screen. You will also

see a button labeled Full somewhere on the right of the screen. Click on that button when you want to redisplay all of the other screen elements.

Changing the Display Magnification

Changing views does not change the size of the text being displayed. By default, when you start Word, text and graphics appear about the same size onscreen as they do on the printed page. The display magnification is 100%. You can change the magnification to display your document larger or smaller than it will be when printed.

Note: Changing magnification does not actually change the font size; it just changes how it appears onscreen.

If you have trouble reading small characters, as I do, you can enlarge the display. For example, set magnification at 200% to display your document at twice the printed size. You can also reduce magnification to display more text on the screen than normal, and you can display a full page or more at one time!

There are two ways to change magnification—with the toolbar and with the View menu. To change magnification from the toolbar, use the Zoom Control on the right side of the toolbar. Click on the down arrow to display the magnification options.

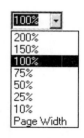

Click on the magnification that you want to use—select either a percentage or the Page Width option. Page Width adjusts the magnification so you can see the full width of the widest line of text. Select 200% from the Zoom Control to enlarge the display.

2

In Page Layout view, the Zoom Control list also includes the Whole Page and Two Pages options. Select the Whole Page option to reduce the display so you see an entire page on the screen. Select the Two Pages option to see two whole pages. These magnifications let you see the overall layout and design of a page.

You can access more zoom options if you use the Zoom dialog box, shown in Figure 2-9. To display this box, select Zoom from the View menu.

From the dialog box, you can select one of the listed magnifications, and you can also set a custom percentage between 10% and 200%. The Whole Page and Many Pages options are dimmed in Normal view because that view is not page oriented. In Page Layout view, select Many Pages to display a thumbnail display of two or more pages on the screen. Click on the button with the picture of a monitor to display a graphic illustrating a multiple-page layout.

Drag over the layout to highlight the number of pages and layout you want, or just click on the lower-rightmost page. For example, to display four pages, two on top and two on the bottom, drag over the layout or click on the center page in the bottom row, as shown here, to select pages.

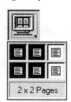

The Zoom dialog box

Figure 2-9.

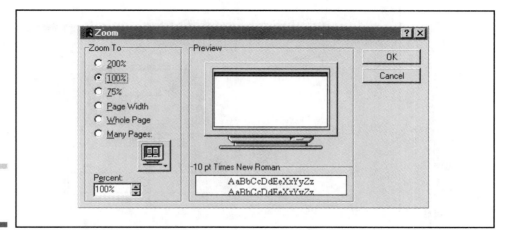

When you release the mouse button, a sample of the layout will appear in the Preview panel, as shown in Figure 2-10.

When you first click on the Many Pages button, the thumbnail displays six pages, three on top and three on the bottom. To display more pages, drag the mouse past the right edge of the thumbnail display, as shown here.

Changing views and magnification lets you customize your screen for the way you like to work, but remember that small magnifications may be difficult to work with. Displaying multiple pages at one time is useful primarily for previewing the overall look of the document, but it is not very easy to work with. Figure 2-11, for example, shows the screen with four pages. While you can see the overall layout of the pages, you certainly cannot read the text.

Tip: A magnification of 100% is a good choice if you are using the default page and margin setting, and Normal view—you will be able to see the full width of the line onscreen. If your lines scroll off the right of the screen, try the Page Width setting. Your text may appear smaller, but you'll be able to read each line without scrolling. Page Width is also effective in Page Layout view.

Showing Invisible Codes

One other change you can make to the screen is to display invisible codes. Pressing keys such as TAB and ENTER affects the format of the text, but they

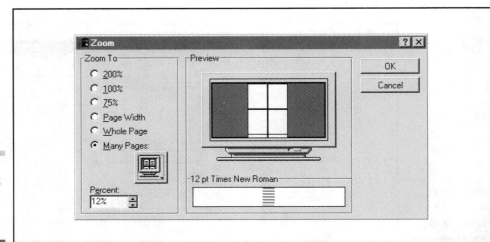

The Preview panel showing the sample layout
Figure 2-10.

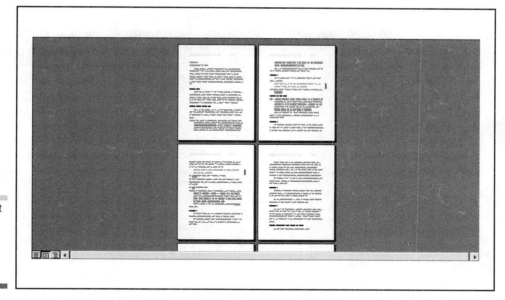

The document
window,
displaying
four pages
Figure 2-11.

do not normally display characters on the screen. These keystrokes, however, do insert special codes into the document that affect the format.

 Sometimes it is easier to edit your document, or to visualize its format, if you display these codes. To display them, click on the Show/Hide button on the Standard toolbar.

Word will display the codes, as shown in Figure 2-12. It shows spaces with small dots, tabs by the right arrow, and places where you pressed ENTER as the paragraph symbol (¶). To turn off the display of codes, click on the show/hide button again.

Previewing a Document Before Printing

Even with Page Layout view, you may have trouble visualizing exactly how your document will appear when printed. So before you print your document, use Word's Print Preview. Print Preview can display one or more entire pages of your document at one time, showing how it will appear when printed. Print Preview actually simulates printing your document and gives you some capabilities not found in Page Layout.

 Preview your document now. Select Print Preview from the File menu, or click on the Print Preview button in the Standard toolbar. Figure 2-13 shows how a document appears in Print Preview display.

Move the mouse pointer anyplace on the letter; the pointer will look like a small magnifying lens. To quickly enlarge a portion of the page, point to the

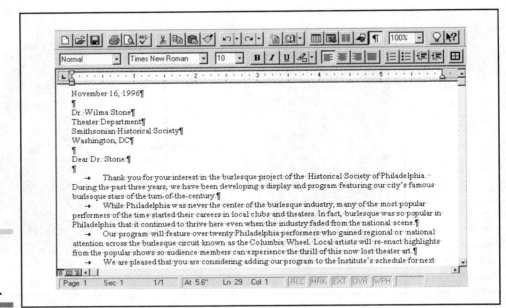

Invisible codes revealed!
Figure 2-12.

text you want to enlarge with the magnifying lens and click the mouse button. Click the mouse again to return to the other view. Click the mouse to enlarge the display, and then click again to reduce it. When you are finished previewing the document, click on the Close button.

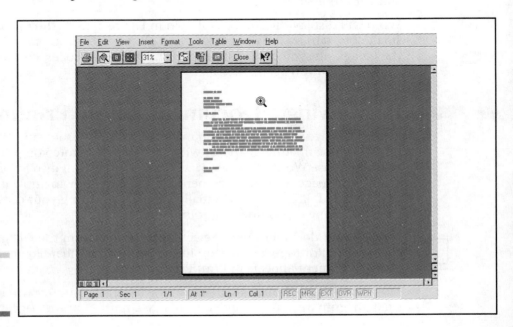

Your letter in Print Preview
Figure 2-13.

Caution: To exit Print Preview, be sure to use the Close button in the Print Preview toolbar, not the Close command in the File menu.

The Print Preview toolbar contains the following options for adjusting the display and working with your document.

2

Button	Name	Function
	Print	Prints the document without first displaying the Print dialog box.
	Magnifier	Changes from Magnifier to Editing mode. When you turn off the magnifier function, the button appears not to be pressed down, and the mouse pointer looks like the I-beam. You can use the I-beam to position the insertion point in the document to add or edit text from the preview window.
	One Page	Displays one page of the document at a time.
	Multiple Pages	Displays more than one page at a time.
100% ▾	Zoom	Adjusts the displayed magnification, just like the Zoom button on the Standard toolbar.
	View Ruler	Toggles the ruler display on and off.
	Shrink to Fit	Adjusts the document's spacing to reduce the number of pages. Use this button when just a few words or lines appear on the last document page.
	Full Screen	Removes the title bar, menu bar, scroll bars, and status bar from the screen. Has the same effect as selecting Full Screen from the View menu.

Changing Toolbars

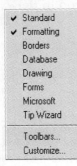

One other way you can customize the screen is to turn the toolbars off and on, and to change how the buttons appear. To turn a toolbar off or on, point the mouse on any toolbar already on the screen, and then click the right mouse button. You'll see the shortcut menu, shown here. The check marks next to a toolbar name mean that the toolbar is turned on—that it is being displayed. Click on the name of the toolbar that you want to turn off or turn on. The toolbars that appear onscreen when you exit Word will automatically appear when you next start Word.

Chances are you won't want to remove the Standard and Formatting toolbars from the screen. They are so useful that they'll save you countless keystrokes and the trouble of working your way through menus and dialog boxes. To make them even more useful, you can customize their appearance and move them to other locations on the screen, even outside the Word window onto the Windows 95 desktop.

Moving a toolbar is as easy as dragging. Point the mouse to any blank area on the toolbar between or surrounding the buttons. Do not point to a button on the toolbar. Hold down the mouse button and then drag the mouse. As you drag, a gray box representing the toolbar will move along with the pointer. Release the mouse button when the box is where you want the toolbar to appear.

If you drag the toolbar somewhere above the text area, or to the bottom of the screen above the status bar, the buttons on the toolbar will appear in one row, just like the default layout. If you drag the toolbar to the far left or right of the screen, the buttons will be in one column. If you drag the toolbar into the typing area, however, it will appear as a small window, complete with a title bar and control button, as you see here.

You change the size and shape of the toolbar by dragging one of its borders, just as you can change the size and shape of any window in Windows. Click on the control button to turn off the toolbar. To turn it back on, you'll need to display the shortcut menu and select the name of the toolbar.

In addition to changing the position of a toolbar, you can adjust certain aspects of its appearance. Right-click on a toolbar and then select Toolbars

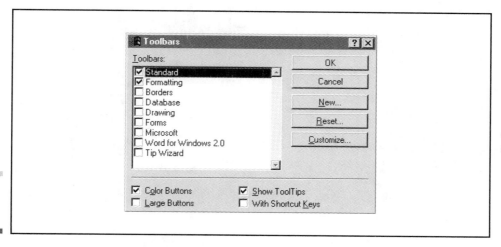

The Toolbars
dialog box
Figure 2-14.

from the shortcut menu, or choose Toolbars from the View menu. Word will
display the dialog box shown in Figure 2-14.

♦ Select *Color Buttons* to toggle between color and black-and-white buttons.

♦ Select *Large Buttons* to increase the size of the buttons. The buttons will
be easy to see, but some of them will now be off the right edge of the
screen. To see all of the buttons, drag the toolbar to
a new position and change it to a rectangular
window.

♦ Select *Show ToolTips* to toggle on or off the display
of the button name under the mouse pointer.

♦ Select *With Shortcut Keys* to display the ToolTip along with its
corresponding key combination, as shown here.

Now close the document on the screen, without saving your changes to it,
and then exit Word.

You now know the fundamentals of editing documents and customizing
their appearance on the screen. These capabilities, however, only touch
upon Word's amazing power and versatility. In the next chapter, you'll learn
even more ways to edit your documents, how to move and copy text, and
how to have Word enter text for you!

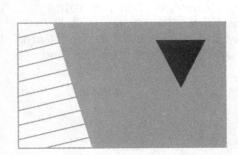

More Editing

3

When you have to write an important document, don't worry first about the structure—just concentrate on what you want to say. Once your ideas start to take shape, you can then use Word's versatile editing resources to organize your thoughts. In this chapter, you will learn how to move and copy text within a document, and how to let Word insert text and correct mistakes for you. What you'll learn here will save you hours of work, and many headaches.

Moving and Copying Text with Drag and Drop

Sometimes you type text only to discover it would be better in another location in your document. One of the great advantages of Word is that you can easily move text from one place to another. You can even make a duplicate copy of text in another location.

Using the mouse, you can move or copy text that you've selected as easily as dragging. When you *move* text, you delete it from one place in your document and insert it into another location. When you *copy* text, you make a duplicate of selected text and place the copy in another location—the text in the original location is not affected.

You can easily copy and move text using a method called *drag and drop*. This means that you drag the selected text to where you want to insert it, and then release the mouse button to drop it into place. Here's how to *move* text using drag and drop:

1. Select the text, using either the mouse or the keyboard.
2. Point anywhere in the selected area so the mouse pointer is shaped like an arrow.
3. Press and hold down the mouse button, and then drag the mouse to where you want to insert the text. As you drag the mouse, a small box and a dotted insertion point will accompany the pointer, as you can see here.

The cow quickly jumped over the moon.

4. Release the mouse button when the dotted insertion point is where you want the text to appear.

If you want to *copy* text, rather than move it, press and hold down the CTRL key while you release the mouse button. When you hold down CTRL, a plus sign will appear with the pointer, confirming that you are making a copy of the text.

The cow quickly jumped over the moon.

You can use drag and drop to move or copy text anywhere in the document, even in areas that have scrolled off the screen. When you drag the pointer past the top or bottom of the window, the screen will scroll automatically.

Tip: It is sometimes difficult to control the speed at which your screen scrolls as you drag the mouse. If the screen scrolls too fast, you may have difficulty placing the insertion point where you want it. I can't tell you how many times I've had to scroll up and then down several times to get it right. You may be able to reduce the magnification so you don't need to scroll the screen. But if you can't avoid scrolling, and have difficulty when trying to drop text into any area not visible on the screen, use the cut and paste method discussed later in this chapter.

3

You do not have to hold down the CTRL key while you are dragging, only when you release the button.

If you change your mind about moving the text while you are dragging, just move the pointer back to the selected text and then release the button. If you've already dropped the text, and then change your mind, use the Undo Move command from the Edit menu, or select Move from the Undo list.

Open the document Letter to Historical Society. Let's use drag and drop to move a sentence to another paragraph. Drag to select the first sentence of the paragraph beginning with "Our program will feature". Be sure to select the period at the end of the sentence.

> Our program will feature over twenty Philadelphia performers who gained regional or national attention across the burlesque circuit known as the Columbia Wheel. Local artists will re-enact highlights from the popular shows so audience members can experience the thrill of this now lost theater art.
>
> We are pleased that you are considering adding our program to the Institute's schedule for next year. We are looking forward to your visit to Philadelphia, and to sharing with you the exciting story of Philadelphia burlesque.

Now point to the selected sentence, hold down the mouse button, and drag the text to move the dotted insertion point to the end of the first paragraph, like this:

> Thank you for your interest in the burlesque project of the Historical Society of Philadelphia. During the past three years, we have been developing a display and program featuring our city's famous burlesque stars of the turn-of-the-century.
>
> While Philadelphia was never the center of the burlesque industry, many of the most popular performers of the time started their careers in local clubs and theaters. In fact, burlesque was so popular in

Release the mouse button. Word moves the sentence to the first paragraph, automatically inserting a space before it.

Now use drag and drop to copy the words "Historical Society of Philadelphia" below the signature block. Drag over the words in the first paragraph. Point to the highlighted words with the mouse and drag them to the end of the document. As you drag past the bottom of the window, the document will scroll up. Notice that if you did not press ENTER after typing the title, "President", you cannot move the insertion point below the title, only after it.

Jane W. Wilcox
President

Now press and hold down CTRL and then release the mouse button. Click the mouse to deselect the text. If the title and the society name appear on the same line, move the insertion point after the word "President" and press ENTER.

Jane W. Wilcox
President
Historical Society of Philadelphia

The signature block will now look like the one you see here.

Save the document, close it, and then click on the New button in the toolbar to begin a new document.

Moving and Copying Text Through the Clipboard

The *Clipboard* is an area in the computer's memory where Windows temporarily stores information. You can place text into the Clipboard and then later take it from the Clipboard to insert elsewhere. When you move text using the Clipboard, it's called cut and paste. You cut the text from one location and paste it elsewhere. When you copy text with the Clipboard, it's called copy and paste. You make a copy of the text and then paste it elsewhere.

Remember: Use the Clipboard when you find that scrolling a long document when dragging is inconvenient, or if you get tired of holding down the mouse button until you locate the correct location.

To move text using cut and paste, first select the text you want to move. Then cut the text into the Clipboard by clicking on the Cut button in the Standard toolbar. The selected text is now in the Clipboard.

You can also cut text to the Clipboard by using one of these techniques:

♦ Select Cut from the Edit menu.
♦ Press CTRL-X.
♦ Select Cut from the shortcut menu that appears when you click the right mouse on the selected text.

Tip: Practice using the shortcut menu when you edit your documents. It is easier to right-click and then select Cut from the shortcut menu than it is to move the mouse all the way to the toolbar or menu bar. The Cut and Copy options will be dimmed in the shortcut menu if text is not selected.

Next, place the insertion point where you want to insert the text. Then paste it into the document by clicking on the Paste button. Word will insert whatever is in the Clipboard into the document.

You can also paste the contents of the Clipboard using one of these techniques:

3

◆   Select Paste from the Edit menu.
◆   Press CTRL-V.
◆   Select Paste from the shortcut menu that appears when you right-click.

Note: The Paste option will be dimmed in the shortcut menu if no text is in the Clipboard.

To *copy* text rather than move it, follow the same steps as above but click on the Copy button. You can also select Copy from the Edit menu, press CTRL-C, or select Copy from the shortcut menu.

Caution: Windows can only store one thing in the Clipboard at a time. So think about the consequences. If you cut some text in preparation to move it, then absentmindedly cut or copy something else, the text you want to move is erased from the Clipboard. Click on the Undo button twice to restore both cut portions of text, and then start over.

The contents of the Clipboard will remain there until you cut or copy something else, or until you exit Windows. This means that you can insert the same text over and over again in your document, as long as you do not cut or copy something else. To insert the Clipboard contents in multiple locations, just position the insertion point and select Paste at each spot.

Moving Text with the Spike

While the Clipboard is certainly useful, it does have its limitations. Suppose, for example, that you want to move a number of selected portions of text to one location. Because the Clipboard can only store one thing at a time, you'd have to cut and paste each section individually, moving back and forth through your document.

It's not much easier with drag and drop. Sure, you can drag and drop the first selection to the next, then select both sections, and drag them to the third, and so on. But dragging text through a long document while scrolling the screen can be difficult.

The solution is to use the *spike,* a special Clipboard area that can store more than one item at a time. Each item you add to the spike is inserted after any items already there. So you can move through a document, cutting selected text into the spike, collecting individual sections into a group. You can then insert the entire contents of the spike elsewhere in the document.

Note: Wonder where the term "spike" came from? Have you ever seen those nails that a secretary uses to impale "while you were out messages" or a waiter uses to stick orders for the chef? Each new sheet of paper is added to the nail without removing those already there. Word's spike works the same way.

There is no mouse or menu equivalent for adding information to the spike. You can insert the contents of the spike into your document, however, using the AutoText command. More on that later.

To add text to the spike, select the text and then press CTRL-F3. Windows will cut the selected text and place it into the spike. Repeat the same procedure for each section of text that you want to cut and collect into the group—select it and press CTRL-F3.

When you've collected all of the text you want to move, place the insertion point where you want to insert the text and press CTRL-SHIFT-F3. The contents of the spike will appear in your document. Word automatically inserts a carriage return after each entry in the spike, so each entry you saved will appear as a separate paragraph.

Unlike the Clipboard, which retains its contents after you paste, the spike is cleared when you press CTRL-SHIFT-F3. But also unlike the Clipboard, if you do not clear the spike, Word will retain its contents even when you exit Windows. The next time you start Windows and Word, the spike will contain what was saved there.

Note: Word will sound a warning beep if the spike is already empty when you press CTRL-SHIFT-F3.

If you want to insert the contents of the spike but not empty it, type the word **spike** and then press F3. The insertion point must be positioned after the word "spike," with no intervening characters other than a space or carriage return. You must type the word "spike" as a separate word. There can be no characters immediately in front of it, such as "addspike".

Inserting with AutoText

3

Sometimes you find yourself writing the same word or phrase over and over again. You may repeat it several times in one document, or use the same phrase in a number of documents that you write. It's not bad if you have to repeat a small word several times. But imagine having to repeat a complex scientific or medical term, or the full name of some company or governmental agency. How many errors could occur if you had to type **laryngopharyngography** 10 or 20 times in the same report? Sure, you could copy the word and then paste it where you want it. But then the word would be deleted from the Clipboard if you had to cut or copy something else.

When you have a word or phrase that you use frequently, use AutoText. AutoText lets you insert a word, phrase, or entire section of text by typing an abbreviation for it. So you could create an AutoText entry for laryngopharyngography, for example, and then insert it by typing **lar**.

You can have an AutoText entry for your name and address, for your telephone number, for standard closings, or for anything that you want to insert easily and quickly. In fact, you can have an unlimited number of AutoText entries defined because Word automatically saves the AutoText on your disk.

Upgrade: The AutoText button is no longer on the Standard toolbar.

To use AutoText, you first create an AutoText entry, linking a word or phrase with its abbreviation. To create an AutoText entry, select the text you want to assign to an abbreviation, and then select AutoText from the Edit menu. Try it now by typing your full name in a new document window. Select your name, and then choose AutoText from the Edit menu to display the dialog box shown in Figure 3-1.

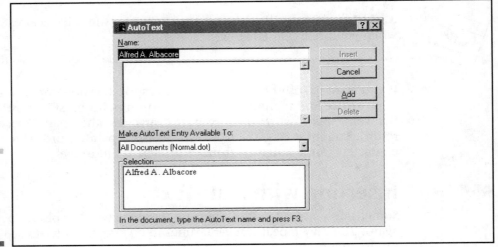

The AutoText
dialog box for
creating an
AutoText entry
Figure 3-1.

Note: The list labeled Make AutoText Entry Available To is used when
you are working with various templates. You will learn about templates in
Chapter 11.

Your name will be highlighted in the Name text box, and it will appear in
the Selection box. You use the Name text box to designate the abbreviation
that you can use to insert the complete phrase into your document. Type
your initials, which will replace the highlighted text in the box. Click on
Add to link the abbreviation with the text.

You want to use abbreviations that identify the AutoText entry but don't
take as long to type. Abbreviations that are too short may not really save
you time. For example, several months from now, will you remember that F
represents Federal Communications Commission? Using FederalCC, on the
other hand, isn't that much of a shortcut. Of course for this example, FCC is
a perfect abbreviation!

The next time you need to insert the text into a document, type the
abbreviation and press F3. So type your initials now and press F3.

The abbreviation must be followed by a space or carriage return, although
there could be some blank spaces between the abbreviation and the insertion
point when you press F3. If there are any other characters after the abbreviation,
such as FCCB, Word will sound a beep because it cannot find the abbreviation
in the AutoText list. Type **ABC** and then press F3. Word will sound a beep
because ABC is not an AutoText entry.

Tip: You actually do not have to type the full abbreviati characters to uniquely identify the AutoText entry. For exam only one AutoText abbreviation that starts with the letter l, y type **l** and press F3, rather than **lar**.

If you forget what abbreviations you used, or you want to delete an AutoText entry, you'll need to display the AutoText dialog box. Without any text selected, choose AutoText from the Edit menu. The dialog box shown in Figure 3-2 will appear, with the first abbreviation ready to be selected.

Tip: If you have any text in the spike, you will see the word "spike" in the Name list. This indicates that the spike is actually an AutoText entry. You can insert the contents of the spike by selecting its name in this dialog box.

3

If your initials are not already selected, click on them now. The full text that the abbreviation represents appears in the Preview panel. Double-click on your initials to insert the full text into the document, or select the abbreviation and then click on Insert.

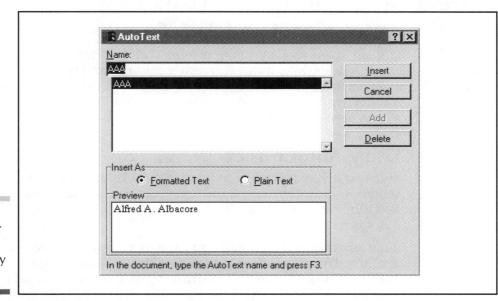

The AutoText dialog box for inserting an AutoText entry
Figure 3-2.

Display the AutoText dialog box once again. Notice the option buttons labeled Formatted Text and Plain Text. Choosing Formatted Text will insert the text with all of the formats from the text you originally selected. If you select the Plain Text option, the text appears using the formats of the paragraph in which the insertion point is located.

Tip: To print a list of your AutoText entries, select Print from the File menu, pull down the Print What list, select AutoText Entries, and click on OK.

To delete an AutoText entry, select it from the Name list and then click on Delete. To edit an AutoText entry, insert the text into the document, edit it, and then save it again as an AutoText entry using the same abbreviation.

Remember: To clear the spike without inserting its text into your document, select the spike entry in the AutoText box and click on Delete. The spike will be re-created the next time you add something to it.

Streamlining Your Work with AutoCorrect and AutoFormat

It is easy to get spoiled with a program such as Word. Not only will Word check your spelling, it can also correct mistakes and insert special symbols and characters as you type. This magic is performed by two special Word features—AutoCorrect and AutoFormat As You Type. In fact, you may have already seen both of these features in action.

Using AutoCorrect

AutoText is very powerful but it is not automatic. You have to type the abbreviation and then press the F3 key, or open the AutoText dialog box, select the entry, and insert it. If you find that too much work, then use AutoCorrect.

AutoCorrect is actually a built-in feature that you may have already noticed in action. Try typing **adn** and then press the SPACEBAR. Word will automatically change the word to "and". Type **HEllo**, with the first two letters uppercase. Press ENTER—Word changes the second letter to lowercase. If you type **i** for the pronoun I, Word will automatically make it uppercase.

These automatic corrections are provided by AutoCorrect. AutoCorrect actually watches as you type, correcting these and some other common mistakes on the fly. You can customize the way AutoCorrect works, and you can add your own AutoCorrect entries. For example, if you frequently misspell certain words, you can have Word correct the spelling as you type. You can also create AutoCorrect entries to insert text when you type an abbreviation—without the need to press F3. For instance, you can have Word insert a person's full name when you type their initials, or insert the full name of a state when you type its two-letter abbreviation.

Create an entry now to insert the words "personal computer" when you type the abbreviation **pc**. Select AutoCorrect from the Tools menu to display the dialog box shown in Figure 3-3.

The two-column list box shows AutoCorrect entries that Word has already defined for you. It includes some common typographical errors and misspelled words, as shown in Table 3-1. The checked items on the top of the dialog box show the defaults for general corrections.

In the Replace box, you type the abbreviation for an automatic entry, or the way you normally misspell a word. Type **pc** in the text box now. In the With box, type the full text you want displayed with the abbreviation, or type the correct spelling of the word that you misspell. Press TAB to reach the With box and type **personal computer**. Choose Add to create the entry and then close the dialog box.

3

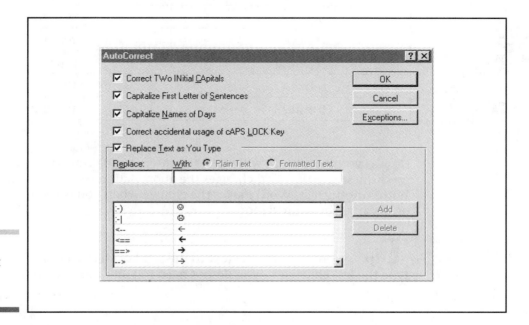

The
AutoCorrect
dialog box
Figure 3-3.

You Type:	AutoCorrect Inserts:
(c)	©
(r)	®
(tm)	™
-->	→
:-(	☹
:-)	☺
:¦	☺
<--	←
<==	⬅
<=>	⇔
==>	➔
adn	and
alot	a lot
don;t	don't
helpfull	helpful
immediatly	immediately
occurence	occurrence
recieve	receive
seperate	separate
teh	the
tonite	tonight

Common
Typographical
Errors and
Misspelled
Words in
AutoCorrect
Table 3-1.

Now as you type, Word will make the insertion for you. Type **pc** and then press the SPACEBAR. Word changes the abbreviation to "personal computer." With AutoCorrect, Word makes the change when you press SPACEBAR, ENTER, or TAB after the abbreviation.

Tip: Word changes the text to the symbol characters as soon as you type the last character—you do not need to enter the space first.

You can create an AutoCorrect entry from text that you've already typed. So if you type a long word, or misspell a word, create an AutoCorrect entry to save and trouble the next time you need to type it. Let's do that now. Suppose you frequently misspell the word "deceive" as "decieve". Type **deceive** and then double-click on the word to select it. Now choose AutoCorrect from the Tools menu. The selected text automatically appears in the With text box, and you can select either the Plain Text or Formatted Text option buttons. Type the way that you misspell the word—**decieve**—and then click on Add. Click on Close to return to the document, type **decieve** (spelled incorrectly) and then press the SPACEBAR. Word will correct the word for you.

Watch Your Case with AutoCorrect

3

When you create an AutoCorrect entry, pay attention to the case of your characters. If you enter the Replace and With text in lowercase characters, Word will automatically insert text based on the case of the abbreviation, as shown here:

You Type:	AutoCorrect Inserts:
pc	personal computer
PC	PERSONAL COMPUTER
Pc	Personal computer
pC	[*nothing*]

AutoCorrect uses the case of the abbreviation to determine the case of the insertion. But Word won't be so understanding if you use any uppercase characters in the Replace or With phrases in the AutoCorrect dialog box. If you designate the Replace phrase with an uppercase letter, as in **Pa**, then you must enter **Pa** or **PA** for AutoCorrect to work. And, Word will insert the full text exactly the way you entered it in the With box. So if you create an AutoCorrect entry to replace Pa with pennsylvania, entering **Pa** or **PA** will replace it with all lowercase letters. If you tell Word to replace Pa with Pennsylvania, then it will match the case, like this:

You Type:	AutoCorrect Inserts:
Pa	Pennsylvania
PA	PENNSYLVANIA
pa	[*nothing*]

AutoCorrect Options

AutoCorrect does have its disadvantages. For example, suppose you have an AutoCorrect entry that inserts the word Maine after you type **Ma**. Word cannot distinguish when you really want to address your mother as Ma in a letter. I don't think she'd appreciate getting a letter addressed to Dear Maine. To turn off AutoCorrect, and to otherwise customize how it operates, check out the options in the AutoCorrect dialog box.

Click on the Replace Text As You Type check box to turn off automatic replacement of the AutoCorrect entries. You can now type **pc** without replacing it with personal computer. To control the default options for general corrections, click to turn off or on their check boxes. The Correct Accidental Usage of cAPS LOCK Key option is especially useful. If you press the CAPS LOCK key by mistake, your sentence will start with a lowercase letter, followed by all uppercase letters. AutoCorrect detects this capitalization, turns off the CAPS LOCK key, and reverses the case of the characters.

If you type abbreviations or words that do have mixed capitalization, click on the Exceptions button. A dialog box will appear with two pages—First Letter and Initial Caps. In the First Letter box, enter an abbreviation that you do not want Word to treat as the end of a sentence. For example, if you type **Set the margin at 5 in. and then click on OK**, Word will capitalize the letter *a* in the word *and*, thinking that it begins a sentence. To avoid this problem without having to turn the Capitalize First Letter of Sentences feature off, enter **in.** as an exception. In the Initial Caps page, enter any words—such as special trade names and logos—that may have the first two letters capitalized.

Tip: If you press an arrow key immediately after typing an AutoCorrect entry, AutoCorrect will not take effect. For instance, if you decide that you want the first two letters of an existing word capitalized, edit the word and then press an arrow key to move the insertion point.

Using AutoFormat As You Type

In addition to AutoCorrect, Word also will insert and format text for you through a feature called AutoFormat As You Type. If you surround a word in quotes, for instance, Word automatically changes straight quotes into "Smart Quotes," as shown here.

Word changes "straight quotes" into "Smart Quotes"

AutoFormat will also superscript ordinal numbers (changing 1st to 1st for example), change fractions such as 1/2 to fraction characters such as ½, and change two hyphens (--) to an em-dash (—). AutoFormat can also insert lines, format headings, and create bulleted and numbered lists as you type. (You'll learn about lines and headings in Chapter 9, and about lists in Chapter 13.)

To select which changes AutoFormat makes for you as you type, select Options from the Tools menu, and then click on the AutoFormat tab to see the options shown in Figure 3-4. To turn a feature off or on, select or deselect its check box.

Note: Turning an option on or off will not automatically affect text that you've already typed. However, it will affect text if you move the insertion point after the word in question and then press SPACEBAR, ENTER, or TAB. In Chapter 9, you'll learn more about using AutoFormat to format existing text.

3

Inserting the Date and Time

You probably add the date to letters, memos, and faxes. You might even add the time to faxes, logs, journals, messages, and other documents when the time of distribution or printing is important. Rather than manually typing

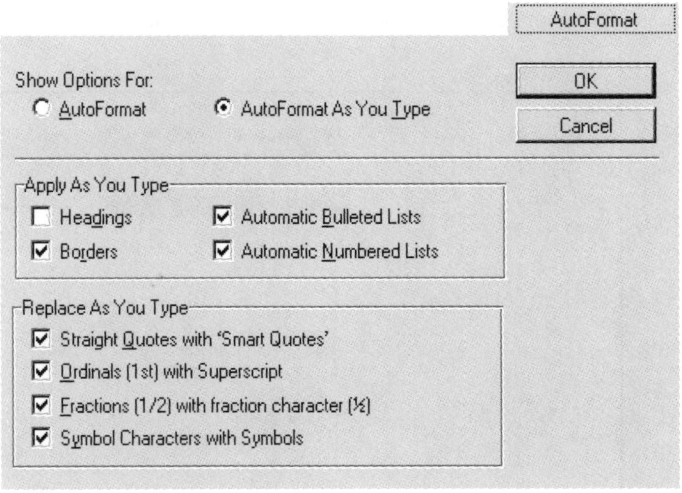

Use the
AutoFormat
section of
the Options
dialog box
to control
AutoCorrect
Figure 3-4.

AutoFormat

Show Options For:
  ○ _A_utoFormat   ⦿ AutoFormat As You _T_ype

OK

Cancel

┌─Apply As You Type─────────────────────────
│ ☐ _H_eadings   ☑ Automatic _B_ulleted Lists
│ ☑ Bo_r_ders   ☑ Automatic _N_umbered Lists

┌─Replace As You Type───────────────────────
│ ☑ Straight _Q_uotes with 'Smart Quotes'
│ ☑ _O_rdinals (1st) with Superscript
│ ☑ _F_ractions (1/2) with fraction character (½)
│ ☑ S_y_mbol Characters with Symbols

the date or time, let Word do it for you. Word can add the date and time in two ways—as text or as a field. Both methods will display the same information on the screen, but there are important differences between them.

When you have Word insert the date or time as *text*, Word enters it as a series of characters, just as if you had typed it yourself. You can edit or delete individual characters, just as you can edit any text that you've typed.

When you have Word insert the date and time as a *field*, however, you will *see* the date or time appear on the screen, but Word has actually entered a code called a field. The field tells Word to display the current date or time that the document is opened or printed. For instance, suppose it is 10:30 A.M. when you write a fax to your attorney, and you insert the time as a field. You will see 10:30 A.M. on the screen, just as if you had typed 10:30 A.M. or you had Word insert the time as text. When you later open or print the document, however, you can have Word automatically change the time to the current time. So for instance, if you do not get a chance to send the fax until 2:15 P.M., you can have Word automatically update the field so 2:15 P.M. appears on the fax.

To insert the date or time, select Date and Time from the Insert menu to display the dialog box shown in Figure 3-5. The dates and times shown in the Available Formats list are the actual date and time you display the box. Notice that there are choices that show just the date, some that show a combined date and time, and several that only show the time. Select one of the formats that displays the time with seconds.

If you want to insert the date or time as *text* so Word cannot change it, make certain that the Update Automatically (Insert as Field) check box is not checked. To insert the date or time as a *field*, make certain the box is checked.

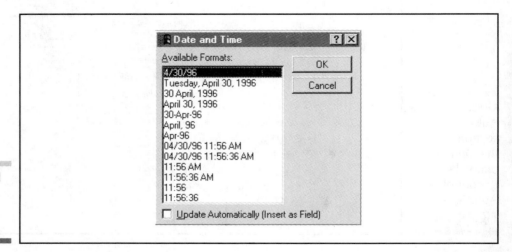

The Date and Time dialog box

Figure 3-5.

For now, make certain that the check box is not selected, and then click on OK to insert the time as text. Press ENTER to move to the next line. Now insert the same time as a field. Choose Date and Time from the Insert menu, click on the check box to insert the time as a field, and then select OK.

While the field will appear in a gray box when selected, the times are the same, except that they vary by a few seconds. Click on the first time, the one inserted as text, and add 1 to the hour—that is, if the time appears as 3:41:02 P.M., change it to 4:41:02 P.M.

Tip: If you hear a beep when you're editing the time in the field, don't be alarmed. You cannot delete the first character in a field by placing the insertion point before it and pressing DELETE. Likewise, you cannot delete the last character in a field by placing the insertion point after it and pressing BACKSPACE. To delete the first character, move the insertion point after it and press BACKSPACE; to delete the last character, move the insertion point before it and press DELETE.

3

12:58:54 AM
11:59:01 AM

Now click on the second date, the one inserted as a field. The entire date appears in a gray rectangle.

Add one to the hour. So far, both dates still look the same. Now drag the mouse over both dates to select them and press F9. Word updates the field to the current time but does not change the time inserted and edited as text. The F9 key is the universal command for updating all types of fields in Word. To delete the time, or any field in Word, drag the mouse over it and then press DELETE.

Tip: You do not have to select a field to update with F9. Just click on the field so it appears in the gray highlight, and then press F9.

Inserting Dates and Times with Keystrokes

You can also insert the date and time as a field using shortcut key combinations. To insert the date as a field, press ALT-SHIFT-D. To insert the current time as a field, press ALT-SHIFT-T. The format of the date and time shown in the field depends on your most recent selections in the Date and Time dialog box.

Remember: Each time you start Word, the first format will be selected when you open the Date and Time dialog box. However, Word will retain your most recent selection for the Update Automatically (Insert as Field) option.

Changing Pages

You know that as you type, Word automatically begins a new page as each becomes filled. There may be instances, however, when you want to start a new page even though the one before it is not filled, such as when you type a short cover letter before typing an attachment.

To end one page and start another before the page becomes full, press CTRL-ENTER. This is called a *hard page break*, and it appears as a dotted line with the words "Page Break" in the center of the screen.

--- Page Break ---

To delete a hard page break, click on the line and press DELETE. Word will combine the text with the page before it, and add soft page breaks where needed.

The line that Word inserts between pages automatically as you type is called a *soft page break*. You cannot delete a soft page break yourself, but as you insert or delete text above the soft page break, Word will adjust its position so it includes a complete page of text. Of course, if you delete enough text on the last page of your document, the page break line will disappear.

Close the document now on your screen, without saving it.

Caution: I've seen beginning Word users insert soft page breaks by pressing ENTER until the page break line appears. Don't make that mistake. Let Word paginate the document for you, or insert hard page breaks when you definitely want a new page to begin. Filling pages with blank lines will make editing and formatting your document a nightmare.

The techniques you've learned in this chapter will streamline your work. Practice moving and copying text until you feel comfortable with the mouse and the Clipboard. Create AutoText and AutoCorrect entries for text that you use often, and to correct your most common mistakes. And even though the spike is a keyboard technique, don't forget how useful it can be.

Searching and Replacing Text

4

Word not only makes it easy to *do* things, it makes it easy to *find* things as well. You can have Word search your entire document, or just parts of it, to find a specific word or phrase. Better yet, you can have Word replace text for you just as easily. So when you need to find a word or phrase, or make replacements, stop scrolling and let Word do it for you! In this chapter, you will learn all about Word's powerful Find and Replace commands.

Searching Your Document

The Find command can be a real time-saver. Suppose you're looking for a specific reference in your document. You know it's there but you don't know exactly where. Instead of reading the entire document to look for the reference, use the Find command. The Find command scans your document, looking for the first occurrence of the word or phrase that you specify. After it finds the word or phrase, you can repeat the command to find the next occurrence, and so on, until your entire document has been searched.

Open the Biography of Sliding Billy Watson document. If it is already open, move the insertion point to the beginning. Then to search your document, select Find from the Edit menu, or press CTRL-F to display the dialog box shown in Figure 4-1.

The insertion point is in the Find What text box. This is where you tell Word

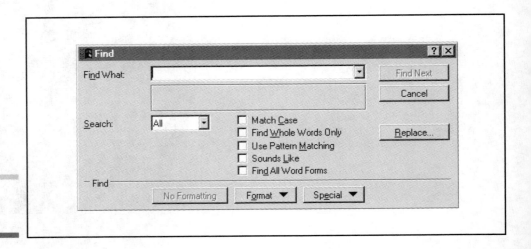

what word or phrase to search for. Type **Watson** and click on the Find Next button. Word locates and highlights the first occurrence of the characters following the insertion point.

Word will scroll the window so the highlighted word is near the top of the screen. If you cannot see the word, move the Find dialog box to the bottom of the window by dragging its title bar.

The Find
dialog box
Figure 4-1.

Remember: Word will search your document starting at the position of the insertion point. If the insertion point is not at the beginning of the document, the first occurrence of the word found may not be the actual first reference to it in the document.

The Find dialog box remains onscreen so you can continue searching for the next occurrence or change the search options. To find the next occurrence, click on Find Next again or press ENTER. The word "Watson" is not located again, so a message box appears telling you that Word has finished searching the document. Click on OK to clear the box from the screen. The highlight disappears and Word returns the insertion point to its original position. The Find dialog box is still on the screen in case you want to begin a new search. Select Cancel to clear the box.

Tip: If you close the dialog box and decide you want to continue searching for the same text, press SHIFT-F4. Word begins the search without displaying the Find dialog box.

4

Now let's try another search, this time not starting at the beginning of the document. Click at the beginning of the third paragraph, and then select Find from the Edit menu. The last phrase you searched for during this Word session is still shown in the Find What box. Type **Billy** and click on Find Next. Word highlights the first occurrence of the word following the insertion point. Continue selecting Find Next. When Word reaches the end of the document, it starts over at the beginning until it reaches the insertion point where it started the find operation. Select OK to clear the message box.

Tip: If Word stops and displays a message asking if you want to continue searching from the beginning of the document, select Yes. You'll learn why this message may have appeared in the discussion of the Search box options.

Now try one more search. Type **ever** and then click on Find Next. Word highlights the characters *ever* at the end of the word "However", like this:

Billy was born as Wolf Shapiro on October 12, 1876. His family moved from New York to Philadelphia, where Billy tried to settle down into a quiet family life. However, the call of the stage was too difficult for him to resist. He abandoned his wife and two children for the limelight and fame of vaudeville.

By default, Word looks for the characters that you type wherever they are, even if they are part of another word. So searching for "ever" will also stop at words such as "forever" and "every".

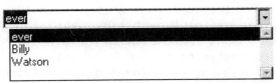

Click on the down arrow at the end of the Find What text box. All of the search phrases you've looked for are retained until you exit Word. To search for the same phrase again, select it from the list. Now let's look at the other options in the dialog box.

♦   The *Search* box determines how Word scans through the document. When set at All, the default value, Word scans down to the end of the document and then moves back to the start of the document to continue the search. You can also choose to search Down or Up. When you select Down, Word pauses at the end of the document and asks if you want to continue searching at the top. When you select Up, Word scans the document from the insertion point toward the beginning of the document. When it reaches the beginning, it will ask if you want to continue searching from the end.

Tip: If you select text first, Word will only scan through the selected text during the Find operation, and the Search option will automatically be set to Down. When Word completes the search, it will ask if you want to continue searching the remainder of the document. The next time you begin a search during the same session, the Search box will still be set at Down. Change the setting to All if you want Word to scan the entire document without pausing.

♦   *Match Case* determines whether Word pays attention to the case of characters. With this option not selected (the default setting), Word ignores case. For example, if you search for **club**, it will find references to "club", "Club", and "CLUB". If you select this option, Word only locates words with the exact case of characters that you enter in the Find What box.

♦   *Find Whole Words Only* determines whether Word locates text that is part of another word. By default, as you know, Word will locate the Find

What characters even if they are part of another word. Select this option to locate the characters only when they are whole words. When this option is turned on, searching for **ever** will not stop at "however", or any other word other than "ever" itself.

♦ *Use Pattern Matching* helps you find words using the question mark as a *wildcard*. When this option is selected, the character ? represents any single character in the search phrase. Searching for **m?l**, for example, will locate the letters *m* and *l* with any other letter between them, such as the *mil* in "family", and *mel* in "limelight".

♦ *Sounds Like* lets you search for words that sound like the Find What text. For instance, searching for **berlesk** will locate "burlesque". When you select this option, Word dims the first three check boxes, so Sounds Like cannot be combined with Match Case, Find Whole Words Only, or Use Pattern Matching.

♦ *Find All Word Forms* is a powerful new feature in Word for Windows 95. It locates all tenses of a word. For example, searching for **sing** with this option selected will locate "sing", "sang", and "sung".

4

 Note: The Replace command button changes the dialog box to the Replace dialog box. The Format and Special buttons let you search for formats and formatting codes. You'll learn about these commands in the next few sections of this chapter.

Replacing Text Automatically

Making a mistake is only human, but making the same mistake more than once is downright annoying. Have you ever typed a document only to discover that you've made the same mistake several times? It's no fun scanning the entire document to make the same correction over and over. But even multiple mistakes can be fun with Word.

The Replace command will search your document to find text automatically and replace it with something else. You can use it not only to correct errors but to recycle documents. Perhaps you created a sales proposal that mentions a person's name in several places. You may be able to modify the proposal for another prospect by changing just one or two words several times. You can have Word scan the entire document, automatically replacing Mr. Smith with Mrs. Jones. It just takes a few keystrokes. As an example, close the document that you have on the screen and open the Letter to Historical Society document.

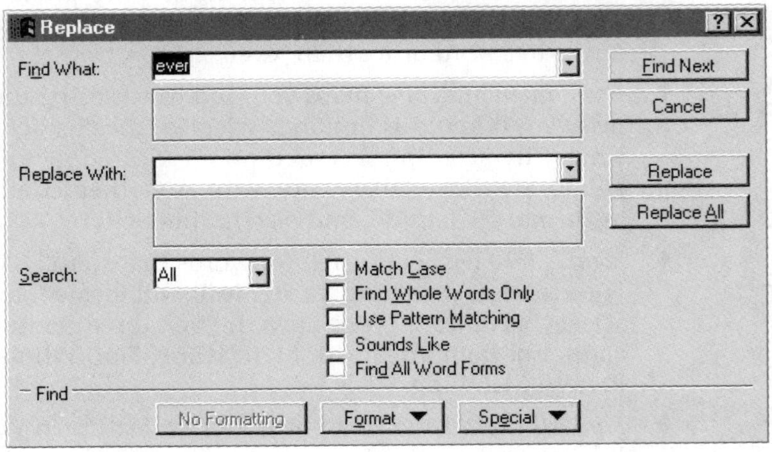

Replace

Find What: ever

Find Next

Cancel

Replace With:

Replace

Replace All

Search: All

☐ Match Case
☐ Find Whole Words Only
☐ Use Pattern Matching
☐ Sounds Like
☐ Find All Word Forms

─ Find ─

No Formatting   Format ▼   Special ▼

The Replace
dialog box
Figure 4-2.

To start a replace operation, select Replace from the Edit menu. Word will display the dialog box shown in Figure 4-2.

Tip: If you select text first, Word will only make replacements in the selected area.

The replace operation actually begins by performing a find to locate the characters that you want to replace, so it includes the same options that you've already learned about. In fact, the options and the Find What text will be the same as you selected in the last Find operation. The Replace dialog box also has a text box labeled Replace With and command buttons labeled Replace and Replace All.

In the Find What text box, you enter the text you want to find and replace. Type **Philadelphia** as the text you want to replace. In the Replace With box, you enter the text you want to insert. Press TAB to reach the box, or click in it, and then type **Camden**.

Caution: If you leave the Replace With entry blank, Word will delete every occurrence of the Find What text when you select Replace All.

Now to make all of the replacements automatically, click on the Replace All button. Word makes all of the replacements and displays a message box telling you the number of occurrences that have been changed. Select OK to clear the box. The Replace box remains onscreen.

Confirming Replacements

You might not want to replace every occurrence of the text in the document. For example, suppose that in your document you refer to the titles of two persons. You call Mrs. Jones President, and you refer to Mr. Smith as Vice President. After completing the letter, you learn that Mrs. Jones' correct title is Chairman. Can you use Replace All to change every occurrence of President to Chairman? Not really. If you do, you would change Mr. Smith's title to Vice Chairman.

4

When you do not want to replace every occurrence of the text, use the Find Next and Replace buttons, instead of Replace All. Try this now by typing **program** in the Find What text box. Press TAB and type **exhibition** in the Replace With box. Now click on Find Next to locate the first occurrence of the word after the position of the insertion point. When you click on Find Next, Word locates the next occurrence of the text and highlights it—just as if you had used the Find dialog box.

Tip: If you cannot see the highlighted occurrence, drag the Replace box out of the way.

You want to leave this occurrence unchanged, so click on Find Next again to locate the next occurrence. This time you want to make the replacement, so click on Replace. Word makes the replacement and then searches for the next occurrence. Click on Cancel to close the dialog box.

Use Replace with Caution

Using the Replace All command can lead to some strange and unwanted results if you are not careful. The default settings of the Replace box ignore case and locate characters even if they are part of another word. With these settings, replacing every occurrence of the text could unintentionally change parts of other words. For example, suppose you make a mistake referring to novels by George Sand as "his." An automatic replacement of "his" to "her" would also change "Buddhism" to "Buddherm", "historian" to "hertorian", and "sophism" to "sopherm". Can you picture what your professor would say about the sentence "As a Buddherm hertorian, he suffered from a degree of sopherm"!

To safeguard against these types of errors, confirm your replacements. If you don't want to take the time, however, combine Match Case with Find Whole Words Only to locate only the exact words that you want to change. For example, locating **his** with Find Whole Words Only turned on would prevent the mistakes just illustrated. Use the Match Case option when the word you want to replace might also appear as a proper noun (or a proper noun might appear as a lowercase term). With Match Case selected, for example, searching for **bill** to replace with **invoice** would not affect the name Bill.

If you do not select Match Case during a replacement, Word will duplicate the case of the text it locates. So it would change "bill" to "invoice", "Bill" to "Invoice", and even "BILL" to "INVOICE".

Finding Formats and Special Characters

Sometimes you want to find information that you cannot type into the Find What box. For example, suppose you want to find a word, but only when it is in italic format. Not only must you tell Word what text to locate but also its format.

You might also want to find and replace text that is coded in a certain way. For instance, suppose you type your entire dissertation with the first line of a paragraph indented by TAB, or with an extra blank line between paragraphs. You are later told that both formats are unacceptable.

It is easy to find formatted text and replace keystrokes such as TAB and ENTER. Both the Find and the Replace dialog boxes contain command buttons labeled Format and Special. You use the Format command to locate text in specific formats, or to replace text with a format. You use the Special command to locate and replace invisible codes, such as TAB, ENTER, and items such as page breaks, fields, and line breaks.

Font...
Paragraph...
Tabs...
Border...
Language...
Frame...
Style...
Highlight

To find or insert a format, first enter the text you want to find or replace in the Find What or Replace With text box. Then click on the Format button to display the list shown here.

Selecting an item from the list will display the Word dialog box that controls that format. For instance, selecting Font will display the Find Font dialog box with a list of font options. Choose the format that you want to find or insert, and then select OK. The format will appear in the Replace dialog, under the text it refers to. For example, Figure 4-3 shows the Replace dialog box set to locate the word "Inquirer" in bold, and replace it with the word "Inquirer" in italic.

Tip: Once you select a format, the No Formatting button is no longer dimmed. Click on No Formatting to remove the formats from the dialog box.

Paragraph Mark	Field
Tab Character	Footnote Mark
Annotation Mark	Graphic
Any Character	Manual Line Break
Any Digit	Manual Page Break
Any Letter	Nonbreaking Hyphen
Caret Character	Nonbreaking Space
Column Break	Optional Hyphen
Em Dash	Section Break
En Dash	White Space
Endnote Mark	

Locating and inserting special characters and codes is even easier. To find a code, place the insertion point in the Find What text box, and then click on the Special button to display a list of the codes you can search for.

4

Click on the item that you want to locate or insert. Word will insert a special code, starting with a caret (^), into the text box. For example, when you want to locate a paragraph mark (which is inserted in a document whenever you press ENTER), Word will insert ^p into the text box.

The Replace dialog box set to change bold to italic

Figure 4-3.

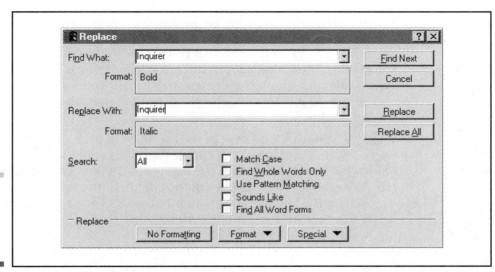

Tip: You do not have to memorize the caret codes for special characters, because you can select the character by name from the list. If you want to type them yourself, however, type the caret by holding down the SHIFT key when you press 6 on the top row of the keyboard. The caret characters are not control codes—do not try to enter them by holding down the CTRL key.

To insert special codes, place the insertion point in the Replace With box, and then click on the Special button to see a list of the codes you can insert.

Note the differences between the Special list that appears when you are entering the Find What text and the list that appears when you are entering the Replace With text. The Find list presents some options that are only valid when searching, such as Any Character (^?), Any Digit (^#), and Any Letter (^$). Since you would not want to use these codes in the Replace With box, they will not appear on its Special list.

| Paragraph Mark |
| Tab Character |
| Caret Character |
| Clipboard Contents |
| Column Break |
| Em Dash |
| En Dash |
| Find What Text |
| Manual Line Break |
| Manual Page Break |
| Nonbreaking Hyphen |
| Nonbreaking Space |
| Optional Hyphen |

Tip: You can replace text with the contents of the Clipboard by selecting the option Clipboard Contents (or using the ^c code) in the Replace With box. Just make certain that you cut or copy the text you want to insert before performing the operation. You cannot use ^c in the Find What box.

Try finding and replacing special codes now in the Letter to Historical Society document that should still be on your screen. Notice that the first line of each paragraph is indented with a TAB. You want to remove the tab's and create double-spaces between all the paragraphs. Select Replace from the Edit menu.

You first want to locate the tab code in front of each paragraph. Click on the Special button and select Tab Character. Word will insert the code in the Find What box. Now click in the Replace With box. You want to replace the tab character with a paragraph mark. Highlight the text in the box (or delete it), click on the Special button, and then select Paragraph Mark. Word will insert the code in the Replace With box, like this:

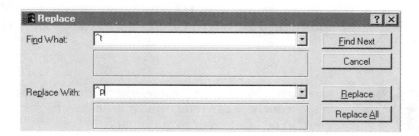

Select Replace All. Word makes the replacement, but there is one problem. There was already a blank line between the salutation and the first paragraph. Just delete the extra blank line yourself.

In our example, we only encountered one extra line that had to be deleted, so it was easy to correct. If you're working with a complex document that has the potential for more problems, use the Find Next and Replace commands, instead of Replace All. You could also use Replace All on selected portions of text that would present no problem.

Close the document on the screen without saving the changes.

Tip: If you want to delete blank lines between paragraphs, enter two paragraph codes in the Find What box and one paragraph code in the Replace With box. And remember, you can delete text or codes by entering them into the Find What box and leaving the Replace With box empty.

Replacing All Word Forms

The new Find All Word Forms feature in Word for Windows 95 is so amazing that you must try it. Type the following sentence: **He was going to sing to the police, but if he sang he'd be in trouble**. Now to avoid using colloquialisms, we want to change "sing" to "speak" and "sang" to "spoke".

Select Replace from the Edit menu. Type **sing** in the Find What text box. Press TAB, and then type **speak** in the Replace With text box. Now click to select Find All Word Forms.

Select Replace All. Word will display a warning that using Replace All with Find All Word Forms is not recommended. Go ahead—click on OK anyway. A message box appears reporting that two replacements have been made. Select OK to clear the message box, and then close the Replace dialog box.

Your sentence now reads: **He was going to speak to the police, but if he spoke he'd be in trouble.** I told you it was amazing!

 C···

aution: When you change documents using the Find All Word Forms option, check them carefully. Some replacements, particularly with forms of the verb "to be," can result in grammatical errors.

Using Multiple Documents and Windows

5

Word lets you have more than one document open at the same time. If you don't think you'll ever need to use this capability, think again. Imagine that it's late at night and you're trying to complete an important letter. You suddenly realize that you need to refer to a memorandum that you wrote last month. Because you have Word, there's no need to rummage through your file cabinets. Just open the memorandum in its own window on the Word screen so you can refer to it as you work on your letter. You can even copy information from one document to the other.

Opening Multiple Documents

The ability to open more than one document at a time is one of the principal reasons that Windows can offer so many powerful features. You can have multiple documents open, switch back and forth between them, even see them all onscreen at the same time.

When you have one document open and you open another one, the first document is moved to the background. It is still open; its window has simply been moved behind the new document window. In fact, each document that you open appears in its own window. Just as the pages in a book are layered over each other, the windows of open documents are layered one on top of the other. But unlike the pages of a book, you can arrange your screen so you can see more than one document at a time, as illustrated in Figure 5-1.

Opening multiple documents makes it easy to copy or move information
Figure 5-1.

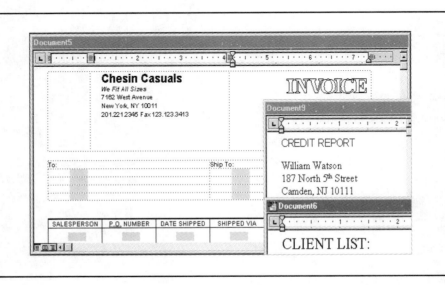

Opening a second, third, or any other document is as easy as opening the first. In fact, you open them in just the same way! To open another document, click on the Open button or select Open from the File menu, select the document you want to open, and click on Open.

To start a new document when one is already open, just click on the New button or use the New command from the File menu.

You can even open more than one document with the same command, as long as they are located in the same *folder*—Windows 95-speak for directory. When the Open dialog box is displayed, click on the first document that you want to open. Then hold down the CTRL key and click on any others. To select several documents listed consecutively, click on the first in the list, point to the last in the list, hold down SHIFT, and click.

You can also select consecutive documents by dragging a box around them. Point to the blank space in front of the icon of the first document you want to select, or to the blank space following the last document. Then drag the mouse to draw a box around all of the documents. As each document name is enclosed in the box, it will become highlighted. As a shortcut, you can drag the mouse to form only part of the box instead of fully enclosing the document names, as shown in Figure 5-2.

When you select Open, Word will open all of the selected documents, placing each in a separate window. The last document opened will be in the foreground—it will be the one shown on the screen.

5

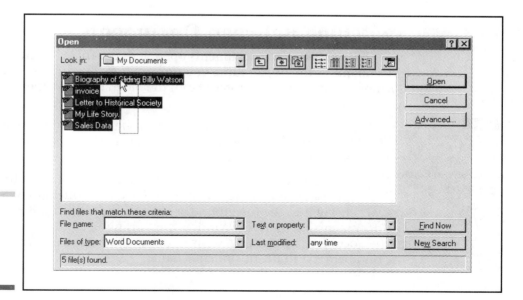

Selecting
multiple
documents
to open
Figure 5-2.

Upgrader: You cannot drag directly over documents to select them in the Open dialog box as you could in Windows 3.1.

Document windows are totally independent. Any changes that you make to a document in one window will not be reflected in another document's window. Each window can be in a different view and a different magnification. So changing views or magnification in one document will not affect the view of the other documents.

Note: Because of the power of Windows, you can even have Word documents, Excel worksheets, tables created from Access databases, and other types of documents open simultaneously. See Chapter 20 for more information about sharing information among applications.

To see how easy it is to open multiple windows, start Word and open the document named Letter to Historical Society. Now open the Biography of Sliding Billy Watson document. The window holding the letter moves into the background, and you see the window containing the biography. The document control menu and the Minimize, Restore, and Close buttons control only the window shown in the foreground. Closing one document window, for example, will not close any other document window.

Switching Between Documents

Now that you have two documents open, let's use them. To switch to a document in the background, you press CTRL-F6. Do so now. The letter document moves into the foreground, the biography document into the background.

```
Window
 New Window
 Arrange All
 Split
 1 Biography of Sliding Billy Watson
✓ 2 Letter to Historical Society
```

You can also change documents using the Window menu. Pull down the Window menu to see a list of the open documents, as shown here.

The check mark next to the document's name means that it is the active document. Click on Biography of Sliding Billy Watson to bring it to the foreground as the active document. Because each of the documents listed in the Window menu is numbered, you can also switch to the document by pressing ALT-W to display the menu and then pressing the number next to the document's name.

Remember: Switching in and out of a document window does not change the position of the insertion point. You can switch back to a window and continue typing or editing exactly where you left off.

Displaying Two or More Windows

While switching between windows is easy, wouldn't it be even easier to refer to a document as you type if you could see both documents at the same time? You're in luck. Word lets you divide the screen into more than one document window.

To display both of your open document windows now, select Arrange All from the Window menu. Word will *tile* the open windows, as shown in Figure 5-3. Tiling means that the windows will be arranged so they do not overlap.

Now that the windows are displayed, you can switch between them by clicking on the document you want to work with. Just point anywhere in the document window and click the mouse.

While you can *see* more than one document at a time, only one can be *active*. That is, only one document at a time can contain the insertion point for you to enter or edit text. The document that was active when you used the Arrange All command will still be the active window. Look again at Figure 5-3.

5

Two documents tiled with the Arrange All command
Figure 5-3.

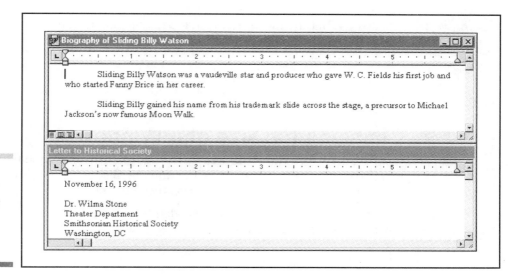

- The title bar of the active window contains a control menu button and Minimize, Maximize, and Close buttons. The title bar of the inactive window contains only the document's name.

- The title bar of the active document will be blue (if your Windows 95 display uses the default settings), and the title bar of the inactive window will be gray.

- Both windows have rulers and scroll bars, but the three view buttons are only in the active window.

No matter how many windows are open, there will be only one menu bar, one set of toolbars, and one status bar. These are part of the Word program window, not a document window. The indicators in the status bar and the toolbars reflect those in the active window. When you change from one document to another, the indicators will change to tell you about the currently active document. The menu bar selections, such as Save and Print, work on the active document.

Remember: The Save All option in the File menu will save all of your open documents.

Word does not tile windows automatically. If you now open a third document, its window will overlap those that are tiled. Select Arrange All from the Window menu to tile all of the open document windows.

Tip: When windows are overlapped, clicking on one or switching to it with CTRL-F6 will bring it to the foreground.

Changing the Size of a Window

Just because Word tiles your windows, it doesn't mean they have to stay that way. To quickly return the active document—Biography of Sliding Billy Watson—to full size, click on its Maximize button.

Now return the documents to their tiled format by clicking on the Restore button of the active document.

If you want to make the document window as small as possible—to get it out of the way until you need it again—click on its Minimize button. Switch to the letter document in the bottom window and click on its Minimize button. Its window will appear as a small title bar at the bottom of the screen.

 Note: If you minimize the window that is at the top of the screen, its minimized title bar will be obscured by the remaining tiled window. You can move the tiled window out of the way, as you will soon learn, or you can change to the minimized document using the Window menu.

To redisplay the minimized document, click on its title bar (if it is not obscured by another window). Word will sound a beep and then display the title bar as shown here, with its control button, Restore, Maximize, and Close buttons.

Click on the Restore button to again display the tiled windows.

You can also customize the size and position of windows using the mouse. Drag one of the corners of a window to change both its height and width at the same time. Drag the left or right border to change the window's width. Drag the top or bottom border to change the window's height. Point to the part of the window you want to drag, so the mouse pointer will have one of these shapes:

5

↕	Drag the top or bottom border
↔	Drag the left or right border
↙↗	Drag the lower-left or upper-right corner
↖↘	Drag the upper-left or lower-right corner

If you again select Arrange All from the Window menu, the document windows will again be tiled. Any custom size and position will be retained.

Note: Word includes a template containing a macro to let you arrange windows horizontally, vertically, tiled, and cascaded (neatly overlapping each other). You'll learn about templates in Chapter 11, and how to use the macro in Chapter 24.

Moving a Window

To move a window, point to the title bar and drag the mouse in the direction you want to move it. As you drag the mouse, a gray box the same size as the window will move along with it. Release the mouse when the box is in the location you want to place the window.

By moving windows and changing their sizes, you can arrange your screen as you want.

Moving Text Between Documents

You can move and copy text from one open document to another whether or not they are displayed at the same time. If the windows are not displayed at the same time, copy or move text using the Clipboard. If both windows are displayed, use the Clipboard or drag and drop.

Moving Text with Drag and Drop

To drag and drop text from one displayed window to another, select the text, point to it with the mouse, hold down the mouse button, and drag the selected text to the other window. When you release the mouse button, the window to which you dragged the text will be active. Remember to hold down the CTRL key if you want to copy the text rather than move it.

Because tiled windows can be small, it may be difficult to drag through a document to locate the position where you want to insert the text you are dragging. So either before or after you select the text, but before you drag it, activate the other document and make sure the place where you want to insert the text is visible. Then click in the other window—the text will still be highlighted—and drag the selected text to its new position.

Try this now with the two documents that you have opened. Select Arrange All from the Window menu to tile the documents. Click in the Letter to Historical Society document window, and then place the insertion point just before the period in the first sentence. Type a comma, press the SPACEBAR, and then type **such as**.

Click in the Biography of Sliding Billy Watson window. Select the name Sliding Billy Watson in the first paragraph. Drag the text to the end of the first paragraph in the letter document window, hold down CTRL, and release the mouse.

Moving Text with the Clipboard

If the windows are overlapped, or stacked in the background, move or copy text using the Clipboard. Switch to the window containing the text you want to move or copy. Select the text and then click on either the Cut button or the Copy button on the toolbar.

Switch to the window containing the document where you want to place the text, and then click on the Paste button on the toolbar.

Note: Remember, you can also use the shortcut menu, the Edit menu, or the key combinations to perform the cut, copy, and paste operations.

You can also use the Clipboard to copy or move text to a new document, or to an existing document that you have not yet opened. After you cut or copy the text to the Clipboard, click on New to start a new document, or open an existing document. Then position the insertion point and click on the Paste button.

5

Now close the letter document without saving the changes, and then maximize the biography document.

Tip: Once you cut or copy text into the Clipboard, you can close the document that it came from. The document does not have to be open for you to paste the Clipboard contents elsewhere. If you forget what you've placed in the Clipboard, open a new document and click on Paste to display the contents of the Clipboard. You can also use the Clipboard Viewer accessory, available from the taskbar.

Two Views of One Document

Sometimes you want to copy or move text from one location to another in a long document, or you want to refer to one page of the document while you are editing another page of the same document. Scrolling with the mouse or hunting for the location to paste text can be difficult and time-consuming. The solution is to display two different parts of the same document in *panes*. Using panes, you can also display the same document in two different views or magnifications; so one pane, for example, could display the document in Page Layout view, the other pane in Normal view. You can cut, copy, and paste text between panes, and even drag and drop text between them.

You create panes using the *split box*, which is the small rectangle above the scroll bar:

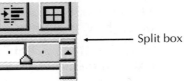

Split box

Point to the split box on your screen so the mouse pointer is shaped like this:

Hold down the mouse button and drag the split box down the scroll bar. As you drag the mouse, a gray line appears across the page indicating the position of the line separating the two panes of the document. When the line is about halfway down the scroll bar, release the mouse. Word will divide the window in two. Your screen should look similar to the one shown in Figure 5-4.

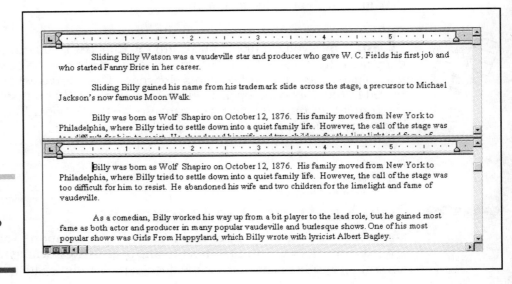

Your document split into two panes

Figure 5-4.

Tip: Double-click on the split box to quickly divide the document into panes.

Creating Panes with the Menu

You can also split a window into panes by selecting Split from the Window menu. Word will display the gray split line across the screen.

Without holding down the mouse button, drag the mouse up or down to position the line, or press the UP ARROW and DOWN ARROW keys. When the line is where you want it, click the mouse or press ENTER to set its position. If you change your mind before setting the position, press ESC.

Working with Document Panes

Each pane has its own ruler bar and scroll bars. To select one of the panes, click in the pane with the mouse or press F6 to move from pane to pane. Click in the top pane now to make it active. The active pane is the one that contains the insertion point.

To scroll a pane, make it active and then use the scroll bar in that pane. You can scroll each pane independently to display two different sections of the same document. So for example, you can refer to something at the start of the document while adding text at the end. Scroll one pane to the top, and scroll the other to the end. Just remember that you are using only one document. Editing and formatting that you make to the document in one pane affect the document in the other pane, even if you are not looking at the same section of text in both panes.

To change the view or magnification of a pane, select the pane, then change the view or zoom settings. With the top pane active, click on the Page Layout View button on the scroll bar, or select Page Layout from the View menu. The view of the bottom pane is not affected. Now click in the bottom pane to make it active, and then select 75% from the Zoom Control. The change only affects the active pane. Your screen will appear as in Figure 5-5.

To move or copy text from one pane to another, use drag and drop. Select the text in one pane, drag it to the desired position in the other pane, then release the mouse button. Hold down CTRL to copy the text. You can also use cut, copy, and paste.

Tip: If you want to see the effects of your editing on the page layout, display one pane in Normal view, and display the other pane in Page Layout

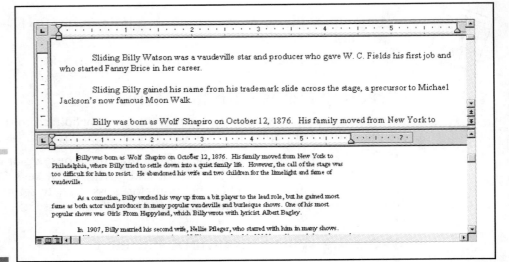

Using a different view and magnification for each pane
Figure 5-5.

view with the magnification set at Whole Page. Changes to the text and layout that you make in the Normal view pane will automatically be reflected in the whole page.

Removing Panes

When you are finished working with the panes, remove the split line. To do this, point to the split box, which is now to the right of the lower ruler, or point to the top of the lower ruler, and then drag it off the top or bottom of the window. You can also remove the split line by selecting Unsplit from the Window menu.

Remove your window panes now by dragging the split line up off the top of the scroll bar. The full window will now appear in Normal view with 75% magnification. Change the display to 100%. If you remove the split line by dragging it up, the view and magnification setting of the bottom pane will be applied to the entire document. If you drag the split line down, the setting of the top pane will apply.

Tip: Double-click on the split box to quickly remove the window panes.

Multiple Windows for a Single Document

It is possible to display a document in *more* than two views and magnifications, and to view more than two locations in it at the same time. This is useful, for instance, if you want to see full-page views of different parts of the document. Use the New Window option in the Window menu. Each time you select New Window, Word opens another window containing the active document, adding the notation :2, :3, and so forth to the title bar, as in Letter:2.

Select New Window from the Window menu to create a window titled Biography of Sliding Billy Watson:2. Select New Window again to create a window titled Biography of Sliding Billy Watson:3. Now select Arrange All to tile the three documents, as shown in Figure 5-6.

As with panes, you can display each window in its own view and magnification, and changes you make to one window will be reflected in the text in all of the other windows. Remember, you are still only working with one document. And you can cut, copy, and paste or drag and drop selected text between windows, making it easy to move information between sections of a large document.

Now close the active tiled window by clicking on its Close button or by double-clicking on its control button. In the same way, close the currently active tiled window. Finally, maximize the remaining window.

5

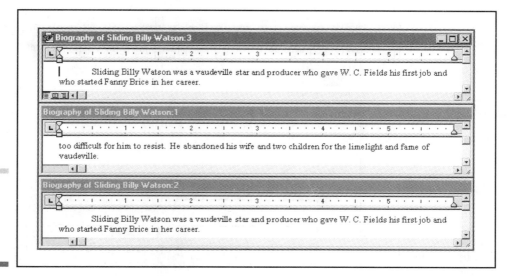

Multiple tiled
windows for
the same
document
Figure 5-6.

Caution: When you want to close one of the document windows, but not all of them, use the Close button or control button in that window. If you select Close from the File menu, Word closes all of the document windows.

Inserting a File into a Document

So far we've been moving text within a document, or from one open document to another. However, its not really necessary to open a document in order to copy all of it into another document.

Remember: Inserting a document does not delete it from the disk. It copies its contents and places it in the active document.

To insert one entire document into the open document, place the insertion point where you want to insert the contents, and then select File from the Insert menu. Word will display the dialog box shown in Figure 5-7. Select the document that you want to insert and then click on OK. Word inserts the document using the page layout setting of the active document. You can now edit the inserted text, just as if it were originally part of the document.

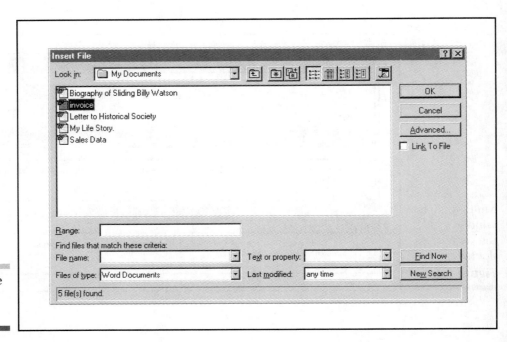

The Insert File
dialog box
Figure 5-7.

Note: Some of the options in the Insert File dialog box are used for more advanced functions, such as sharing information between Windows applications and creating links to other documents. You will learn about these functions in Chapter 20.

Now close the document that you have open, without saving it.

That's it for Part 1. You now know the basics of creating and editing documents in Word and working with more than one document at a time. Practice these techniques as you write. Because you can move and copy text, and change it as much as you want, concentrate on the content—getting across your ideas—rather than the structure or order of your paragraphs. You can always edit your document using the wonders of Word.

5

PART 2

Formatting Documents

Formatting Characters

6

When you edit a document, you change its content. When you *format* a document, you change its appearance. As with editing, you can format text as you type it or anytime after, so you don't have to worry about the format when you're struggling to find the right words. In this book, formatting is divided into three areas—characters, lines and paragraphs, and pages.

Character formatting affects the shape, size, and appearance of characters. Use these formats to make your document visually appealing and to emphasize important points.

A Font Primer

A *typeface* refers to the general shape or design of characters. For example, *roman* is a generic name for a very popular, and classic, typeface. A roman typeface is characterized by small strokes at the ends of its letters, called *serifs,* and by combinations of thick and thin lines within the same letter. Roman typefaces are easy to read, so designers have created hundreds of other typefaces using its same general characteristics. For example, Times Roman is widely used in newspapers, magazines, and other publications; but there are many typefaces that have roman characteristics, such as Times New Roman, which comes with Windows, and Garamond.

Times New Roman

Garamond

Typefaces that do not have the cross strokes are called *sans serif.* They may be block style, where all lines that make up the character are the same size, or they may be a variation of roman, using both thick and thin strokes. A few examples of sans serif typefaces are shown here.

ARIAL

UNIVERS

HAETTENSCHWEILER

A set of characters in one typeface, one size, and one style (such as bold or italic) is called a *font.* A font usually contains numbers, punctuation marks, and the uppercase and lowercase letters of the alphabet. Most fonts also contain accented characters and special symbols. For instance, Figure 6-1 shows a complete font of a typeface called Arial.

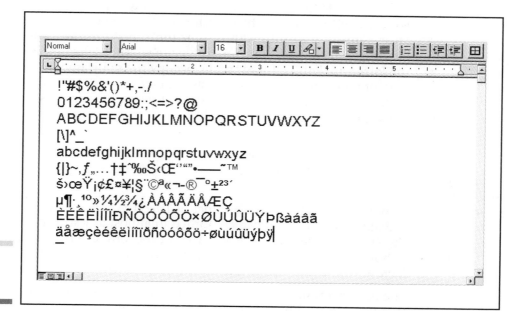

The Arial
typeface
Figure 6-1.

Note: In Word for Windows, the term "font" refers to any size type of a particular typeface, rather than a single point size. To choose a typeface, you select from Word's Font list.

A *family* is a collection of fonts based on the same typeface. By making the typeface a little wider or narrower, darker or lighter, each font has a different effect but the same basic characteristics. The three fonts you see here, for instance, are in the Arial family.

6

Arial
Arial MT Black
Arial Narrow

Fonts are measured in *points*. There are 72 points in one inch, so a 12-point font measures 1/6 of an inch. The font size is not the actual size of a character. Rather, it is the total space occupied by the characters on the line. This includes the distance from the top of the highest letter (capital *M*, for instance) to the very bottom of the lowest letter (such as lowercase *y*).

Font size only measures the overall height of characters—there is no uniform measurement of a font's width. Some fonts, however, are called *monospaced*, because each character takes up the same width; the uppercase letter *M* and the lowercase letter *i*, for example, occupy the same amount of space horizontally. Most fonts used today are *proportionally spaced*. This means that each character takes up only the space it needs, as you can see by comparing the same text in both types of fonts:

```
Monospaced     ABCiiiibm
Proportional   ABCiiiibm
```

Windows lets you use other types of fonts in addition to TrueType that can be printed in any size, including PostScript and Intellifont. However, you may need additional software or hardware, such as Adobe Type Manager, Intellifont for Windows, or a PostScript printer or software.

Windows 95 comes with a number of *TrueType fonts*. A TrueType font is actually a typeface that can be printed in almost any size and any style. So the Times New Roman typeface, a TrueType font, can be regular, bold, italic, or bold and italic at the same time. You can make it as small as 1 point or as large as hundreds of points, but the typical range is from 8 to 72 points.

The maximum size that you can print, and the number of different fonts that you can use on a page, will depend on your printer. There are even some printers, such as daisy wheel and older dot matrix printers, that cannot print TrueType fonts at all.

Your printer may also have fonts built into it. These fonts may be TrueType, just like the ones that come with Windows, or they may be PostScript or some other type of font that can be printed in any size or style. Your printer may also contain some fixed-size fonts. These are fonts that can only be printed in one size and style. So the fonts available to you will depend on the printer that is connected to your system. Many laser printers, for example, come with at least a roman, a sans serif, a monospaced, and a small monospaced font. Using your printer's built-in fonts will usually result in faster printing times, since Windows does not have to send all of the font information to the printer.

Character Formatting with the Toolbar

There are literally thousands of combinations of character formats that you can apply to your document. You can access all of these formats using the Format command from the menu bar. Many of the most common formats used in documents are also provided as buttons on the Formatting toolbar:

Tip: Any time you've just formatted some text, you can quickly apply the same format to selected text by pressing F4, or by selecting Repeat from the Edit menu. The Repeat command in the menu will specify the type of formatting you performed last.

The toolbar has buttons for both character and line and paragraph formats. When you click on a button to apply a format, it will appear pressed down. In fact, you can tell from the button's appearance which format, or combinations of them, you have applied to your text. When you move the insertion point into text that you've already typed, Word will automatically depress the buttons to indicate the format already applied. For example, if you click on a word that is boldfaced and centered on the page, the buttons representing those formats will appear pressed down, as you can see here.

 You can also tell what formats are applied to text by using the Help button on the Standard toolbar. Click on the Help button and then click on the text. Word will display a message box showing the character and paragraph formats applied to it, as shown in Figure 6-2. The formats labeled Paragraph Style and Character Style refer to formats applied by a special Word feature called *styles*. You will learn all about styles in Chapter 15. The formats labeled Direct are those that you applied using the toolbar or the Format menu. Press ESC when you're ready to clear the message box from the screen.

6

Use the Help function to display the formats applied to your text
Figure 6-2.

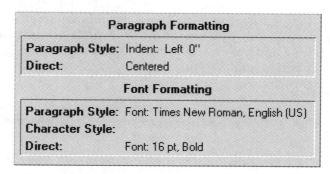

The Big Three—Bold, Italic, and Underline

Three of the most popular character formats are **bold**, *italic*, and underlining, by themselves or in combination. These are quick and easy to apply because buttons for them are on the Formatting toolbar.

Tip: Shortcut key combinations for the three most-used character formats are CTRL-B for bold, CTRL-I for italic, and CTRL-U for underlining.

To format text as you type it, just click on the appropriate button and then type. Try it now by typing **Your bill is** and then pressing the SPACEBAR. Click on the Underline button in the toolbar and then type **seriously overdue**. Word underlines the words and the spaces between them as you type.

Now turn off underlining by clicking on the Underline button again. This stops the formatting and changes the button so it no longer appears pressed down. This type of action is often called a *toggle*, named after a toggle switch that turns a light on and off.

Note: Not all toolbar buttons act as toggles.

Press the SPACEBAR, type **and we will be forced to take**, and then press the SPACEBAR again. Click on the Bold button and then click on the Italic button in the toolbar. To use a combination of the formats, click on each button that you want to apply. Type **legal action**, and then click on the Bold and Italic buttons again. You can click the buttons in any order. Type a period and then press ENTER. Your sentence should look like the one shown here.

Your bill is <u>seriously overdue</u> and we will be forced to take *legal action*|

To format text that you've already typed, select the text first and then click on the button. You can format a single word by clicking anywhere in the word and then choosing the button from the toolbar—you do not have to select the word first.

Tip: You can select a rectangular section of text by holding down ALT while you drag. Use this technique if you want to format a specific column in a list.

If you format characters by mistake, or just change your mind, select the text. The formats applied will appear as depressed buttons. Click on the button representing the format you want to remove.

Tip: You can quickly remove all formats applied to text by pressing CTRL-SPACEBAR.

Try removing and reformatting the text on your screen. Drag the mouse over the words "seriously overdue". The Underline button will appear pressed down. Click on the Underline button to remove the format from the selected text. Click on the word "seriously" and then click on the Italic button. Your sentence should now be formatted like the one shown here.

Your bill is *seriously* overdue and we will be forced to take **legal action**|

Close the document on the screen, without saving it, and start a new document.

Note: The format buttons will not appear pressed down if you select some text that is not formatted. For example, if you select a word that is bold along with a normal word, the Bold button will not appear pressed down. What happens when you then click on a format button depends on the format of the first word. For example, if the first word is bold and the next is normal, clicking on the Bold button will remove the bold format, making both normal. If the first word is normal and the second is bold, both will become bold.

6

Selecting Fonts from the Toolbar

Remember: Word for Windows uses the term "font" to mean any individual typeface, regardless of its point size. Thus 10-point Courier and 16-point Courier are, in Word's terminology, the same font.

When you start Word, or create a new document, a default font will be set for you. In most cases, the default font is 10-point Times New Roman.

The Formatting toolbar contains text boxes and drop-down lists for selecting the font and the size of its characters. To select a font, click on the down-pointing arrow next to the Font text box. Word will display a list of fonts available to you. The list will have a scroll bar if there are more fonts than can be displayed.

 Tip: You can set the font of your text as you type it, or you can change the font—even of a single character—by selecting the text first. To change the font of a single word, however, just place the insertion point in the word before selecting the formats.

The fonts are listed in alphabetical order. However, after you start using Word to select fonts, you'll see several fonts listed at the beginning of the list, separated from the rest by a double line. These are the fonts that you've used recently. Word places them first to make it easy for you to select the fonts that you use most often.

To select a font, click on its name in the list. When the font list is displayed, you can scroll the list by typing the first characters of the font name. You can also click in the Font text box and then type the name of the font you want to use. Word will display a warning message if you type the name of a nonexistent font.

 Tip: To access the Font list with the keyboard, press CTRL-SHIFT-F, and then press the DOWN ARROW key to open the box and select a font.

To practice changing fonts, type the text shown here:

> By combining Word's character formats, I can create professional-looking documents. My letters, memos, reports, and faxes will look like they're from the pages of a design magazine. I will be so popular at work that my company will offer me a promotion with a raise in pay and a company car. In fact, other companies will be calling me night and day with wonderful offers.

Press ENTER twice when you are finished typing the sample text. Now let's choose a different font for the next sentence. Pull down the font list and click on Arial, and then type **It's nice to dream, isn't it?** The text appears in the Arial font. Click on the word "promotion" in the first paragraph, pull down the font list, and click on Courier New. Drag over the words "company car" and format them with the Courier New font in the same way. Your text should now look like this:

> By combining Word's character formats, I can create professional-looking documents. My letters, memos, reports, and faxes will look like they're from the pages of a design magazine. I will be so popular at work that my company will offer me a promotion with a raise in pay and a company car. In fact, other companies will be calling me night and day with wonderful offers.
>
> It's nice to dream, isn't it?

To select a font size, click on the down-pointing arrow next to the Size text box. Word will display a list of the available sizes. The sizes shown in the list depend on the font being used. With TrueType fonts, the list will contain the sizes 8, 9, 10, 11, 12, 14, 16, 18, 20, 22, 24, 26, 28, 36, 48, and 72. You can select one of these sizes, scrolling the list as needed, or you can type another size directly in the text box. Use the text box, for example, to choose half-point sizes, such as 8.5, and for sizes smaller than 8 points or larger than 72 points. While half-point sizes are allowed, you cannot enter other fractional numbers.

Tip: To access the Size list with the keyboard, press CTRL-SHIFT-P, press DOWN ARROW to display the list, and then press UP ARROW or DOWN ARROW to select a font. You can also change the font size without using the toolbar—press CTRL-SHIFT-> to increase the size of selected text to the next point size, and press CTRL-SHIFT-< to reduce the font size.

6

To return to the default font and size, select them from the list boxes or press CTRL-SPACEBAR.

Let's change the sizes of some of the characters in our sample text. First, let's make sure that the boss knows we want a promotion and company car. Click on the word "promotion", pull down the Size list and select 18. Select the words "company car", and change them to 18 points in the same way. Now select the last sentence in the document, pull down the Size list, and select 8—we don't want to think this is really just a dream, do we? Your text should look like this:

> By combining Word's character formats, I can create professional-looking documents. My letters, memos, reports, and faxes will look like they're from the pages of a design magazine. I will be so popular at work that my company will offer me a promotion with a raise in pay and a company car. In fact, other companies will be calling me night and day with wonderful offers.
>
> It's nice to dream, isn't it?

If you are unsure what font and size have been applied to a character, just move the insertion point in front if it. The name of the font and its size will appear in the text boxes in the Formatting toolbar. You can also see the font and size by clicking on the Help button and then clicking on the text.

Now on your own, experiment with the different fonts and sizes that are available to you. Try some very small sizes and some very large ones. Print out a copy of your experiment to see how your printer handles it. Close the document when you're done and start a new document.

Note: Check your printer's manual to learn its limitations. Newer laser printers, for example, are only limited by their memory—to print larger type and more fonts, add memory. Older laser printers have definite limits, such as fonts up to 14 inches and only 16 fonts per page with the Hewlett-Packard LaserJet II, and only 18-point fonts with 8 per page on the original LaserJet.

More Options with the Font Dialog Box

The character formatting options in the toolbar are used most frequently, but they are only a sampling of Word's formats. To see all of the character formats, select Font from the Format menu, or right-click in the text window and then select Font from the shortcut menu. Click on the Font tab to display the options shown in Figure 6-3. Make your choices from the Font page of the dialog box, watching the preview panel to see their effects, and then click on OK to apply the settings to your text.

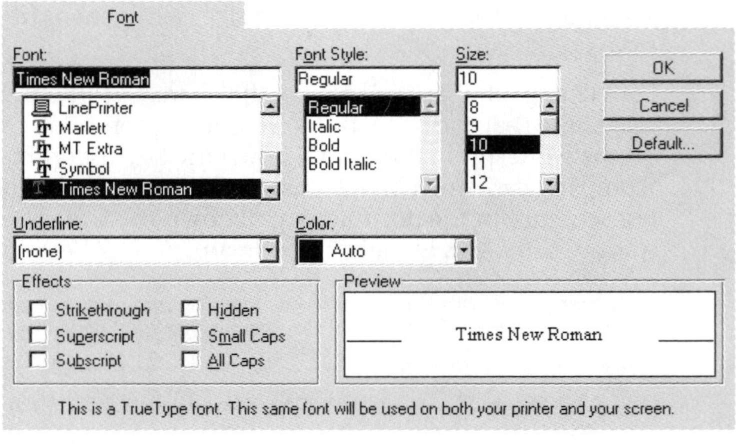

In the Font dialog box, click on the Font tab to see all of the character formats provided with Word

Figure 6-3.

Tip: The shortcut menu is especially effective when you want to apply formats to selected text. After dragging to select the text, leave the pointer on it, right-click, and then click on Font. Just remember, if you click the right mouse button on a word with a wavy underline, the Spell Check shortcut menu appears.

Now take some time to look at the options in the box.

♦   You can select a *font, type size,* and *type style* from the list boxes. When you close the dialog box, the font and size you select will be shown in the font and size boxes in the toolbar. The styles you select will be reflected in the look of the Bold and Italic buttons in the toolbar. You can later change the font, size, and style using either the toolbar or the dialog box.

♦   You can select *underlining,* and the *style of the lines,* from the Underline list. Your options are None, Single (a single line), Words Only (spaces between words will not be underlined), Double (a double line), and Dotted (a dotted line). Only the Single option will result in the Underline button in the toolbar appearing pressed down—to turn it off, click on the Underline button.

Tip: To turn off the other underline styles from the toolbar, double-click on the Underline button.

6

♦   You can select an *effect.* The options are Strikethrough, Superscript, Subscript, Hidden, Small Caps, and All Caps. Superscript and Subscript are exclusive—only one can be selected at a time. Small Caps converts all lowercase characters that you type to uppercase letters, but in a size smaller than the font's regular size. All Caps formats text in all uppercase characters. You will learn how to use the Hidden effect later in this chapter.

~~Strikethrough~~

Super[script]

Sub[script]

SMALL CAPS

Tip: Use the Small Caps option for special effects, for example, when you want the text in all uppercase letters but still want to distinguish the first letter in a word. Type the word with an initial uppercase letter and then format it in Small Caps.

♦   You can select a *color* from the Color drop-down list. If you do not have a color printer, how your printed output looks will depend on the printer you are using. In some cases, Word will print all of your text in black. In other cases, Word will match the color with an appropriate shade of gray—light colors such as yellow will print in a light shade of gray; darker colors such as red will print in a darker shade.

Caution: You may think that this will never happen, but I've seen it done. Do not select the White color. If you do, you won't see what you are typing over the white window background. If this should happen to you, select the text—or at least what you think is the text—and then choose another color.

You can change the default font that Word uses with every new document. Select the font, size, and style, and then click on the Default button. A dialog box will appear asking you to confirm your choice. Select Yes to accept the new default.

Remember: The new default is actually applied to the template being used by the current document, so it only affects other documents using that template. If you have not selected any particular template, then the default will be used for every new document. See Chapter 12 to learn more about templates.

Table 6-1 shows all of the shortcut key combinations for character formats.

Changing Case

If you want to type all uppercase letters, press the CAPS LOCK key on your keyboard. With Caps Lock turned on, you can type uppercase letters without holding down SHIFT. If you do hold down SHIFT, typing a letter will insert it in lowercase.

Your keyboard might have a lighted Caps Lock indicator. This means that a small light will appear on the key, or elsewhere on the keyboard, to indicate

Style	Key Combination
Normal	CTRL-SPACEBAR
Italic	CTRL-I
Bold	CTRL-B
Underline	CTRL-U
Double Underline	CTRL-SHIFT-D
Small Caps	CTRL-SHIFT-K
All Caps	CTRL-SHIFT-A
Subscript	CTRL-=
Superscript	CTRL-SHIFT-=
Select Font	CTRL-SHIFT-F
Select Font Size	CTRL-SHIFT-P
Increase Font Size	CTRL-SHIFT->
Decrease Font Size	CTRL-SHIFT-<

Shortcut Key
Combinations
for Character
Styles*

Table 6-1.

*All Are Toggles Except for the Font and Font Size Combinations.

that the function is turned on. Word itself does not display any message or indicator in the status bar. As you learned in Chapter 3, AutoCorrect will turn off Caps Lock key if you accidentally turn it on. But if you select to turn off this particular AutoCorrect feature, and press CAPS LOCK by mistake, you could type several paragraphs before looking up at the screen and realizing that all of your cases are reversed. Instead of deleting and retyping the text, you can change its case from the Format menu.

As an experiment, press on CAPS LOCK and then, starting on a new line, type **THE RAIN IN SPAIN FALLS MAINLY ON THE PLAIN**. Select the text—it represents the text that you want to change—and choose Change Case from the Format menu to display this dialog box:

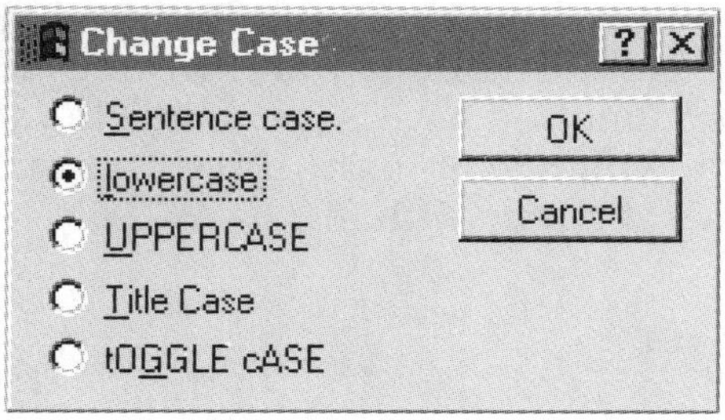

6

Tip: To change the case of the word to the immediate left of the insertion point, don't bother selecting it first. When you select Change Case, Word will highlight the word automatically. If the insertion point follows a space, and there is a word on its right, Word will select the word to the right.

The sample text next to each option button illustrates how the text will appear. Choose Lowercase and then click on OK. Every character is changed to lowercase. Leave the text selected, display the Change Case dialog box, select Sentence Case, and then click on OK. Word will automatically uppercase the first letter of the sentence, and it will lowercase any others that are uppercase except for the pronoun *I*. Again, leave the text selected, and then choose tOGGLE cASE from the Change Case dialog box to have Word reverse the case of all characters. Finally, select Title Case from the Change Case dialog box. Word now capitalizes the first letter of every word. As a summary, here's the original sentence, along with several revised versions that show the effects of the various Change Case options:

> THE RAIN IN SPAIN FALLS MAINLY ON THE PLAIN
> the rain in spain falls mainly on the plain
> The rain in spain falls mainly on the plain
> tHE RAIN IN SPAIN FALLS MAINLY ON THE PLAIN
> The Rain In Spain Falls Mainly On The Plain

Close the document on your screen and start a new one.

Tip: To quickly change case, select the text and press SHIFT-F3. Each time you press SHIFT-F3 the case will rotate through uppercase, lowercase, and sentence case.

Changing Character Spacing

Some fonts are monospaced and some are proportionally spaced, but in both cases, the space occupied by each character, and the space between characters, is determined by the font itself. Sometimes the default spacing doesn't quite suit your purposes. You might be creating a newsletter, for example, and the headline you're writing just won't fit within the column. Or the headline you have is just a little too short, but using a larger font makes it too high to fit in the space. Fortunately, we're Word users and we don't have to put up with it.

To customize character spacing—both vertically and horizontally—select the characters that you want to adjust. (If you only want to change the spacing in a single word, click once on the word to position the insertion point in it.) Then choose Font from the Format menu and click on the Character Spacing tab to see the options shown in Figure 6-4. The Character Spacing page contains three sets of options: Spacing, Position, and Kerning.

Adjusting Horizontal Spacing

Let's try adjusting the horizontal spacing of characters. Type **Word Sales Soar Suddenly**, select the text, and then select Font from the Format menu. Click on the Character Spacing tab. You use the Spacing box and the By text box to its right to change the spacing between characters. Pull down the Spacing list to see the options Normal, Expanded, and Condensed. You select Expanded to increase the spacing between characters; select Condensed to reduce the spacing. Select Expanded. Word inserts "1 pt" in the By text box, which increases the spacing between characters by one point, as shown in the preview panel. You can enter your own measurement into the box, or you can click on the up arrow to increase the spacing between characters, or the down arrow to decrease the spacing. Now click on

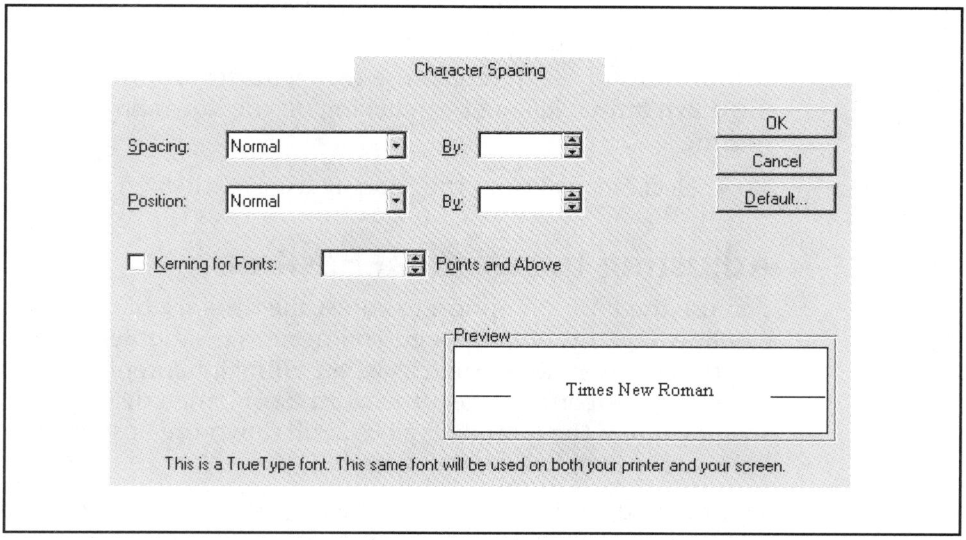

6

Use these options to adjust the spacing between characters

Figure 6-4.

Character Spacing		
Spacing: Normal	By:	OK
Position: Normal	By:	Cancel
☐ Kerning for Fonts:	Points and Above	Default...
	Preview	
	Times New Roman	

This is a TrueType font. This same font will be used on both your printer and your screen.

the up arrow ten times to increase the spacing to two points. Here's how the text will appear with normal spacing and with the expanded spacing:

Word Sales Soar Suddenly
Word Sales Soar Suddenly

Pull down the Spacing list and select Condensed. The setting in the By box does not change, so the text in the Preview panel appears condensed by two points.

It is important to remember that the value in the By box determines how much extra spacing will be inserted (expanded) or how much spacing will be reduced (condensed). A setting of two points when condensed means that the space between characters is reduced by two points. A setting of two points when expanded means the spacing is increased by two points. If you type a larger number in the By box now, the spacing between characters will be reduced further—condensed by a larger amount.

Clicking the up arrow always increases spacing, and clicking the down arrow always decreases spacing, regardless of whether you select Expanded or Condensed. Click now on the up arrow ten times. Each time you click, the value in the By box is decreased by 1/10 of a point, because decreasing the setting will increase the spacing between characters, as shown here.

To condense the characters further, you need to click on the down arrow. Remember, clicking on the down arrow always reduces the spacing.

Now select Normal from the Spacing list and click on OK.

Adjusting the Vertical Position

You use the Position option to adjust the distance of characters from the baseline. Use this option when you need to position characters at some exact position between lines, such as when filling in a preprinted form, or to create a special effect. Select the word "Soar", then display the Character Spacing tab of the Font dialog box. Pull down the Position list to see the options Normal, Raised, and Lowered.

Select Raised, and then click on the up arrow next to the By box until it is set at 6 points. Clicking on the up arrow always raises text; clicking on the down arrow always lowers text. Select OK to see the following effect on the text:

Word Sales ^{Soar} Suddenly

Kerning

The Kerning for Fonts option turns on or off automatic kerning. *Kerning* is a way of spacing certain pairs of characters that allows them to be closer without appearing condensed, just more properly spaced. This includes combinations such as *WA*, *Te, Yo*, and so forth. When kerning is turned on, Word moves these combinations of letters closer together.

Kerned	Not Kerned
WA	WA
Te	Te
Yo	Yo

Notice that in the kerned sample, the characters *W* and *A* are closer together because they have opposite slants. The shape of the *A* fits into the opposite shape of the *W*. The combination *Te* and *Yo* are kerned because the lowercase characters tuck under overhanging strokes of the *T* and *Y*.

Where you turn on kerning will determine how Word performs the function:

♦ To kern a specific set of characters, place the insertion point between them.

♦ To kern a section of text, select it first.

♦ To kern as you type, place the insertion point where you are going to start typing.

6

Display the Character Spacing dialog box and check Kerning for Fonts. Word inserts the current point size of the font into the Points and Above box. This means that it will only kern characters that are that point size or larger. If you want to kern smaller characters as well, enter the measurement in the text box. To kern only larger characters, enter a larger point size in the box. Clicking on the down arrow, by the way, won't go below 8 points; so to kern smaller fonts, you must type the size in the text box.

Tip: Kerning is most effective with larger fonts. With smaller fonts, the effects of kerning, and any reduction in the space between characters, will be difficult to discern.

Special Characters and Symbols

Most fonts usually contain symbols and accented characters in addition to the characters shown on your keyboard keys. These characters and symbols are useful when you are writing scientific or technical documents, or writing in a language other than English—although an American might need to enter the £ currency symbol when writing to England. Since your keyboard does not show you what to press to enter these characters, Word has a special dialog box just for that purpose.

Typing International Documents

When you want to insert an international character in your document, select Symbol from the Insert menu to display the options shown in Figure 6-5. With the Symbols section selected, the symbols dialog box will show the characters available in the current font—the font in effect at the position of the insertion point. To insert a character in the document, double-click on it, or click on it once and then select Insert. When you click on a character, Word enlarges it in the display to make it easier to see.

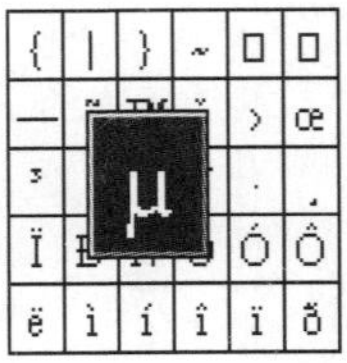

Note: The small rectangles in some sections of the dialog box indicate that there is no special symbol or character at that position in the font. If you select one of these sections, Word will insert the actual rectangle into the document.

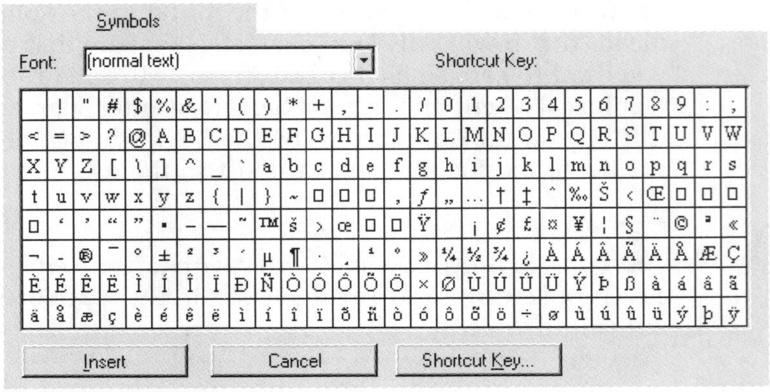

The Symbols options in the Symbols dialog box lets you insert special characters

Figure 6-5.

When you are finished inserting characters, click on the Close button. The character will appear in the size and style of the characters at the insertion point. So, if you insert a character into a phrase that is bold and underlined, the character will be bold and underlined.

Now let's take a close look at the Symbols page. When you are using certain standard roman and sans serif fonts—such as Times New Roman, Courier New, and Arial—the Font text box will contain the notation [normal text]. With other fonts—such as Desdemona—the name of the font will appear in the box. If you want to insert a character in another font, pull down the Font list and make a new selection. For example, Windows comes with a special set of graphic symbols called Wingdings, shown in Figure 6-6. If you want to insert one of these symbols in your text, pull down the Font list, scroll the list until you come to Wingdings, and click. There is also a font called Symbol that includes Greek characters, mathematical symbols, and arrows.

Note: The Font list on the Symbols page will not list the "normal" fonts. If you want to enter a special character in a normal font other than the one you are already using, insert the character using the Symbols dialog box, then select the character in the document, and choose the font from the Font list or Font dialog box.

Notice the Shortcut Key prompt to the right of the Font text box. Word has assigned shortcut key combinations for many of the special characters. If you know the key combination, you can type the character directly from the keyboard rather than having to select it from the dialog box.

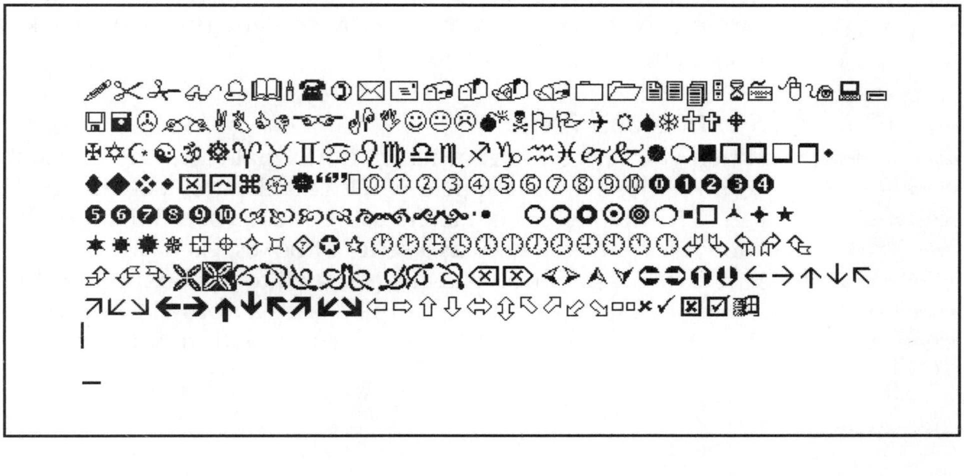

6

Wingdings
Figure 6-6.

Note: The Shortcut Key command button at the bottom of the dialog box lets you customize the keyboard, so you can designate some other combination that will insert the character. You will learn more about customizing the keyboard in Chapter 24.

When the font is set at [normal text], clicking on a character in the Symbols dialog box displays its keyboard combination at the Shortcut Key prompt. Some of the combinations use the CTRL key. For example, when you click on the Ñ character, the combination will appear as Ctrl+~,N. This means that you can enter the character by holding down CTRL while you press SHIFT-~, then releasing all of the keys and typing **N**. "Shift" does not appear in the shortcut key combination, but you must press the SHIFT key to enter characters that are in the "uppercase" position on the keyboard, such as ~, ^, and :.

Tip: Here's an easy way to remember some of the key combinations. The vowels accented with ', `, ^, and ~ are created by pressing CTRL and the accent, then pressing the letter. (Use the colon to accent with an umlaut, as in Ä.) Word will beep if you try to create a character that does not exist!

Technically, all of the international characters and other symbols in the font can be inserted using ALT and a series of four digits. When Word has assigned its own CTRL key combination, it shows that as the shortcut.

Other combinations appear with "Alt", such as Alt+Ctrl+C to enter the copyright symbol ©, or Alt+0163 for the English pound symbol £. To insert the copyright symbol, press all three keys at the same time: ALT-CTRL-C. When Alt is followed by numbers, you must press and hold down ALT as you type the number using the keypad on the right side of the keyboard. So, for example, to insert the pound sign, hold down ALT and type **0163**. Remember, in order to use the keypad for entering numbers, you must first turn on the Num Lock function (by pressing the NUM LOCK key) so the Num Lock light on your keyboard is lit.

Symbols and Fonts
When you select a font other than [normal text], the shortcut key combinations do not appear when you click on a character. However, you can still enter these characters using the keyboard. Picture the characters shown for [normal text] as a series of boxes, each one storing a character. Each key combination is really assigned to the box, not just to the character shown in the box. So for example, using a normal font, the Õ character is shown as having the Ctrl+~,O key combination. It is shown in the second

row from the bottom of the box, 14 characters from the left. If you select another font that uses the standard character set in the Symbols box, you'll see the same character at that position. But if you click on the character, the key combination will not appear. Still, if you select that font when typing a document—either from the Font list in the toolbar or from the Font dialog box—pressing CTRL-~ and then the letter O will insert the symbol in the current font.

You can see how this works when you use the Wingdings font. If you select Wingdings in the Symbol dialog box, you'll see this character where the Õ would appear in the normal text font:

No shortcut key will be shown when you click on the character. However, if you select the Wingdings font when typing, pressing CTRL-~ and then the letter O will insert that character into the document.

Tip: Try this experiment. Type the letters of the alphabet in both uppercase and lowercase using Times New Roman or some other "normal" font. Make a copy of the characters and paste it so you have two sets. Then select the second set of characters and choose Wingdings from the Font menu. You will see which keys you can press to insert Wingdings characters when that font is selected.

6

Typographic and Other Symbols

To insert typographical characters, such as dashes and the registered symbol, select the Special Characters tab from the Symbols dialog box to access commonly used characters that do not appear on the keyboard. The options are shown in Figure 6-7. Listed next to each character is its name and a shortcut key combination, if one has been provided by Word. Double-click on the character that you want to insert, or select it and choose Insert.

Remember: AutoCorrect and AutoFormat will automatically replace some text with special characters.

Select Special
Characters
from the
Symbols box
to insert
typographic
and other
commonly
used
characters that
do not appear
on the
keyboard
Figure 6-7.

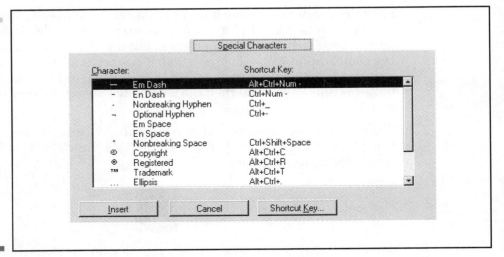

Working with Hidden Text

One of the options available in the Font menu is Hidden for *hidden text*.
When you apply this format, you can choose whether or not the text
appears onscreen and on your printout. Hidden text is useful for typing
reminders and notes to yourself that you do not want to print with
the document.

Before typing hidden text, click on the Show/Hide button in the toolbar so
you can see the normally invisible codes. When Show/Hide is on—that is,
looks pressed down—you'll be able to see the hidden text as you type it.
Then display the Font dialog box, select the Hidden effect, and choose OK.
You can also turn the Hidden style on or off by pressing CTRL-SHIFT-H. Now as
you type, the characters will appear with a dotted underline, like this:

Speak·with·Joan·about·the·raise.··But·not·more·than·$.¶

Turn off the Hidden effect now by clicking on the style again in the Font
dialog box or pressing CTRL-SHIFT-H. Click on the Show/Hide button to
remove the codes from display—the hidden text will disappear as well. Click
on Show/Hide again to display the codes; the hidden text also reappears.

Tip: If you want to see the hidden text without the codes, select
Options from the Tools menu, click on the View tab, select Hidden Text in
the Nonprinting Characters section, and then choose OK. To print hidden
text, you must select Options from the Tools menu, then select Hidden Text
from the Print options; this will be explained further in Chapter 21.

Hidden text will only be printed if it is displayed onscreen when you print the document. So if you do not want the hidden text to appear on your printout, make certain it does not appear onscreen.

Duplicating Formats with Format Painter

With all of the format options that Word makes available, there are certainly a large number of possible combinations. If you've gone to the trouble of selecting a combination that you like for one section of text, you do not have to make the selections all over again for some other text. For example, suppose you choose a font, size, and style combination for a subtitle. You can quickly apply the same combination to another subtitle. This is called *format painting*, and you do it using the Format Painter button in the toolbar.

Close the document that you have on the screen and start a new one. Type **Heading One**, press ENTER, and type **Heading Two**. Select the words "Heading One" and click on the Bold and Underline buttons. With the text still selected, pull down the Size list and select 18. Click the mouse to deselect the text. It should now look like this:

<u>**Heading One**</u>
Heading Two

When you want to copy a format, place the insertion point in the text that uses that format and then click on the Format Painter button. Do that now. Click anywhere in the text "Heading One" and click on the Format Painter button. The mouse pointer appears as an I-beam and a small paintbrush. Select "Heading Two"—the text that you want to apply the format to. When you release the mouse button after selecting the text, Word will apply the formats and turn off the Format Painter function. You've just formatted the text in bold, underlining, and 18 points without selecting the individual options from the toolbar.

6

<u>**Heading One**</u>
<u>**Heading Two**</u>

If you want to apply the same formats to more than one section of text, double-click on the Format Painter button. After you select text and release the mouse button, the Format Painter function stays on, and the paintbrush will remain with the I-beam. Select any other sections of text to which you want to apply the same format. To turn off the Format Painter function, click on the Format Painter button again or press ESC.

Note: To copy formats with the keyboard, press CTRL-SHIFT-C to turn on Format Painter, select the text you want to format, and then press CTRL-SHIFT-V. The Format Painter button will not appear pressed down when you use these key combinations.

Formatting characters can add impact and visual appeal to any document. However, don't lose track of the primary purpose of your document, which is to be read. Beginning Word users sometimes have a tendency to over-format, trying to use every possible combination of character shape and size on the page. Keep in mind, however, that heavily stylized documents are often difficult to read, and they tend to lose their impact because the visual clutter overpowers the text.

Formatting Paragraphs

7

When you want to add some style and flair to your document, apply paragraph formats. Paragraph formats affect the alignment of text on the page. Probably the first two paragraph formats that you'll want to learn are centering text between the margins and changing the line spacing. But, again, Word offers much more. In this chapter, you will learn how to adjust the alignment of text between the margins, how to change line spacing, how to indent text, and more.

As with character formats, you can format paragraphs as you type them or anytime afterward. Before looking at paragraph formats in detail, however, there are some important concepts that you should keep in mind.

Paragraphs in Word

To Word, a paragraph is any text ending with a carriage return—where you press ENTER. It is not a grammatical structure, as we're taught in school, but a physical one. So all of the formats discussed in this chapter also apply to single lines, such as headings and titles, that you end by pressing ENTER. If you are typing a letterhead, for example, each of the lines is considered a separate paragraph.

Paragraph formats are stored in the paragraph mark—the paragraph symbol that you see when you click on the Show/Hide button. If you delete that mark, you remove the formats that you've selected for the paragraph. The paragraph will be merged with, and take the formats applied to, the paragraph that follows it.

When you press ENTER after typing a paragraph, its formats are carried to the next line as well. If you press ENTER after typing a centered title, for example, the next line you type will be centered. So paragraph formats do not end when you press ENTER.

You have several ways to select paragraph formats: you can use the Formatting toolbar, you can use shortcut key combinations, and you can use a dialog box. Unlike character formats, paragraph formats are not toggles. To change formats, such as to stop centering and return to the default left alignment, you must select a new alignment.

You can format a single paragraph by placing the insertion point in it and then selecting the format. To format multiple paragraphs, select them first. This also includes setting tabs. If you change the position of tabs, only the current or selected paragraphs will be affected. To adjust tabs for the entire document, select all of the text first—or set the tabs before you start typing a new document.

Remember: Paragraph formats affect only the paragraph in which the insertion point is placed, selected paragraphs, or new text starting at the position of the insertion point.

Aligning Text Between the Margins

Probably the first paragraph format you'll want to use is centering. You may need to center your address on a letterhead, or a title on a report. Word provides four options for aligning text between the margins: Left, Center, Right, and Justify.

♦ With *left alignment*, lines of text align evenly at the left margins, with an uneven right margin.

♦ *Centered alignment* centers the text between the left and right margins, with uneven left and right margins.

♦ *Right alignment* creates even right margins, with an uneven left margin.

♦ *Justify* adds spaces to the lines of text so they are aligned evenly on both the left and right.

You can select alignment options using the toolbar, shortcut keys, or a dialog box. We'll look at using the dialog box a little later. The quickest method is to select one of the alignment buttons from the toolbar.

To center a title, a line of text, or an entire paragraph as you type it, click on the Center button on the Formatting toolbar or press CTRL-E. The insertion point will move to the center of the screen, and as you type, Word will shift characters to keep them centered between the margins. When you press ENTER after typing the text, the center format will automatically be applied to the new line.

When you want to stop typing centered text, click on the Align Left button or press CTRL-L.

7

To center text that you've typed, place the insertion point anywhere in the paragraph, and then click on Center or press CTRL-E. To center several paragraphs, select them first. If you change your mind and want to realign text, place the insertion point in it, or select multiple paragraphs, and then click on Align Left or press CTRL-L.

Note: If you click on the Align Left button before you pressENTER after the paragraph, the text will become left aligned.

Try centering text now by adding a title to the document Biography of Sliding Billy Watson. Open the document, and then press ENTER twice to insert two blank lines before the first paragraph. Place the insertion point on the first blank line and use the Size list in the toolbar to change the size to 16 points. Now click on the Center button in the Formatting toolbar. The insertion point will move to the center of the screen.

Notice that the Col indicator in the status bar shows that you are on the first character, even though the insertion point is in the three-inch position. Type **The Sliding Billy Watson Story** and press ENTER. The insertion point appears in the center of the next line. Change the font size for this line to 14 points, type **A Biography**, and press ENTER. Click on the Align Left button to move the insertion point back to the left margin. Change the font size to 10 points and use the Date and Time option from the Insert menu to enter the date. Your document should look like mine:

The Sliding Billy Watson Story
A Biography

May 11, 1996

       Sliding Billy Watson was a vaudeville star and producer who gave W. C. Fields his first job and who started Fanny Brice in her career.

Other Alignment Formats

 Click on the Align Right button or press CTRL-R to align text on the right. When you select Align Right, the insertion point will move to the right margin, and text that you type will shift toward the left.

 Click on the Justify button or press CTRL-J to align text on both the left and right. When you select Justify, text will shift to the right, as usual. However, when Word reaches the right margin, it will decrease or increase the spacing between words to align the text on the left and right. Word justifies every line of a paragraph except the last.

You can turn off both of these formats by clicking on Align Left or pressing CTRL-L.

 Caution: Some justified lines may contain too much extra space, making them unsightly. See "Hyphenating Text" later in this chapter to correct the spacing.

To stop or cancel the formats, click on the Align Left button or press CTRL-L. Remember, these buttons are not toggles.

To experiment with these alignment options, click on the date in the document on your screen, and then click on the Align Right button. The date shifts over to the right of the screen.

Click on the Center button to see how the date looks centered, and then click on Align Left to return the date to the left margin. Now place the insertion point anywhere in the third paragraph and click on the Justify button. As you can see here, Word will add extra space to expand each line, except the last, to the right margin.

> Billy was born as Wolf Shapiro on October 12, 1876. His family moved from New York to Philadelphia, where Billy tried to settle down into a quiet family life. However, the call of the stage was too difficult for him to resist. He abandoned his wife and two children for the limelight and fame of vaudeville.

Click on Align Left to cancel justification, and then save the document.

Changing Line Spacing

Large sections of single-spaced text can be hard on the eyes and difficult to read. By adjusting the line spacing, you can give your document more impact. Line spacing is just like other paragraph formats. You can set it for text you are about to type, or change the spacing of existing text. You can set it for individual paragraphs, large sections of text, or for the entire document.

Set and change line spacing using either shortcut key combinations or a dialog box. There is no button for line spacing on the Formatting toolbar, although you can add spacing buttons by customizing the toolbars, as will be explained in Chapter 24. To set and change line spacing, use these key combinations:

Keystroke	Format
CTRL-1	Single spacing
CTRL-5	1.5 line spacing
CTRL-2	Double spacing
CTRL-0 (zero)	Double spacing between paragraphs

7

Press the combination before you type to set the spacing for new text. To change line spacing, place the insertion point in the paragraph, or select multiple paragraphs, and then change the spacing. Try it out now. Click in the first paragraph of the biography document (not on the title or date) and then press CTRL-2 to double-space. The space setting affects the lines within paragraphs as well as the spacing between paragraphs:

Sliding Billy Watson was a vaudeville star and producer who gave W. C. Fields his first job and

who started Fanny Brice in her career.|

Sliding Billy gained his name from his trademark slide across the stage, a precursor to Michael

If you select double spacing, for example, Word double-spaces as it wraps text to the next line. When you press ENTER to end a double-spaced paragraph, Word double-spaces before the next paragraph. Except for the CTRL-0 command, the keystrokes are not toggles. After typing double-spaced text, for example, return to single spacing by pressing CTRL-1. Press CTRL-1 now to single-space the paragraph.

The actual spaces created by line spacing are dependent on the font size. If you are using the default 10-point font, for example, double spacing will insert 10 points of space between lines; 1.5-line spacing will insert 5 points between lines. If you are using an 18-point font, double spacing inserts 18 points, and 1.5-line spacing inserts 9 points.

Remember: Double spacing does not insert a blank line. If you double-space and then click on the Show/Hide button, you will not see extra paragraph marks between lines or paragraphs. The only way to delete the extra lines is to change the spacing.

The CTRL-0 command requires a little explanation. When you press CTRL-0, Word inserts an extra line only when you press ENTER. For example, to double-space only between paragraphs, a very common format, type using the default single spacing but format paragraphs with CTRL-0. The extra space is in addition to the paragraph spacing already in force. If you are typing double-spaced text, for example, there will be three lines between each paragraph. If you are using 1.5-line spacing, there will be two and a half lines between paragraphs. The CTRL-0 combination is a toggle. Press it again to turn off the extra spacing.

Using the Paragraph Dialog Box

You can set text alignment, spacing, and other formats from the Paragraph dialog box, shown in Figure 7-1. Use the box just as you do the toolbar and key combinations. To format new text, select the options before typing. To format a single paragraph, place the insertion point in it before selecting options from the dialog box. To format multiple paragraphs, select them before choosing your options.

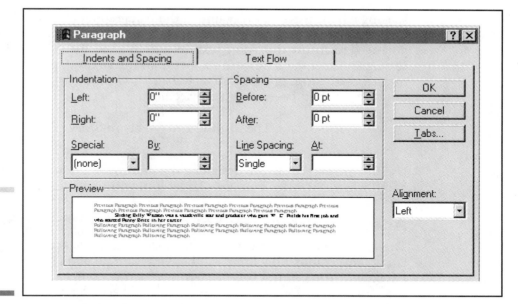

Use the
Paragraph
dialog box
to format
paragraphs
Figure 7-1.

To display the dialog box, select Paragraph from the Format menu, and then click on the Indents and Spacing tab. You can also display the box by right-clicking on the text and choosing Paragraph from the shortcut menu. The dialog box has a number of options. We will concentrate on the Spacing section and the Alignment pull-down list.

To change the alignment of text, pull down the Alignment list to display the options you see here. Select an alignment from the list and then click on OK. The corresponding button on the toolbar will be pressed down. You can later cancel or change the alignment using Undo, the toolbar, shortcut keys, or the dialog box.

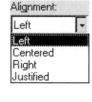

To set or change line spacing, pull down the Line Spacing list to display the options shown here. The Single, 1.5 Lines, and Double options work just the same as their corresponding shortcut keys. To use some other spacing, such as three lines or two and a half lines, select Multiple and then enter the line spacing in the At box. Use the Exactly and At Least settings for text that contains fonts or graphics of various sizes. When you format some text within a paragraph in a larger font size than other text on the line, the spacing between it and the line above is based on the largest character on the line. If you want Word to maintain a fixed line spacing, regardless of font size, select Exactly and enter the measurement in points in the At box. The designated line

7

spacing will be used for every line in the paragraph, even those without large type. This option is most commonly used in desktop publishing and when you need to ensure that some text fits within a specific space. However, setting an exact measurement smaller than the largest type size on the line may cause the tops of some letters to be *clipped*—they won't appear onscreen or on the printed page, as you can see here.

The Sliding Billy Watson Story
A Biography

Use the At Least setting to designate the minimum amount of space that Word will insert when you use a larger font within a paragraph.

Adding Extra Blank Space Between Paragraphs

The CTRL-0 command forces Word to add an extra space when you press ENTER. This command tells Word that you want an extra line before every paragraph. You can test this by starting a new document and then pressing CTRL-0. The insertion point moves down the space of a line, adding the space before the current paragraph. You can create the same effect, and enter a specific measurement, using the Paragraph dialog box. In Figure 7-1, you can see the Before and After text boxes in the Spacing section.

The Before option determines how much extra space Word inserts before each paragraph. The After option determines how much extra space Word inserts after each paragraph. Select either Before or After, and then enter the spacing in points.

When you are typing, the Before and After options may appear to create the same effect. For example, between two paragraphs, adding 12 points after the first would create the same affect as adding 12 points before the second. The difference between Before and After is the spacing between those paragraphs and others using the default setting. For example, setting 12 points before will add extra space between a paragraph and one before it that uses the default setting, as shown here on the left; setting 12 points after will use the default setting between those two paragraphs, but add extra space after the formatted text, as shown here on the right:

Paragraph One

Paragraph formatted with space Before
Paragraph Three

Paragraph One
Paragraph formatted with space After

Paragraph Three

Keeping Paragraphs Together

You know that as you type, Word divides your document into pages. As one page becomes full, Word automatically adds a soft page break and begins a new page. By default, Word will divide text in a way that avoids widow or orphan lines. A *widow* is the first line of a paragraph that appears by itself at the bottom of a page. An *orphan* is the last line of a paragraph that appears by itself on the top of a page. Word will adjust the text so the widow or orphan line appears with the rest of the paragraph. Widow and orphan control, as it is called, only takes effect when one line of a paragraph is involved. It will not, for example, move a two-line widow to the next page; neither will it prevent a title or subtitle from appearing at the bottom of the page, with the first paragraph relating to that title starting on the next. If you want to control the way sections of text flow from page to page, use the Text Flow options in the Paragraph dialog box. These options are shown in Figure 7-2.

Widow/Orphan Control is selected by default. Deselect the option if you do not want Word to adjust widows and orphans for you. To prevent a page break from occurring anywhere in a paragraph—sort of a widow and orphan control for more than one line—click in the paragraph and then select Keep Lines Together in the Paragraph dialog box. To keep a title on the same page as the paragraph that follows it, click in the title and then select Keep with Next. This option will keep any two paragraphs on the same page. To have Word insert a page break before a paragraph, no matter how else the text flows, click in the paragraph and select Page Break Before.

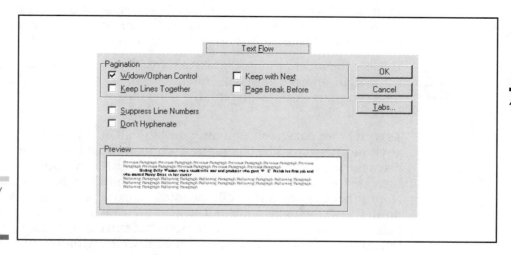

The Text Flow options
Figure 7-2.

7

The Suppress Line Numbers option controls the appearance of line numbers. You will learn about line numbering in Chapter 9. Select Don't Hyphenate to prevent Word from applying automatic hyphenation. You will learn about hyphenation later in this chapter. The Tabs command button will let you set tab stops.

Indenting Paragraphs

If you want to indent the first line of a paragraph, just press the TAB key. But you might want to indent every line of a paragraph from the left margin, or from both the right and left margins. You might also want to automatically indent the first line of every paragraph to save yourself the trouble of pressing TAB. You can control paragraph indentations from the toolbar, ruler, and from the Paragraph dialog box.

Tip: To indent a single paragraph, place the insertion point anywhere in the paragraph before using the indent function. To indent several paragraphs, select them first. As with other formats, indentation will be carried to the next paragraph when you press ENTER.

Let's look first at indenting text using the toolbar and the dialog box.

When you want to indent every line of a paragraph from the left margin, press CTRL-M or click on the Increase Indent button. Each time you do, Word moves the indentation to the next tab stop to the left. As you will soon learn, Word sets tabs every half-inch. If you click on Increase Indent once, the paragraph will be indented one half-inch; if you click on it twice, the paragraph will be indented one inch; and so on.

To clear the indentation—that is, to move the paragraph back toward the left margin—press CTRL-SHIFT-M or click on the Decrease Indent button. Each time you press Decrease Indent, the paragraph will move one tab stop toward the left.

As with other paragraph formats, you can indent text as you type it or anytime afterward. The biography document should still be on your screen. Place the insertion point anywhere in the fourth paragraph and click on the Increase Indent button once. All of the text shifts one half-inch to the right. Notice that the first line is still indented an extra half-inch because you pressed TAB when you typed it. Click on Increase Indent again, to shift the text over another half-inch. Now press CTRL-SHIFT-M twice to remove the indentation. Close the document on your screen without saving the changes, and then click on New to start a new document.

Indenting with the Dialog Box

You can have even more control over paragraph indentations using the Paragraph dialog box's Indents and Spacing page. From the dialog box, you can indent paragraphs from both the left and the right, and you can indent the first line of every paragraph automatically. You control these formats using the options in the Indentation section. Refer to Figure 7-1 to see these options as we review them.

To indent text from the left margin, enter the indentation distance in the Left text box. To indent text from the right margin, enter the distance from the right margin in the Right text box. To indent the first line of every paragraph, pull down the Special list and select First Line, and then enter the indentation distance in the By box.

 Tip: To later cancel first-line indentation, select (none) from the Special list.

Hanging Indentations

The other option in the Special list is Hanging. A hanging indentation is the exact opposite of first-line indentation—every line *except* the first is indented, as shown here.

> This paragraph is an example of a hanging indentation because every line except the first is indented at the tab stop. Create a hanging indentation using the CTRL-T key combination or by selecting Hanging in the Special list of the Paragraph dialog box.

To create a hanging indentation, select Hanging from the Special list. Then in the By box, enter the distance that you want every line except the first to be indented. If you want to create a hanging indentation with the keyboard, press CTRL-T. Each time you press CTRL-T, the hanging indentation will increase to the next tab stop. Cancel hanging indentation, or just reduce the distance, by pressing CTRL-SHIFT-T.

7

 Note: Word includes built-in features for creating numbered lists and outlines, two formats that often use hanging indentations. You'll learn about lists in Chapter 13, and outlines in Chapter 19.

Indenting with the Ruler

You can also create indentations—from the left, right, first line, and hanging—using the ruler. To indent text from the right, drag the Right Indent Marker, which is the small triangular object at the right end of the ruler, to the position at which you want to indent the text.

Remember: The numbers along the ruler indicate the distance from the left margin, not from the left edge of the page. Word has a default left margin of 1.25 inches, so the number 1 on the ruler represents 1 inch from the margin but 2.25 inches from the left edge of the paper. The larger tick marks between the numbers represent half-inch positions. The smaller tick marks are one-tenth inch positions.

To indent text from the left, you use the left section of the ruler. There are actually three separate indentation controls:

▽	First Line Indent Marker
△	Left Indent Marker
▭	Paragraph Indent Marker

The First Line Indent Marker controls the position of the first line of every paragraph. To indent the first line, point to the First Line Indent Marker and drag it to the indentation position. For example, to indent the first line one half-inch, drag the marker to the position indicated here.

Note: When you insert a tab at the beginning of an existing paragraph, Word moves the First Line Indent Marker to the first tab stop position instead of actually inserting a tab code.

To indent every line except the first, creating a hanging indentation, drag the Left Indent Marker. As you drag the marker, the Paragraph Indent Marker moves along with it. To indent every line of the paragraph, including the first, drag the Paragraph Indent Marker—all of the other markers will move along with it.

Tip: To learn which parts of the ruler to drag, create the indentation using the toolbar, shortcut keys, or the Paragraph menu, and then look at the positions of the markers in the ruler.

Setting Tabs

Tab stops not only control the distance moved by the Increase Indent and Decrease Indent buttons, they let you create columns and other effects. You can use the mouse to quickly set and delete tab stops on the ruler, or you can work with tabs using a dialog box. Word lets you set four types of tab stops, as shown in Figure 7-3. The default *left* tab aligns a column along the left. Characters that you type shift normally to the right of the tab stop. A *right* tab aligns characters on the right. As you type, your text shifts toward the left of the tab stop. Use a *center* tab to center text at the tab stop. As you type, text shifts alternately to the left and to the right. Use a *decimal* tab to align

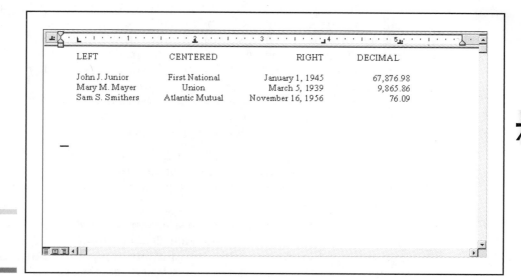

Types of
tab stops
Figure 7-3.

7

a column of numbers on the decimal point. As you type, the characters shift toward the left until you type the decimal point. Decimal values then shift to the right. There is a fifth type of tab—a *bar* tab for drawing lines between columns—that you can only set from the Tabs dialog box, discussed later.

Remember: As with other formats, setting, moving, and deleting tab stops affect only the paragraph in which the insertion point is placed, selected paragraphs, or new text starting at the position of the insertion point.

It is really easiest to set tabs with the ruler. On the far left of the ruler is a button that represents the type of tab. The shape of the button changes to illustrate the type of tab that you set:

L	Left Tab button
⊥	Center Tab button
⌐	Right Tab button
⊥•	Decimal Tab button

Each time you click on the Tab button, the tab will change to one of the four types—clicking four times cycles through all four. To set a tab, first select the type of tab, then click on the ruler where you want to set the tab stop. If you hold down the mouse button while pointing on the ruler, a vertical line will appear down the screen so you can see the tab stop position in relation to the text. When you release the mouse button, Word places the tab-type graphic at the position to indicate the tab stop. If you decide not to set the tab before you release the mouse, drag the mouse down into the typing area before you release it. When you set a tab, Word deletes its default tab stops to the left. For example, if you set a tab at the 1.75 inch position, the default tab stops at .5, 1.0 and 1.5 inches will be deleted.

You can also move and delete tabs using the mouse and the ruler. To delete a tab stop, point to its marker in the ruler, and then drag the mouse down into the typing area. To move a tab stop to a different position, drag its indicator to a new position on the ruler.

When you set, delete, or move a tab stop, any selected text, or the paragraph in which the insertion point is located, will adjust automatically. For example, if you use TAB to indent the first line of a paragraph at the half-inch position, setting a new left tab stop at .75 inches will delete the previous tab stop, and the first line of the paragraph will shift to the new tab stop position.

Note: Changing tab stops will not affect indentations—not even the indentation created when you insert a tab at the beginning of an existing paragraph.

Close the current document, without saving it, and start a new one. Now for practice, place a centered tab at 2 inches, a right tab at 4 inches, and a decimal tab at 5.5 inches. Type **Sandra Kaufman** at the left margin, press TAB to reach the tab stop at 2 inches, and type **President**. Press TAB to reach the 4-inch position and type **209-23-1923**. Press TAB to reach the 5.5-inch position, type **80,000.00**, and then press ENTER. In the same way, complete the columns as shown here, pressing ENTER after the last line.

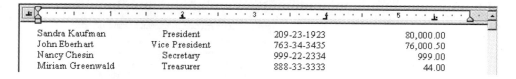

Sandra Kaufman	President	209-23-1923	80,000.00
John Eberhart	Vice President	763-34-3435	76,000.50
Nancy Chesin	Secretary	999-22-2334	999.00
Miriam Greenwald	Treasurer	888-33-3333	44.00

When you're done, save the document with the name Club Officers.

Setting Tabs with the Dialog Box

The Tabs dialog box gives you even greater control over tab stops, although it may not be as easy to use as clicking the mouse. To adjust tabs, select Tabs from the Format menu to display the dialog box shown in Figure 7-4.

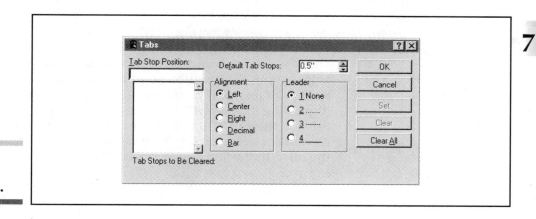

The Tabs
dialog box
Figure 7-4.

7

Tip: To set a tab and display the dialog box in one step, double-click on the tab stop position along the ruler.

The Default Tab Stops setting indicates Word's default tab stops every half-inch. To set a tab from the dialog box, type its position in the Tab Stop Position box, choose the type of tab, and then click the Set command button. The position will appear in the Tab Stop Position list. Each time you set your own tab, either from the dialog box or the ruler, its position will be added to the list. To change the type of the tab, click on it in the list and then click on the alignment option. The bar tab type, by the way, draws a vertical line on the screen at the tab stop position. In the ruler, a bar tab is indicated by a small vertical line, as you can see here.

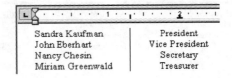

Remember: Tab stops are paragraph oriented. If you set tabs in one paragraph, move the insertion point to another paragraph, and then display the dialog box, your custom tabs will not be listed. You will only see them if you are in the paragraph that you formatted with tab stops. To delete a tab stop, click on its position on the list box, and then click on the Clear command button. To delete all of your custom tabs, reinstating Word's defaults, click on the Clear All command button. If you want to set a series of evenly spaced tabs, such as every .75 inch along the ruler, enter the spacing in the Default Tab Stops box.

Your Club Officers document should still be on the screen. Make certain the insertion point is in the blank line under the last line of text, and then select Tabs from the Format menu to display the dialog box. The three custom tabs that you set are listed in the Tab Stop Position list, shown here. Click on Clear All and then click on OK. Your tab stops no longer appear in the ruler, indicating that Word's default tab stops are again in effect.

Using Tab Leaders

Normally when you press TAB, the insertion point moves to the next tab stop along the ruler, inserting spaces between it and the previous position. In the Tabs dialog box, you can select a *leader,* which is a character that will appear in each space leading to the tab. You can choose to have no leader, a series of dots or dashes, or a solid underline.

Let's add dot leaders to all of the tab stops in the Club Officers document. First, select all four lines of text. Do not drag the mouse beyond the last line. The best way to do this is to point to the end of the fourth line and then drag up to the start of the first line. When you release the mouse button, the tab stops should still be indicated in the ruler.

Now choose Tabs from the Format menu to display the Tabs dialog box, which was shown in Figure 7-4. Click on 2" in the Tab Stop Position list, click on option 2 in the Leader section, and then click on Set. In the same way, select dot leaders for the 4" and 5.5" tab stops, and then select OK. Click the mouse to select the text. You'll see the dot leaders at each column, like this:

Sandra Kaufman	President	209-23-1923	80,000.00
John Eberhart	Vice President	763-34-3435	76,000.50
Nancy Chesin	Secretary	999-22-2334	999.00
Miriam Greenwald	Treasurer	888-33-3333	44.00

To see how the leaders look when you type, place the insertion point at the end of the fourth line and press ENTER. Press TAB to reach the first tab stop. Word will insert the dot leaders. Press BACKSPACE once to delete the tab, removing all of the leaders.

The New-Line Command

7

Because all of the formats discussed in this chapter are paragraph oriented, you must select text if you want to apply a format to more than one paragraph. This includes changing tabs. When you created the Club Officers document, for example, you pressed ENTER after each line, so each line is considered another paragraph. In order to change the tabs to create dot leaders in each one, you had to select all four lines first. If you just placed the insertion point on one of the lines, your tab stop changes would only affect that line.

To make formatting easier in cases like this, press SHIFT-ENTER at the end of each line as you type, instead of ENTER alone. Pressing SHIFT-ENTER inserts a new-line code, moving the insertion point to the next line without ending the paragraph. All four lines of Club Officers, for instance, would be treated as one paragraph. You could then change the tab settings, or any other paragraph formats, by clicking on any one of the lines rather than selecting them all.

Copying Paragraph Formats with Format Painter

You learned in Chapter 6 how to copy formats from one section of text to another using Format Painter. Format Painter copies paragraph formats as well as character formats. However, to copy paragraph formats, you must select the paragraph mark at the end of the paragraph. That's where the paragraph's formats are stored. The best way to select the paragraph mark is to drag past the end of the paragraph. The selection should include what appears to be a blank space at the end of the paragraph.

> Sliding Billy Watson was a vaudeville star and producer who gave W. C. Fields his first job and who started Fanny Brice in her career.

To be certain that the paragraph mark is selected, click on the Show/Hide button. After you select the paragraph mark, click on the Format Painter button, and then select the text that you want to format.

Hyphenating Text

When you justify text on both the left and right, Word inserts extra space to fill out the line. Sometimes the extra space is just too obvious:

> Local   performers   will   reenact highlights from popular shows so members of the audience may experience the thrill of this now lost theater art.

You hyphenate text to reduce these extra spaces. Hyphenation will divide some words between lines, adding enough characters at the right to avoid large blank spaces between words. You can have Word hyphenate automatically as you type, or you can have it hyphenate a selection of existing text. To turn on hyphenation, select Hyphenation from the Tools menu to display the following dialog box:

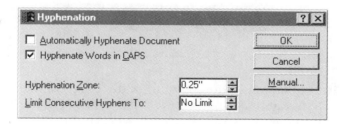

Click on the option labeled Automatically Hyphenate Document, and then select OK. Now as you type, Word will decide if a word can be hyphenated at the right margin, and add the hyphen for you.

Customizing Hyphenation

Word will hyphenate a word at the right margin, if it is suitable to be hyphenated—when the extra space in a paragraph is at least one quarter of an inch. This is called the *hyphenation zone*. You can adjust the zone to control how many words Word will hyphenate. A smaller setting results in less extra space, but increases the number of hyphenated words. A larger setting reduces the number of hyphenated words, but increases the amount of extra space. To change the setting, enter the measurement in the Hyphenation Zone box.

Often, Word will hyphenate words in several lines in a row. Too many consecutive hyphens may look strange to the reader. To limit the number of consecutive hyphens, enter the maximum number you would prefer in the Limit Consecutive Hyphens To box.

Making Hyphenation Decisions

Automatic hyphenation is convenient, but you may not like some of Word's choices for the hyphenation position. And with the feature turned on, you cannot delete the hyphen that Word adds to the document. If you want to remove an automatic hyphen, you must turn the feature off for the entire document.

7

As an alternative to letting Word make the hyphenation decisions, you can make them yourself. Display the Hyphenation dialog box, and then click on the Manual command button. Word will switch to Page Layout view, if you are not already in it, and then scan the document for words that can be hyphenated. For each word, you'll see a dialog box, like this one:

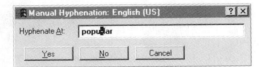

The blinking insertion point indicates the recommended hyphenation point. You may also see one or more other hyphens in the word, which are there to suggest alternative locations. Click on Yes to accept the recommended location, or click on the word where you want the hyphen to appear and then click Yes. You can also indicate the position by pressing RIGHT ARROW or LEFT ARROW to move the insertion point. Click on No if you want the word to wrap to the next line unhyphenated. You can later delete the hyphens inserted by manual hyphenation.

Tip: To hyphenate only a portion of the document, select it first, and then display the Hyphenation dialog box.

Typing Hyphens

You can always hyphenate words yourself by pressing the HYPHEN key at the end of the line. However, manual hyphenation is quite time-consuming, and if you later insert or delete text before the hyphenated word, the word may move onto one line while retaining the hyphen, like this:

> Hyphenating words manually by pressing the hyphen key can result in prob-
> lems if you later edit the text.

> Hyphenating words manually by pressing the hyphen key often results in
> prob-lems if you later edit the text.

The hyphen really doesn't belong in the word, so it will appear as a spelling error. Instead of pressing the HYPHEN key alone to insert the hyphen, press CTRL-HYPHEN, called an *optional hyphen*. Word will only display the hyphen character if it wraps the word between lines at that position. If the entire word fits on one line, the hyphen will not appear. You can also insert a *nonbreaking hyphen* by pressing CTRL-SHIFT-HYPHEN. Use this to keep social security numbers, phone numbers, and other hyphenated terms on the same line.

Note: You can control whether or not optional hyphens are displayed using the View page of the Options dialog box which is opened from the Tools menu. You'll learn more about this dialog box in Chapter 21.

Formatting Pages and Sections

8

For all of your documents so far, you've been starting Word and just typing. You haven't worried about the page margins or the page size because Word provides standard default settings. If you like the way your documents look using the default settings, you don't have to change them. But chances are you won't want to use the same settings for every document that you type. You may want to print a document on something other than standard 8½ × 11-inch paper—perhaps on legal-sized paper or an envelope. You may also want to change the margins to fit more text on the page—or to pad your document so it fills more pages. To make these changes, you must change the page layout.

Section Fundamentals

Before learning how to change the page layout, you should understand a Word concept called sections. *Sections* let you have more than one page format in the same document. If you want to type a letter and an envelope in one document, for instance, you need to have two sections. One section will be formatted in the size of the letter, the other section will be formatted in the size of the envelope. Or perhaps you want to print a newsletter using the format shown in Figure 8-1. As you can see, you'll need three sections—

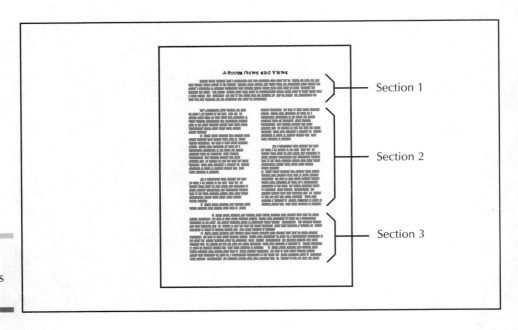

A document
page using
three sections
Figure 8-1.

In this chapter you'll learn how to change page size, margins, and orientation. You will learn how to add headers, footers, and page numbers in Chapter 9.

a single-column section at the top of the page, followed by a two-column section and then another one-column section.

With the newsletter example, all three sections are on the same page. With the letter and envelope example, each section is on its own page. You can combine different left and right margins, and column layouts, on one page with multiple sections, but formats such as page size and top and bottom margins apply to an entire page. Because sections add some complexity to page formatting, you'll first learn how to change page formats for an entire document. Once you understand the basics of page layout, you'll be able to handle sections with ease.

Changing Margins

The top, bottom, left, and right margins determine how much text you can fit on a page. The left and right margins determine the length of the lines; the top and bottom margins determine the number of lines that fit on the page. Word uses default left and right margins of 1.25 inches and top and bottom margins of 1 inch. When you want to fit more text on a page, make the margins smaller. When you want to fit less text on a page—to stretch that nine-page book report to meet your teacher's ten-page requirement, for example—make the margins larger. You can change the margins with the ruler as well as with a dialog box.

Remember: You can change the length of text lines using either indentation or margins. Use indentations when you want to change the line length of selected portions of text; use margins when you want to change the line length of the entire document.

Setting Margins with the Ruler

To change margins with the ruler, you must be in either Page Layout or Print Preview view. In these views, you drag the boundary markers shown in Figure 8-2 to change the margins. The boundary markers are the lines between the white and gray areas of the ruler.

When you point to a margin boundary, the mouse pointer will be shaped like a two-headed arrow. To change the top or bottom margin, place the pointer on the appropriate boundary, as shown here. Drag the top boundary to change the top margin; drag the bottom boundary to change the bottom margin. You can drag the boundaries either up or down, to increase or decrease the margins.

8

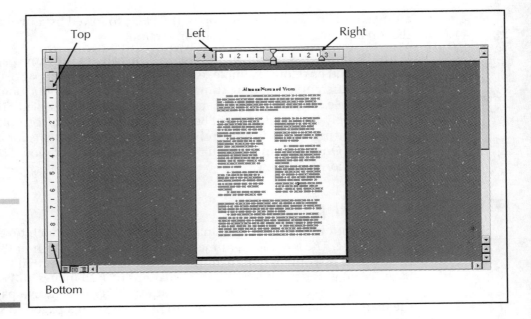

Use these boundary markers to change margins
Figure 8-2.

To move the left or right margin, point to the appropriate boundary on the horizontal (top) ruler, as shown here.

Drag the boundary on the left side of the ruler to change the left margin; drag the boundary on the right side of the ruler to change the right margin. You can drag the boundaries either to the left or right, to increase or decrease the margin.

Tip: To see the rulers in Print Preview mode, click on the View Ruler button in the Print Preview toolbar.

Hold down the mouse button and drag the boundary along the ruler to the desired margin position. As you drag the mouse, a dotted line appears down or across the screen to help you judge the width of the margin. You can drag the boundaries either up or down to increase or decrease the size of the margins.

As you drag the mouse to increase margins, the gray section of the ruler will increase. The large tick marks along the ruler indicate half-inches, and the small tick marks are tenths of an inch. Use the tick marks to judge the distance you are changing the margins.

If you want to be more exact, hold down ALT while you drag the mouse. Word will display the exact measurements in inches along the ruler. When you press ALT and drag the left boundary, for example, you'll see the size of the margin and the length of the text line:

As you press ALT and drag a boundary on the horizontal ruler, Word displays the sizes of the left and right margins, along with the line length. When you drag a boundary on the vertical ruler, Word displays the sizes of the top and bottom margins, as well as the number of inches of text space between the margins. If you want to display all four margin boundaries, select Whole Page from the Zoom Control in the toolbar or from the Zoom dialog box from the View menu. You can only select Whole Page when you are in Page Layout or Print Preview view.

Remember: If you change your mind after adjusting the margins, select Undo Formatting from the Edit menu, or reverse the action with the Undo button or list.

If your document is not divided into sections, changing margins with the ruler will affect the entire document, regardless of the position of the insertion point. For example, if you are on page 10 of a 50-page document, changing the margins will affect all 50 pages. You will learn how to create and use sections later in this chapter.

Open the Biography of Sliding Billy Watson document and change to Page Layout view. Pull down the Zoom Control and select 75% magnification. This will let you see the margin widths as you drag. Now try increasing the left and right margins by .25 inch. Point to the left margin boundary, hold down ALT, and drag the mouse to the right until the indicator reads 1.5".

Point to the right margin boundary, hold down ALT, and drag the mouse to the left until it reads 1.5". Now set the top margin to .5 inch. Point to the top margin boundary, hold down ALT, and drag the mouse up until it reads 0.5. The rulers should look like this:

8

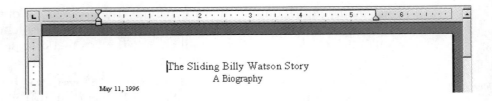

Setting Margins with the Dialog Box

Changing margins with the ruler is as easy as dragging, but you may find it difficult to set an exact margin width. To set an exact margin position, or to change more than one margin at a time, select Page Setup from the File menu, and then click on the Margins tab to display the options shown in Figure 8-3. The settings shown in the figure correspond to the margins you just set using the ruler. If you did not change the margins, the default 1-inch top and bottom margins, and 1.25-inch left and right margins will be shown. Enter your settings in the Top, Bottom, Left, and Right text boxes, and then select OK.

Tip: To quickly display the Page Setup dialog box, double-click on the top or sides of the ruler. In Page Layout view you can also display the dialog box by double-clicking on the upper-left or upper-right corner of the page when you do not have a header, or the lower-left or lower-right corner when you do not have a footer.

Some printers, most commonly laser printers, cannot print very close to the edge of the paper. The dimension depends on your printer but it is usually

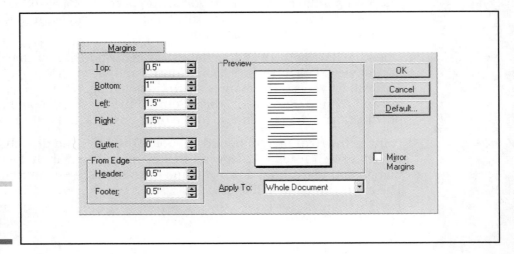

The Margins
options
Figure 8-3.

about one quarter of an inch. If you make one or more margins small enough so text would appear on these nonprintable areas, Word will display a warning box when you exit the Page Setup dialog box. The warning box gives you two options, Fix and Ignore. Select Fix to have Word reset the problem margins so they are just wide enough to clear the nonprintable areas. Select Ignore to accept the narrow margins, although text in the nonprintable areas may not print.

T ip: If you want to use the same margins for every new document, click on the Default command button in the Page Setup dialog box, and then select Yes from the dialog box that appears.

Formatting Pages for Books

Pages destined to be bound—if only in a three-ring binder—present some additional formatting opportunities. In most cases, the binding will take up some of the space on each page. In a ring-binder, for example, some space is taken up by the punched holes. When you open a book, this space in the middle between the two pages is called the *gutter.* Half of the gutter is on the right side of even-numbered pages; the other half is on the left side of odd-numbered pages. To compensate for this space, so that the text will still appear centered between the margins when readers open the book, set the width in the Gutter text box in the Margins page of the Page Setup dialog box.

When you bind pages in a book, you should also consider how two consecutive pages appear when the book lies open. This is called the *two-page spread.* Many books, for example, leave some extra space on the outside edges of the page for margin notes, cross-references, or just some space to break up large sections of text. To leave extra space on the outside of the pages, the margins on the left of odd-numbered pages and on the right of even-numbered pages must be expanded. The opposite is true if you want the extra space on the inside edges of the page. To format pages with extra inside or outside margins, you use the Mirror Margins option in the Page Setup dialog box.

In Chapter 9 you will learn how to create headers and footers for odd- and even-numbered pages.

When you select Mirror Margins, the Preview panel will illustrate two pages instead of one, and the Left and Right margin options change to Inside and Outside. Set the Inside margin to determine the space on the right side of even-numbered pages and the left side of odd-numbered pages. Set the Outside margin to determine the space on the left side of even-numbered pages and the right side of odd-numbered pages. As you set margins and select options in the Page Setup dialog box, watch the Preview panel to see the effects on the document. Figure 8-4, for example, shows a page layout with a .75" gutter, a 1-inch inside margin, and a 2-inch outside margin.

8

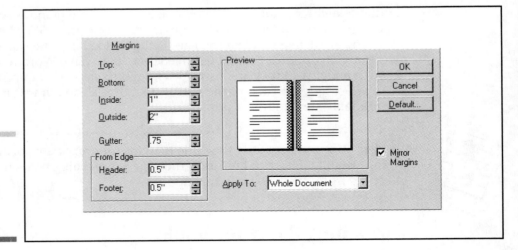

Margin
settings for
mirrored
margins and
gutter
Figure 8-4.

Changing Page Size

Word's default page size is 8½ × 11 inches. To use a different page size, such as legal size, you click on the Paper Size tab in the Page Setup dialog box, and select from the options shown in Figure 8-5.

Word has already defined the dimensions of certain standard-sized papers. To choose one of these sizes, pull down the Paper Size list, shown here, and make your selection.

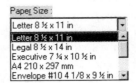

Now let's format the document on your screen to print on legal-sized paper. Select Page Setup from the File menu and click on the Paper Size tab. Pull down the Paper Size list and select Legal 8½ × 14 In. Select OK to accept the setting. Now click on Print Preview to see the format of your page, as shown in Figure 8-6. Close the Preview window.

If you want to use a size that is not already defined, you have to enter its measurements in the Width and Height boxes. If you want to change both the width and height, select Custom Size from the Paper Size list, and then enter the dimensions in the Width and Height boxes. If one of the defined page sizes has one of the dimensions already, select it from the list and then

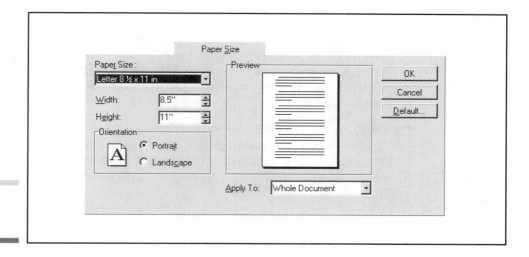

The Paper
Size options
Figure 8-5.

change the other dimension. When you type a dimension in the Width or
Height box, the Paper Size changes to Custom automatically.

Tip: Watch the Preview panel to see the shape of your paper size.

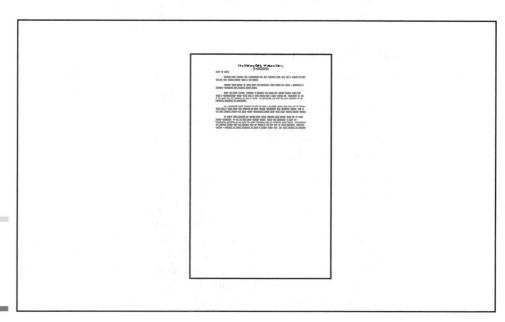

Print Preview,
showing
legal-sized
paper
Figure 8-6.

8

Changing the paper size does not change the default margins, so you may want to check the margins before selecting OK. For example, suppose you have some small personal stationery, say 4 inches wide and 6 inches high. If you enter these custom settings and then select OK, Word will retain the default 1.25-inch left and right margins. This means that each line will only be 1 inch wide.

 T**ip:** You can move from page to page of the dialog box while the dialog box is displayed. The settings are not applied until you select OK from any of the pages. So you can change paper size and then margins in one step before applying them to the document.

Page Orientation

One other factor that determines the width of your lines and the number of lines per page is the *orientation*. The default setting is *portrait*, in which your lines of text print across the narrow dimension of the page. You can also select *landscape* orientation, in which your lines print across the longer dimension of the page. Landscape orientation is useful when printing wide tables and other documents that require long lines. Of course, with landscape orientation you can fit fewer lines on the page.

To change orientation, display the Paper Size options of the Page Setup dialog box and click on either Portrait or Landscape in the Orientation section.

The Paper Source

Your printer may be equipped with more than one paper source or tray. You may have one tray containing letterhead paper, another holding plain paper, and yet another with envelopes. One of the sources is usually the default—the tray your printer uses unless you give it a special command. If you want to use paper in a tray other than the default, you must select it in the Page Setup dialog box.

Word may automatically select a tray other than the default when you select the envelope page size.

Look at the feed options that are available for your printer. Display the Page Setup dialog box, and then click on the Paper Source tab to see the options shown in Figure 8-7. The available choices depend on your printer, so your options may be different from those shown in the figure. Notice the two lists—First Page and Other Pages. In the First Page list, select the source that you want to use for the first page of the document. In the Other Pages list, select the source you want for the second and subsequent pages. If you want every page to be from the same source, select the same options in both lists. Close the dialog box.

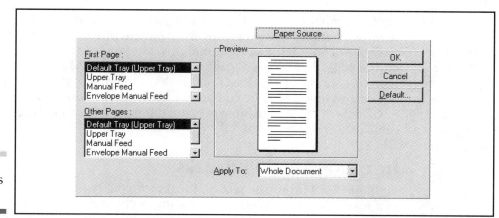

The Paper
Source options
Figure 8-7.

Using Sections

Now that you know how to format pages, you are ready to delve into Word's
sections. Remember, sections let you have more than one page format—such
as different page sizes, margins, and sources—in the same document. Each
place in your document where a new section begins is called a *section break*.
You can go about formatting sections in two ways. You can first insert a
section break and then apply the formats to it. Or you can have Word insert
the section break for you when it applies page setup formats.

Types of Section Breaks

Before learning how to create sections, you should understand the types of
section breaks. The type of break determines how Word applies the formats
of the section. Here are descriptions of the options:

Option	Effect
Next Page	The section break is also a page break, and the section starts after the section break line. The option is also called New Page.
Continuous	The section break does not insert a page break. Multiple formats that can be combined on one page, such as left and right margins, will appear on the same page. Formats that cannot be combined, such as page size and top and bottom margins, will begin after the next page break.
Even Page	The section break is also a page break, and Word forces the next page to be even numbered.
Odd Page	The section break is also a page break, and Word forces the next page to be odd numbered.

8

If you select a page setting that cannot exist on the same page as the previous section, Word will insert a page break for you, and the format will continue on the next page.

Some explanation may be needed so you understand these types of breaks. Say, for example, that you want some paragraphs at the top of the page to have the default left and right margins, but you want the remaining text on the page, and on every page thereafter, to have 2-inch margins. You therefore want to enter a section break on the first page—after the text with the default margins—but you do not want the section break to be a page break as well. This is possible because different left and right margin settings can exist on one page.

Inserting Section Breaks

To have Word insert the section breaks for you, type your document until you reach the location where you want to change the page format, or place the insertion point in existing text where you want to change the format. Select Page Setup from the File menu and select the tab (Margins, Paper Size, and so on) containing the option you want to change. Adjust the formats as desired, and then pull down the list labeled Apply To.

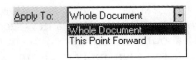

The Whole Document option will apply your changes to the entire document, without inserting a section break. The other option, This Point Forward, will insert a section break and apply the format to all of the text from the insertion point to the end of the document or to the next section break, whichever is first.

If your document already contains sections, you will see a third option in the Apply To list, This Section. Use this option to apply the format only to the current section. If you select text before displaying the Page Setup dialog box, the Apply To option will be set at Selected Text. This setting will insert section breaks before and after the text.

Remember: Although you'll see an Apply To option on each page of the Page Setup dialog box, the setting you select on one page applies to all of the others as well.

The default section break when you choose This Point Forward will also set a page break. If you want to insert another type of section break, click on the Page Layout tab and make a selection from the Section Start list.

When you've entered all of the settings on the Page Setup page, click on OK. If you've selected This Point Forward in the Apply To box, you'll see that Word has inserted a section break:

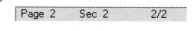

As you scroll through a document that contains sections, the Sec indicator in the status bar will show you which section you are in.

Page 2	Sec 2		2/2

Anytime you want to use a different page format, or return to the default, place the insertion point where you want the format to begin, select Page Setup, and then choose your settings.

Now let's format the document on your screen, Biography of Sliding Billy Watson, to print on two different orientations of paper. Follow these steps, starting with returning the document to 8½ × 11-inch paper.

1. Select Page Setup from the File menu and click on the Paper Size tab.
2. Select Letter 8½ × 11 In and click on OK.
3. Place the insertion point after the third paragraph and select Page Setup from the File menu.
4. Click on the Paper Size tab and choose the Landscape option button.
5. Pull down the Apply To list and select This Point Forward.
6. Click on the Layout tab and confirm that Section Start is set at New Page.
7. Click on OK.

To see how the format looks, click on the Print Preview button in the toolbar. If you do not see both pages in Print Preview, pull down the Multiple Pages button and drag across to select two pages. Your preview should resemble Figure 8-8. Close the Print Preview window.

Using the Break Dialog Box

Another way to create a section is to enter the section break yourself and then apply the formats to it. To insert a section break, select Break from the Insert menu to display the Break dialog box.

The Insert section of this box has options for inserting a page break (which is just like pressing CTRL-ENTER) and for inserting a column break. Select the

8

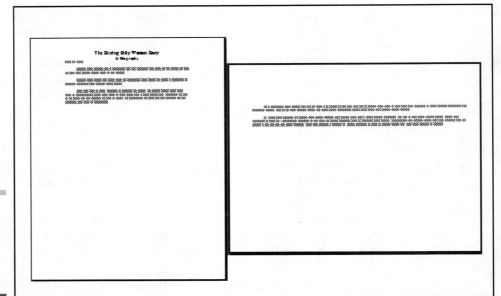

Portrait and
landscape
orientations in
the same
document
Figure 8-8.

You will learn
how to create
and use
columns in
Chapter 16.

type of break you want to insert and click on OK. Close the dialog box and
then use the Page Setup box to format your page, choosing This Section in
the Apply To list.

Removing Section Breaks

If you change your mind about your page formats, you can always reverse
them by selecting Undo Page Setup from the Edit menu or the Undo list.
You can also delete a page break line. However, just as paragraph formats
are stored in the paragraph mark after the paragraph, so are section formats
stored in the section break line after the section. If you delete the section
break that Word has inserted, you will actually delete the formats applied
to the text above the section break line. The previous text will become
formatted according to the page setting of the text that is below the line.

To see how this works, click on the section break line in your document and
then press DELETE. The two pages are combined into one landscape-oriented
page. Now close the document on your screen *without* saving the changes.
The default margins and page sizes will still be in effect when you next open
the document.

Aligning Text Vertically

As an example of using sections, and to learn more about the Layout options in the Page Setup dialog box, let's create a title page. A title page usually contains some text that is centered both horizontally and vertically on the page. Following the title page is the first page of the document. You could create the title page manually, by pressing ENTER until the text appears to be centered. However, all of these extra carriage returns could be a problem if you later insert or delete text. So rather than create the page manually, let Word do it for you using page setup options.

Open the Biography of Sliding Billy Watson document, and then press ENTER to insert a blank line at the top of the document. Select Break from the Insert menu, click on Next Page, and then select OK. Word will insert a section break at the beginning of the document, like this:

···End of Section··

The Sliding Billy Watson Story
A Biography

Place the insertion point above the section break line. The insertion point should still be centered because the first line of the document is a centered title. Type the title of your report, **The Biography of Sliding Billy Watson**, press ENTER, and then type your name as the proud author.

Next, format the page as a title page. Select Page Setup from the File menu. Click on the Layout tab to see the options shown in Figure 8-9.

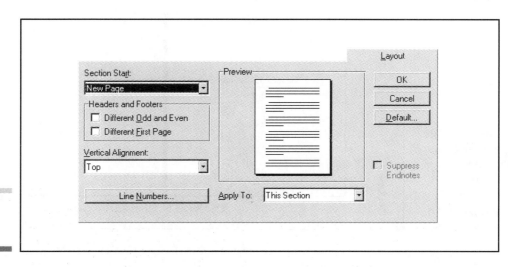

The Layout options
Figure 8-9.

8

Pull down the Vertical Alignment list, shown here, and select Center.

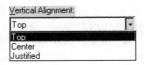

Tip: If you want to center every page in a document, for a presentation or printed handouts, for example, set the Vertical Alignment option at Center and choose Whole Document from the Apply To list.

Now Word will center the text between the top and bottom margins. Make certain that the Apply To option is set at This Section and then click on OK. To confirm the alignment of the text, click on Print Preview and check the text. With both pages displayed, your document should look like mine in Figure 8-10. Close the Print Preview window. Select Save As from the File menu, type **Watson Report**, and then select OK. This saves the two-section document without overwriting the original document.

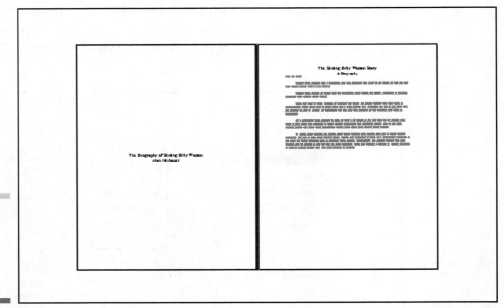

The title page
and first page
of the
document in
Print Preview
Figure 8-10.

If you don't want your text centered, the Vertical Alignment option has two other choices—Top and Justify. When set at Top, the text will start at the top of the page, the default page setup. When set at Justify, Word will spread out the lines on the page evenly between the top and bottom margins.

Envelopes and Letters

One of the most typical reasons to use two paper sizes in one document is to create a letter and its envelope. As you know from the previous discussion, this would require two sections—one for the letter-sized paper, another for the envelope. This is such a common word processing task, however, that Word handles the formatting of sections for you, even creating the envelope automatically.

Open the Letter to Historical Society document so you can create an envelope for it. The letter includes the address of the recipient, so Word will use it for the envelope. Select Envelopes and Labels from the Tools menu and click on the Envelopes tab to display the options shown in Figure 8-11. (If the Envelopes page of the Envelopes and Labels dialog box is aready active, you won't need to click on the Envelopes tab.) Word copies the mailing address from the letter and displays it in the Delivery Address box. If the address is incorrect, click in the box and edit the address. To include your return address on the envelope, select the Return Address box and type your address.

You will learn about printing labels in Chapter 14.

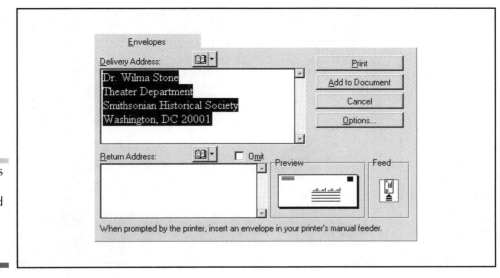

The Envelopes options in the Envelopes and Labels dialog box
Figure 8-11.

Remember: If your letter contains more than one address, select the address you want to appear on the envelope before displaying the dialog box. Word will use the selected text for the mailing address.

Now look at the Preview and Feed panels. The Preview panel shows the size and shape of your envelope and how the text will look. The Feed panel shows the direction to feed the envelope and which surface is fed as the top. Now click on Add to Document. A dialog box will appear asking if you want to save the return address as the default for other envelopes. Select No or Yes as it pleases you. Word will insert the envelope at the beginning of your document, separated from the letter with a section break, as you can see in Figure 8-12. It formats the page size and paper sources for both parts of the document. If you want to confirm that the envelope is using the correct paper source, place the insertion point in its section and display the Paper Source options of the Page Setup dialog box.

Tip: If you want to print the envelope without adding it to the document, click on Print from the Envelopes options.

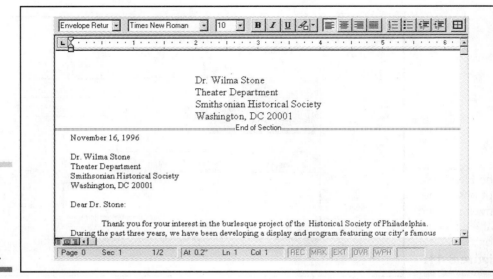

Word inserts the envelope at the beginning of the letter
Figure 8-12.

Enhancing Envelopes

You have many options for customizing envelopes. One of the most common customizations is adding a bar code. The automatic sorting equipment at the post office reads the code to speed your letter's progress. There are two sets of options—envelope options and printing options. Since you already have an envelope on the screen, let's add a bar code to it now. Select Envelopes and Labels from the Tools menu. Notice that the Add to Document button has been replaced by Change Document because the letter already includes an envelope. Click on the Options command button to display the dialog box and click on the Envelope Options tab to see the options shown in Figure 8-13.

 Tip: You can access the envelope options by clicking on the Preview panel of the Envelopes page. You can access the printing options by clicking on the Feed panel.

Now to add the bar code, click on Delivery Point Bar Code—the POSTNET bar code using the ZIP code in the delivery address will appear just above the address in the Preview panel. If you choose to include a delivery point bar code, you will also see the FIM-A Courtesy Reply Mail option on the dialog box. The FIM-A code identifies the front side of the envelope for automated presorting equipment.

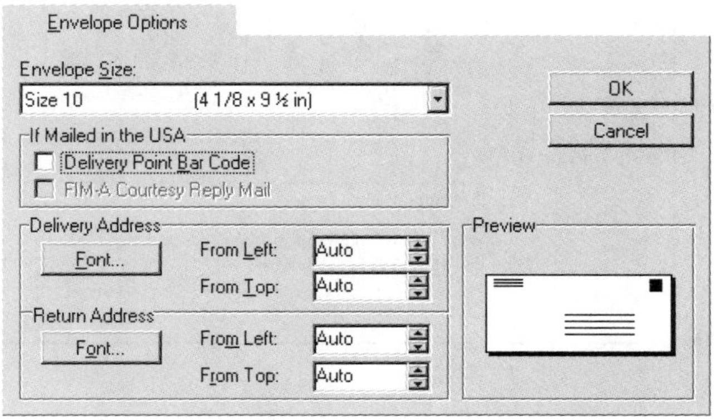

More
Envelope
options
Figure 8-13.

8

The other envelope options determine the size of the envelope, the font used to print the delivery and return addresses, and the position of the addresses. If you want to select another standard envelope size, or set a custom size, pull down the Envelope Size list. If you want to print the address in another font, select the appropriate font button, and then choose a font from the dialog box that appears. To change the position of either address, enter the measurement in the appropriate From Left and From Top boxes.

Click on OK to return to the Envelopes page and select Change Document. The bar code will appear above the address on the envelope, as you can see here.

> |ı.|ıllıı.llıı.llıııı.lllıı.ll
> Dr. Wilma Stone
> Theater Department
> Smithsonian Historical Society
> Washington, DC 20001

If your envelopes do not print correctly, you may have to change the paper source or feed settings. Let's take a look at these options. The Envelopes page of the Envelopes and Labels dialog box should now be displayed on your screen, so click on the Feed panel to see the options shown in Figure 8-14. The dialog box contains six buttons showing possible ways to feed an envelope

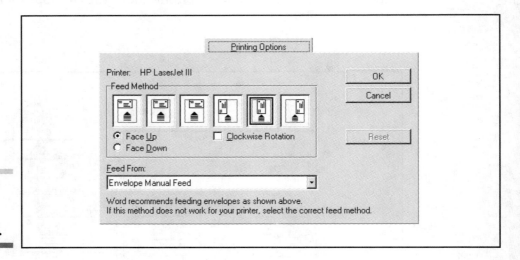

The Printing options for envelopes
Figure 8-14.

through a printer. The selected option is the method Word recommends for your printer. If you are having difficulty feeding the envelope through your printer, however, select one of the other buttons. Each button illustrates the orientation of the envelope, the direction of feed, and which side to face up.

If none of the buttons shows the proper feed for your printer, you can alter the suggested feed methods. Click on Face Up or Face Down to change which side of the envelope faces up in the feed tray. You can also click on Clockwise Rotation to change the leading edge when you print in landscape orientation—controlled by the three feed buttons on the right. Between these options and the six buttons, every possible feed direction is made available for your selection. To change the feed tray, select another option in the Feed From list.

Remember: If you change the feed options and want to return to the default methods, click on Reset.

Close the dialog box and try printing the envelope and letter. If you have a laser printer, you may see a message indicating that you must insert an envelope in the manual feed tray. Insert an envelope using the orientation shown in the Feed panel of the Envelopes page. After Word prints the envelope, it will print the letter.

Using the Address Book

Rather than typing an address, you can insert one into a letter, envelope, or other document using the Insert Address button. You'll find the button on the Standard toolbar as well as in the Envelopes and Labels dialog box. If you've already entered addresses into the book, pull down the list next to the button to display the recipients' names.

Barbara Elayne Cohen
Billy Preston
Adam Chesin

Cancel

To access the address book for more information, or to add addresses to it, click on the button to display a dialog box like the one shown in Figure 8-15.

8

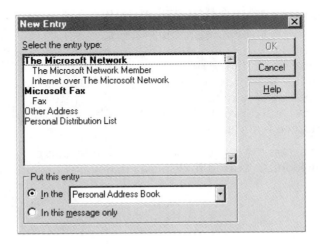

You can create your own personal address book
Figure 8-15.

To insert an address into the document, double-click on a name. To enter a new address, click on New. Word will display the dialog box you see here, in which you can designate the type of address.

Select the type of address and then click on OK to see the dialog box shown in Figure 8-16. Use the tabs to enter this type of information:

♦ *Business* stores the recipient's first and last name, the complete address, and information about the recipient's company.

♦ *Phone Numbers* stores a variety of numbers for the recipient, including home, business, mobile, and pager.

♦ *Notes* lets you enter descriptive information about the recipient.

♦ *New Address* includes the recipient's name, E-mail address, and E-mail type.

T ip: Your ability to access an address book and use the mail options depends on your hardware and your Windows setup. If you use Microsoft Office, Word can use Schedule+ to maintain the address book.

Mail Options

With E-mail and online services becoming so popular, chances are you may not be printing and mailing your letters and other documents but sending them electronically—through a modem, over a network, or by fax. If your

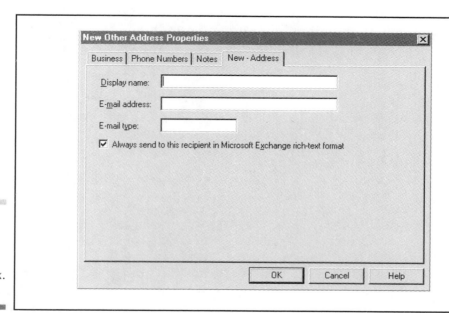

Enter information about the recipient in this dialog box.
Figure 8-16.

8

computer is so equipped, you can send your
documents using the File menu options
shown here.

Send...
Add Routing Slip...
Post to Exchange Folder...

Select Send to start Microsoft Exchange and
to transmit the current document immediately. Select Add Routing Slip to
route the transmission to more than one recipient. Select Post to Exchange
Folder to store the document for transmission later.

Enhancing Pages and Text

9

To give your document more impact, you can enhance pages with headers, footers, page numbers, and even lines and borders. These elements not only add visual appeal but they help to identify your document. In this chapter, you will learn how to embellish the pages of your document to provide the reader with useful information as well as to make reading your document easier and more pleasant.

Using Headers and Footers

Pages of a long document can easily get separated. They can get out of order or misplaced, or perhaps one page gets stuck in the copying machine and never makes it into the document at all. Headers and footers help to identify the pages of your document, as well as the document itself, and they can even create pleasing visual effects that grab and hold the reader's attention. A *header* is text or graphics that prints at the top of every page. A *footer* is text or graphics that prints at the bottom of every page. Two common uses of a header or footer are to number pages and to repeat the document's title on each page.

Word offers a number of options for positioning headers and footers. You can have a header or footer, or both, in your document, and you can control their exact position on the page. You can have a different header or footer on odd and even pages. You can have a different header and footer for the first page of your document, and you can have different ones in each section. To start with the most basic, and common, method, let's place a header and footer on every page of your document.

Open the Biography of Sliding Billy Watson document to use as a sample, and then switch to Normal view if you are not there already. To best show how headers and footers work, divide the text into several pages. Place the insertion point after the second paragraph and press CTRL-ENTER to insert a hard page break. Do the same after the third paragraph so the document now has three pages. You can enter a header or footer while on any page—Word will apply it to the entire document, unless other sections already have their own.

Select Header and Footer from the View menu. Word will switch to Page Layout view, as shown in Figure 9-1, and display the header area within the top margin of the document as well as the Header and Footer toolbar.

In the header area, you type the text that you want to appear on the top of each page, or use the toolbar buttons to insert other elements. If you look at the ruler, you'll notice that Word has formatted the area with a center tab in the center of the page and a right-aligned tab at the right margin. These tabs let you easily align three objects—on the left, centered, and on the right.

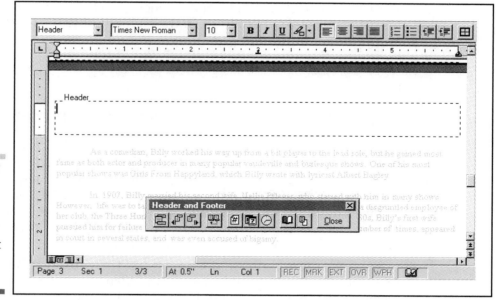

Word displays
the header
area and the
Header and
Footer toolbar
in Page Layout
view
Figure 9-1.

 Now let's create a header and footer for your document. Make sure the header area is displayed—if not, click on the Switch Between Header and Footer button in the Header and Footer toolbar. Type your name and then press TAB to reach the center tab stop. Type the title of your report, **Biography of Sliding Billy Watson**, and then press TAB to reach the right tab stop.

 Now click on the Date button. Word inserts the date as a field, so the current date will print with the document no matter when you get a chance to print it. If you also want to display the time, click on the Time button. Your header should now look like this:

 Tip: Text in the header and footer uses the document's default font. To use another font, select it from the toolbar or Font menu before typing, or select the text and then choose the font. Headers and footers can contain more than one line of text—just press ENTER at the end of a line, or let Word wrap long lines for you.

9

To switch between the header and the footer, click on the Switch Between Header and Footer button. Click on the button now to display the footer area at the bottom of the page:

The footer is also formatted with a center and right-aligned tab, and you can add any of the elements from the toolbar. Press TAB to reach the center tab stop position. Type **Page**, press the SPACEBAR, and then click on the Page Numbers button in the Header and Footer toolbar. Although the current page number appears for now, Word has inserted a field so that the actual number of each page will appear in the footer.

Click on the Close button in the Header and Footer toolbar. Word removes the toolbar and header and footer areas and returns the screen to your previous view. But where's your header? Headers and footers will appear on the screen in Page Layout view and in Print Preview, but not in Normal view. Switch to Page Layout view now—using either the buttons next to the scroll bar or the View menu. You'll see the dimmed header above the text.

If you have to edit a header or footer, you can always select Header and Footer from the View menu. But if you are in Page Layout view, you can also double-click on the dimmed header, or the dimmed footer, that you see on the screen. Double-click on the header area now. Word will display the Header and Footer toolbar and the header area. When you create or edit a header or footer, the text of the document will appear dimmed. This is useful because you can see the spacing between the header or footer and the text. If you find the dimmed text distracting, click on the Show/Hide Document Text button in the Header and Footer toolbar. The Show/Hide button toggles off and on the display of the dimmed text. Now click on the Close button.

The Show Previous and Show Next buttons are used when your document contains more than one section, or when you have different headers and footers for the first page, for odd pages, or for even pages. When your document is divided into sections, the buttons show the header or footer in the next or previous section. For example, if you are looking at the header area, clicking on Show Next will show the header for the next section—not for the next page in the document. When you are using different headers for odd and even pages, and looking at the odd page footer, clicking on Show Next will show the footer for the next even-numbered page, if there is one.

By default, headers and footers are placed a half-inch from the edge of the page. You can adjust that position using the Page Setup dialog box. To display the dialog box, select Page Setup from the File menu, or click on the Page Setup button in the Header and Footer toolbar. Click on the Margins tab, and then enter new positions in the From Edge section of the dialog box, which you see here.

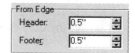

For example, enter **1"** in the Header box of the From Edge section to position the header so it starts 1 inch from the top of the page. You can also adjust the position of the header or footer by dragging. When you display the header in Page Layout view, for instance, Word will change the ruler to show the height of the header area.

To change the position of the header, drag the top and bottom boundaries—the lines between the white and gray areas of the ruler that show the header or footer depth. When you drag the boundary, the insertion point will be shaped like a two-headed arrow, as you can see here:

Options in the Page Setup dialog box also let you designate different headers and footers for odd and even pages or a different one just for the first page. To select these options, display the Page Setup dialog box and click on the Layout tab. You'll see the options in the Headers and Footers section:

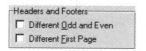

For example, if you are binding your pages, you may want the page number in a header always to appear on the outside edge of each page—just like the page numbers in this book. The page numbers of even-numbered pages are on the left of the header; the numbers on odd-numbered pages are on the right side. To create this format, select the Different Odd and Even option and then click OK. When you then display the header or footer area of the pages, Word will clearly indicate which you are creating, as you can see here.

9

Odd Page Header

To enter an odd page header or footer, display any odd-numbered page and then type the header or footer. To enter an even page header or footer, display any even-numbered page. Unlike creating a header or footer for every page of the document—where you can be on any page when you create it—you must be on an odd or even page to create an odd or even header or footer.

The Different First Page option lets you have a different header and footer just for the first page. In many cases, for instance, you do not place a page number on the first page, and you do not need any identifying items because it contains its own title.

You can select one or both of the options. Choosing both will let you create a header and footer just for the first page, a different header and footer for other odd-numbered pages, and a header and footer for even-numbered pages. If you select these options after creating a header or footer, change to Page Layout view and check your document. For example, selecting Different First Page will delete the header and footer from the first page of the document, so you must then display the page and create a new header or footer for it. The header and footer area will indicate its placement.

Tip: To prevent the header and footer from appearing on the first page, select Different First Page and do not create a header or footer on it.

Since there are many variations that you can create, let's modify the headers and footers in our sample document. We'll create one header and footer for the first page and then others for odd and even pages. Follow these steps:

1. Press CTRL-HOME to move to the beginning of the first page.
2. Select Page Setup from the File menu and click on the Layout tab.
3. Select both Different Odd and Even and Different First Page.
4. Select OK.
5. Select Header and Footer from the View menu. The header that you created for every page of the document does not appear on this page.
6. Press TAB twice to reach the right margin.
7. Click on the Date button in the toolbar.

8. Click on the Show Next button in the Header and Footer toolbar. The Even Page Header area appears. It too is blank because the original header that was on page 1 is now used for odd pages.

9. Type **Page**, press the SPACEBAR, and then click on the Page Numbers button in the toolbar.

10. Press TAB and type the name of the document—**Biography of Sliding Billy Watson**.

11. Press TAB and type your name.

12. Click on the Show Next button. The original header appears for odd-numbered pages.

13. Delete the date code on the right of the header.

14. At the right margin, type **Page**, press the SPACEBAR, and then click on the Page Numbers button in the toolbar.

15. Click on the Switch Header/Footer button.

16. Delete the page number in the footer.

17. Click on Close.

You now have one header for the first page and different headers for odd and even pages. The odd and even headers are reversed, so the page number appears on the outside edge. Figure 9-2 shows how the pages appear in Print Preview. Now close the document without saving it.

Headers, Footers, and Sections

You know that you can use sections to have different page formats in one document. This also applies to headers and footers. Each section in a document can have its own headers and footers—even different ones for its first page and for odd and even pages. By default, however, Word carries the header and footer to the next sections. To see how this works, open the

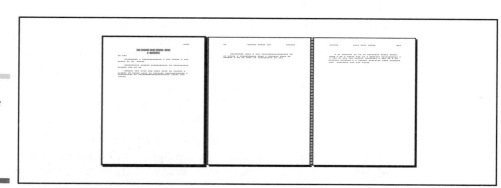

Headers and footers for the first page and for odd and even pages

Figure 9-2.

9

Watson Report document. The document contains two sections—a title page section followed by one page of text.

Place the insertion point anywhere in the title page—the first section—and then select Header and Footer from the View menu. Click on the Switch Header/Footer button to display the footer area. Press TAB to reach the center tab stop and then click on the Date button. Now click on the Show Next button in the toolbar. Word will display the footer area for the next section:

Footer -Section 2-   Same as Previous

05/12/96

The words Same As Previous along the top of the footer area mean that the footer is linked to the footer in the previous section. Also notice that the Same As Previous button in the toolbar appears pressed down. Because we do not want the date to appear at the bottom of every page—only the title page—click on the Same As Previous button. The notation Same As Previous is removed from the footer area. Delete the date code in the footer. With Same As Previous turned off, deleting the date here will not affect the footer in the previous section. Close the Header and Footer toolbar. Display the document in Print Preview to confirm that the footer appears only on the title page.

Tip: If you later decide that you want to continue the footer from the previous section, display the footer area and click on Same As Previous again. A message appears asking if you really want to delete the footer that you entered for that section and link the footer with the one in the previous section.

Page Numbers

If all you want to include in a header or footer is a page number—with no other text—you don't even have to create a header or footer. The Page Numbers command from the Insert menu lets you insert page numbers and change their position and the type of numbers that appear. You can number every page of your document consecutively, or you can use sections to start with page 1 at the beginning of every chapter, or you can use roman numerals for a table of contents and index.

To see how this works, close the document you have on the screen without saving the changes. Reopen the Biography of Sliding Billy Watson document and insert page breaks after the second and third paragraphs as you did before. To number pages, place the insertion point anywhere in the document. If the document contains more than one section, place the insertion point in the section that you want to number. Now select Page Numbers from the Insert menu to display the following dialog box:

You use the Position list box to select where to place the number, on either the Top of Page (Header) or the Bottom of Page (Footer). The bottom of the page is selected by default, so let's leave it that way.

Caution: If you already have a page number in a header, selecting Top of Page (Header) will delete the number and insert your choice from the Page Numbers dialog box instead. However, if you use the Page Numbers dialog box to insert a number, and you later add a page number to the header using Headers and Footers from the View menu, then both numbers will appear. The same situation applies to footers.

You use the Alignment list to select the position of the number between the left and right margins. Your options are Left, Center, Right, Inside, or Outside. The Inside and Outside options alternate the placement of numbers on the odd and even pages. Selecting Inside, for example, will place even numbers on the right of the page and odd numbers on the left. Pull down the Alignment option and select Center. Select OK.

Tip: If you do not want the page number to appear on the first page, deselect the Show Number on First Page check box.

Changing the Page Number Format

By default, Word inserts numbers using 1, 2, 3, and so on. You can also choose to number pages with roman numerals or letters. To select a number format, display the Page Numbers dialog box, and then click on the Format button to display the dialog box shown in Figure 9-3.

9

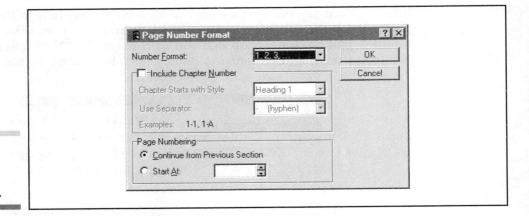

Page
numbering
formats
Figure 9-3.

Pull down the Number Format list to select from the options shown here.

If you divide your document into sections, you can even use a different method for each. So you can use roman numerals for your table of contents and index while using regular numbers for the text itself. Changing number formats, however, does not automatically restart the first number to 1, so you must do so using the Page Numbering section in the Page Number Format dialog box.

Tip: Use the Include Chapter Number section with long documents divided into chapters. To use this feature, your document must be formatted with heading numbers, which are discussed in Chapter 15.

As an example, let's add another page at the beginning of your document to represent an index. Follow these steps:

1. Move the insertion point to the beginning of the document and press ENTER to insert a blank line.

2. Select Break from the Insert menu, click on Next Page, and select OK. Word will insert a section break line at the beginning of the document.

3. Place the insertion point in the first section.

4. Select Page Numbers from the Insert menu and click on Format.

5. Select lowercase roman numerals in the Page Number Format dialog box.

6. Select OK twice to return to the document.

If you display the page numbers in Page Layout view or in Print Preview, you'll see that the "introduction" is numbered "i" but the first page of the document is numbered "2". That's because the default setting is to number pages consecutively from section to section, regardless of the number formats themselves. You have to change this setting to begin numbering with each section. Here's how:

1. Move the insertion point to the beginning of the second section.

2. Select Page Numbers from the Insert menu and click on Format.

3. Click on the Start At option. Word will insert the number 1 in the text box, indicating that the first page in the section will be numbered 1:

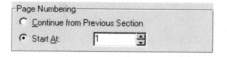

4. Select OK twice to return to the document.

Display the document in Print Preview to confirm that the first page of the text, following the introduction, will now be numbered "1". Close the document without saving it.

Formatting Pages and Text Automatically

It is usually easier to concentrate on writing the text of a document if you leave the formatting for later. You can always go through the completed document to format text, add sections, and adjust the layout. You can also have Word format the entire document for you. To format your entire document automatically, place the insertion point anywhere in the document you want to format, and then click on the AutoFormat button in the toolbar.

Word will scan your document, formatting text and adjusting the layout. It will format titles, subtitles, and headings throughout your document. It will even superscript the characters in ordinals such as 1st and 2nd, and will change the fraction entries 1/4, 1/2, and 3/4 to the symbols ¼, ½, ¾.

Word distinguishes titles, subtitles, and headings based on their current format and using a set of rules that may seem somewhat contrived. For text

9

to be converted into a title, for example, it must be centered at the beginning of the document, it must start with an uppercase letter, and it must not wrap at the end of the line. It must be followed by a blank line or a subtitle—another line of text meeting the same criteria as the title. A heading is text that starts with an uppercase letter and ends with a carriage return, without wrapping at the end of the line. Subheadings are headings that are indented. Figure 9-4, for instance, shows a document before and after AutoFormat was applied.

Note: You really don't need to concern yourself with Word's rules for AutoFormat. Just type your text, using titles and headings where you want. You can always apply AutoFormat and then scan your document, adjusting the formats to suit your taste.

Using the Style Gallery

Word applies formats based on *styles*. There is a style for each element that you can include in your document, such as titles, headings, and body text. The styles applied when you use AutoFormat are those that are made available to every new document. Once you apply AutoFormat, however, you can select from additional collections of styles that will apply different formats to the elements in your document.

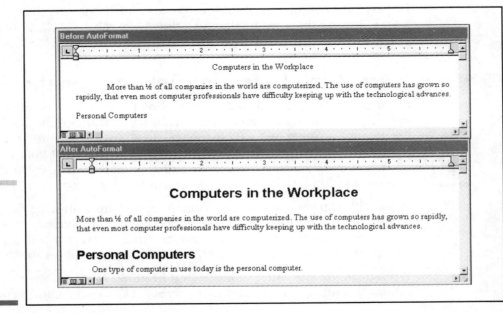

Sample text before and after formatting with AutoFormat
Figure 9-4.

Note: You'll learn more about styles in Chapter 12.

After you apply AutoFormat to a document, choose Style Gallery from the Format menu to display the dialog box shown in Figure 9-5. The list of templates on the left of the dialog box represents the collections of styles. To see how a template will affect your document, click on the template in the list and then on the Document option in the Preview section. Your document will appear in the Preview panel. You can also select Example to see a sample document that uses most of the styles, or you can select Style Samples to see the name of each style in its format. Select OK from the dialog box to apply the formats to your document.

Using the AutoFormat Dialog Box

Clicking on the AutoFormat button in the toolbar formats your entire document. If you do not like the applied formats, you can select Undo AutoFormat or Undo Style Gallery from the Edit menu. These commands undo all of the styles that have just been applied. If you want to have

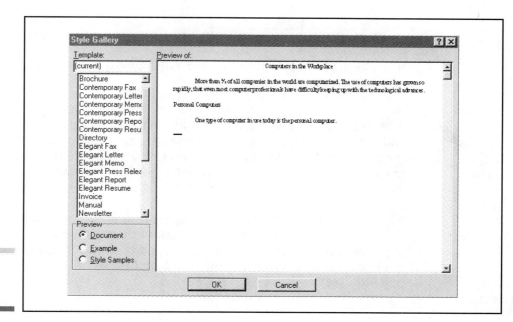

The Style
Gallery
Figure 9-5.

control over the individual styles applied to each element of the document, select AutoFormat from the Format menu, and then select OK from the dialog box that appears. Word will perform the AutoFormat, then display the dialog box shown here.

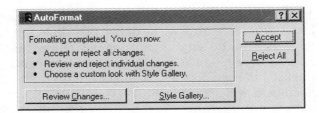

The four command buttons on the dialog box let you Accept all of the formats; Reject All of the formats, removing those just applied; display the Style Gallery to select another template; or Review Changes. If you opt to review the changes, Word highlights the first text that was changed and displays this dialog box:

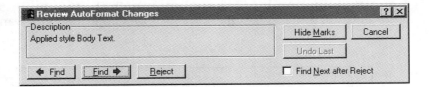

If the Reject button is dimmed in the dialog box, press ENTER or click on the Find button.

Note: Word also displays revision marks on the document. Click on the Hide Marks button in the Review AutoFormat Changes dialog box to remove the marks from display. Revision marks indicate where changes have been made. You will learn more about revisions in Chapter 23.

Choose Reject to undo the change to the text, and then click on one of the Find buttons to move forward or backward through the document, stopping at the next or previous change. To accept a change, just click on one of the Find buttons. If you change your mind about the last item you rejected, click on Undo Last.

Tip: Click on Find Next After Reject to have Word automatically move to the next change in the document when you click on Reject.

When you have finished reviewing the changes, close the Review AutoFormat Changes dialog box. Word displays the AutoFormat dialog box again. Select Accept to accept those changes that you did not reject, or choose Reject All to remove all of the changes from the document.

Highlighting Text with Borders and Shading

You may have some text in your document that you want to especially emphasize or bring to the reader's attention. You can always use a different font or font size for the text, or indent it from the left or right to call attention to it with the extra margin space. But when you really want to emphasize text, consider surrounding it in borders or shading the background behind it.

You can add borders and shading using a toolbar or a dialog box. To use a toolbar, click on the Borders button on the far right of the Formatting toolbar. Word will display the Borders toolbar, shown here.

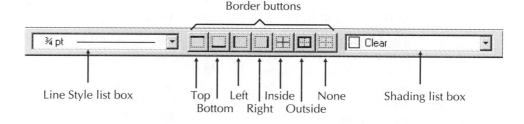

Border buttons

Line Style list box   Top   Left   Inside   None   Shading list box
          Bottom   Right   Outside

Tip: You can also display the Borders toolbar by right-clicking on a toolbar and then selecting Borders from the shortcut menu, or by using the Toolbars dialog box that was discussed in Chapter 2.

Borders and shading are paragraph-oriented formats. This means that you can format an individual paragraph just by placing the insertion point in it, or format several paragraphs by selecting them first. Next, pull down the Line Style list and select the line thickness or type that you want to use for a border. Then click on the buttons that represent where you want the border to appear. For each of Top, Bottom, Left, or Right buttons you select, Word will insert a line in that position. For example, to place horizontal lines above and below the text, click on the Top and Bottom buttons. To place vertical lines along the left and right margins, click on the Left and Right buttons. To insert lines between a number of selected paragraphs, click on the Inside button. To surround the text in a box—all four lines—click on the Outside button. Click on both Inside and Outside for everything!

As with other formats, the appearance of the Top, Bottom, Left, Right, and Inside buttons illustrate which lines have been applied to the paragraph or the selected text. If the paragraph has a line on top, for example, the Top button will appear pressed down. If you use the Outside button to surround the text with a box, then the first four buttons will appear pressed down, but not the Outside button itself.

To remove an individual line from the text, simply click on the appropriate pressed-down button. To remove all of the lines at one time, click on the No Border button.

When you enclose text in a box, Word extends the box from the left to the right margin, even if you've selected a short title centered on the page:

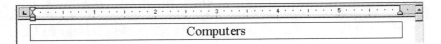

To make the box narrower so it only surrounds the text, use either the ruler or the Paragraph dialog box to indent the paragraph on the left and right.

The Shading list on the Borders toolbar lets you add shading, stripes, or a grid pattern to the background of the text. You can add a background even if you do not insert borders. To add a background, just pull down the Shading list and select your choice. Keep in mind that dark shading and patterns can make your text very difficult to read. To remove shading from text, select the Clear option in the list. Fill shades of 80% and above will result in reversed text—white text on the dark background.

Computers

Creating Borders with AutoFormat As You Type

If you only want to insert a horizontal line across the screen, the quickest way is to use AutoFormat As You Type. Type at least three hyphens or equal signs and then press ENTER. Word will replace the hyphens with a single line across the screen, or the equal sign with a double line across the screen. If Tip Wizard is turned on, you'll see a message reporting the change:

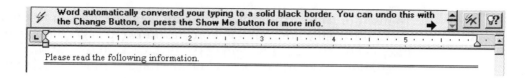

Please read the following information.

To undo the horizontal line and reinsert the hyphens or equal signs, click on the Change button.

 Tip: If Tip Wizard is turned off, the Tip Wizard button will flash. Click on the button to display the tip.

Using the Borders and Shading Dialog Box

As an alternative to using the Borders toolbar, you can use the Borders and Shading dialog box. Display the dialog box by selecting Borders and Shading from the Format menu. To add or remove borders, click on the Borders tab. The options shown in Figure 9-6 will appear on your screen.

The three options in the Presets section let you quickly remove all borders (None), surround text in a box (Box), or create a shadow box (Shadow). A shadow box has two thicker border lines to give the illusion of a shadow.

The Borders options in the Borders and Shading dialog box
Figure 9-6.

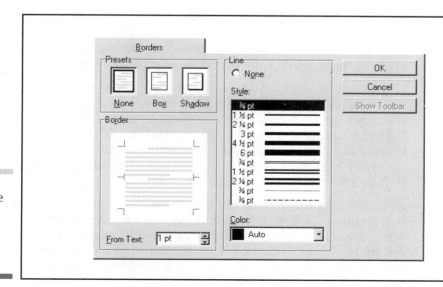

9

To insert or remove individual lines, use the illustration of text in the Border section. The gray horizontal lines represent two paragraphs. For example, to insert a line on the left margin of the text, click on the left side of the illustration. Word will display a line like the one shown here, indicating that it will be inserted.

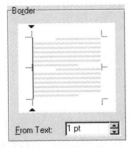

The small triangles at the top and bottom of the line show what is currently selected. To insert a line on the top of the paragraph, click above the first gray line. To insert a line below the paragraph, click below the last line. To insert a line between selected paragraphs, click between the two sample paragraphs.

Remove an individual line in the same way—click on the line that you want to remove. Word inserts lines 1 point from the text. You can increase or decrease this setting in the From Text box.

The border lines actually extend into the margins, although you may hardly notice with the default thin border line and the 1-point distance settings. As you increase the thickness of the lines, or increase the spacing from the text, you will start to notice the border lines in the margin area.

Use the options in the Style section of the Borders page to determine the thickness and type of the lines. Click where you want to insert a line and then click on the style in the Style list. The option you choose in the Style list will be applied to the selected line and any other lines that you insert. To change a line style, click on the line in the Border section and then choose the style. As an example, let's create a box with thin lines on the sides and thicker lines on the top and bottom.

Open the Biography of Sliding Billy Watson document. Click in the third paragraph of the document, and then select Borders and Shading from the Format menu. To insert the thinner lines on the left and the bottom, make certain the 3/4 pt option is selected in the Style section, and then click on the left and right sides of the sample in the Border section.

Now click on the top of the Border section to insert a thin line, and then click on the 6 pt line in the Style box. Finally, click on the bottom of the sample to insert the currently selected style at that location as well. Select OK. Your box should look like mine:

> Billy was born as Wolf Shapiro on October 12, 1876. His family moved from New York to Philadelphia, where Billy tried to settle down into a quiet family life. However, the call of the stage was too difficult for him to resist. He abandoned his wife and two children for the limelight and fame of vaudeville.

To add shading using the dialog box, click on the Shading tab to display the options shown in Figure 9-7. Select the density of the shade, or the pattern, in the Shading list. You can also select the foreground and background colors. Look at the Preview panel as you select options.

Practice adding borders and shading until you feel comfortable with the function, and then close the document without saving it.

Tip: If you have a color printer, select the color of the lines and foreground and background colors.

Numbering Lines

Legal documents, such as contracts, pleadings, and depositions, often have line numbers down the left margin; so may printed copies of computer

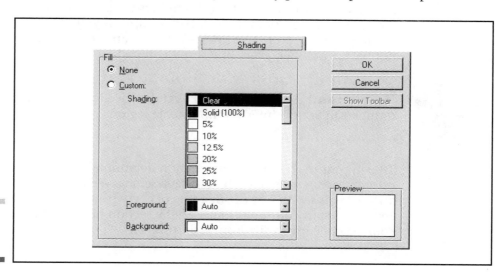

The Shading
options
Figure 9-7.

9

programs and macros. The numbers make it easy to reference a specific line in the document. If you did not have Word, you could try to type the numbers yourself, but then you'd have to press ENTER after each line—just as you did on that old-fashioned typewriter. Fortunately, and to the delight of many legal assistants and secretaries, Word can number lines automatically for you.

When you want to number lines, select Page Setup from the File menu and then click on the Layout tab. Click on the Line Numbers command button to display the dialog box you see here.

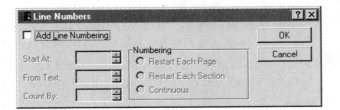

When line numbering is not turned on, most of the options in the box will be dimmed. To turn on line numbering, and to select options from the dialog box, select the Add Line Numbering check box. You can then specify what number to begin with, the distance from the text to the number, and whether you want every line to be numbered or just some lines at regular intervals. The Line numbers actually print in the margin area, about one quarter inch from the text. To change that distance, enter the measurement in the From Text box. The setting in the Count By box determines how the number is incremented. Using the default, each line is numbered 1, 2, 3, 4, 5, and so on. If you do not want numbers to appear at each line, specify the increment in the Count By box. For example, if you enter 5 in the box, line numbers appear every five lines—5, 10, 15, and so on. While each line may not have a number, every line is still counted.

Caution: Making the From Text distance too large may place the numbers in your printer's nonprintable region.

The options in the Numbering section determine how the count is restarted on each page or section. With the default setting—Restart Each Page—numbering always begins with 1 at the first line of every page. Select Restart Each Section to start counting from 1 after a section break. Select Continuous to count consecutively, without restarting.

The line numbers will not appear onscreen in Normal view. You will see them in Page Layout view and in Print Preview, but you cannot edit them. The only way to change numbering is to select options from the Page Setup dialog box.

Word's line numbering function is a page format. This normally means that if you want different formats in one document, you must insert a section break. For example, suppose you want to number two series of lines on a page, but start each series with the number 1. You would need to insert a continuous section break between the two series of lines and turn on numbering in each section. In the second section, however, you'd need to select the Restart Each Section option.

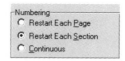

If you want to number paragraphs, instead of individual lines, use the numbered list feature explained in Chapter 13.

If you just want to turn off numbering for a selected portion of text, however, you do not need a section break. Select the text and then choose Paragraph from the Format menu. Click on the Text Flow tab and select Suppress Line Numbers.

Word will not number the lines and will not include them in the count. In this example, for instance, numbering was suppressed for one line. Word displays the line, as shown here, but does not count it.

```
1    Adam
2    Alan
3    Albert
     Charles
4    Dan
5    David
```

PART 3

Moving Beyond the Basics

Proofing Your Documents

10

Your document should be not only attractive, but also correct. Your spelling and grammar should be perfect, and your vocabulary should be varied and suitable for your readers. Checking your document for spelling, vocabulary, and grammar is called *proofing*, and Word has all of the proofing tools that you need.

The *spelling checker* compares all of the words in your document with those in Word's dictionary. The *thesaurus* lets you find synonyms for words, and even look up a word's meaning. The *grammar checker* checks your document for common grammatical mistakes and reports its readability.

Tip: Although Word's proofing tools are a great help, they are not foolproof. Misspelled words, improperly used words and phrases, and grammatical errors can still find their way into a document even after you've proofed it. The proofing tools should be used as supplements to your own proofreading.

Automatic Spell Check

As you already know, Word checks your spelling as you type. A word that is not in Word's dictionary, a duplicated word, or an improperly capitalized word will be underlined with a wavy red line.

You can correct the word yourself to remove the wavy line, or click the right mouse button on the word to see a shortcut menu, as shown in the following illustration. You can select the correct spelling from the menu or select Ignore All to accept the word as it is spelled.

The Add option in the shortcut menu inserts the word into a dictionary so it is no longer reported as misspelled. The Spelling option begins Word's interactive spelling checker. You'll learn more about this option later in this chapter. For now, let's look at some options for the automatic spell check. Select Options from the Tools menu, and then click on the Spelling tab to see the options shown in Figure 10-1.

If you type many technical terms, jargon, or proper names, Word will display a lot of wavy lines in your document. If you find the lines distracting, you can either turn off automatic spell check or hide the lines from display. To turn off spell check, deselect the Automatic Spell Checking box. When you turn off this option, it is dimmed, and the Hide Spelling Errors in Current Document check box becomes selected. When you select OK, all wavy lines in the document will disappear, and Word will no longer

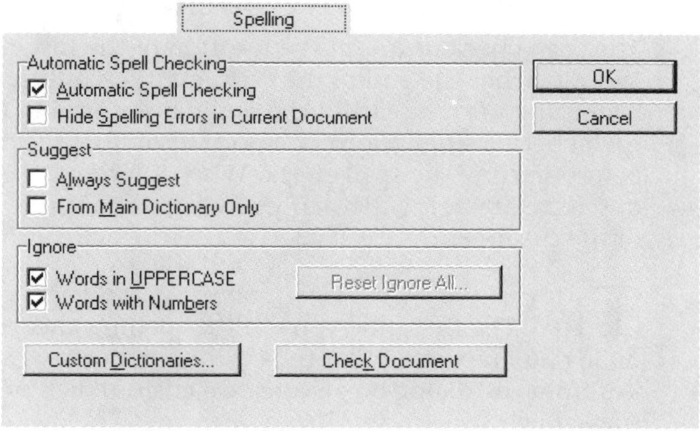

The Spelling
options
Figure 10-1.

check your spelling as you type. If you later turn spell check back on, Word
will redisplay the wavy lines and spell check your text.

You can also leave automatic spell check turned on while the Hide Spelling
Errors in Current Document check box is selected. Word will continue to
check your document, but it won't display the lines. When you're ready to
correct the document, display the dialog box and deselect the Hide option.

At the bottom of the dialog box is a button that will be labeled either Check
Document or Recheck Document. If spell check has already started working
on your document, the label will be Recheck Document. Click on the button
to have Word recheck the document after you change the spelling options
or select a new custom dictionary. The button is labeled Check Document if
this is the first spell check for the document in the current Word session.

Interactive Spell Check

Rather than correct each misspelled word as you type, you can spell check
your entire document at one time. One way is to ignore the wavy lines that
appear and continue typing. When you're done with the entire document,
start at the beginning and scan through the document looking for each
misspelled word.

As an alternative, you can use Word's interactive spelling checker. The
interactive checking scans through the document for you, locating each
misspelled word and displaying alternative spellings for you without the
need to click the mouse.

Starting Interactive Spelling

The spell check begins at the location of the insertion point. When Word reaches the end of the document, it continues checking at the beginning until it reaches the original position of the insertion point. To spell check a single word or a portion of text, select the word or the text before starting the spell check. When Word completes checking the spelling of selected text, it will ask if you want to continue checking the remainder of the document.

Tip: The first time you use the spelling checker, Word may display a dialog box reporting that the custom dictionary cannot be found. Select Yes from the dialog box to create a custom dictionary and to continue the spell check.

To begin checking your spelling, click on the Spelling button in the Standard toolbar, select Options from the Tools menu and then click on the Spelling tab, or simply press F7. You can also select Spelling from the automatic spell check shortcut menu. When Word finds a word that is not in its dictionary, it highlights the word in the text above the Spelling dialog box and displays a list of possible spellings, as shown in Figure 10-2. The suggested alternatives are usually words that are spelled similarly to the word not found, but there may also be some words that sound the same. The Not in Dictionary prompt shows the word the way it is spelled in your document. The Change To prompt shows the selected word in the list of suggested spellings. If Word cannot find any suggested spellings, the (no suggestions) notation will appear in the list. You now have several options depending on whether the word is spelled correctly or incorrectly.

The Word Is Spelled Incorrectly

If you see the correct spelling in the list, double-click on it, or select it and then choose either Change or Change All. Word inserts the correctly spelled word and then searches for the next error. The difference between Change and Change All determines how Word reacts when it locates the same misspelling again. When you choose Change, Word will report the next occurrence as a possible error so you can again select from the list. When you choose Change All, Word will automatically replace other occurrences of the same misspelling. Change All is useful when you know you've misspelled the same word in the same way several times in the same document.

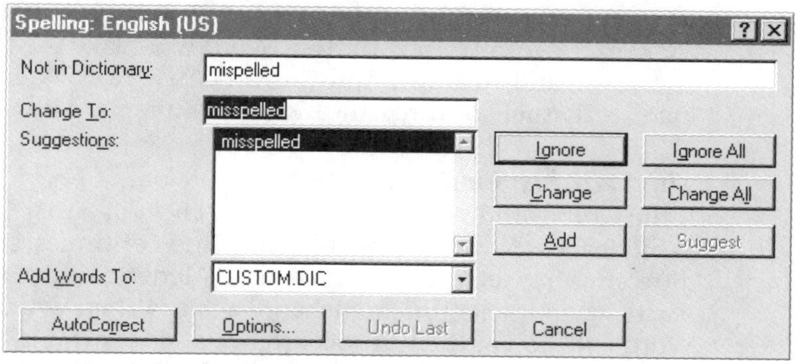

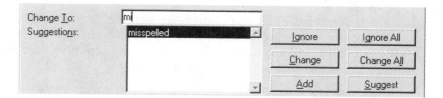

The Spelling
dialog box
Figure 10-2.

If you do not see the correct spelling, or if no suggestions are listed, type
another spelling for the word in the Change To box, and then click on either
the Change button or the Suggest button, which becomes visible when you
begin typing your new word.

If you select Change, word looks in the dictionary for the new word; if it
isn't there, Word will ask whether you want to use the replacement anyway
and continue, or look up your replacement for possible alternatives. If you
select Suggest, Word looks up the word you typed and displays alternative
spellings for it.

Tip: If you forget a space between words, as in MicrosoftWord, the
combination will be reported as not in the dictionary. Just edit or retype the
words, with the space, in the Change To box and select Change.

The Change All option only affects the current document. If Word locates
the same misspelling when checking another document, it will again report

it as an error. When you know it's a word that you frequently misspell, click on the correct spelling in the list, or type it in the Change To box, and then click on the AutoCorrect button. Word will make the replacement in your document and create an AutoCorrect entry. Now whenever you type the incorrectly spelled word, AutoCorrect will replace it with the correct spelling.

The Word Is Spelled Correctly

If the word is indeed spelled correctly, click on either Ignore or Ignore All. Word leaves the word as you typed it and continues the spell check. The difference between Ignore and Ignore All determines how the spell check reacts when it encounters the word again. When you choose Ignore, Word will stop at the next occurrence and report it as a possible error. When you choose Ignore All, Word skips over all occurrences of the word in the document.

The Add option works the same as in automatic spell check—it inserts the word into the dictionary so the same word will not be reported as misspelled in other documents.

More Spelling Options

Now let's look at some other options in the Spelling dialog box.

If you select Change or Ignore by mistake, click on the Undo Last button to return to the previous word. If you've just changed the word, the original spelling will appear. Until you take some action in the Spelling dialog box, the Undo Last button will be dimmed.

To delete a word from the document, clear the contents of the Change To box. The Change and Change All buttons will change to Delete and Delete All. Select Delete to erase the single occurrence of the word; select Delete All to erase them all.

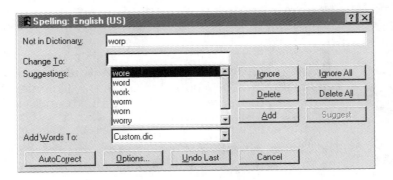

Caution: Undo Last does not work with the Delete All command.

If Word encounters two of the same correctly spelled words in a row, such as "do do", the second occurrence of the word is highlighted and the Not in Dictionary box will be labeled Repeated Word. The Change To box will be empty, and all but the Ignore and Delete buttons will be dimmed. Choose Delete to erase the duplicate, or choose Ignore to leave it alone. To replace the word with another, type it in the Change To box—the Delete button will become Change so you can make the replacement.

Tip: Word ignores common pairs of duplicate words, such as "had had" and "that that".

Finally, you might want to see the reported misspelling with more text than appears onscreen, or you may want to edit text during the spell check. Just click in the document and make your changes. The Spelling dialog box remains on the screen, as shown here, but the Ignore button will be labeled Resume. Click on Resume when you want to continue checking the spelling.

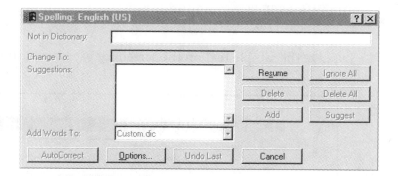

To practice using the interactive spelling checker, start by turning off automatic spell check so you can type some text with mistakes. Select Options from the Tools menu, and then click on the Spelling tab. Deselect the Automatic Spell Checking box and click on OK. Now type the following text, including all of its mistakes:

Representives of the Patrite Company will visit the plant on on Friday to discuss health insurance benefits. The Patrite Company hasbeen contracted to provide benefits to all union members.

Follow these steps to correct the text using the interactive spelling checker:

1. Place the insertion point at the beginning of the document and click on the Spelling button in the Standard toolbar. Word stops at the very first word—"Representives"—and displays the dialog box that you see in Figure 10-3. Notice that the suggested correct spelling starts with an uppercase letter because the misspelled word begins with one.

2. Click on Change to make the replacement and to continue to the next unknown word—"Patrite".

3. "Patrite" is spelled correctly, and because you use it more than once in the same document, click on Ignore All. Word now stops at the duplicate of the word "on".

4. Select Delete to erase the duplicate and to find the next error, the words "has been" that have no space between them. If you look carefully in the Change To box, you'll see that Word is suggesting "has-been". That's not want you want.

5. Click anywhere in the Change To box, delete the hyphen between the words and insert a space.

6. Select Change. Word displays a message reporting that the spell check is complete.

7. Select OK.

Leave the sample text on the screen for use later in this chapter.

Word stops at the first spelling error in the document

Figure 10-3.

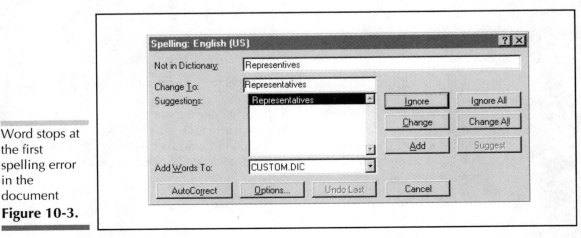

Settings for Uppercase Characters and Numbers

By default, the automatic and interactive spelling checkers ignore words in all uppercase characters and words that contain numbers. To change these, and some other spelling settings, display the Spelling options shown earlier, in Figure 10-1, by selecting Options from the Tools menu, then clicking on the Spelling tab.

To proofread capitalized words and those that contain numbers, deselect the check boxes labeled Words in UPPERCASE and Words with Numbers. You can also choose whether Word automatically looks up suggested spellings by selecting or deselecting the Always Suggest check box. And tell Word to look up words only in the main dictionary, not in your custom dictionary, by clicking on From Main Dictionary Only.

Tip: The Always Suggest option only affects the interactive spelling checker. Word always looks up suggestions for the automatic spell check.

When you choose Ignore All from either the automatic or interactive spelling checker, the word is added to a temporary list used until you exit Word. If you decide that you do not want to ignore these words during the remainder of your session, click on the Reset Ignore All button. A dialog box will appear asking you to confirm that you want to erase the Ignore All list. Select Yes to erase the list, or select No to retain it for the remainder of the Word session.

Tip: If you have a slower computer, there may be some delay as Word looks up suggested words. If you usually type the replacement word yourself, deselect the Always Suggest option. When you do want Word to find alternative spellings when checking a document, click on the Suggest button in the Spelling dialog box.

The Custom Dictionaries command button displays a dialog box that lets you create or use other dictionaries. For example, you may purchase a dictionary with medical or legal terms, or you may want to store your own technical words in a separate dictionary. You can select which custom dictionaries Word will use during the spell check process.

Checking Foreign Language Documents

Your version of Word will include a dictionary in your language. When you purchase Word in France, for example, your dictionary will contain French words. If you type documents using words from another language, Word will not find them in the dictionary. It will report them as possible errors, and no suggested alternatives will be located.

The solution is to purchase another dictionary in the language that you use. However, because your document now contains sections of text in a language other than the default, you must tell Word which dictionary to use for which text.

To designate a language other than the default for a section of text, select the text and then choose Language from the Tools menu to see the dialog box shown here:

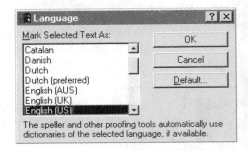

Scroll the list and select the language that corresponds to the dictionary you want to use. When Word spell checks your document, it will use the appropriate dictionary. For example, suppose you type a proposal containing paragraphs in both English and French for a Canadian client. If you have the English language version of Word, select each of the paragraphs that are in French and choose the language from the dialog box. (You can choose either French or French Canadian, by the way, depending on the dictionary you purchase.) When you spell check your document, Word will use the English dictionary for English text and the French dictionary for the French text.

If you select a language for text but do not have the dictionary on your system, Word will display an error message when it reaches the text. Select OK to skip the section and to continue with the next section of text in another language.

Tip: If you type a section of text using technical terms, jargon, or accented words that you know are correct but not in the dictionary, you can mark the text so Word skips over it when spell checking. Select the text, display the Language dialog box, and then choose (no proofing) from the top of the list.

Improving Your Vocabulary

Word's thesaurus is a handy tool to have around:

10

♦ You can look up a word because it doesn't quite convey the correct meaning, and the thesaurus may list an alternative word that means exactly what you want to say.

♦ You can look up a word because you've repeated the same word several times already and you want a little variety in your writing.

♦ You can look up a word to understand its meaning, such as distinguishing "cloth" from "clothe", and "whether" from "weather".

♦ You can look up a phrase, such as "point of view", to find words or other phrases with the same meaning.

♦ You can even look up antonyms for adjectives, to find a word with the opposite meaning.

To look up a word, place the insertion point anywhere in the word and select Thesaurus from the Tools menu, or press SHIFT-F7. To look up a phrase containing more than one word, select the entire phrase first. Word will display the thesaurus dialog box, such as the one shown in Figure 10-4 for the word "point". The word you are looking up appears in the looked up box, and one or more meanings for the word appear in the meanings box. More than one meaning will appear when the word has several connotations. For example, "point" can be used as a noun to refer to a detail (such as "trying to make a fine point"), a time ("some point in the future"), or a small speck ("a thousand points of light"). It can also be used as a verb, as in "point out the person in the lineup".

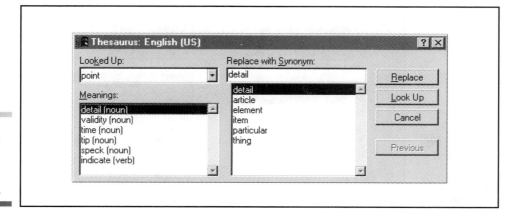

Looking up
synonyms for
the word
"point"

Figure 10-4.

Select the meaning that best represents what you are trying to say. Word will list synonyms in the Replace with Synonym list. Choose the synonym that you want to insert in your document and then select Replace.

If none of the synonyms is quite right, select the word that has the closest meaning and choose Look Up. Word will now use that word for the lookup, finding meanings and synonyms for it. Continue selecting meanings and looking up suggested synonyms until you find just the right word.

Tip: To return to a word that has already been looked up, pull down the Looked Up list and click on the word.

The Meanings box may also list the options Related Words and Antonyms. Select Related Words to show the root of the word, such as "point" for "pointing". Selecting Antonyms lists words with the opposite meaning.

If Word cannot find your word in the thesaurus, the Looked Up box will be labeled Not Found, and an alphabetical listing of words and phrases will appear in the Meanings box. Double-click on a word or phrase in the list that has the same meaning that you want to convey—Word will use it for the lookup, displaying related meanings and synonyms.

As an example of using the thesaurus, click on the word "discuss" in the sample text on your screen. (If you've closed the sample document, just start a new one and type **discuss**.) Pull down the Tools menu and select Thesaurus. Word will display the options shown in Figure 10-5. Since the

Looking up
synonyms for
the word
"discuss"
Figure 10-5.

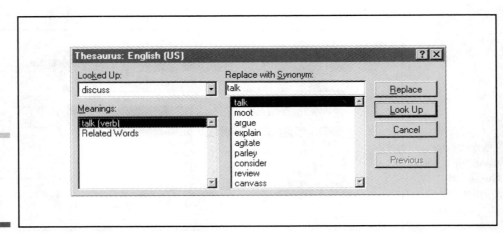

company will actually be explaining benefits to the employees, select the word "explain" in the Synonyms list and click on Replace.

Now let's see how Word handles a phrase, rather than a single word. Type **up to a point**, select all four words, and press SHIFT-F7 to start the thesaurus. Word recognizes this expression as meaning "to some extent", and it lists synonyms that have that connotation. Click on "partially" in the synonym list and then select Replace. Close the document without saving it.

10

Improving Your Grammar

As you know, the spelling checker cannot tell if you are using the wrong word if the word is correctly spelled. So for example, it will not report that "affect" is spelled wrong when you should be using the word "effect". If you have trouble with words such as these, and if the terms split infinitive, dangling participle, and passive tense give you anxious flashbacks to high school English class, then take advantage of the grammar checker.

The grammar checker does just that—it checks your grammar and, to some extent, your writing style. To check your document for correct grammar, select Grammar from the Tools menu. Word finds the first possible error and displays a description of the problem and, in some cases, a suggested correction, as shown in Figure 10-6. If Word can correct the problem for you, the Change button will not be dimmed. Click on Change to correct the problem and move on to the next. If the Change button is dimmed, make a mental or written note so you can correct the problem later, or click in the

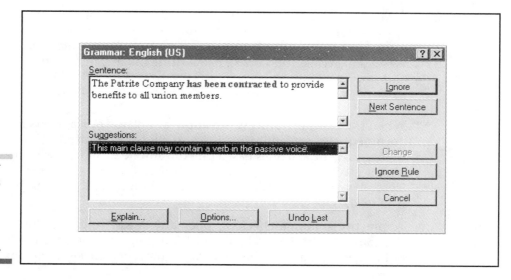

The grammar checker finds mistakes and suggests corrections.

Figure 10-6.

document, make the change, and select Start, which has replaced Ignore in the dialog box.

Tip: If Word encounters a spelling error, it will display the Spelling dialog box. Select Change to replace the text with Word's suggestion, or select Ignore to move on to the next problem.

Use the other command buttons in the dialog box to take these actions:

♦ Select *Ignore* to skip the current problem. Word will continue checking, and it may even find another problem in the same sentence.

♦ Select *Next Sentence* to skip the sentence entirely, even if it has other problems.

♦ Select *Ignore Rule* to skip other problems that violate the same rule of grammar. For example, if Word reports a passive sentence, selecting Ignore All will make it skip any other passive sentence errors.

♦ Select *Cancel* to stop the grammar checking process, by accepting any changes that you've already made.

♦ Select *Explain* when the description of the problem is not detailed enough to help make the correction. Read the explanation in the dialog box that appears, and then click on its Close box.

♦ Select *Undo Last* to return to the previously reported error.

Note: Word actually checks your document for two categories of errors—grammar and style. Grammatical errors are those that violate the formal elements of writing, such as subject/verb agreement or the use of A versus An. Style errors correct bad writing habits, such as the use of clichés and sexist expressions.

When the checking process is complete, a dialog box appears reporting document and readability statistics, as shown in Figure 10-7. You have to interpret the statistics based on your intended audience. Generally, higher grade levels require more reading skills. The opposite is true for the Flesch Reading Ease scale—the higher the number, the easier the document is to read.

To practice grammar checking, open any one of your own documents. Start the grammar checker and see how Word can improve your writing. If you do not understand a rule when an error is detected, click on Explain.

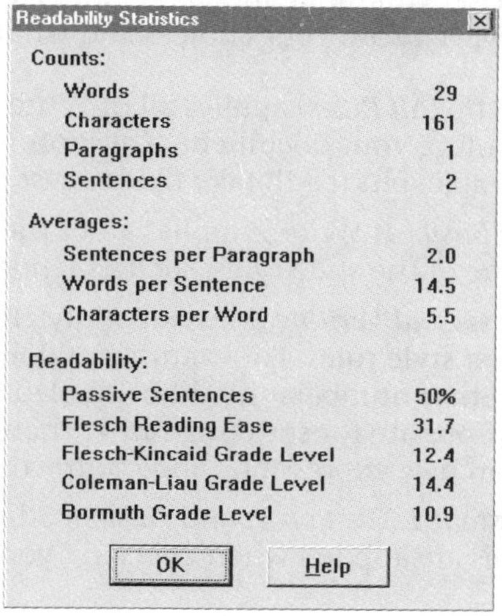

Word displays
readability
statistics after
checking your
grammar
Figure 10-7.

Grammar Options

While there are plenty of books that cite rules of grammar, correct grammar
is not always an exact science. Some writing styles may have conventions
that violate strict grammatical rules, so a sentence that would be considered
inappropriate in one type of writing, such as a formal proposal to a client,
would be acceptable in another setting, such as a personal letter. To apply
the appropriate rules of grammar to a document, or to customize which
rules are applied, select Options from the Grammar dialog box, or choose
Options from the Tools menu and then click on the Grammar tab. The
Grammar options are shown in Figure 10-8.

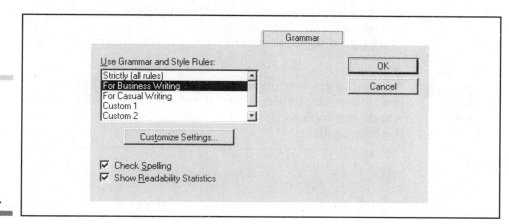

Adjust the
grammar
checker for
the type of
document
you're
working on
Figure 10-8.

In the User Grammar and Style Rules list, select which set of rules you want to apply. Here are your choices and what they do:

◆ *Strictly (All Rules)* applies all of Word's grammatical and style rules when proofing your document. This option will catch as many errors as possible, but it will take the longest to complete.

◆ *For Business Writing* applies all of the grammatical rules, but it overlooks some of the style rules, such as reporting homonyms, clichés and jargon.

◆ *For Casual Writing* does not apply all of the grammatical rules, and even fewer style rules. For example, it does not check the format of dates, whether numbers should be spelled out, or constructions that are more appropriate for speaking rather than reading. It ignores style rules such as archaic expressions and contractions.

◆ *Custom 1, Custom 2,* and *Custom 3* let you determine which grammatical rules are applied when checking your document.

The grammar page also allows you to turn off or on spell check as part of the grammar checking process, and to select whether or not to display the readability statistics at the end.

To create a custom set of rules, or to modify any of the others, click on Customize Settings to display the dialog box shown in Figure 10-9. Start by selecting the set you want to modify by choosing it in the Use Grammar and Style Rules list. Next, select the option button for the category of rule you want to modify—either grammar or style. A list of the grammatical problems that you can check for that category will appear in the list box. A check mark next to an item means that it will be applied when your document is checked. To turn off or on any item, just click on it. If you are unsure what the rule means, select it in the list and click on Explain. Word will display the same information it does if you select Explain while checking your grammar. After you complete setting the options for one category, repeat the procedure for the other category. If you change a set of rules and then change your mind, select the set in the list and click on Reset All.

Caution: When you click on an item and select Explain to read its description, the setting of that item's check box will be toggled off or on. If you do not want to change the setting, just read its explanation and click on the item again.

Customize the Grammar checker by selecting problems to be flagged
Figure 10-9.

The Catch section of the Customize Grammer Settings dialog box controls lets you search for four general grammatical problems:

♦ *Split Infinitives* determines the number of words allowed between the word "to" and the verb. The default setting of one word, for example, would allow you to write "to boldly go" but not "to very boldly go". The options are Always, By More Than One Word, By More Than Two Words, By More Than Three Words, and Never. Selecting Never will accept all split infinitives. To absolutely, positively, assuredly warn you of all split infinitives, select Always.

♦ *Consecutive Nouns* determines the number of consecutive nouns that will be considered an error. The default is More Than Three in a Row. Other options are More Than Two in a Row, More Than Four in a Row, and Never. If you change the setting to More Than Two in a Row, for example, Word will warn you of sentences such as "He purchased a home foundation tester".

♦ *Prepositional Phrases* determines the number of consecutive phrases that will constitute an error. For example, the option More Than Two in a Row would flag a sentence such as "The ball rolled down the stairs through the hallway under the chair".

♦ *Sentences Containing More Words Than* warns you about run-on sentences. The default setting will not report this error in sentences up to 35 words long. Change the setting to accommodate your audience. If you're writing for very young children, for example, specify a smaller number of words.

When you have finished customizing the catch section, you must select OK in both the Customize Grammar Settings dialog box and in the Grammar section of the Options dialog box. Selecting OK in one box and Cancel in the other will ignore your changes.

Tip: The three custom sets of rules begin with all of the grammatical and style rules selected. To create your own custom set, display the Customize Grammar Settings dialog box, and then choose which custom set you want to modify. In the Grammar and Style lists, select which rules you do not want to apply—click on the rule to remove the check mark. Then select OK in both dialog boxes to save your settings. You cannot change the names of the custom set.

Using Word's Templates and Wizards

11

If there is one theme that applies generally to Word, it is ease of use. Features such as AutoText, AutoCorrect, and AutoFormat are designed to make you more productive, to relieve some of the burden of routine and monotonous tasks. Two features that exemplify this theme best are Wizards and templates. Both of these features help you create a completely formatted document with a few clicks of the mouse. Wizards will even help you with the contents.

Upgrader: Word 7 offers an improved New dialog box, additional Wizards and templates, and access to an address book for name and addresses in faxes and other Wizard documents.

Wizards and templates are tied to another powerful Word feature called styles. In fact, it is difficult, if not impossible to discuss one topic without mentioning the other. A style is just a collection of formats that you can apply to text. You'll learn all about styles in Chapter 12.

Word Magic with Wizards

A *Wizard* is a special Word feature that takes you step-by-step through formatting a document. In a series of dialog boxes, the Wizard lets you select formatting options and enter text. When you're done, the formatted document appears so you can complete the text, customize it if you want, and then print it. Word comes with Wizards for these types of documents:

♦ *Newsletters* come complete with masthead and graphics, with text in one to four columns.

♦ *Resumes* come in three styles.

♦ *Memos* are formatted for either preprinted letterhead or blank paper, in three styles.

♦ *Letters,* for business or personal communication, offer prewritten styles that you simply edit to your taste.

♦ *Faxes* come in either portrait or landscape orientation, in three styles.

♦ *Agendas,* for meetings and conferences, come complete with all of the headings and categories, in three styles.

♦ *Awards and certificates* use either preprinted paper or Word's own design, in four styles.

♦ *Calendars,* in either portrait or landscape orientation, can start and end on any date, in three styles.

♦ *Pleadings,* for legal purposes, have extensive options for formatting according to your court's guidelines.

♦ *Tables,* in either portrait or landscape orientation, come complete with column and row headings, in six styles.

Your Personal Secretary

When you use a Wizard to create resumes, letters, fax cover pages, and other documents, Word automatically inserts your name and address for you. The default name will be the one entered when Word was installed on your computer. If you are not the primary user of Word on your system, or if you want to use a different mailing address, you can change the name and address information as you follow the Wizard.

If you do not share your computer with another user, however, you should check the name and address information that Wizards will use. Select Options from the Tools menu, and click on the User Info tab to display a dialog box much like the one shown in Figure 11-1. Make sure your name, initials, and mailing address are correct. If not, click a text box and edit or enter the appropriate information. When you're done, click on OK. Word now has the information it needs to complete the Wizards.

11

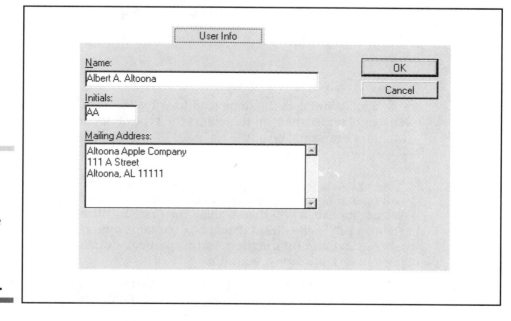

Check the User Info tab so Word inserts the correct name and address into Wizard documents

Figure 11-1.

T ip: Enter your company name as the first line of your address in the Mailing Address box. Word will then use the company name in appropriate locations in Wizard documents.

Starting a Wizard

You start a Wizard using the New command in the File menu. Let's use a Wizard to create a fax cover page. Select New from the File menu now to display the New dialog box. The icon labeled Blank Document on the General page represents the default template that Word will use for every new document. There are no Wizards available on the General page, so click on the Letters & Faxes tab to display the dialog box shown in Figure 11-2.

T ip: You'll find Wizards for agendas, awards, calendars, pleadings, resumes, and tables in the Other Documents tab.

There are eight icons in the dialog box. Six of the icons represent templates, but the two that have little magic wands are Wizards.

Fax Wizard.wiz   Letter
                  Wizard.wiz

T ip: Word uses the same icon for all Wizards in the New dialog box. The label under the icon represents the type of document, and it always includes the word "Wizard".

Now to create a fax cover page, double-click on the Fax Wizard icon. Word will open a blank document window and take a few moments to prepare the Wizard for use. It will then display the first Fax Wizard dialog box, shown in Figure 11-3. Each Wizard dialog box contains options to select or text boxes where you enter information. In this particular dialog box you select either portrait or landscape orientation.

Most dialog boxes have a preview panel that shows a sketch of how the document will look. As you select options, the preview panel changes, giving

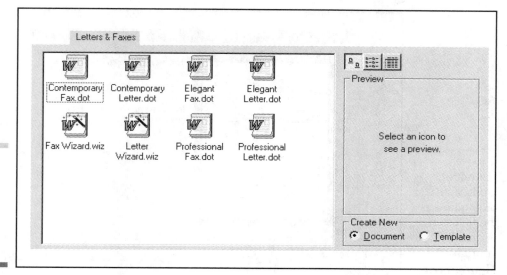

Wizards and templates on the Letters & Faxes page of the New dialog box

Figure 11-2.

11

you a chance to see each of the available styles or options applied to the document. So if you select the Landscape option, the preview panel will show the fax that you see here:

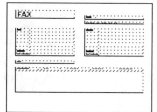

At the bottom of Wizard dialog boxes are four command buttons:

♦ *Cancel* stops the Wizard and clears the blank window that the Wizard created.

♦ *Back* returns to the previous Wizard dialog box in the series, if there was one.

♦ *Next* accepts your selections and text and moves to the next Wizard dialog box.

♦ *Finish* completes the document using your selections up to that point, bypassing any remaining Wizard dialog boxes. To create a document using all of the default settings, for example, select Finish in the first dialog box.

Note: The Back option is dimmed in the first dialog box, and the Next option is dimmed in the last box.

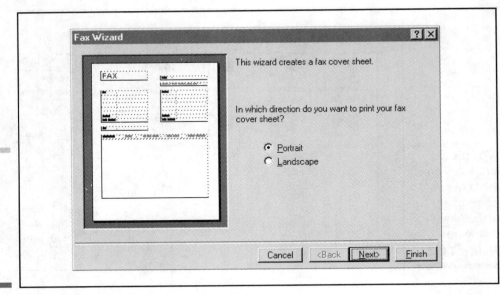

Choose portrait or landscape orientation as the first step in creating your fax

Figure 11-3.

Select Next to see the second Fax Wizard dialog box, where you can choose from three styles—Contemporary, Modern, and Jazzy. Click on each style to see how it looks in the preview panel. Choose the Modern style, and then click on Next to see the third dialog box, shown in Figure 11-4. This dialog box contains your name and address. Confirm that your name and address are correct, and then click on Next.

Now, in a series of remaining dialog boxes, Word will ask for the following information:

♦ Your voice and fax telephone numbers

♦ The name, company, and address of the recipient

♦ The recipient's voice and fax telephone numbers

 Upgrader: In dialog boxes that ask for name and address information, you can also click on the Address Book command button. Before you can use Address Book, either Microsoft Exchange or Schedule+ must be installed on your computer.

Complete the dialog boxes with some sample information, clicking Next after each. The final dialog box asks if you want to display help information

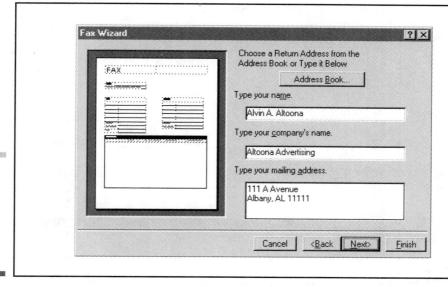

The Fax
Wizard dialog
box for
inserting your
name and
address
Figure 11-4.

as you complete the fax. Click on Finish to display the complete fax, as
shown in 75% magnification in Figure 11-5.

The fax will contain the date, your address, and the recipient's address that
you entered in the Wizard dialog boxes. You can now click on options in the
Remarks section and type the text of the fax or cover page. Print out a copy
of the fax to see how it looks, and then close the document without saving it.

Tip: If your computer has a fax modem, and you've installed the
appropriate software in Windows 95, you can fax the document directly
from the File menu or from the Print dialog box.

The document completed by some Wizards will contain illustrative text as
an example of the type of information you can enter. Edit or delete the text
as necessary. Many Wizard documents will prompt you to enter additional
information, particularly when you do not complete some of the Wizard
dialog boxes. The prompts will appear in square brackets, as shown here.

To:	[Click here and type names]
CC:	[Click here and type names]
From:	Alvin A. Altoona
RE:	[Click here and type subject]

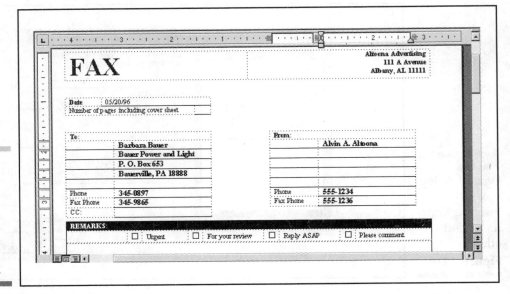

The Completed fax, reduced to 75% to show the heading information
Figure 11-5.

Click on the prompt to enter your own information. When you click on a prompt, it will be highlighted, so it will be erased when you start typing. Complete the information requested and then save or print the document.

Tip: If you do not have information to enter at a prompt, click on the prompt and press DELETE. If you do not delete the prompt, it will print with the document.

Word Remembers

Word saves your settings, selections, and text in Wizard dialog boxes on your disk. For example, suppose you create a fax in landscape orientation and change your address in the dialog box. The next time you run the Wizard, it will be set at landscape and the edited address will appear. Word saves the information so you can customize the default options. If you want to use these same settings, just run the Wizard and click on Finish. If you want to change some of the settings, select Next to display the dialog box you want to change.

Tip: The Wizard settings are stored in a file called Wordwiz.ini in your Windows 95 directory. To reset all of the Wizard settings to their defaults, delete the Wordwiz.ini file. You can also edit the file to change individual settings.

Word Templates

A template is a special type of document that contains built-in formats and text. When you want to type a document for which a template is available, you start a new document using the template and then customize it for your needs.

11

In a way, a template is like a form that has headings, graphics, and standard information already printed on it. But it is more than that. Most templates have prompts that show you where to enter your personalized information, and some templates have extensive details on how to use the styles and formats that are available. The Manual template, for example, has eight pages of information and tips on how to create a user or style manual.

Note: A template is just like the documents that Wizards create except that no dialog boxes appear, so you have to enter all of the information yourself.

Word comes with a number of templates that help you create common types of documents. In some cases, there are even different styles. Word has templates for reports, memos, letters, faxes, press releases, and resumes in three styles—contemporary, elegant, and professional. There are also templates for these documents:

- Manuals
- Newsletters
- Theses
- Brochures
- Directories
- Invoices
- Purchase orders
- Weekly time schedules

For example, suppose you want to write up a purchase order. Instead of worrying about the format and style, you start a new document based on the Purchase Order template. You only need to enter the name and address information and other details of the purchase order. The form and format are taken care of by Word.

To use a template, select New from the File menu, and then click on the tab for the type of document you want to create. Templates use the icon shown here, with the name of the document type.

Note: You'll find templates for brochures, directories, manuals, newsletters, press releases, and theses on the Publications page of the New dialog box; and templates for invoices, purchase orders, resumes, and weekly time schedules on the Other Documents page.

Double-click on the template you want to use, and then wait until Word displays the document on the screen. As with Wizard documents, the template may contain illustrative text and prompts in square brackets.

Remember: Be sure to delete any prompts that you do not replace with your own text.

Some templates also contain fields. For example, look at the document using the Purchase Order template in Figure 11-6. The fields are indicated by the gray areas. When you open the template, the insertion point will be in the first field, and a message in the status bar will prompt you for an entry. Enter the information requested and then press TAB to move to the next field. Continue in this way until the document is complete. You will no doubt also want to change the sample text that is not in a field, such as "Your Company Name". In order to edit these parts of the document, you must select Unprotect Document from the Tools menu.

Tip: If you want to return to completing the information requested in the fields, select Protect Document from the Tools menu, click on the Forms option button in the dialog box that appears, and then select OK. You'll learn all about protecting documents and using forms in Chapter 23.

11

> **Your Company Name**
> *Your Company Slogan*
> Your Company Street Address
> City, State ZIP
> 000.000.0000 Fax 000.000.0000
>
> PURCHASE ORDER
>
> The following number must appear on all related
> correspondence, shipping papers, and invoices:
> P.O. NUMBER:
>
> To: Ship To:
>
> | P.O. DATE | REQUISITIONER | SHIP VIA | F.O.B. POINT | TERMS |
> |---|---|---|---|---|
> | | | | | |
>
> | QTY | UNIT | DESCRIPTION | UNIT PRICE | TOTAL |
> |---|---|---|---|---|
>
> Enter the purchase order number

Even though templates have names, the title bar will contain the generic type of name—Document1, Document2, and so on. This indicates that you have not really *opened* the template but are just using it as a basis for your own document. Any changes that you make to the text or formats will not affect the template itself, just the current document.

Creating Your Own Templates

Templates are so useful that you may want to create your own. Are there certain types of documents that you create periodically? Rather than set the layout and formats each time and type text that you want in every copy, create a template. For example, suppose you frequently write legal documents. Each time you start such a document, you change the page size to legal, type your letterhead, add a line down the left margin of the page, and turn on line numbering. Instead of doing this for every new legal document you type, create a template with these formats. Then when you need to type a legal document, just use the template.

Let's create such a document now. To create a new template, select New from the File menu. In the New dialog box, click on the Template radio button.

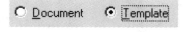

This tells Word that you are creating a template rather than a document. Now if it is not already selected, click on the Blank Document icon in the General page of the New dialog box. You select a template—not a

Wizard—that you want to use as the basis of your own template. In most cases, this will be the Blank Document icon because it represents the normal template—default styles and no special text. Click on OK to see a blank document window labeled Template1. To change the paper size, select Page Setup from the File menu, and then click on the Paper Size tab. Pull down the Paper Size list and select Legal 8½×14 In. To add line numbers, click on the Layout tab and then on the Line Numbers command button. In the dialog box that appears, click on Add Line Numbering.

You now want to place a vertical line down the entire length of the page. To make the line appear on every page, it should be inserted in the header. If you make the header the full length of the page, however, there won't be room for any text, because normally your text begins after the header. Word to the rescue. The trick is to set the top page margin to –1, a negative number. This tells Word to start the text at 1 inch regardless of the size of the header. Do this now. Click on the Margins tab and enter **–1** in the Top text box. Now select OK to return to the document.

Caution: With Top set at –1 for the page setup, if you type text in the header that extends past the top margin, it will overlap with the text on the page.

Select Header and Footer from the View menu. You'll notice that the header area extends down the entire page, as shown in Figure 11-7. Click on the Border button to display the Borders toolbar, and then click on the Left Border button.

Even though the header is the full length of the page, the border is only one line high because the paragraph is only one line long. To automatically extend the line down the page, select Paragraph from the Format menu, select Exactly in the Line Spacing list, and enter **80li** in the At box. Click on OK—the line now extends down the margin. Choose Close in the Header and Footer toolbar.

Note: The abbreviation "li" indicates lines.

The next step is your letterhead. Click on the Center button and type your name, address, and telephone number as the letterhead. Press ENTER twice when you're done, and then click on the Align Left button. If you change to Page Layout view, you'll see that the line numbering begins with your

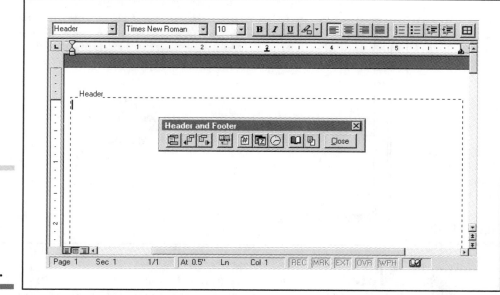

Using the
header to
place a line
down the
entire length
of the page
Figure 11-7.

letterhead. Since you don't need to number these lines, select the letterhead
and the two blank lines after it, choose Paragraph from the Format menu,
and then click on the Text Flow tab. Select Suppress Line Numbers and click
on OK. In Page Layout view, your document should appear as in Figure 11-8.

Your template is now complete, so let's save it. Choose Save from the File
menu. Type **Legal** as the template name and then click on Save. Word saves
new templates in the Templates directory with the extension DOT. Close the
document window.

Using Your Templates

If you
installed Word
as part of
Microsoft Office,
Templates
will be a
subdirectory
of the office
suite—such as
C:\Office95\
Templates.

When you want to type a legal document, you
do not have to worry about the formats. Just
start a new document based on the Legal
template. Choose New from the File menu and
click on the General tab if that page is not
already displayed. You'll see a template icon labeled Legal.

Double-click on the Legal template to display your letterhead. It is formatted
on legal-sized paper, with line numbers, and with a vertical line down the
left margin. All you need to do is move the insertion point beyond the
letterhead and type your legal document. Enter a few lines of sample text
and display the document in Print Preview. Print out a copy if you have
legal-sized paper. Close the document when you're done.

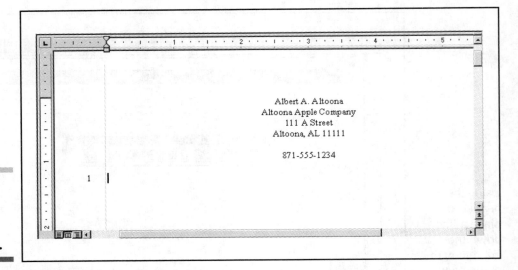

The Legal
template in
Page Layout
view
Figure 11-8.

Note: In addition to styles and formats, a template can have its own AutoText entries, toolbars, menus, and macros that you may need for a specific type of document. You'll learn about custom toolbars, menus, and macros in Chapter 24.

Deleting Templates

You can delete templates that you are no longer using. If you are already in Word, the quickest way to delete a template is to select New from the File menu, and then click the right mouse button on the template. Word will display the shortcut menu that you see here.

Select Delete from the shortcut menu. Windows will display a message asking you to confirm that you want to delete the file. Select Yes.

Upgrader: The ability to delete, cut, copy, and otherwise manipulate files from the Open and New dialog boxes is a new feature of Windows 95.

Depending on how your system is set up, your deleted files may be placed in the Windows 95 Recycle Bin. Files in the Recycle Bin are not actually deleted from your disk. Windows places them in the bin just in case you later change your mind and decide you do not want to delete them. If you want to undelete a file, or actually delete it from the disk, double-click on the Recycle Bin icon in the Windows 95 desktop. To erase the file, select Empty Recycle Bin from the File menu. To undelete the file, select Restore from the File menu.

Tip: If you accidentally delete the Normal template, don't worry. Word will re-create the template the next time you start the program; however, any custom features, such as AutoText entries and custom default formats, will be lost.

Creating Templates by Example

Although creating a template is easy, you might not plan ahead of time. You may have already typed and formatted individual documents that would be perfect for templates. For example, you may have typed and formatted a legal document using all of the formats available from the Legal template. Similarly, you may have created memos, invoices, purchase orders, and company forms—typical categories of documents that you type periodically. Do you need to repeat the formats and retype the standard text to create a template for each category of document? Of course not!

Word lets you use an existing document to create a template. Using a memo as an example, you can open one of your memo documents and delete from it all of the text except what you want to appear on the template. You would probably not delete the memo title, and headings such as To, From, Date, and Subject. When the document looks just as you want it to for the template, select Save As from the File menu. Enter a template name in the File Name text box. Make the name generic, so it represents the type of document, such as Memorandum. Then pull down the Save as Type list to see the options shown here.

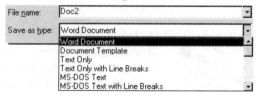

Choose Document Template from the list. Next, check the location where the file will be saved. When you create a template using the New dialog box, Word automatically saves it in the default directory where other general templates are stored. So when you select New from the File menu, your template will be listed, just as you saw when you used the Legal template. When you create a template by example using the Save As Type list, however, Word saves the template in whatever directory is shown in the Save In box. Technically, you can save your template in any location. However, it will only appear in the New dialog box if it is saved in the default Templates directory. Pull down the Save In list and select the drive and directory for the default templates. Finally, click on OK to save the template with the DOT extension.

Tip: The General page of the New dialog box represents the contents of the Templates directory. The other pages—such as Letters & Faxes and Memos—are subdirectories under Templates.

Modifying Templates

When you create a document using a template from the New dialog box, you are not changing the template itself. You can modify a template, even those supplied with Word, by opening the template into a document window. To modify a template, select Open from the File menu. Use the Look In list to select the Templates directory or the other location where you may have saved your own templates. Pull down the Files of Type list and select Document Templates. Double-click on the template you want to open.

Tip: By default, Word lists only documents with the DOC extension in the Open dialog box. So when you change to the template directory, you will not see your templates listed. Choosing Document Templates from the Files of Type list will display files with the DOT extension.

With the template opened in a document window, modify the text or formats so the template is the way you want it for new documents. Then click on the Save button or select Save from the File menu.

Caution: Some settings are retained from one function to the next during the current Word session. If you just changed the directory in the Look In text box, that same directory will be the default when you next display the Save As or Open dialog box. If you just opened a document template, then Document Templates will again be used as the default Files of Type when you try to open another document. Remember to select the correct directory and file type for the next save or open operation. The next time you start Word, however, the original default values will be used.

Changing the Normal Template

The default layout settings used for every new document are stored in the Normal template. If you want to change the default settings, don't bother opening the template. To change the default page size, margins, paper source, or layout, make your selections from the Page Setup dialog box and then click on the Default button. To change the default font and size, select your options in the Font dialog box and then click on Default.

11

If you later change your mind and want to restore all of the default settings, delete the Normal template—the file Normal.dot in the Templates directory.

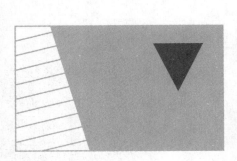

Formatting with Style

12

Templates and Wizards streamline your formatting because they are based on *styles*—a powerful feature of Word that can save you countless hours of formatting and reformatting. Styles let you apply even the most complex combinations of formats easily and consistently over any number of documents.

A Style Primer

A style is just a collection of formats that you can apply to text. Remember format painter? With format painter you can apply the formats in one paragraph of text to another paragraph. Think of a style as a place to store the formats before you apply them. You can store many different styles—collections of formats—and then apply them to text whenever you want.

There are two general types of styles, character and paragraph. A *character style* can only contain font formats—such as the typeface, size, style, effect, and color of characters—and language options. A *paragraph style* can contain any font or paragraph format that you can apply to text, including line spacing, text flow options, borders, and text alignment. You can apply both a character and paragraph style to the same text. Here's a summary of the types of formats that can be applied with each type of style:

Character style	Font, font size, character effect, underlining, color, character spacing, kerning, and language
Paragraph style	All of the above, as well as all paragraph formats, text flow, tabs, borders and shading, frames, and paragraph numbering

Using Word's Styles

The Normal template has about 75 styles defined for you—styles for all of Word's built-in features, such as footnotes, tables of contents, and indexes. When you create an envelope using the Envelopes and Labels option from the Tools menu, for example, Word formats the mailing address according to a built-in style. That is how Word knows where to position the address on the envelopes, what font to use, and how wide each line can be without printing too close to the right edge of the envelope.

You can take advantage of these built-in styles to format your own documents. So for example, if you are creating an envelope yourself, without using the Tools menu, you can use Word's styles to format the envelope address for you.

To learn about styles, start a new Word document. You can see what style is applied to the text at the location of the insertion point by looking in the Style box—the first text box in the Formatting toolbar. The word "Normal" means that you are using the Normal style, with the default font, line spacing, and text alignment that Word automatically applies to new documents. You can apply another style to text by selecting it from the pull-down list.

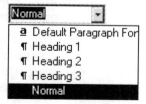

The list displays only a basic set of the styles in the Normal template. As you apply or create other styles, however, they will be added to the list. To display all of the styles, hold down SHIFT while you pull down the list. The list will now contain a scroll bar so you can see all of the built-in styles.

12

Note: If you attach a template to a document, additional styles will be shown in the list. You'll learn how to attach a template later in this chapter.

Paragraph styles are preceded by the paragraph symbol (¶); character styles by the underlined letter *a* (a). To apply a style, select it from the list.

Upgrader: In earlier versions of Word, paragraph styles appeared in boldface, character styles in normal text.

You apply styles the same way you apply individual font or paragraph formats. To apply a paragraph style to a single paragraph, or a character style to one word, place the insertion point anywhere in the paragraph or word. To apply a style to more than a paragraph or word, select the text first, and then choose the style.

You can also apply a style to text you are about to type. Select the style from the list, then type your text. To return the Normal or some other style, select it from the Style list. You can have more than one character style in a paragraph, but only one paragraph style.

Tip: You can use shortcut keys to apply basic styles. Press CTRL-SHIFT-N to apply the Normal style; ALT-CTRL-1 for Heading 1; ALT-CTRL-2 for Heading 2; ALT-CTRL-3 for Heading 3. You can also cycle from Heading 1 through Heading 9 by pressing ALT-SHIFT-RIGHT and ALT-SHIFT-LEFT. Pressing CTRL-SPACEBAR will not delete character formats applied to text by a style, only those you apply manually.

Some styles will remain in effect when you press ENTER, so subsequent text will appear in the same format. Other styles end when you press ENTER, so subsequent text is in the Normal style. This is useful for formats that you only want to apply to one paragraph, such as headings or titles.

Use the built-in styles now to see how this works. Make sure a blank document window is onscreen, and then pull down the Style list and select Heading 1. The Formatting toolbar indicates that the style is Arial, 14 points, bold:

The style also is formatted with 12 points before and 3 points after the paragraph. Type **My Life Story** and press ENTER. The text you entered appears in the Heading 1 style, but the Formatting toolbar now indicates that the Normal style is in force. Word reverts to the Normal style to save you the trouble of selecting it yourself after you type a heading. Now type the text for the first paragraph (press ENTER at the end):

> It was a cold and stormy night when my mother huddled by the open fire to give birth. The wind howled with a viciousness that frightened the horses, but my mother remained calm and at peace. I was to be her tenth child, but she already knew that I was to be special.

Pull down the Style list and select Heading 2. The Formatting toolbar indicates that this heading style is Arial, 12 points, bold and italic. It also is formatted with 12 points before and 3 points after the paragraph. Type **A Remarkable Infant** and press ENTER. Word again reverts to the Normal style. Now complete the document as shown in Figure 12-1. Use the Heading 2 style for the other subtitle. Save the document with the name My Life Story.

Note: Word will use My Life Story as the default name because it is the first paragraph of the document.

Applying Styles with the Style Dialog Box

You can also apply styles through the Style dialog box. Click anywhere in the title My Life Story. Select Style from the Format menu to display the dialog box and then look in the List section. If the setting is Styles In Use, then the dialog box only displays the styles currently applied to the document. Pull down the list and select All Styles. You will now see a list of

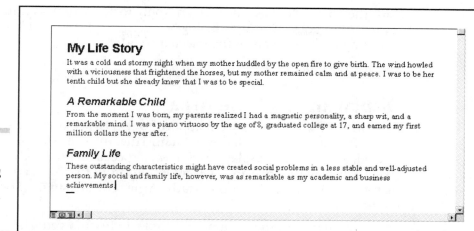

Type this
document to
practice using
Word's
built-in styles
Figure 12-1.

the styles in the Normal template, as shown in Figure 12-2. When you select a
style from the list, Word illustrates its formats in the Paragraph and Character
Preview panels, and lists the formats in the Description box. Scroll through the
list until you see the style Title. Click on the style to see its description.

Note: When you display the Style dialog box, the style applied to the text
at the current location of the insertion point will be highlighted in the list.

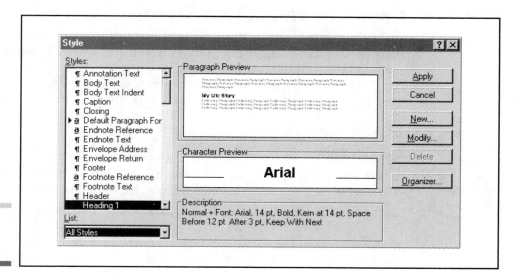

The Style
dialog box
Figure 12-2.

With the Title style selected, click on Apply to apply that style to the text at the insertion point. The Style dialog box closes and the text is formatted according to the formats of the selected style.

Save the document.

Displaying the Style Area

You'll learn more about the Options dialog box in Chapter 21.

You can always see what style is applied to text by looking in the Style box of the toolbar. The box will now contain Title, the style that you just applied. You can also display a *style area*, a special section to the left of the text. To display the style area, select Options from the Tools menu, and then click on the View tab. Enter the width of the style area in the Style Area Width box.

When you return to the document, Word will insert a vertical line down the left margin and show the names of styles applied to text:

Title	**My Life Story**
Normal	It was a cold and stormy night when my mother huddled by the open fire to give birth. The wind howl with a viciousness that frightened the horses, but my mother remained calm and at peace. I was to be tenth child but she already knew that I was to be special.

To change the size of the style area, enter a new setting in the View dialog box or drag the vertical line to the left or right. To remove the style area, enter **0** in the Style Area Width box or drag the vertical line off the left edge of the screen.

Creating Your Own Styles

You may decide that you want to use combinations of formats other than those provided in Word's built-in styles. You can create your own styles— even add them to the Normal template or to another template. The easiest way to create a style is *by example*. Format text using the options that you want to save in a style. Place the insertion point in the text, and then click on the Style box in the toolbar. Type the name you want to give to the style and press ENTER.

Note: Styles by example are always paragraph styles. To create a character style, use the Style dialog box, as explained in the next section.

Word will record the paragraph formats of the text in the new style. If you also want to record character formats with the style, select a word in the paragraph which has the formats you want to save. Keep in mind that Word actually records the formats applied to the first selected character and applies it to the entire style. For example, suppose you select the only underlined word in the paragraph. Word will record the underline format in the style and underline the entire paragraph.

Note: A style that you create by example can only be used in the active document. It will appear in the Style list whenever you open the document, but not in any other. To use the style with all new documents, it must be added to the template, as explained in "Creating Styles with the New Style Dialog Box" and "Modifying Styles with the Dialog Box."

12

Let's create a custom style now called Thesis Title. Select the title in the document on your screen. Now pull down the Font list and select Arial MT Black, and then pull down the Font Size list and select 24. Select Font from the Format menu, click on All Caps in the Effects section, and then click on OK. Click the mouse to deselect the text. Now with the insertion point still in the title, click on the Style box in the Formatting toolbar, type **Thesis Title**, and press ENTER. You've just created a style.

Note: When you pull down the Style list, you'll see your custom style listed.

Creating Styles with the New Style Dialog Box

To create character styles and more sophisticated paragraph styles, use the New Style dialog box. Choose Style from the Format menu, and then select New to see the dialog box shown in Figure 12-3. Type the style's name in the Name text box, remembering that style names are case sensitive. Then select either Paragraph or Character in the Style Type list, depending on the types of formats you want to apply.

When you create a style, you can base it on another style. This means that the style begins with all of the formats of the other style. For example, suppose you want to create a title style that uses the same formats of Heading 1 but is also centered between the margins. If you base your new style on Heading 1, you'll only have to select center alignment to complete the definition of your new style. Pull down the Based On list in the New Style dialog box and select the style that you want to use as the basis for your new style.

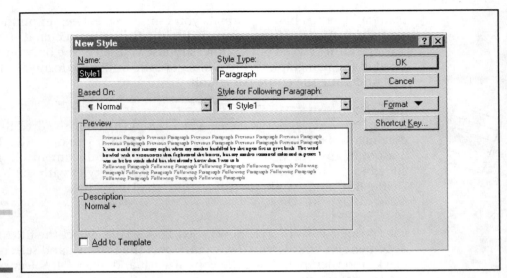

Creating a
new style
Figure 12-3.

Tip: Word will use the style at the location of the insertion point in your document as the basis for the new style. If you've already applied the style you want to use as the base style, place the insertion point in it before displaying the New Style dialog box.

Next, pull down the Style for Following Paragraph list, and select the style to take effect when you press ENTER after typing text in your new style. The default will be set to the same name of your style, meaning that the formats will be carried down to the next paragraph. If you want the style to affect only one paragraph at a time, select the Normal style.

Remember: You cannot select a Style for Following Paragraph for character styles.

Now you have to choose the formats that you want to apply to the style. Click on the Format list to see the options shown here.

Note: All of the formats except Font and Language will be dimmed for character styles.

You use the Shortcut Key command to assign the style to a key combination. You'll learn more about custom key combinations in Chapter 24.

Choose an option from the list to display the appropriate dialog box. For example, if you select Paragraph from the list, Word will display the Paragraph dialog box. Choose formatting options from the dialog box and then click on OK. Repeat the procedure for each type of format that you want to apply.

Notice the check box in the lower-left corner of the New Style dialog box labeled Add to Template. When this box is not checked, your style will be available only for the current document. If you start a new document, your new style will not be available. If you want to use your style with every document that uses the current template, select the Add to Template option. If you are using the Normal template, the style will be available with every new document.

12

Tip: If you create a style by example and want to add it to the template, select the style in the Style dialog box, click on Modify, and then select the Add to Template check box. You'll learn more about modifying styles soon.

Finally, click on OK to accept the new style and to return to the New Style dialog box. You can now use your style just as you can any other.

Modifying Styles

You can modify a style, even those in the Normal template, to change the formats that it applies. When you change a style, all text formatted by the style in the current document will change automatically to reflect the new formats. For example, suppose you use the Heading 1 style to format a series of headings. The style is Arial, 14 points, bold. If you change the style to Times New Roman, 18 points, all of the headings will immediately be changed to that style.

You can modify a style by example or by using the Style dialog box.

Modifying a Style by Example

To illustrate changing a style by example, let's modify the Heading 2 style. You must select text that is already formatted using the style, so drag to select any one of the subtitles formatted by the Heading 2 style. The style name will be shown in the Style box in the toolbar.

Next, use the toolbar or dialog boxes to format the text as you want to modify the style. If you recall, the style is Arial, 12 points, bold and italic. Pull down the Font Size list and select 16 to change the point size. Click on the Bold and Italic buttons in the toolbar to turn off these formats, and then click on the Underline button to turn it on. The heading will now look like this.

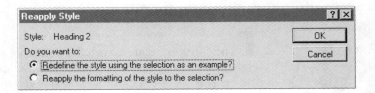

Now pull down the Style list in the toolbar and select the same style already applied to the text. In this case, just click on the Style text box—the style name Heading 2 will be selected. Press ENTER. Word will display the Reapply Style dialog box, shown here. Choose the Redefine option to change the style. All of the paragraphs that were formatted with the Heading 2 style conform automatically to the new formats.

Remember: Choosing the Reapply option instead of Redefine cancels your changes and reapplies the existing style formats to the text.

Modifying Styles with the Dialog Box

You can also modify a style with the Style dialog box. This way you can change the based-on style and the style for the following paragraph, and you can add the style to the template. For example, the Thesis Title style that you created previously will retain the format when you press ENTER. That's because it is based on the Title style that had this same attribute. Since your title will probably only be one line long, let's change the style to revert to the Normal style after pressing ENTER.

To change the style, place the insertion point in the title and select Style from the Format menu. You'll see that Thesis Title is selected in the list of styles. Click on the Modify command button to display the Modify Style

If you want to modify a different style, just select it in the list. You cannot modify the style named Default Paragraph Font. To change the default font, modify the Normal style.

dialog box, which has the same options as the New Style dialog box, just a different title.

Pull down the Style For Following Paragraph list and select Normal:

If you want to change any of the other formats in the style, do so now using the Format command button. You can also select the Add to Template check box to save the changes in the template. Select OK to return to the Style dialog box and then click on Close. Save and then close the document.

12

Note: If you've selected Add to Template, the change will affect every new document, but not existing documents. To apply the modified style to other documents, see "Styles and Templates" later in this chapter.

Finding and Replacing Styles

You know that you can search for formats using the Find dialog box, and replace them using the Replace dialog box. The same is true for styles. To find where a style is used in your document, select Find from the Edit menu, pull down the Format list, and select Styles. Word will display the dialog box you see here, listing only the styles already applied in the document.

Select the style you want to search for in the list and then click on OK. The style will be listed in the Format section under the Find What text box. Click on Find Next to locate the next occurrence of text using that style.

Using a similar technique, you can replace one style with another using the Replace dialog box. Select the Find What box, pull down the Format list, choose Style, and then select the style that you want to replace. Next select Replace With and use the Format list to choose the style you want to insert. However, remember that Word only lists the styles currently used in the document. So for example, if you want to reformat all Heading 1 text to use the Title style, the Title style must already be used in the document at least once.

Tip: If you want to replace a style with one that is not yet used in the document, move the insertion point to any blank line and apply that style using the Style dialog box. It will then be listed when you perform the Replace operation. After the replacement, reapply the Normal style to the blank line.

Styles and Templates

Styles and templates are very closely connected. As you become more experienced with Word, you'll learn how to take advantage of this connection to make formatting even easier. Let's look at a few ways in which this connection can be useful.

The Style Gallery

When you used the AutoFormat command in Chapter 9, Word formatted your document using built-in styles. For example, it applied title and heading styles to text that it detected as being headings. You also learned to use the Style Gallery to apply other formats to your text. Selecting a template from the Style Gallery actually reformats text that already has styles applied to it. It will also make the template's styles available in the Style list and in the Style dialog box.

If you have not applied styles to your document, either from the list or with AutoFormat, you may not see much difference to the document when you select a template from the Style Gallery. The selection will only affect paragraphs if the Normal style is different. Once you apply styles, the change will be more evident. For example, if you used the Heading 1 style from the Normal template, Word will apply the Heading 1 style from the template you select in the Style Gallery.

Applying Modified Styles

When you modify styles in a template, the changes only affect the active document and any new documents that use that template. The changes are not applied to any existing documents using the template.

To apply the modified styles to an existing document, open the document, and then select Templates from the File menu. Word will display the Templates and Add-ins dialog box, shown in Figure 12-4. Select the Automatically Update Document Styles check box and then choose OK.

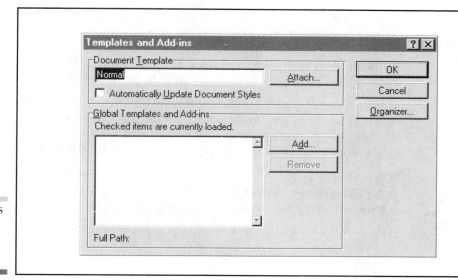

The Templates
and Add-ins
dialog box
Figure 12-4.

Attaching a Template

Now that you know about templates, you may have existing documents that
you'd like to format using one of Word's templates or one of your own. It's
not too late. To apply the styles of a template to an existing document, you
attach the template.

Attaching a template makes its styles available to the active document, as
well as its AutoText entries, macros, and other custom features. To attach a
template to the open document, select Templates from the File menu to see
the Templates and Add-ins dialog box. Select Attach to see the Attach
Template dialog box. This box is just like the Open dialog box, except by
default it lists template documents in the Templates directory. Use the dialog
box to select the template you want to attach, and then select OK to return
to the Templates and Add-Ins dialog box.

Note: Attaching a template does not insert any text from that template
into the current document. For example, attaching the Fax template will
not display the text that appears if you start a new document using
that template.

To automatically apply the styles to existing text, click on the Automatically Update Document Styles check box and then choose OK. Word will reformat any text using a style with the same name as a style in the attached template. For example, it will reformat paragraphs using the Heading 1 style with the formats of the Heading 1 style in the template.

Whether you choose to update styles automatically or not, any style with the same name as one in the attached template will be replaced. The original Heading 1 style, for example, will be replaced by the new Heading 1 style, so any text to which you now apply the style will use the new formats.

 Remember: Attaching a template also replaces AutoText entries and macros with any that have matching names in the new template.

Using Global Templates

If you want to use AutoText and macros from another template but not its styles or any standard text, then make the template *global*. To create a global template, choose Templates from the File menu to display the Templates and Add-ins dialog box, and then

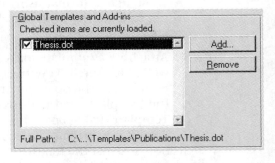

select Add. You'll see the Add Template dialog box, which is the same as the Attach Template box but with a different title. Select the template that you want to make global, and then click on OK to return to the Templates and Add-ins dialog box. The name of the template will appear in the Global Templates and Add-ins list with a selected check box, as you can see here.

The check mark indicates that any macros and AutoText entries of the template will be available for use in the document. You can add more than one global template.

The next time you start Word, the global templates will still be listed in the Templates and Add-ins dialog box, but the check box will not be selected. Select the check box if you want to make the template's resources available.

Tip: When you no longer want to use a global template, select its name in the Global Templates and Add-ins list, and then click on Remove. To temporarily make the resources unavailable, uncheck the check box.

Templates and AutoText

When you attach a template, you can use it in AutoText entries. You can also create new AutoText entries and decide which template to store them in, the Normal template or the attached template. When you define the AutoText entry, pull down the Make AutoText Entry Available To list, for options like these:

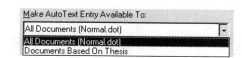

Choose All Documents (Normal.dot) to store the entry in the Normal template so it is available for all documents. If you select the Documents Based On option, the entry will be available only for documents using the named template.

Copying Items Between Templates

As you create templates, you may find that you'd like to use styles and AutoText entries from a combination of templates. Rather than attaching or using a global template, you can copy objects from one template to another. For instance, you can copy a style from one of your custom templates to the Normal template so it is available for every document.

To copy items between templates, first select Templates from the File menu, and then click on the Organizer button to display the dialog box shown in Figure 12-5. Click on the tab for the type of item you want to copy—a style, an AutoText entry, a toolbar, or a macro.

Tip: You can also select Organizer from the Style dialog box.

12

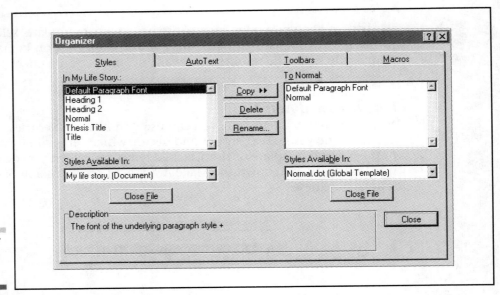

The Organizer
dialog box
Figure 12-5.

There are two sides to the dialog box. You must list the resources that you want to copy on one side, and the name of the destination template—where you want to copy the items to—on the other side. The default settings show the styles that you used in the document on the left, and the Normal template on the right.

Note: Although the default box shows one side labeled In and the other side labeled To, it really doesn't matter which template is listed in which box because you can select and move an item from either box.

If you do not see the item that you want to copy in the list on the left, pull down the Styles Available In list. You can then choose to display all of the styles in the attached template, or those in the Normal template.

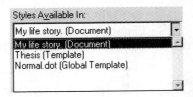

If you want to copy styles in some other document or template, click on the Close File command button. The button will be renamed Open File. Click on Open File, and then select the document or template containing the styles you want to copy.

Next, make certain that the template you want to copy the styles to is listed in the right side of the dialog box. If it is not, use the Styles Available In list or the Close File/Open File command button on the right.

Select the item that you want to copy from one side to the other. When you select an item from a list, it automatically becomes the In list, and the other becomes the To list. Word will adjust the Copy button so the arrows point to the To list—the list where no item is selected. Click on Copy to copy the selected item from one list to the other.

Tip: Choose Delete to delete the selected item, or choose Rename to change its name.

12

Creating Tables and Lists

13

When you want information to have real impact, consider formatting it as a list or table. Lists and tables are easy to read because they usually contain less text than the same information presented in paragraph format. Attractively formatted tables are especially easy to read, and they convey an air of precision.

Typing Lists with Bullets and Numbers

Word has several built-in features that let you create numbered lists and bulleted lists with a click of the mouse. Here are examples of both types of list:

1.	Call Mom	•	Call Mom
2.	Go to the bank	•	Go to the bank
3.	Return gift	•	Return gift
4.	Pay bills	•	Pay bills

A numbered list inserts a number in front of each paragraph; a bulleted list inserts a bullet. The default bullet is a small circle, although you can change it to an arrow, diamond, asterisk, or any other character in any font—even Wingdings. You can create lists as you type, or by selecting existing text.

Creating a Numbered List

To automatically number existing paragraphs, select the paragraphs, and then click on the Numbering button in the Formatting toolbar. Word will number the paragraphs consecutively starting with the number 1, and format the paragraphs with hanging indentations at the quarter-inch position.

To create a numbered list as you type, click on the Numbering button in the Formatting toolbar. Word will insert the number 1 at the left margin and format the paragraph with a hanging indentation.

Tip: You can customize the indentation level and the type of numbers using the Bullets and Numbering dialog box.

Type the text for the paragraph and then press ENTER. Word will insert the next number in the series. Continue typing the list in the same way, pressing ENTER after each paragraph to insert another number. To stop numbering paragraphs, press the Numbering button again. You can also turn off numbering by pressing ENTER on a numbered line without any other text.

Upgrader: With previous versions of Word, pressing ENTER while in a list always inserts the next number, even if there is no text on the line.

If you type text after the list and then later turn numbering on, Word will start a new list with the number 1. When you want some unnumbered paragraphs within the list, start by numbering them all. Then place the insertion point in paragraphs that you do not want numbered and click on the Numbering button. Word will remove the number from the paragraph and automatically renumber following paragraphs.

When you remove the number from the last paragraph in the list, Word will also clear the hanging indentation. The hanging indentation will be retained only if the paragraph is followed by other numbered text in the series.

Creating a Bulleted List

To create a bulleted list, click on the Bullets button in the Formatting toolbar. If you select text first, Word will insert the bullet character in front of each paragraph and format the text with a hanging indentation.

13

The Bullets button is a toggle, just like the Numbering button. To remove bullets, place the insertion point in the paragraph and click on the Bullets button.

Using the Shortcut Menu

If you click the right mouse button in a numbered or bulleted list, Word will display the shortcut menu with the options you see here. You use Promote and Demote when typing a multilevel list. You'll learn about this type of list later in this chapter. If you select Skip Numbering, Word removes the number or bullet from the paragraph but retains the hanging indentation. To begin inserting numbers or bullets again, click on the Numbering or Bullets button.

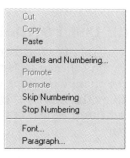

When you click on Stop Numbering in the shortcut menu, Word turns off the numbering or bullets function. It removes the number or bullet from the current paragraph and clears the hanging indentation.

Using the AutoFormat As You Type Feature

Another way to create a numbered or bulleted list as you type it, is to use the AutoFormat As You Type feature. Just start typing the first line of the list. For a numbered list, type a number or letter, followed by a period (1., A., a., I., or i.). For a bulleted list, type an asterisk (*) or hyphen (-). Then press the SPACEBAR or TAB to insert space, and type the first entry of the list.

As soon as you press ENTER after the line, AutoFormat goes into action and converts the list to an automatic list. If you are creating a numbered list, Word inserts the next number in the sequence (2., B., b., II., or ii.) and turns on hanging indentation. If you are typing a bulleted list, Word replaces the asterisks with a round bullet, or the hyphen with a square bullet, inserts the bullet on the next line, and turns on hanging indentation.

If Tip Wizard is turned on, you'll see this message, reporting that the numbering or bulleted list feature has been turned on:

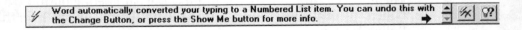

> Word automatically converted your typing to a Numbered List item. You can undo this with the Change Button, or press the Show Me button for more info.

T ip: If Tip Wizard is turned off, the Tip Wizard button will flash in the toolbar. Click on the button to display the message.

 If you do not want Word to start the automatic list feature, click on the Change button in the Tip Wizard.

Customizing List Formats

You have more control over the format of lists using the Bullets and Numbering dialog box shown in Figure 13-1. Use the dialog box to turn the list on or off, or to change the type of numbers or bullets, or to adjust the indentation. Display the box by selecting Bullets and Numbering from the Format menu, or from the shortcut menu when you click the right mouse button in the text.

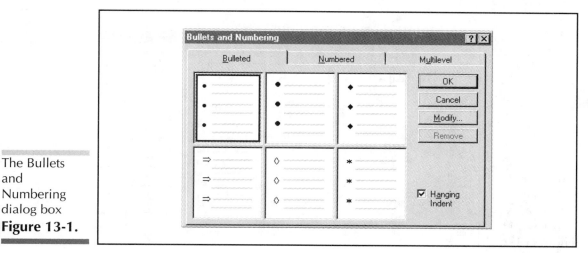

The Bullets and Numbering dialog box **Figure 13-1.**

13

The bullet or numbering style that you select from this dialog box will remain in effect during the current Word session, even for new documents and existing documents that you open. For example, if you choose an arrow for the bullet, then later turn bullets on from the toolbar, Word will insert an arrow, not the round bullet.

To stop typing the list, click on the Bullets button, select Stop Numbering from the shortcut menu, or display the Bullets and Numbering dialog box and select Remove.

Selecting Bullet Formats

The Bulleted options contain six bullet styles. All of the styles, except the second, will be inserted in the same point size as the text. If you are typing 8-point text, Word will insert an 8-point bullet; if you are typing 18-point text, Word will insert an 18-point bullet. The second bullet style inserts a 14-point bullet regardless of the text size. You can also select whether or not to use hanging indentations. If you deselect the Hanging Indent check box, only the first line of each bulleted paragraph will be at the quarter-inch position. Following lines will align at the left margin below the bullet.

When you select OK from the dialog box, Word will return to the document and begin inserting bullets in the selected format.

For even more choices, click on the Modify command button in the dialog box to see the options shown in Figure 13-2. For each of the six bullet styles, you can select a point size and color. Set the point size to Auto to have Word

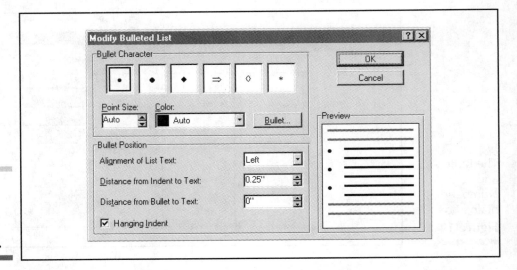

Use these
options to
modify a
bulleted list
Figure 13-2.

insert the bullet in the same size as the text, or enter a fixed point size. To
select a different character for the bullet, click on the Bullet command
button. You can then select a character and a font. You adjust the alignment
of the text and bullet using these options:

♦ *Alignment of List Text* determines the position of the bullet in the space
before the first line of text. Your choices are Left, Center, and Right.

♦ *Distance from Indent to Text* determines the distance of every text line
from the left margin.

♦ *Distance from Bullet to Text* determines any additional indentation of the
first line of text. By default, this is set at 0, meaning that the first line is
indented according to the Distance from Indent to Text setting. You can
increase this setting to indent the first line farther.

Selecting Number Formats

When you want to customize list numbering, click on the Numbered tab in
the dialog box to see the options shown in Figure 13-3. Select from one of
the numbering styles to turn on numbering and to insert the first number
(or letter) into the text. As with bullets, you can also select or deselect
hanging indentations.

To customize the numbering scheme, click on the Modify command button
to display the dialog box shown in Figure 13-4. Select the type of number in
the Number list. These are your options:

1, 2, 3

I, II, III

i, ii, iii

A, B, C

a, b, c

1st, 2nd

One, Two

First, Second

You can also enter one or more characters to come before and after the number. For example, if you want to insert numbers like **>>1<<**, enter **<<** in the Text Before box, and enter **<<** in the Text After box. Other options in the dialog box let you select the font for the inserted numbers, specify the starting number, and adjust the position of the number and the alignment of the text.

13

Multilevel Lists

The Multilevel page of the Bullets and Numbering dialog box lets you insert multiple levels of letters or numbers depending on the indentation of the

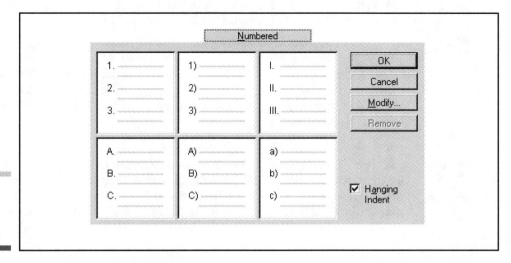

Numbered
list
options
Figure 13-3.

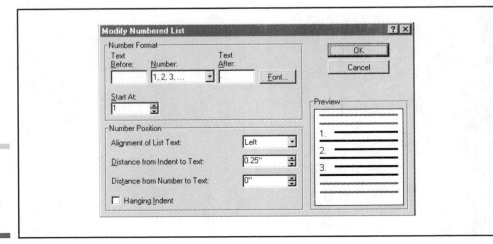

Use these
options to
modify a
numbered list
Figure 13-4.

text, just like an outline. The different Multilevel options are shown in
Figure 13-5. With multilevel lists, the inserted number increases, or the letter
increments, each time you increase the indentation. Increase indentation
using the Increase Indent button in the toolbar, by pressing ALT-SHIFT-RIGHT,
or by selecting Demote from the shortcut menu. Decrease indentation by
clicking on the Decrease Indent button, by pressing ALT-SHIFT-LEFT, or by
selecting Promote from the shortcut menu.

T ip: When you are not in a multilevel list, pressing ALT-SHIFT-RIGHT and
ALT-SHIFT-LEFT cycles through Heading 1 to Heading 9.

Select Modify from the Multilevel options to customize the letters or
numbers inserted at each level. Word offers the same options as those
available for modifying numbers, but you can also select which indentation
level to customize.

T ip: Word also provides a more powerful outlining feature that you'll
learn about in Chapter 19. Multilevel lists simply insert level numbers based
on indentation. The outlining feature also inserts level numbers, but it lets you
manipulate outline families and heading formats to organize your document.

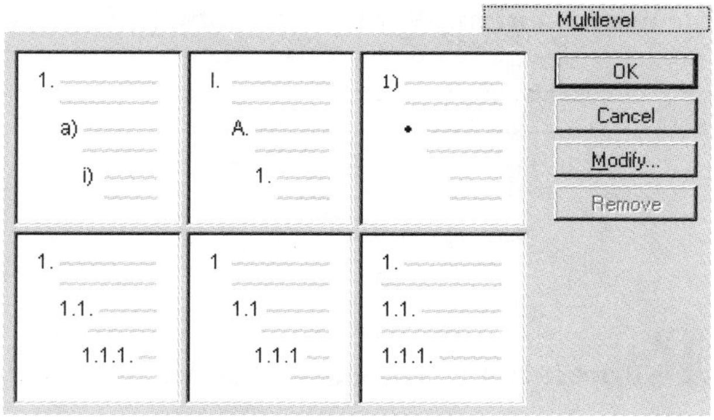

Multilevel
lists look like
outlines
Figure 13-5.

Creating Tables

13

A table lets you enter text in neatly arranged rows and columns. You can insert grid lines in the table and perform math calculations, similar to using a spreadsheet such as Microsoft Excel or Lotus 1-2-3. Tables can add a great deal of impact to a document. They make it easier to read columns of numbers, and they help show relationships and trends that cannot easily be expressed in text. You can create a table by dragging the mouse or by selecting from a dialog box.

Building a Table

Create a table now using the mouse. To create the table with the mouse, click on the Insert Table button on the Standard toolbar. A miniature grid will appear representing the rows and columns of a table.

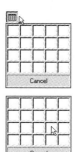

If you want to create a table no larger than five columns or four rows, click in the square on the grid that represents the lower-right corner of the table. For example, create a table of four columns and three rows now by clicking on the square you see pointed to here.

If you want to create a table with more than five columns or four rows, hold down the mouse button and drag down and to the right. As you drag, squares in the grid become selected and the number of rows and columns will be indicated at the bottom of the grid. Drag the mouse until you select the number of rows and columns that you want in the table, and then release the mouse button. Word inserts dotted grid lines in your blank table:

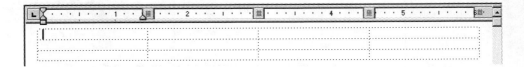

Remember: You can add or delete rows and columns at any time.

The table extends from the left to the right margin, with equal-sized columns. The grid lines indicate the size of each cell—the intersection of a row and column where you enter text—but they will not print. As with a spreadsheet program, each cell in the table is referenced by its row and column numbers, for example, the upper-left cell as A1. The ruler shows the width of the cells.

Other Ways to Create Tables

It is easy to create a table with the mouse and the toolbar button, but Word gives you four other ways: using a dialog box, using a Wizard, converting existing text, and inserting a Microsoft Excel worksheet. You'll learn how to insert an Excel worksheet in Chapter 20, so let's look at the other methods here.

Using the Insert Table Dialog Box

The Insert Table button can create a table as big as 16 rows and 10 columns. To create a table up to 31 columns and even thousands of rows, select Insert Table from the Table menu to display the dialog box you see here. Enter the number of columns and rows desired in the appropriate text boxes, and then click on OK.

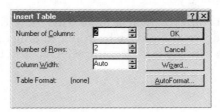

Using Table Wizard

You can create a completely formatted table by using the Table Wizard. To insert a table into the current document, select Wizard from the Insert Table dialog box. To start a new document with a table, select New from the File menu, and then double-click on Table Wizard from the Other Documents options. Word will display a series of dialog boxes prompting you to select:

♦   The overall layout style

♦   The number of columns

♦   Automatic column headings with months, quarters, days, numbers, or years

♦   The number of rows

♦   Automatic row headings with months, quarters, days, numbers, or years

♦   Alignment of text and numbers in cells

♦   Portrait or landscape orientation

The Wizard ends by displaying the AutoFormat dialog box to select borders and shading and the font and color of text.

13

Note: You'll learn more about AutoFormat later in this chapter.

Converting Between Tables and Text

Name	Age	Grade
Jane	15	B
Peter	18	A
Adam	18	A

If you've already typed information in columns separated by tabs or commands, you can automatically convert the text into a table. For example, suppose that before reading this chapter, you had typed the text shown here.

Since the information would look better as a table, select the text, and then choose Convert Text to Table from the Table menu to display the dialog box shown in Figure 13-6. Word will suggest the number of columns based on the format of the text, and the character used to indicate the division into columns will be selected in the Separate Text At section. Since the sample table uses tabs between information in each line, the dialog box is set for using tabs as the separator. Choose OK to convert the text into a table.

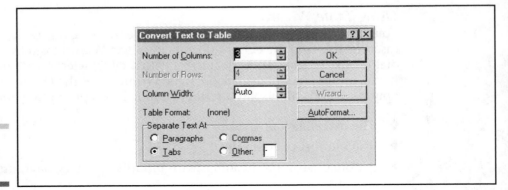

Tip: If you select a table, the menu option will be Convert Table to Text. This option removes the grid lines and displays the information as text. You can select to separate the data in each cell by paragraph marks (creating a paragraph from each cell), tabs, commands, or any other character.

Entering Text into Tables

After you create the table, you are ready to enter text into it. To enter text, place the insertion point in a cell and type. You can place the insertion point by clicking in the cell or by pressing TAB, SHIFT-TAB, or the arrow keys. If you type more text than can fit in a cell, Word will automatically wrap the text and increase the row height. It will not widen the cell automatically.

Caution: Do not press ENTER to move out of a cell. When you press ENTER, the height of the current cell will increase by one line. To delete the extra line, press BACKSPACE.

Make sure the insertion point is in the first cell in the first row, and type **Client**. By default, everything you type in a cell—text and numbers—is left-aligned. Press TAB to reach the next cell in the row and type **Sales Rep**. Now complete your table so it looks like this:

Client	Sales Rep	Amount Due	Invoice Date
Wilson Hats	Maxwell	1600.00	5/1/96
Sterling, Inc.	Nancy	2500.00	2/12/96

When you're done, save the table with the name Sales Data.

T ip: Use the Formatting toolbar and the Font and Paragraph dialog boxes to format text in cells just as you format any text in the document.

Working with Tables

Table
Insert Rows
Delete Cells...
Merge Cells
Split Cells...
Select Row
Select Column
Select Table   Alt+Num 5
Table AutoFormat...
Cell Height and Width...
Headings
Convert Text to Table...
Sort...
Formula...
Split Table
✔ Gridlines

Word provides a number of special ways to work with tables. When the insertion point is in a table, pull down the Table menu to see the options shown here. You can also click the right mouse to display a shortcut menu with table options. Some of the options in the Table menu and shortcut menu will vary depending on whether or not rows, columns, or cells are selected. For example, If nothing is selected, the menu will appear as shown here. If you select a cell, the Insert Cells option will replace Insert Rows. If you select a column, the first two options in the menu will be replaced with Insert Columns and Delete Columns.

13

To format an entire row or column at a time, select the row or column first. Place the insertion point in any cell in the row or column, and then choose Select Row or Select Column from the Table menu. To format the entire table, choose Select Table from the Table menu.

You can also select cells, rows, and columns with the mouse. You can select individual cells in two ways. If you point to the cell so the mouse pointer is shaped like an I-beam, select the cell by clicking three times. If you point to the left margin of the cell so the pointer is shaped like an arrow, you only have to click once.

To select a column, place the mouse pointer on the top grid line of the column—the mouse pointer will be shaped like a down-pointing arrow—and then click. To select a row, place the mouse in the left margin outside of the row—the pointer will be shaped like a diagonal arrow—and click. To select multiple cells, rows, or columns, drag over them with the mouse.

Let's format the first row so the column labels are in 12-point text, bold, and centered in the cells. Click in any cell in the row, pull down the Table menu, and choose Select Row. Now click on the Center and Bold buttons in the Formatting toolbar. Pull down the Font Size list and select 12 points. When you deselect the text, your table should look like this:

Client	Sales Rep	Amount Due	Invoice Date
Wilson Hats	Maxwell	1600.00	5/1/96
Sterling, Inc.	Nancy	2500.00	2/12/96

Changing Cell Width and Height

Word gives you complete control over the size of rows, columns, and cells. Use the Split Cells option in the Table menu to divide one or more cells into columns. For example, suppose you want to add a new column for telephone numbers under the Sales Rep label, like this:

Client	Sales Rep		Amount Due	Invoice Date
Wilson Hats	Maxwell	555-1234	1600.00	5/1/96
Sterling, Inc.	Nancy	567-0956	2500.00	2/12/96

Select the two cells under the column heading. Pull down the Table menu and select Split Cells to see this dialog box:

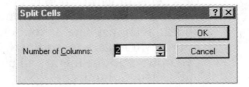

Select the number of columns you want to create—the default is 2—and then choose OK.

Note: If you've made the change to the table, select Undo Split Cells from the Edit menu.

Use the Merge Cells command in the Table menu to combine two or more adjacent cells in a row into one. Select the cells that you want to combine and then choose Merge Cells. Any contents in the cells will be combined. Merge Cells is useful when you want to use one column label for two existing columns of data.

Note: You will learn how to actually insert rows or columns in the section, "Changing Table Size."

The Cell Height and Width option on the Table menu lets you adjust the width of columns, the spacing between the text in columns, the height of rows, and the alignment of rows between the margins. The dialog box has two sections. Clicking on the Column tab will display the following options.

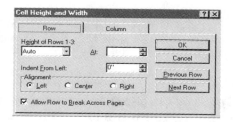

The Width of Column text box shows the width of the current column. Increase or decrease the width as desired. Spacing Between Columns indicates left and right "margin" space within each cell. You can increase or decrease this setting, although it is best to have some margin space so the text in columns does not run together. The AutoFit command button adjusts the column width to accommodate the longest entry in the column. To change the widths of other columns, click on the Previous Column or Next Column button.

Tip: To adjust the width of several columns at one time, select the columns before displaying the dialog box.

13

Clicking on the Row tab in the dialog box displays the options you see here.

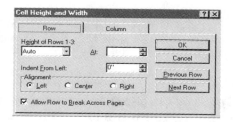

By default, the row height is set at Auto. Word will adjust the row height to accommodate the font size and the amount of text that you enter. You can also choose Exactly or At Least, and then enter a point size in the At box. The Indent option determines the distance of the row from the left margin. The Alignment option specifies the position of the row between the margins, used primarily after you've adjusted the table so it no longer is the full page width. The Allow Row to Break Across Pages option determines whether Word will divide the text in a row between pages. When unchecked, Word will keep a row all on one page.

Tip: If you do not select a cell or a row before displaying the dialog box, the settings will affect every row. To adjust the height of an individual row, select the row or a cell in the row first.

You can also adjust the width of columns and the height of rows with the mouse and the ruler. When you place the insertion point in a table, the horizontal (top) ruler indicates each column width, and you'll see column markers—the gray boxes with cross-hatching—indicating the space between columns.

When you point to a column marker, the pointer will take the shape of a two-headed arrow. To adjust the width of a column, either select the entire column, or place the insertion point anywhere in the column but make sure that *no* cells are selected. Then drag the column marker.

If individual cells in the column are selected, however, changing that column's width with the column marker will only affect those cells, not the entire column. Not all of the cells in the column will have the same width, for example where the Sales Rep column was selected here before the column width was changed.

Client	Sales Rep	Amount Due	Invoice Date
Wilson Hats	Maxwell	1600.00	5/1/96
Sterling, Inc.	Nancy	2500.00	2/12/96

Tip: You can also change column widths by dragging a grid line between columns. Dragging a grid line when no cells are selected affects the entire column. When cells are selected, the change affects only the selected cells.

Adding Printable Grid Lines

The dotted grid lines that you see around the table are there to indicate the size and position of cells. They will not actually print, and they will not appear in Print Preview. When you're using the table to display data in rows and columns, printed grid lines can add visual impact. You can even add shading to highlight specific rows, columns, or cells. You add shading and grid lines around and within a table using the Borders toolbar or the Borders and Shading dialog box from the Format menu.

Tip: To remove the dotted grid lines from the screen, select Gridlines from the Table menu. The option has no effect on printable lines added with the Borders command.

Selecting an option from the toolbar or dialog box affects only the cell containing the insertion point or a group of selected cells. To insert a border around the entire table, for example, select the entire table and then click on the Outside Border button. You can also add grid lines between each cell within the table by clicking on the Inside Border button.

Let's do that now to the table. If the Borders toolbar is not displayed, click on the Borders button in the Formatting toolbar. Make sure the insertion point is in the table, then choose Select Table from the Table menu. Now click on the Inside Border button and on the Outside Border button. Click the mouse to deselect the table.

You can also insert and delete individual cell lines using the Top, Bottom, Left, and Right border boxes. You can choose from a selection of grid lines in the Line Style list and add shading with the Shading list. For example, try shading the top row of the table. Select the first row of the table, pull down the Shading list in the Borders toolbar, and choose 30%. Your table should now look like this:

 13

Client	Sales Rep	Amount Due	Invoice Date
Wilson Hats	Maxwell	1600.00	5/1/96
Sterling, Inc.	Nancy	2500.00	2/12/96

Changing Table Size

You may create a table, only to realize later that you did not make it the correct size. When this happens, you'll need to insert or delete rows or columns.

 Tip: Use the Split Table command to divide a table into two tables. Place the insertion point in the row where you want to start the new table, and then choose Split Table from the Table menu. This command only splits tables horizontally—from row to row—not vertically between columns.

Inserting Rows

If you only need to insert an additional row at the end of the table, place the insertion point in the last cell of the last row and press TAB. Word will insert a blank row. To insert several rows at one time, and to add rows elsewhere within the table, use the Insert Rows command.

Start by selecting the row that you want to insert a new row above, or place the insertion point anywhere in the row but do not select any cells. Then click on the Insert Table button in the toolbar—the button will be labeled Insert Rows—or select Insert Rows from the Table menu. Word will move the current row down, inserting a new row above it.

Note: If you have individual cells selected, Word will open a dialog box, as described shortly in "Inserting Cells."

For example, let's insert a new row after the column headings in a table. Select the second row in the table, and then click on the Insert Table button. Word will insert the row and leave it selected.

Tip: To insert several rows at one time, select the same number of rows in the table. For instance, to insert two rows, select two rows and then click on the Insert Table button.

Now deselect the table and enter the following information:

Client	Sales Rep	Amount Due	Invoice Date
Ajax Plumbing	Nancy	2501.87	4/15/96
Wilson Hats	Maxwell	1600.00	5/1/96
Sterling, Inc.	Nancy	2500.00	2/12/96

Inserting Columns

To insert columns into your table, use the Insert Columns command. Word adds columns to the left of the selected column, so select the column that you want to insert a new column before. Then click on the Insert Table button—the button will be labeled Insert Columns—or select Insert Columns from the Table menu.

Tip: To insert several columns at one time, select the same number of columns in the table.

Inserting Cells

You can also insert individual cells into a table. When you insert cells, you have the option of shifting cells down or to the right. Start by selecting the cell where you want to insert a new cell, then click on the Insert Tables button—it will be labeled Insert Cells—or select Insert Cells from the Table menu. You'll see the dialog box shown here.

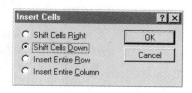

Choosing Insert Entire Row or Insert Entire Column will add a row or column. If you select Shift Cells Right, Word will add a cell just to that row:

Client	Sales Rep	Amount Due	Invoice Date	
Ajax Plumbing		Nancy	2501.87	4/15/96
Wilson Hats	Maxwell	1600.00	5/1/96	
Sterling, Inc.	Nancy	2500.00	2/12/96	

If you select Shift Cells Down, Word inserts a new row at the end of the table and shifts down only the cells in the current column.

13

Deleting Rows, Columns, and Cells

It's as easy to delete rows, columns, and cells as it is to insert them. To delete a row or column, select it and then choose Delete Rows or Delete Columns from the Table menu. If you do not have a complete row or column selected, the menu option will be labeled Delete Cells, and it will display the dialog box shown here.

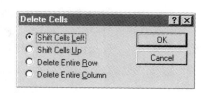

Choosing Delete Entire Row or Delete Entire Column will delete the row or column even though it is not entirely selected. Choosing Shift Cells Left deletes the cell, reducing only that row by one column. Choosing Shift Cells Up erases the contents of the cells, shifting up the remaining cell in that column.

Special Table Formatting

You know that the AutoFormat and Style Gallery commands in the Format menu will format your entire document for you. Well, the Table AutoFormat command in the Table menu does the same for tables. To format the entire table, place the insertion point anywhere in the table, and then select Table AutoFormat from the Table menu. Word displays the dialog box shown in Figure 13-7.

The Formats list contains a series of complete table formats. Click on the formats to see how the sample table in the Preview panel will appear. When you find a format that you want for your table, click on OK. Choosing the Classic 3 format, for instance, will change our sample table to this:

Client	Sales Rep	Amount Due	Invoice Date
Ajax Plumbing	Nancy	2501.87	4/15/96
Wilson Hats	Maxwell	1600.00	5/1/96
Sterling, Inc.	Nancy	2500.00	2/12/96

The check boxes in the dialog box indicate what type of formats will be applied. By default, the command will apply the borders, shading, and font of your selected format, and AutoFit will make the columns the proper width. If the format calls for it, heading rows containing column labels and the first entire column will be formatted differently than the other rows and columns. Customize the formats by selecting the appropriate check boxes. For example, deselecting Heading Rows will format the first row of the table like the remaining rows.

Creating Headings

In most tables, the heading row is usually the first row of the table. It contains labels that explain the contents of the columns. If your table is

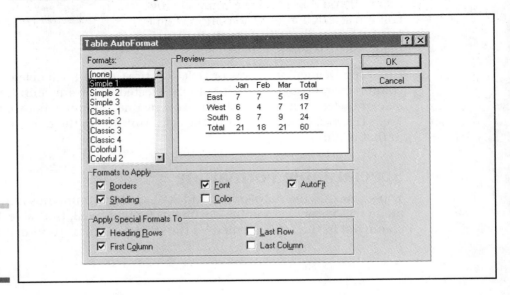

The Table
AutoFormat
dialog box
Figure 13-7.

long, it will be divided into more than one page. If you scroll to the top of the second or subsequent pages, you'll see a row of information but not the column labels, so it may be difficult to interpret the information. When you create headings, you designate one or more rows that will automatically appear at the start of each page where the table is continued.

To create a heading, select all of the rows that you want to repeat on each page, and then choose Headings from the Table menu. You can designate as many rows as you want as the heading, but you must select at least the first row.

Performing Calculations in Tables

A Word table has many of the same characteristics as a spreadsheet. Information is presented in rows and columns, and each cell is referenced by its row and column position. And just like a spreadsheet, you can perform calculations on the numbers in your table. For example, you can display the sum of values in a row or column, compute averages, and insert formulas that reference cells and other values.

The quickest calculation you can make is to total the values in rows or columns. If you want to calculate the total of the Amount Due column in our sample table, for instance, you can insert a new blank row at the bottom of the table, place the insertion point in a blank cell in the Amount Due column, and then select Formula in the Table menu to display the dialog box shown here.

The default formula =SUM(ABOVE) indicates that it will calculate the sum of the values above the current cell. You can also select a format in which to display the resulting value. When you select OK, Word will compute and display the value in the cell.

If you place the insertion point in a blank cell to the right of a row, the default formula will be =SUM(LEFT). Word will calculate and insert the total of the values in that row.

13

Your calculations are not limited to totals. You can create your own formulas using cell references, numeric values, and mathematical operators. For example, entering **=A10-A9** will calculate and display the difference between the values in cell A10 and A9. Note that all formulas must start with the equal sign.

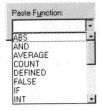

In addition to formulas, you can also use *functions*. The default formula using the word "SUM" is an example of a function. It automatically includes all of the values above or to the left of the cell. So the formula =SUM(LEFT) might perform the same math as =A1+B1+C1+D1+E1+F1, and so on. To choose another function, such as AVERAGE, select it from the Paste Function list.

Word will insert the function in the Formula text box. Edit the formula so it includes the cell references or values that you want to use in the calculation. For instance, you can compute an average on a range of cells using ABOVE, BELOW, LEFT, or RIGHT, as in =AVERAGE(ABOVE), or you can use specific cells, as in =AVERAGE(A1, A2, A3).

Tip: Word inserts the result of a calculation as a field. If you change the value in a referenced cell, you can recalculate the results to reflect the new value. Select the result, the entire table, or the entire document, and then press F9. You can edit the formula by clicking in the cell and selecting Formula from the Table menu. You can also press ALT-F9 to display the codes of all of your fields, rather than the field results. You can then edit the formula directly in the table cell, and then press ALT-F9 and F9 to redisplay the updated results.

Sorting Lists, Tables, and Text

If you do not like the order of information in a list or table, you can always rearrange it using drag and drop, or cut and paste. In many cases, however, you want to place the information in either alphabetic or numeric order. Rather than manually rearranging your table or list, let Word do it for you by *sorting*. Sorting lets you arrange text, numbers, or dates in either ascending or descending order. For example, here's a list of words shown first in its original order, then sorted both ways.

Original List	Ascending	Descending
Peter	Adam	Steven
Nancy	Barbara	Peter
Steven	Marc	Nancy
Adam	Nancy	Marc
Barbara	Peter	Barbara
Marc	Steven	Adam

Let's sort our sample table now using the values in the Amount Due column. To sort the order of rows in a table, place the insertion point anywhere in the table and select Sort from the Table menu to display the dialog box shown in Figure 13-8. You can sort the table on up to three columns. Pull down the Sort By list and select the column that you want to sort by first, in this case Amount Due.

Word can usually detect the type of information in the column and set the Type option automatically. For example, when you select Amount Due, Word will change the Type setting from Text to Number. If the setting is not correct, pull down the Type list and select either Text, Number, or Date, depending on the type of information in the column. Finally, select Descending for the sort order so the clients owing you the most money are at the top of the list. Your options should be set like this:

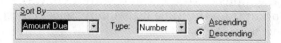

13

To sort on more than one column, repeat the procedure for one or both of the Then By sections, choosing a column, type, and order. Finally, look at the choices in the My List Has section. If your table has column headings in the first row, select Header Row. Word will sort all of the rows except the first, leaving the column headings in the first row. If your table does not have column headings, choose No Header Row to sort every row of the table.

Now select OK to sort the table so the rows appear in order.

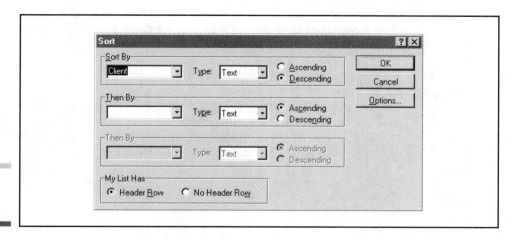

Sorting table rows
Figure 13-8.

Note: If you select the entire table before using the Sort command, the No Header Row option will be selected. If you do indeed have a header row, select the Header Row option. If you select specific rows first, Word will sort just the selected row, and you cannot choose a My List Has option.

Sorting Text

The Sort command will also let you arrange the order of paragraphs and other text not in a table. To sort a list or paragraphs of text, start by selecting the text that you want to sort—or select nothing to sort the entire document—and then choose Sort Text in the Table menu. The Sort By option will be set at Paragraphs and the Type will be set at Text. If the paragraphs in your list start with numbers or dates, choose the appropriate option from the Type list. Finally, select either Ascending or Descending, and then click on OK.

You can also sort text in columns—where values are separated by tabs, commas, or some other character, as in these two lists:

Name, Age Amount			Name	Age	Amount
Marty, 23, 560			Marty	23	560
Paul, 34, 187			Paul	34	187
Ray, 46, 876			Ray	46	876
Wilma, 17, 987			Wilma	17	987

The separate items in each line are called *fields,* and you can sort the data by fields just as you can sort a table by columns. When you display the Sort Text dialog box, pull down the Sort By list and select the field you want to sort by. Choose the type and the sort order, and select any other additional fields in the Then By sections. If you don't select specific rows, you can also choose whether or not your data has a header row. Click on OK to sort the information.

Sorting Options

In most instances, Word will sense the type of separator you used for your data—a tab, comma, or some other character. If your fields are not listed in the Sort By list, or if you want to confirm the separator, choose Options from the Sort dialog box to display the following choices:

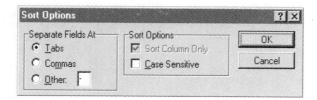

Choose the appropriate option in the Separate Fields At section. You have the added option of choosing Case Sensitive, which will cause Word to place a word starting with lowercase letters before the same word starting with uppercase letters.

You can also display these options when sorting tables. The Separate Fields At section will be dimmed, but you can choose the Case Sensitive option. If you have selected specific columns before using the Sort command, you can also check Sort Columns Only to sort only the data within those columns.

Caution: If your table has row labels in the first column, sorting selected columns is usually not appropriate.

13

Working with Pictures and Graphics

14

While lists and tables can add some visual impact to a document, nothing does it better than pictures. You can enhance your documents with pictures that are supplied with Word, pictures from other applications (even WordPerfect!), and pictures that you create yourself. You can also enhance your documents with special graphic effects using text.

Note: If you did not install the Word clip art files when you installed Word, do so now so you can practice using pictures in your documents. Exit Word, run the Word or the Microsoft Office Setup program, and install the Word clip art files. If you are using Microsoft Office, the Word Clip Art option will be in the Office Tools section.

Picture Basics

To insert a picture into a document, pull down the Insert menu and select Picture. If you installed the Word clip art files when you installed Word, you'll see the Insert Picture dialog box listing graphic files in the Clipart subdirectory. To see what a graphic looks like before you insert it, click on the Preview button in the Insert Picture dialog box's toolbar, and then select the graphic. The preview window displays a copy of whatever graphic is selected in the file list, as shown in Figure 14-1. Double-click on the name of the picture file you want to insert, or select it and then choose OK.

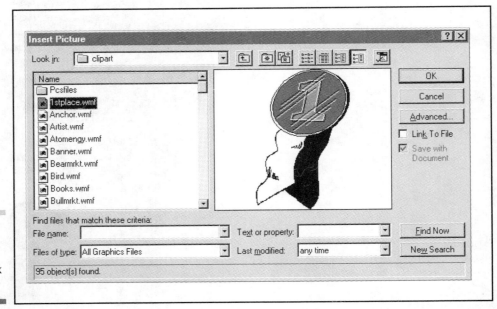

Select a picture to insert from this dialog box
Figure 14-1.

Note: The types of pictures that you can insert into your document depend on how Word is installed on your computer.

Let's try inserting a picture. Open the Biography of Sliding Billy Watson document, place the insertion point in front of the third paragraph, and select Picture from the Insert menu. Scroll the list and double-click on Theater.wmf. The graphic will appear in the document at the position of the insertion point, as shown in Figure 14-2. Use the Save As option from the File menu to save the document with the name Theater Picture.

You are not limited to inserting just the graphic files in the Clipart directory. Use the Look In list if the picture you want to insert is on another disk or in a different directory. For example, you may have created a picture with the Paint accessory and saved it on the desktop. To access the picture, pull down the Look In list and select Desktop.

You can also create the graphic in Paint, or some other application, copy it to the Clipboard, and then paste it into your document. After you copy the picture, switch to or open Word, and then click on the Paste button, or select Paste from the Edit menu.

Linking Files for Dynamic Graphics

14

You can use the Insert Picture dialog box to *link* the graphic file. Linking allows Word to replace the graphic in the document with the most recent

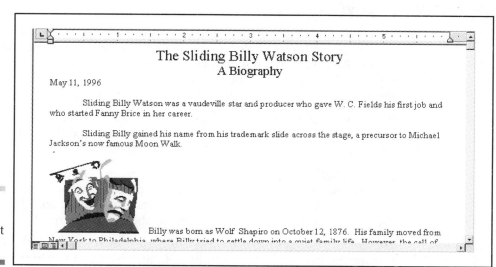

A picture
inserted into
your document
Figure 14-2.

version of it on the disk. For example, suppose you draw a picture in Paint and then insert it into your document. If you later change the picture in Paint, the original version will still appear in the document. By linking the picture, however, Word will be able to insert the edited version when you open or print the document. To link the picture, select it in the Insert Picture dialog box, and then click on the Link To File check box:

When you insert a picture, a complete copy of it is stored with your document. So if the picture file is 8,000 bytes large, your document will increase in size by that amount. If you select to link the picture, however, you can then deselect the Save with Document check box.

Now only the link will be saved in the document, rather than the entire picture itself. While your document will be smaller, Word will first have to retrieve the picture from the disk when you open the document. If you copy your document to a floppy disk, be sure to copy the graphic file as well.

Note: You'll learn more about linking documents in Chapter 20.

Inserting Clip Art

Microsoft Office comes with additional picture files as part of the ClipArt Gallery. The ClipArt Gallery is a program that helps you select and manage picture files. When you install Office, you must install the ClipArt Gallery as well as ClipArt graphics files. Both the ClipArt Gallery and the ClipArt files are in the Office Tools section of the Setup program.

If you've installed both the ClipArt Gallery and graphics, you can insert a picture by selecting Object from the Insert menu and then clicking on the Create New tab to display the dialog box page shown in Figure 14-3.

Double-click on Microsoft ClipArt Gallery in the Object Type list. The first time you select the Gallery, a dialog box may appear reporting that clip art files need to be added to the Gallery. Click on Add All, and then wait until the ClipArt Gallery window appears, as shown in Figure 14-4.

The Gallery divides pictures into categories, such as people, buildings, transportation, and U.S. maps. By default, the categories box is set at All

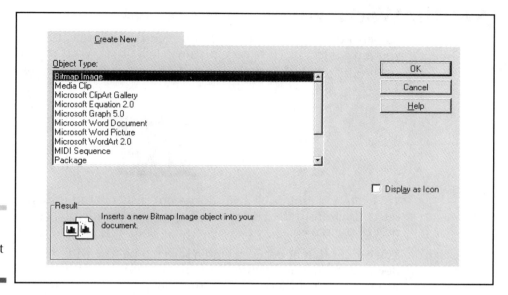

Selecting a
new graphic
object to insert
Figure 14-3.

Categories, so you can scroll the Pictures list to display thumbnail sketches
of all of the available pictures. If you are interested in a specific type of
picture, select it in the Categories list. Only pictures in that category will be
shown. Double-click on the picture that you want to insert, or select it and
click on Insert.

14

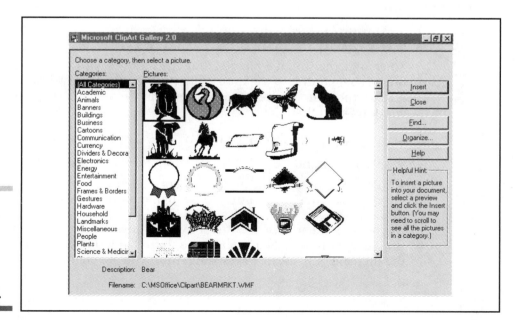

The ClipArt
Gallery
contains
pictures
divided into
categories
Figure 14-4.

Working with Pictures

To perform a function on a picture, such as to change its size or delete it, you must select it. To select a picture, click on it. Word will insert a border around the picture, as you can see here, with eight small boxes called *handles*.

To delete a picture from your document, select it and then press DELETE, or select Clear from the Edit menu. To deselect the picture, click in some other part of the screen.

The border that appears around a selected picture will not print with the document. To add a printable border around the picture, use the Borders toolbar or the Borders and Shading dialog box. For example, to enclose the picture in a box, select the picture and then click on the Outside Borders button. To enclose the picture in a shadow box, choose the Shadow option in the Borders and Shading dialog box.

Note: The "white" area around a picture in a box is opaque, so you cannot add a shading pattern to the picture background.

Changing the Size of Pictures

To change the size of a picture, drag the handles with the mouse. Point to one of the handles so the mouse pointer changes to a two-headed arrow—the same pointers that appear when you change the size of a window—and then drag:

♦   Drag the handle on the left or right side to change just the width.

♦   Drag the handle on the top or bottom to change just the height of the box.

♦   Drag a handle in one of the corners to change the height and width of the box while maintaining the original proportions.

As you drag the mouse, a dotted box will show the size of the picture, and the word "Scaling" will appear in the status bar along with the percentage of the increase or decrease of the dimension you are changing.

You can also crop the picture by holding down SHIFT as you drag a handle. Cropping doesn't change the size of the picture, just the amount of it that shows. When you crop a picture, the mouse pointer will look like this:

As you drag the mouse, the word "Cropping" will appear in the status bar, along with the area and amount being cropped. A negative number indicates you are adding white space around the picture box; a positive number means you are reducing the amount of space or the amount of the picture that shows. When you crop the picture smaller, you are not actually deleting the parts of the picture that no longer appear—you are just hiding it. If you later crop the picture by dragging the mouse away from the picture, you will again see more of the original picture.

Just to be sure you understand the difference between scaling and cropping a picture, here is a picture and how it appears scaled and cropped to the same size:

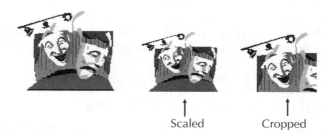

Scaled   Cropped

14

Changing Size with the Picture Dialog Box
You can also change the size of a selected picture and crop it by selecting Picture from the Format menu to see the dialog box shown in Figure 14-5. Enter a positive number in the Crop From section to crop smaller and a negative number to crop larger. As you change the crop setting, the height and width settings will adjust to show the resulting picture size.

Change the size of the picture using either the Scaling or Size settings. Use the Scaling text boxes to change the picture by percentages, for example, enter **200** to double one of the dimensions. Use the Size text boxes to enter a specific height or width.

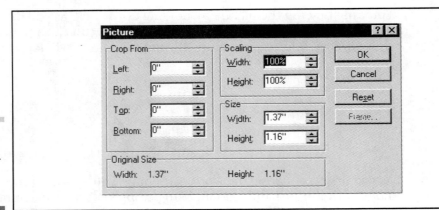

Use the
Picture dialog
box to scale or
crop a picture
Figure 14-5.

Tip: Click on Reset to return the picture to its original size.

Moving Pictures

You can move a picture within the document the same way you move text. Once you select the picture, you can use the Cut, Copy, and Paste commands to copy or move it. You can also drag and drop it with the mouse—remember to hold down CTRL when you release the mouse to copy the picture.

Introduction to Frames

A *frame* is a nonprintable box that you place around a picture so you can move it anywhere on the page—including into the margin area, below the endmark, even overlapping text and other pictures. Until you place a frame around a picture, you can only move it within text, to a location where you could place the insertion point. Once you insert a frame, you can move it anywhere, and even *wrap* text around it.

Let's insert a frame around the theater picture. Click on the picture to select it, and then choose Frame from the Insert menu. If you are in Normal view, a dialog box will appear asking if you want to change to Page Layout view. Select Yes since you can only work with frames in Page Layout view. As you can see, a frame of small diagonal lines appears around the picture:

Billy was born as Wolf Shapiro on October 12, 1876. His family moved from New York to Philadelphia, where Billy tried to settle down into a quiet family life. However, the call of the stage was too difficult for him to resist. He abandoned his wife and two children for the limelight and fame of vaudeville.

As a comedian, Billy worked his way up from a bit player to the lead role, but he gained most fame as both actor and producer in many popular vaudeville and burlesque

T ip: You can also click the right mouse button on the picture and select Frame Picture from the shortcut menu.

Now in Page Layout view you can move the picture anywhere. Point to the picture so the mouse pointer looks like a four-pointed arrow, then drag the picture to the desired location. Once you add a frame, text will flow around the picture, and you can move two or more framed pictures so they overlap. For example, drag the theater picture to the center of the page so text flows around it, as shown in Figure 14-6. Because pictures are not transparent, overlapping pictures will partially obscure each other.

In Normal view, framed objects always appear at the left margin of the page. To see the actual position of the frame, change to Page Layout view or Print Preview. Now save and close the document, and then click on New to open a blank document window.

14

When you frame a picture, you can move it anywhere in the text, and text will even flow around it
Figure 14-6.

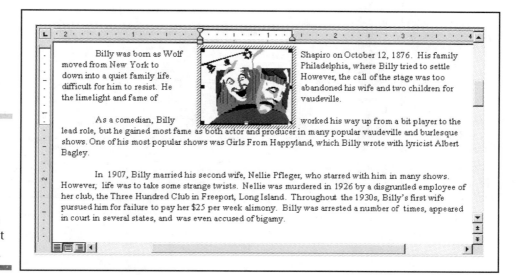

Note: White space added by cropping the picture is transparent.

Framing Text

You can insert a frame around text as well as a picture. As with a framed picture, you can drag and drop framed text anywhere in the document. Figure 14-7 shows how a text frame can be used to call attention to an important point and to add some visual interest to the page. The size of the frame changes automatically as you add or delete text within it, but changing the size of the frame does not change the size of the characters within it.

To surround text in a frame, select the text and then choose Frame from the Insert menu. Unlike the default frame around a picture which does not include a printable border, framed text is surrounded by a single-line border. You can enlarge the frame to add extra space around the text, but you cannot make the frame smaller than the text itself. If you select less than an entire paragraph, Word inserts the frame around the selected text and separates it from the remainder of the paragraph.

Use a text frame to call attention to certain text
Figure 14-7.

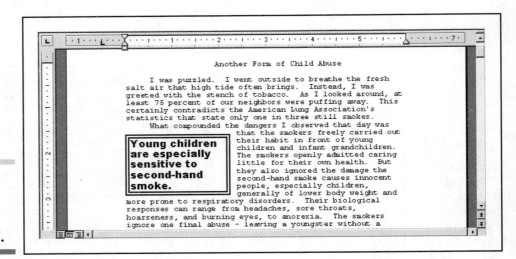

Note: You cannot crop a text frame.

The border only surrounds the text itself; it does not necessarily fit the entire frame. The size of the frame depends on how you selected the text. If you select a single line that ends with a paragraph mark, such as a title or a heading, both the frame and border only extend around the text.

 Note: In Normal view, the border around a single line will appear to extend across the page.

If you select a paragraph with lines ended by word wrap, and the text is indented from the left, the single-line border will only extend from the indentations, while the frame is from margin to margin:

> Sliding Billy Watson was a vaudeville star and producer who gave W. C. Fields his first job and who started Fanny Brice in her career.

14

Click on the text if you want to edit it. When you first click on the text, the frame appears but not the handles. To display the handles, point to the frame and then click the mouse.

You can format text within a frame just as any other text in a document. Selecting alignment options, however, affects the position of the text in the box, not in relation to the page. For example, selecting the Center button in the Formatting toolbar centers the text within the box, it does not center the box on the page. To center the frame, you must drag it into position or use the Frame dialog box discussed later.

Working with Frames

You can remove a frame if you no longer want it around a graphic or text. To remove the frame, select it and then choose Frame from the Format menu to display the dialog box shown in Figure 14-8. Click on Remove Frame and select OK. You can also display the Frame dialog box by clicking the right mouse button on the frame, then selecting Format Frame from the shortcut menu that appears.

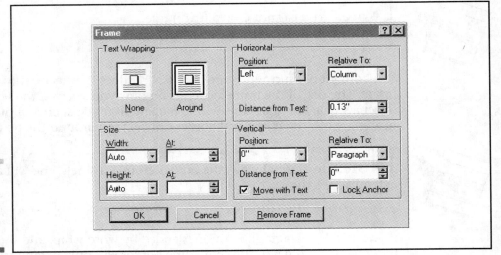

Use the Frame dialog box to remove or adjust a frame
Figure 14-8.

Caution: If you select a frame and then press DELETE, the frame and its contents will be deleted.

You can also use the Frame dialog box to control the placement, size, and effects of a frame. The Text Wrapping option determines how text flows around a frame. If you choose None, no text will appear next to the frame, just above and below it. If you select Around, text will appear around the sides of the frame as long as there is more than one inch between the frame and the margin.

Use the Size options to set the width and height of the frame. Enter a specific size or select Auto to make the frame just large enough for its contents.

The Horizontal options determine the position of the frame in relation to the edge of the paper, margin, or column, as selected in the Relative To list. You can enter an exact position or select from Left, Right, Center, Inside, or Outside. To center the frame between the left and right edges of the paper, for example, select Center from the Position list and select Page from the Relative To list. The Distance From Text setting determines the space between the left and right edges of the frame and any text flowing around it—the default setting is .13 inches.

The Vertical options determine the position of the frame in relation to the top or bottom edge of the page, margins, or paragraph. You can enter an exact position, or select Top, Bottom, or Center relative to the margin or page. You can also specify the spacing between the top and bottom edges of the frame to text.

The Move with Text and Lock Anchor settings determine how the frame will move as you add, delete, or move text. A frame is attached, or *anchored*, to its nearest paragraph. To see which paragraph the frame is attached to, click on the Show/Hide button in the toolbar and then select the frame. You'll see a small anchor symbol next to the attached paragraph:

→ Billy·was·born·as·Wolf·Shapiro·on·October·12,·1876.··His·family·
moved·from·New·York·to·Philadelphia,·where·Billy·tried·to·settle·down·into·a·
quiet·family·life.··However,·the·call·of·the·stage·was·too·difficult·for·him·to·
resist.··He·abandoned·his·wife·and·two·children·for·the·limelight·and·fame·of·
vaudeville.¶
¶
→ As·a·comedian,·Billy·worked·his·way·up·from·a·bit·player·to·the·lead·

If editing moves the paragraph to another page, the anchored frame will move along with the text. To keep the frame in the same position, regardless of where the text appears, deselect the Move with Text check box. When you want to ensure that the frame remains anchored to the same paragraph, select the Lock Anchor check box. When you display the anchor, an icon of a padlock appears along with it, indicating that the anchor is locked.

Tip: To attach the frame to another paragraph, unlock the anchor, and then drag the anchor icon to the new paragraph.

Pictures, Text, and Frames

When you insert a frame around a selected graphic, the frame and the graphic are the same size. You cannot select the graphic and frame separately because they are treated as one object, and because pictures are opaque, you cannot add a shade within the frame. However, you can create a text frame and then insert a graphic into it.

Create the frame by inserting it around existing text or by drawing a blank text frame. To draw a blank text frame, make sure that nothing is selected in the document, and then choose Frame from the Insert menu. The mouse pointer will change to a small plus sign, and you will be asked if you want to change to Page Layout view if you are not yet in it. Now drag the mouse in the document to create a rectangle the size of the frame you want. When you release the mouse, an empty frame will appear with the insertion point ready for you to enter text. Now type some text. If you do not want any text in the frame, type something anyway; otherwise the frame will adjust automatically to the size of the picture that you insert. With the insertion point still in the frame, insert a picture.

You will now be able to select the picture separately from the frame itself. Since you can select them individually, you can create a separate border around each. You can also add shading or patterns to the area within the frame that is not occupied by the picture. Select the frame, not the picture, and then choose a shading option so the shading appears around the picture, as illustrated here.

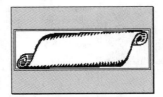

Special Effects with Microsoft's WordArt

Word provides several ways for you to create your own graphics. With Microsoft's WordArt you can create special graphic effects from TrueType fonts, to use a logo, heading, or just as an eye-catching graphic. You can form text into slants, curves, and even buttons. You can fill characters with colors and patterns, and add outlines and shadows. You can also rotate text to give the impression of portrait and landscape text on the same page. For example, here are just some of the effects that you can create with WordArt:

To start WordArt, choose Object from the Insert menu, click on the Create New tab, and then double-click on Microsoft WordArt 2.0. A dialog box appears in which you enter the text that you want to format, and the WordArt toolbar replaces the other toolbars already on the screen, as shown in Figure 14-9. Table 14-1 lists the functions of the WordArt Toolbar buttons.

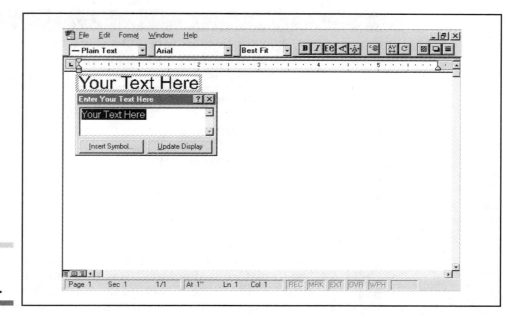

The WordArt
screen
Figure 14-9.

14

Button	Function
— Plain Text	Select a shape to form the text.
Arial	Choose a font.
Best Fit	Choose a font size, or select Best Fit to fit the text to the box size.
B	Make the text bold.
I	Make the text italic.
Ee	Format all of the characters as the same size regardless of their case.
◁	Rotate the text on its side.
⁺Ａ⁻	Expand the text to fit within the box.
ᶜ≡	Determine how the text aligns in the box—the options are center, left, right, stretch, justify, letter justify, and word justify.

The WordArt
Toolbar
Buttons
Table 14-1.

Button	Function
AV ↔	Adjust the spacing between characters—options are very tight, tight, normal, loose, very loose, and custom. You can also choose to kern pairs of characters.
↻	Rotate and slant the text.
▨	Select patterns and colors for text.
◲	Select a shadow pattern.
≡	Select a border thickness and color to outline the characters.

The WordArt
Toolbar
Buttons
(*continued*)
Table 14-1.

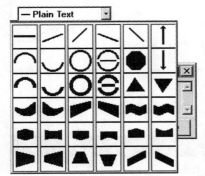

In the Enter Your Text Here box, type the text that you want to format using WordArt. To enter a symbol or special character in the text, click on the Insert Symbol button, and then select the font and character from the dialog box that appears. Next, pull down the Shape list, shown here, and select the shape that you want the text to take.

Choose a font and size for the text, or leave the size set at Best Fit to have WordArt fit the text in the box for you, and add any special effects using the other toolbar buttons. Figure 14-10, for example, shows a WordArt graphic using a fill pattern, border, and shadow effect. As you enter text and select options, the WordArt graphic will appear in the box on the screen. When you create just the effect that you want, click outside of the dialog box to restore the Word screen and display the WordArt graphic. You can change the size and shape of the WordArt graphic, and add a frame or border just as you can for an inserted picture.

Remember: If the image does not change to match your selections, click on Update Display in the dialog box.

If you want to edit the text of the WordArt graphic, or change any of its effects, double-click on the graphic, or click the right mouse button on it and choose Edit WordArt 2.0 from the shortcut menu. WordArt will start, displaying the text in the Enter Your Text Here box. Make any changes that you want, and then click outside of the dialog box to return to Word.

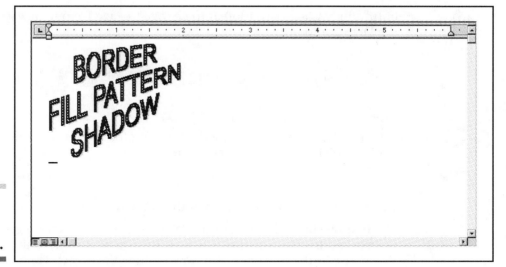

A sample
WordArt
graphic
Figure 14-10.

Now try to recreate this WordArt graphic:

Select Microsoft WordArt 2.0 from the Insert Object dialog box. In the
WordArt dialog box, type **Romeo** and press ENTER. Type **and**, press ENTER
again, and type **Juliet**. Now pull down the Style list and select one of the
three-line button formats.

Now on your own, experiment with the shadow, fill, outline, and other
buttons to see how artistic you can be! When you're done, click outside of
the WordArt window to insert the graphic into the document.

14

Creating and Editing Drawings

You know that you can create a drawing in the Paint accessory and then
paste or insert it into your document, but you can also draw directly on the
Word screen. Word includes a set of basic drawing tools that let you create
freehand and geometric objects. To create a drawing, click on the Drawing

button in the Standard toolbar to change to Page Layout view and display the Drawing toolbar:

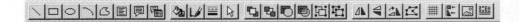

 Tip: You can also display the Drawing toolbar by selecting it from the Toolbars dialog box or shortcut menu.

Table 14-2 shows the functions of the Drawing toolbar buttons.

The first five buttons on the left of the toolbar let you create geometric objects and freehand shapes. Click on the tool you want to use, then drag the mouse in the document window to draw the object. Hold down SHIFT while you drag to draw a straight line with the line tool, a square with the rectangle tool, and a circle with the ellipse tool. When you release the mouse button, the object will appear with handles, so you can move the object or change its size.

Button	Function
＼	Draw lines.
▢	Draw rectangles or squares.
○	Draw ellipses or circles.
＼	Draw arcs.
⬠	Create free-form objects.
▤	Create text boxes.
▦	Create callouts.
▤	Format the appearance of callouts.
▨	Select a fill color or pattern.
▨	Select a line color.
▤	Select a line and arrowhead style.

The Drawing Toolbar Buttons
Table 14-2.

Button	Function
	Select objects.
	Bring an object to the front of another drawing object.
	Send an object behind another drawing object.
	Bring an object to the front of text.
	Send an object to the back of text.
	Combine selected objects into a group.
	Ungroup a group, changing its members back to individual objects.
	Flip an object along its horizontal axis.
	Flip an object along its vertical axis.
	Rotate an object counterclockwise in 90-degree increments.
	Change the shape of a free-form object.
	Control snap-to-grid and the size and origin of the grid pattern.
	Align drawing objects in relation to the page or each other.
	Create a picture.
	Insert a frame.

The Drawing Toolbar Buttons (*continued*)
Table 14-2.

14

You can move a drawing object anywhere on the page, even though it is not in a frame. When you release the mouse button, the drawing tool is turned off, so it no longer appears pressed down. This means that to draw a second object of the same type, you have to click on the button again.

The Text Box tool lets you create boxes similar to a framed paragraph. The difference is that the text box can overlap other text and objects on the page. To use the tool, click on it, then drag the mouse to form a rectangle the size you want. Release the mouse button and type the text in the rectangle. Text boxes have a default single-line border, but you can change that with the Borders toolbar or Borders and Shading dialog box. Text boxes do not automatically increase in size as you enter text—to display more text, you must select and enlarge the box.

A callout is similar to a text box, but includes a line pointing to some other object, as shown here.

To create the callout box, click on the Callout button, point to where you want the callout line to begin, and then drag the mouse to where you want to type the note or reference. Release the mouse and then type the text of the callout. To change the appearance of the callout box or line, select the callout and click on the Format Callout button. A dialog box will appear in which you can change the type of line, choose the distance between the line and the text, and choose a border to go around the text.

The toolbar contains buttons that let you change the type and color of lines and the fill color or shade of objects. Clicking on the Fill Color, Line Color, or Line Style button will display options from which to choose. Your choices will affect any selected drawing object, and they will remain in effect for new objects until you change them again.

In order to change the size, position, or characteristics of an object, you must select it. To select an object, point to it so the mouse pointer looks like an arrow with a four-directional pointer, then click the mouse button. You can then drag the object to a new position, drag the handles to change its size, or choose fill and color options from the Drawing toolbar. To select several objects at one time, hold down SHIFT while you click on each object. You can also click on the Select Drawing Objects button, and then drag the pointer to form a box around the objects.

Working with Layers and Groups

Imagine the screen as being several pieces of clear plastic layered over each other. When you draw an object that overlaps another, it appears on the top layer, obscuring text or another object. The layering buttons let you control how drawing objects and text overlap each other. To move one drawing object under another, select the object and click on the Send to Back button. The selected object will be moved to the bottom layer. Here's how the same two objects appear when layered differently:

Use the Bring to Front button to move an object from the background to the foreground.

The Move to Back and Bring to Front buttons only affect the order of drawing objects. To move an object under the text—so the text can be read on top of an object—select the object and click on the Send Behind Text button. Click on the Bring in Front of Text button to return the object to the top layer, above the text. Here are examples of both:

Tip: The layering commands are available in the shortcut menu that appears when you click the right mouse button on a drawing object.

If you draw several objects to create a picture, you can group them into one composite object. As a group, you can select the entire picture with one click of the mouse to move the picture or to change the size and color of the entire drawing. To group a number of objects, select them all and then click on the Group button. To later break down the group into its original individual objects, select the group and click on the Ungroup button.

14

Aligning Objects

Word uses a grid pattern to help you position objects. The grid is an invisible series of evenly spaced horizontal and vertical lines 0.1 inch apart. When you draw an object, it will automatically start and end on a grid line, so every object that you create is in some increment of 0.1 inches. This process is called *snap-to-grid*. To change the spacing of the grid pattern, or to turn off snap-to-grid, click on the Snap to Grid button to display this dialog box:

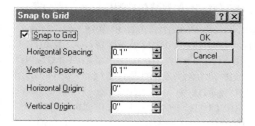

Deselect the Snap to Grid check box, or change the Horizontal Spacing and Vertical Spacing settings for a custom grid pattern. Use the Horizontal and

Vertical Origin settings to determine the starting point of the grid pattern from the left and top edge of the page.

Tip: To turn snap-to-grid on or off as you draw, hold ALT as you drag the mouse.

Even with the grid pattern, it is often difficult to align objects by dragging them. For example, you might want to align objects so their tops are even, or so they are perfectly centered over each other. To align objects with each other, or in relation to the page, select the objects and then click on the Align Drawing Objects button to display the dialog box you see here.

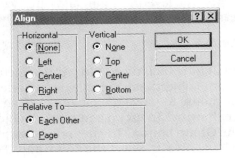

When only one object is selected, the Relative To Page option will be on by default. Select the horizontal and vertical position for the object, and then select OK. For example, to place an object in the exact center of the page, choose Center in both the Horizontal and Vertical sections. When you have more than one object selected, the Relative To Each Other option will be selected. Choose the horizontal and vertical position of the objects in relation to each other.

Creating Pictures

The Create Picture button lets you draw a picture in a separate window, rather than directly on your document. Click on the Create Picture button to display the Drawing toolbar and a drawing area, as shown in Figure 14-11. Use the Drawing toolbar to create your picture within the borders of the drawing box. If you want to create a larger picture, draw or drag objects outside of the box and then click on the Reset Boundary button. When you are finished drawing, click on the Close button to insert the picture in your document.

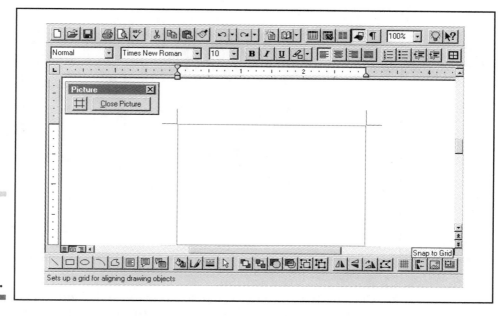

You can
create a
picture in
the drawing
window
Figure 14-11.

The picture is inserted as a single unit, just like a graphic that you insert using the Insert Picture command. It is inserted into the text layer, and like other pictures, you must enclose it in a frame to move it freely within the document. Because the picture is a single unit, you cannot edit its individual drawing objects from within the document. To edit the picture, you must double-click on it to return to the drawing window.

The Insert Frame button will place a frame around a selected picture or drawing object. Once you frame a drawing created directly on your document, however, Word converts the drawing to a picture. You can then only edit it in the drawing window, even if you later remove the frame. You will no longer be able to change it with the Drawing toolbar, and it cannot be layered in relation to the text and other drawing objects.

Editing Drawing Formats

In addition to formatting objects using the Drawing toolbar, you can format them using a dialog box. Double-click on a drawing object, or select it and choose Drawing Object from the Format menu, to see the dialog box shown in Figure 14-12. The box has three tabs.

14

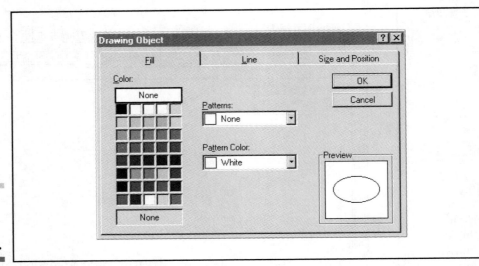

The Drawing
Object dialog
box
Figure 14-12.

◆ Click on the *Line* tab to change the color, style, and thickness of lines; to create a shadow box; to round the corners of rectangles, text boxes, and callouts; and to add arrow heads to the end of lines.

◆ Click on the *Fill* tab to change the fill pattern and color.

◆ Click on the *Size and Position* tab to change the size and position of an object, to adjust the margin between a text box and the text within the box, and to anchor objects to text.

Remember: Changes you make in the Format Drawing Object dialog box will affect the selected object and every new object that you draw.

Pictures, clip art, WordArt, and drawings can help give your documents a professional look. Imagine how your own documents can be improved, and then practice using the techniques that you learned in this chapter. Just don't overdo it. Make sure the graphics relate to the text or supplement it in some meaningful way.

Desktop Publishing

15

...s and graphics can certainly add pizzazz to a document, but you can
...e your documents even further. Columns, captions, drop caps, graphs,
...ations help give your document that published look. When you
...ome Word with a high-quality printer, your capabilities are almost limitless.

Creating Columns

Try using Word's Newsletter Wizard to create a newsletter complete with banner headlines, columns, and graphics.

Newsletters, annual reports, and other published documents may be
formatted in columns, with text flowing from one column to the next on
the page, from left to right. Columns make a document look special, yet
with Word they are easy to create. Once you tell Word the number of
columns you want, it will take care of the text flow for you. As you insert or
delete text, Word shifts text from column to column, or from page to page,
as necessary.

As always, Word has the flexibility to create columns in several ways. You
can type and edit your text in one column across the page, then format it in
columns when you are ready. You can also create the column layout first
and then type your text. You can create columns with the toolbar or from a
dialog box. No matter how you create columns, however, you can always
change their size, spacing, and number.

Using the Toolbar to Create Columns

Columns that you create with the toolbar affect the current section. So if
your document is not divided into sections, all of it will be affected. Before
creating columns, place the insertion point where you want the columns to
begin and then enter a section break. For example, suppose you want to type
some single-column text to be followed by two columns, as shown in Figure
15-1. Type the single-column text, or if you've already typed it, place the
insertion point after it. Then select Break from the Insert menu, choose
Continuous, and then click on OK to insert a section break without a page
break. You can now format the new section into multiple columns without
affecting the single-column text on the page.

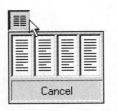

To create columns, pull down the Columns button on
the toolbar to see an illustration of four columns and
the word Cancel.

If you change your mind about the columns, click
anywhere in the document window or click on Cancel.
To create columns, click on the column in the diagram
that represents the number of columns you want. For
example, to create two columns, click on the second column in the diagram.

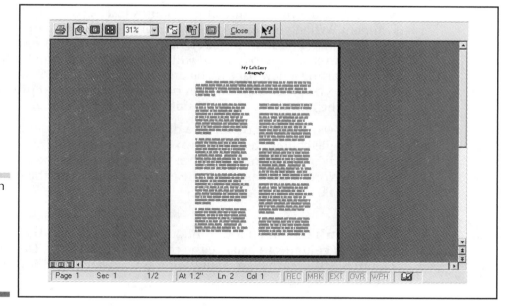

Single-column text followed by two columns requires two sections

Figure 15-1.

Tip: To create five or six columns, drag the mouse beyond the fourth column and then release the mouse button.

The column layout will be created when you release the mouse button. The ruler will show the width of each column and the spacing between them, in much the same way it indicates the space between table columns.

15

Remember: If you change your mind while you're still holding down the mouse button, drag the mouse up into the toolbar or menu bar, and then release the mouse button.

Typing Columns

If you create columns for a section of existing text, all of the text in the section will flow from column to column and from page to page. You will only see the columns side-by-side in Page Layout view and in Print Preview. In Normal view, the columns will appear under each other, separated by a column break line.

Type, edit, and format your text in columns just as you would for any document. When you reach the bottom of one column, Word will begin the next column. If you want to start a new column before filling the current one, press CTRL-SHIFT-ENTER. Word will move the insertion point to the next column, starting a new page if you are on the rightmost column. If you press CTRL-SHIFT-ENTER when the insertion point is in existing text, the text following the insertion point will shift to the next column.

When you want to start typing in a different number of columns, such as to enter single-column text after two columns, insert another continuous section break, pull down the column button, and select the number of columns. Word will balance out the existing columns on the page above the section break.

Remember: Insert a continuous section break after the text on the last page of columns to balance the columns on that page. Do not insert a column break after the last column unless you want the following text to start on a new page.

Changing Column Width

You change the width of columns, and the amount of space between them, by dragging the gray area in the ruler that indicates the space between columns. When you point to the area, the mouse pointer will appear as a two-headed arrow. To create columns of unequal width while retaining the same space between them, drag the gray area by the cross-hatching in the center:

Tip: Hold down ALT while you drag to display column and spacing dimensions in the ruler.

To change the width of columns as well as the space between them, drag one of the lines on the left or right of the gray area, as shown here.

Dragging a line toward the cross-hatching will decrease the space between the columns while increasing the width of the column on that side. Dragging a line away from the cross-hatching will increase the space between columns while decreasing the width of the column. For example, drag the line on the left to widen the space between columns, making the column on the left narrower.

Upgrader: In previous versions of Word, columns created with the toolbar were always equal width, and there was no cross-hatching in the gray area. Unless you changed the setting in the Columns dialog box, you could only drag the gray area to change the spacing between columns—the width of all of the columns would change equally.

In Page Layout view, you can drag the left or right margin boundary to change the width of the columns and their position on the page.

Using the Dialog Box to Create Columns

If you want to create more than six columns, create columns without manually inserting a section break, or specify an exact column width and spacing, then select Columns from the Format menu to see the dialog box shown in Figure 15-2.

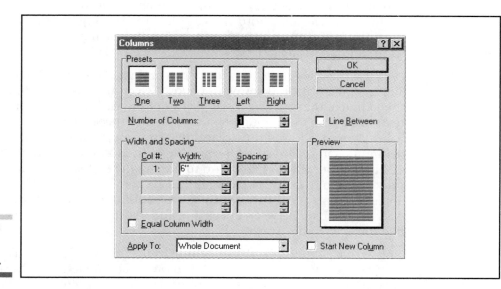

The Columns dialog box
Figure 15-2.

15

As you select options and enter measurements in the dialog box, the graphic in the Preview panel will change to illustrate the column layout. Select the number of columns and their spacing, and then select an option from the Apply To section. Choosing This Point Forward will insert a continuous section break so you can combine column layouts within a document, even on one page. Select Whole Document to apply the style to the entire document, or choose This Section—if it is an option in the list—to apply the layout to the current section.

Select the Line Between check box to insert a vertical line between the columns.

Tip: Click on Start New Column, and select This Point Forward in the Apply To section, to move the text following the insertion point to the top of the next column.

Equal Width Columns

To create columns of equal width, click on the Two or Three preset option, or select the Equal Column Width check box and enter a number in the Number of Columns box. To modify the width of the columns, or the spacing between them, enter a measurement in the Width and Spacing section. When you select Equal Column Width, only the first column will be active; the others will be dimmed.

When you set the width of the first column, all of the columns will change to the same size, and Word will calculate the spacing to fit the columns on the page. If you enter a measurement for the spacing, Word will adjust the width automatically.

Let's use the dialog box now to create columns. Open the Biography of Sliding Billy Watson document, choose Select All from the Edit menu, and then change the font size to 16. (Without increasing the size or adding extra text, there won't be enough text to flow into the second column.) Change to Page Layout view, and then place the insertion point at the left margin— before the tab space—at the beginning of the second paragraph. Now select Columns from the Format menu to display the dialog box. Click on the Two preset option to create two equal-sized columns. Pull down the Apply To list and select This Point Forward to insert a continuous section break. Finally, click on the Line Between check box and select OK. Your columns will look like those in Figure 15-3.

Notice that there is no cross-hatching in the gray area in the ruler. When you set equal width columns you can only drag the left or right side of the area to increase or decrease the gutter size. All of the columns in the section,

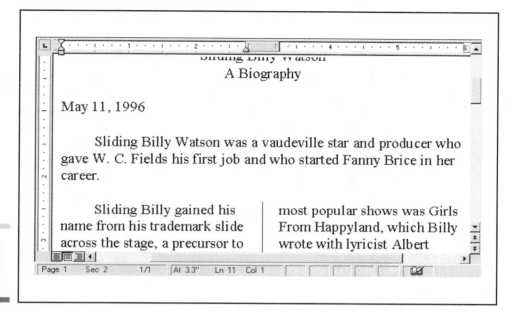

Adding a line between columns
Figure 15-3.

however, will adjust so they are all the same width. If you have three or more columns, as you increase or decrease one gutter, the others will change as well. In Figure 15-4, for example, I've increased the gutter width by one inch, reducing both of the equal-sized columns by a half-inch.

Close the document without saving the changes, and then start a new blank document.

Uneven Columns

To create columns of different widths, click on the Left or Right preset option in the Columns dialog box. Alternatively, you can deselect the Equal Column Width check box and enter a number in the Number of Columns box, and then enter dimensions in the Width and Spacing section. Changing the width of one column will affect the size of the columns to its right while maintaining the same spacing.

Graphics in Columns

Pictures, drawings, and WordArt can be quite effective in columns. Insert a frame around the graphic so you can move it freely within the document. You can also use the Format Frame dialog box to set the position of the frame relative to a column, or columns. When you display the dialog box, the Relative To option in the Horizontal section will be set at Column.

15

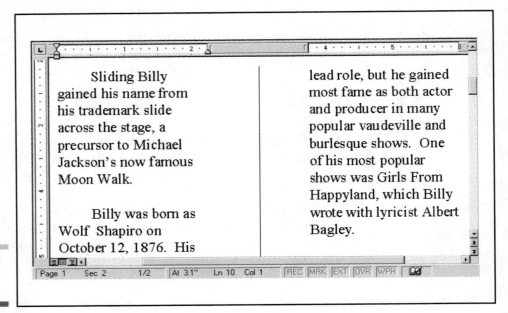

Sliding Billy gained his name from his trademark slide across the stage, a precursor to Michael Jackson's now famous Moon Walk.

Billy was born as Wolf Shapiro on October 12, 1876. His

lead role, but he gained most fame as both actor and producer in many popular vaudeville and burlesque shows. One of his most popular shows was Girls From Happyland, which Billy wrote with lyricist Albert Bagley.

Increasing the gutter width
Figure 15-4.

Pull down the Position list and choose Left, Center, or Right to determine the position of the graphic within the column. If your document has two columns, center the graphic between them by choosing Page or Margins in the Relative To list and Center in the Position list. Figure 15-5, for example, shows a picture centered in one column and a WordArt graphic centered between columns.

Adding Captions

You can also create a table of figures, equations, illustrations, and tables, similar to a table of contents. See Chapter 17 for more information.

Whether you are typing text in one column or multiple columns, you may have a number of pictures, drawings, tables, or charts in a long document. If you want to refer to a graphic in the text, such as "As you can see in Chart 2," or if you just want to identify the graphic, you may decide to add captions.

Before inserting a caption, you should first place a frame around the graphic. If you add a caption to an unframed object, the caption will appear near the object but it will not be connected to it. So, for example, you could move a picture to another location in the document without moving its caption. When you insert a caption in a framed picture, the caption will move with the frame.

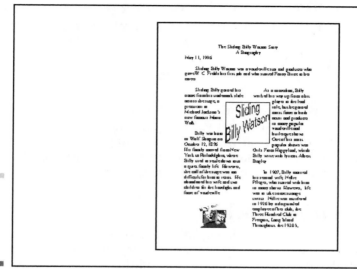

Using
graphics and
WordArt in
columns
Figure 15-5.

Tip: If you insert a caption before adding a frame, select the unframed object and the caption, and then select Frame from the Insert menu. The frame will now include the object and the caption.

To insert a caption, select the frame and then choose Caption from the Insert menu. You will see the dialog box shown here.

15

Pull down the Label list and select the label that you want to appear in the caption—your choices are Equation, Figure, Illustration, and Table.

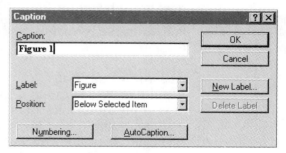

In the Caption box, add any other text that you want to appear along with the label and caption number, and then pull down the Position list to select a location—either Above Selected Item or Below Selected Item.

Select OK to insert the caption. Word automatically numbers the captions in sequence. The first object labeled Illustration will be numbered 1, the second will be numbered 2, and so on. Each label name—Illustration, Figure, Table, and Equation—will have a separate sequence.

Remember: If you delete or insert captions, make certain that Word updates the numbers of those remaining. Choose Select All from the Edit menu and then press F9.

If you insert a caption in the picture's frame, you can then select just the picture or just the frame separately, as you learned in Chapter 14. So you can add a separate border around each, and add shading or a pattern to the area within the frame that is not occupied by the picture, as shown here.

Figure 1 Theater Masks

Customizing Labels

If none of Word's built-in labels suit you, you can create your own labels, and even customize the way Word numbers captions. To create your own label, display the Captions dialog box and then click on the New Label button. Type the name for the label in the dialog box that appears and then select OK. You can now select that label from the Labels list. If you want to delete the label from the list, select it and click on the Delete Label button.

You cannot delete the built-in labels, Figure, Equation, and Table.

To customize the way Word numbers the captions, click on Numbering to display the dialog box shown here.

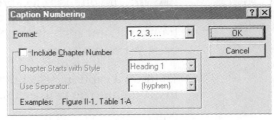

Pull down the Format list and select the type of number you want added to the current label.

Automatic Captions

If you want to add captions to all of your pictures, tables, or other graphics, you can have Word insert them automatically. This way, you do not need to select the object and insert the caption yourself—Word will insert the caption as soon as you insert the object. To turn on this feature, select AutoCaption in the Caption dialog box. You will see the options shown here.

The Add Caption When Inserting list contains the various types of objects that you can insert in a Word document. For each of the items that you want Word to caption, select its check box and then choose the label and position. Use the New Label and Numbering buttons to create your own label or numbering scheme. Select OK to return to the Captions dialog box, and then select OK to return to the document.

Chapter Numbering

The Caption Numbering dialog box also lets you select the Include Chapter Number check box to number objects by chapter. For example, the first figure in chapter 1 would be labeled "Figure 1-1"; the third table in chapter 5 would be "Table 5-3". This is very much like the option to number pages by chapter in the Page Numbering Format dialog box. In order to number captions and pages by chapter, however, you need to do two things—use heading styles and turn on automatic heading numbering.

Word needs to know when one chapter ends and the next begins. By default, Word assumes that each chapter begins with a title formatted with the Heading 1 style. So for instance, Word would assume that all of the text and pages between the first and second Heading 1 styles belong in chapter 1. The text between the second and third Heading 1 style would be in chapter 2. Get the idea?

Refer to Chapter 9 to refresh your memory about page numbering.

However, using heading styles is not enough. In order to number captions and pages by chapters, you must first apply automatic heading numbers. Heading numbering inserts numbers in titles and headings in much the same way a numbered list inserts numbers in paragraphs. Turn on this feature by selecting Heading Numbering from the Format menu to display the dialog box you see here.

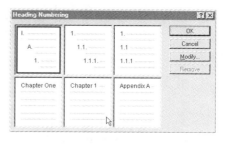

15

Select the style you want to apply, or choose Modify to change a style using techniques similar to customizing a numbered list. If you select either of the three multilevel options, Word will number—or letter—the text according to the heading style number. If you select either of the last three styles, Word will number Heading 1 as chapters. The first text formatted by the Heading 1 style, for example, would be labeled Chapter One, Chapter 1, or Appendix A. The next text formatted by the Heading 1 style would be labeled Chapter Two, Chapter 2, or Appendix B.

When you've done both of these things—used heading styles and turned on Heading Numbering—the Caption Numbering dialog box will display the options for turning on chapter numbering for captions and pages.

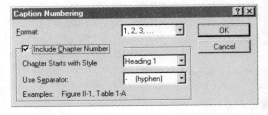

Select the Include Chapter Number check box, and then choose a separator character to use for the number. The default will display numbers with a hyphen, for example, 1-2, and 2-3; but you can also select a period, color, en dash (–) or em dash (—).

If you select any of the three multilevel heading numbering types—the ones without the word "Chapter" or "Appendix"—then you can select another heading style to designate the change in chapters.

Because there are several steps involved when using chapter numbering, let's practice. Pull down the Style list in the toolbar, select Heading 1, and then type **My Childhood.** Press ENTER twice, select Heading 1 again, and type **School Years**. Press ENTER twice, select Heading 1, type **College Years**, and press ENTER twice. Now turn on heading numbers. Select Heading Numbering from the Format menu, click on the Chapter 1 option, and then click on OK. Word will number your chapter titles, like this:

Chapter 1 My Childhood

Chapter 2 School Years

Chapter 3 College Years

Next, add several captions using chapter numbering. Place the insertion point in a blank line following the first heading and select Caption from the Insert menu. Pull down the Label list and select Figure. Now, click on Numbering, select the Include Chapter Number option, and then click on OK twice. In the same way, enter captions under Chapter 2 and Chapter 3. The captions will look like this:

Chapter 1 My Childhood

Figure 1-1

Chapter 2 School Years

Figure 2-1

Chapter 3 College Years

Figure 3-1|

Now close the document without saving it.

Creating Drop Caps

A nice finishing touch for a professional-looking document is a
drop capital, or *drop cap*. A drop capital is a large initial letter or letters
that begin a paragraph:

S liding Billy Watson was a vaudeville star and producer who gave W. C. Fields his first job and who started Fanny Brice in her career. Sliding Billy gained his name from his trademark slide across the stage, a precursor to Michael Jackson's now famous Moon Walk.

To create a drop cap, select the letter or letters that you want to use, and
then select Drop Cap from the Format menu to see the dialog box shown here.

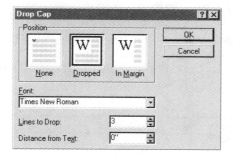

Tip: To create a drop cap from the first letter in a paragraph, you can
place the insertion point to its immediate left before selecting Drop Cap
from the menu.

Now select your options from the dialog box and select OK:

♦ Select the *Dropped* position to place the letter within the paragraph,
   or select the *In Margin* position to place the letter in the margin area.

♦ Select a font from the *Font* list if you want to format the drop capital in a
   font other than the one already used for the text.

♦ In the *Lines to Drop* text box, enter the number of lines high you want
   the letter to be.

♦ Set the distance of the letter from the text in the *Distance to Text* box.

If you are in working Normal view, a dialog box will appear asking if you want to change to Page Layout view—select Yes in order to see the drop capital. Word inserts the drop cap in a frame, so you can adjust its size and position by dragging.

Creating Charts and Graphs

Upgrader: Microsoft Graph uses a new interface that resembles the version of Graph shipped with Microsoft PowerPoint and other applications.

In Chapter 13, you learned how to display text and numbers in a table. Sometimes, however, numbers can have even more impact when presented as a chart or graph, as shown in Figure 15-6. A reader can often see a trend with just one glance at a chart, instead of trying to interpret numbers presented in a table or explained in text. Word lets you create bar, line, pie, and other types of charts—both two- and three-dimensional—and inserts them into your document. You can enter the information for the chart directly in the Graph application, or you can use information already entered into a Word table.

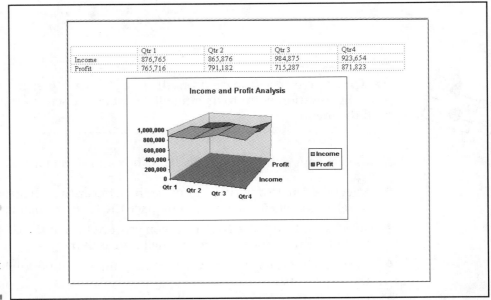

Charts and graphs can add impact to your document
Figure 15-6.

To create a chart entirely from the Graph application, select Object from the Insert menu, and then double-click on Microsoft Graph 5.0. You'll see the chart window with a default sample chart and data, as shown in Figure 15-7. The window also contains the Graph menu bar and toolbar. The File, Window, and Help menu items contain the same options as those in a document window. Table 15-1 shows the new functions available in the Edit and other menus. Table 15-2 shows the functions of the toolbar.

Upgrader: The Insert Chart button (from Word for Windows 6.0) no longer appears in the Standard toolbar. You can always insert the button yourself, as explained in Chapter 24.

The application actually contains two windows—the chart (or graph) and the datasheet. In the datasheet you enter the information that you want to chart. To delete all of the sample information from the table, click on the box in the top left corner to select the entire datasheet, and then press DELETE. The datasheet is just like a spreadsheet, but you enter the row headings in the column to the left of column A, and enter column headings in the row above row 1. Use the other rows and columns for the numeric values that you want to graph. As you enter data into the datasheet, Word will create the chart in the background.

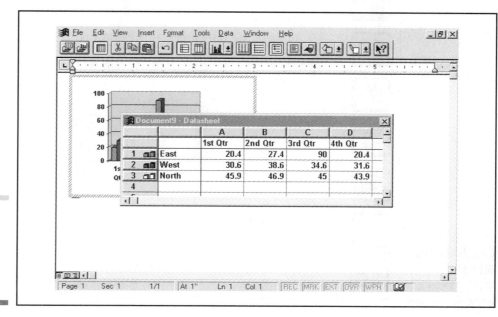

15

The Graph application starts with sample information

Figure 15-7.

Menu Item	Function
Edit	Import data or a chart from a spreadsheet program
View	Switch between the datasheet and chart, select toolbars, and zoom the display
Insert	Add cells, titles, data labels, a legend, axis labels, grid lines, and trend lines
Format	Format the appearance of text and chart elements, the column width, chart type, and 3-D view
Tools	Display options for selecting default colors and chart type, to allow drag and drop of cells, and to move the insertion point to a new cell when you press ENTER
Data	Display data series from row or column information and include or exclude specific rows or columns

Menu Options in Microsoft Graph
Table 15-1.

Button	Function
	Import data from a spreadsheet
	Import a chart from a spreadsheet program
	View the datasheet or the chart (this is a toggle)
	Cut
	Copy
	Paste
	Undo
	Create data series from rows

The Microsoft Graph Toolbar Buttons
Table 15-2.

Button	Function
	Create data series from columns
	Select the chart type
	Turn on or off vertical grid lines
	Turn on or off horizontal grid lines
	Turn on or off the legend
	Create a text box
	Display the Drawing toolbar for drawing on the chart
	Choose a color for chart objects
	Choose a pattern for chart objects

The Microsoft
Graph Toolbar
Buttons
(*continued*)
Table 15-2.

15

To display the chart in the foreground, click on the View Datasheet button. Then select options from the menu bar or toolbar to format the chart as you want it to appear in the document. When you're done, click outside of the chart to return to the document. The chart will appear as a graphic object, so you can add a border, insert a frame, and change its size and position. To edit the chart itself, double-click on it to return to the Graph application.

Experiment with the menu bar and tool bar in the Graph application on your own to learn more about creating charts. You can select or change the type of chart by selecting an option from the Graph Type list pulled down from the Microsoft Graph toolbar. Two-dimensional charts are on the left side of the list; three-dimensional types on the right. For each type of chart, you can also choose from predefined formats. Choose AutoFormat from the Format menu, for example, to display the dialog box shown in Figure 15-8.

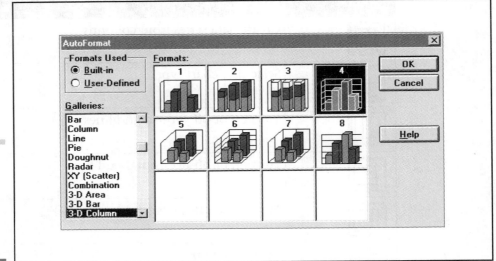

AutoFormat lets you choose from a number of predefined chart formats
Figure 15-8.

As you pick a chart type in the Galleries list, subtypes of it will appear in the Formats list. You can also choose a subtype and customize a chart by selecting Chart Type from the Format menu and then clicking on Options. To customize the rotation, elevation, and other aspects of a three-dimensional chart, choose 3-D View from the Format menu to see the dialog box shown in Figure 15-9.

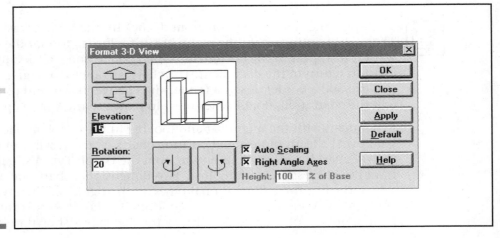

You can fine-tune your chart to present a more effective view of your data
Figure 15-9.

Graphing a Table Created in Word

If you've already created a table in Word with the values you'd like to graph, you do not have to type the same information into the datasheet. Select the rows and columns from the table, and then choose Microsoft Graph 5.0 from the Insert Object dialog box. Word will start the Graph application using Graph Wizard. In a series of four dialog boxes you can select these options:

- ♦ Type of chart
- ♦ Format or subtype
- ♦ Type of data series and row and column labels
- ♦ Use of legends, chart titles, and axis labels

When you select Finish from a dialog box, the datasheet will appear with your table information and the completed chart in the background. Modify or customize the chart using the menu bar and toolbar.

Creating Equations

If you type scientific and technical documents, you might need to type equations. Word helps you create equations as a special type of graphic object. You can get complete details on using the Equation Editor in the Microsoft Word manual and from the on-line help system. Because equations are certainly not used by most people, the Equation Editor will only be discussed briefly here.

To start the Equation Editor, select Object from the Insert menu, click on the Create New tab, and then double-click on Microsoft Equation 2.0. The Equation Editor has three main areas, as shown in Figure 15-10. There's the equation menu bar, an Equation toolbar, and a box where you type your equations. The small dotted rectangle in the box is called a *slot*, and it represents the position of an equation object.

15

You create an equation by typing letters, numbers, and punctuation marks from the keyboard, and by selecting options from the toolbar. The toolbar itself is divided into two sections. The buttons in the top row provide mathematical, Greek, and logical symbols, as well as some other characters or spaces. The buttons on the bottom of the toolbar let you select *templates*. A template represents the position of objects, and they are usually combined with an equation character. For example, the template you see pointed to here represents a fraction. It includes the line between the numerator and denominator, and two slots for the values.

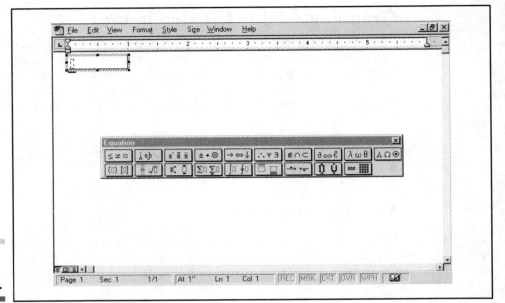

The Equation
Editor
Figure 15-10.

To create an equation, select templates and enter information into the
slots. Often, one template is used within another. For example, let's create
this equation:

$$\sqrt[3]{\frac{X^a}{Y^b}}$$

Start the Equation Editor by selecting Object from the Insert menu, clicking
on the Create New tab, and then double-clicking on Microsoft Equation 2.0.
Click on the fractions and radicals tool—the second button in the bottom
row of the toolbar. Click on the root template for this operation to display it
in the equation window:

Now click on the slot on the outside of the root symbol, and type **3**. Click on
the slot under the root symbol to select it. It's now time to insert the fraction
template in the slot. Pull down the fractions and radicals button again and

select the fraction template. Click on the slot on the top of the fraction and type **X**. To enter the superscript number, you need to select another template. Pull down the superscripts and subscripts button to display these options:

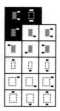

Click on the first template in the top row to insert the template and then type **a.** Now click on the slot on the bottom of the fraction, and type **Y**. Select the superscript template and type **b**.

The equation is complete, so click outside of the equation window to close the Equation Editor and return to the document. Word inserts the equation as a graphic object. This means that you can insert it in a frame, change its size and position, and add a caption, just like any other graphic object:

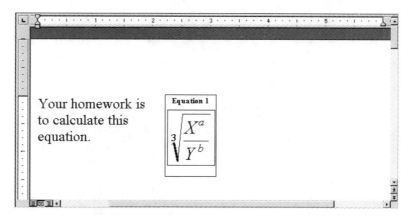

Print out a copy of the equation to see how your printer handles the graphic characters.

T ip: To edit the equation, double-click on it to restart the Equation Editor.

15

Equation Menu Options

You format an equation using the menu bar of the Equation Editor. The File, Edit, Window, and Help menus contain the traditional Windows options, so let's now review the other menu items:

♦ The *View* menu lets you change the displayed magnification in the Equation Editor.

♦ The *Format* menu contains options to align multiple equation lines and adjust spacing.

♦ The *Style* menu lets you edit the styles applied to equation objects, such as text, functions, variables, Greek letters, matrix, and vector quantities.

♦ *Size* lets you select a default point size for characters based on their position on templates, such as regular characters, superscripts and subscripts.

PART 4

Advanced Features

Creating Form Letters

16

Although form letters may have a bad reputation, they are one of the best features of Word. A form letter is merely a document that you want to send to more than one person. Each copy of the letter has the same format, and perhaps much of the text, in common. You just need to change some of the text, even if it's only the address and salutation, to customize the letter for each recipient. Word's form letter command, called Mail Merge, lets you create more than letters. You can use it to print envelopes or labels for an entire mailing list; even create price lists and catalogs.

Principles of Form Documents

The data source can contain information about products, clients, and any other type of information that you might want to use for form documents. I'm concentrating on name and address information for mailing lists because it is a typical use of Word's merge capabilities.

To create a form letter, or to print a series of envelopes or labels, you actually need two things—a mailing list and a form document. In Word, the mailing list is called a *data source*. The data source is like an electronic index card file. Every card in the file, called a *record*, contains all the information you need about each person—such as their first and last names, address, city, state, and ZIP code. Each of these items is called a *field*.

In Word the form document is called the *main document*. You link the main document with the data source so it can access the name and address information. Every place in the document where you want an item from the mailing list, you insert a code, giving the name of the field that you want inserted at that position. So instead of writing a letter and actually typing the recipient's name, for example, you insert a field code for the last name and first name.

Once you have these two parts done, you merge them. Word will automatically insert the information from the mailing list into the appropriate locations in the letter. For example, Word inserts the information from the first record in the data source into the appropriate locations in the first copy of the main document. It then inserts the information from the second record in the data source into the second copy of the main document, repeating the process until all of the records have been used.

You can create the data source and main document in any order. For example, you can write the main document and then complete the data source. Before merging the two parts, however, you have to return to the main document and tell Word what data source to use for the merge operation. You can also create the data source first and then complete the main document. This way, you can link the data source with the main document from the start.

Word will take you step-by-step through creating a main document and a data source using what it calls the Mail Merge Helper. Using the Helper, you actually create a blank main document and then create the data source, or designate one to use that you have already created. You then complete the main document.

Creating a Mailing List

You could create the data source yourself by entering the records into a Word table, with each field in a separate column. Mail Merge Helper, however, will guide you through the process, helping you design the data source to avoid errors during the merge process. Because of the number of steps involved in creating a data source, let's go through the process together this first time. Pull down the Tools menu and select Mail Merge to display the dialog box shown in Figure 16-1. As shown in the dialog box, the first step is to create the main document.

Click on the Create button to see four types of main documents that you can create—Form Letters, Mailing Labels, Envelopes, and Catalogs—as well as the option to convert a main document into a normal document that is not associated with any data source. The Convert option is dimmed because you are not yet working with a main document.

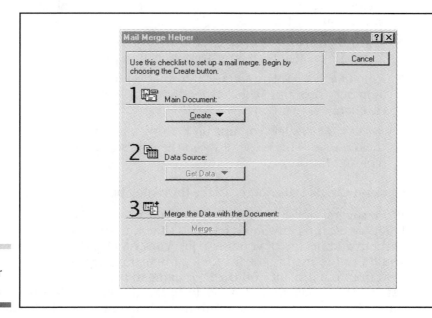

16

The Mail
Merge Helper
Figure 16-1.

Click on Form Letters to see these choices:

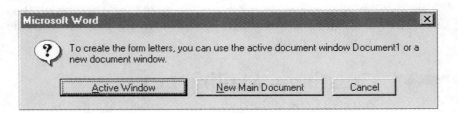

You would select the Active Window option only if the current window is blank, or if it contains text that you want to use in the main document, such as a letter that you want to convert into a form letter. Click on New Main Document to open a new document window and to redisplay Mail Merge Helper. Notice that there is now an Edit command button to the right of Create, and Word shows the type and name of main document.

If you wanted to write the main document before creating or choosing the data source, you would click on Edit. But it's best to deal with the data source next, so you can access its fields when you write the main document. Click on Get Data to display these options:

♦ *Create Data Source* lets you create a new data source, designating the fields and entering information into records. You can add, edit, or delete records at any time.

♦ *Open Data Source* lets you choose an existing data source, including a database created with another application, such as Access or Excel.

♦ *Use Address Book* lets you use information from a Microsoft Schedule + contact list or from the Personal Address Book maintained by Windows Exchange.

♦ *Header Option*s lets you link an existing data source with a separate list of field names. This is useful when the data source is a table without column headings.

Click on Create Data Source to see the dialog box shown in Figure 16-2.

Word suggests a list of fields that are typically used for addressing form letters or creating envelopes or labels. If you want to use all of the fields, without adding any of your own, just click on OK. However, chances are you'll want to modify the list for a particular main document. To remove a field from the list, click on the field name in the Field Names in Header Row list and then click on Remove Field Name button. To add a field to the list, type it in the Field Name box and then click on the Add Field Name button.

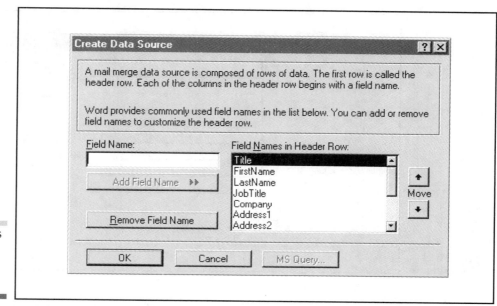

Word suggests
fields for a
mailing list
Figure 16-2.

Remember: Field names cannot include spaces.

For now, let's remove all of the suggested fields and enter our own. Click on the Remove Field Name button 13 times, or until all of the fields are removed from the list. Then, type **Name** and click on Add Field Name.

In the same way, add the fields Address1, Address2, City, State, Zip, Greeting, Last_Order_Date, and Amount_Due. When you've entered the last field, click on OK to see the Save As dialog box. Type **Mailing List** as the data source file name, and then click on Save. A dialog box appears with the options Edit Data Source and Edit Main Document. If you wanted to type the main document now and complete the data source later, you would choose Edit Main Document. But let's enter some information into the data source first. Click on Edit Data Source to display the Data Form dialog box, shown in Figure 16-3.

The Data Form box makes it easy to enter information into the data source, as well as to edit and find records. The insertion point will be in the text box for the first field, so type **Adam Chesin**, and then press ENTER. Word moves

16

Enter and edit
records in the
Data Form
dialog box
Figure 16-3.

Data Form	? X
Name:	OK
Address1:	Add New
Address2:	Delete
City:	Restore
State:	
Zip:	Find...
Greeting:	View Source
Last_Order_Date:	
Amount_Due:	

Record: |◀ ◀ 1 ▶ ▶|

the insertion point to the
next field. Now fill in the
rest of the fields as shown
here, pressing ENTER after
each.

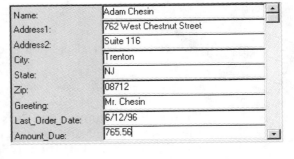

When you press ENTER after
typing the entry for the
Amount_Due field, Word
adds the record to the data
source, clears all of the text
boxes, and places the insertion point in the first text box to start a new
record. Enter the next record using this information, noting that the field
Address2 is left blank:

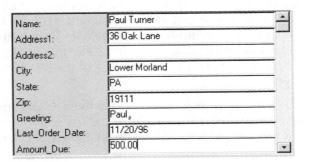

When the insertion point moves back to start the next record, click on OK. Word clears the Data Form box from the screen and displays a blank main document window. The window is the same as any document, except that it includes the Mail Merge toolbar shown here.

Writing the Form Letter

You write, format, and edit a main document using the same techniques you use in any Word document. However, when you come to a place where you want Word to insert information from the data source, you enter a field code.

Click on the Insert Merge Field button to display a list of field names in the data source.

Insert Merge Field

Name
Address1
Address2
City
State
Zip
Greeting
Last_Order_Date
Amount_Due

Tip: You can use the fields in any order in the main document, and you can use a field more than once—or not at all.

Click on the Name field. Word inserts the word "Name" in your document, surrounded by chevrons.

Tip: If a field appears in brackets, such as {MERGEFIELD name}, then the display of merge fields is turned on. Although you can still complete and merge the letters this way, showing the fields in brackets makes it more difficult to read your letter and to judge its spacing on the screen. You can turn off the option by pressing ALT-F9.

16

Press ENTER to move the insertion point to the next line, click on Insert Merge Field, and choose Address1. Press ENTER, pull down the list again, and choose Address2. Press ENTER to move to the next line. You want to place the next three fields on the same line—City, State, and Zip. Pull down the list and choose City. Type a comma, press the SPACEBAR, and insert the State field. Press the SPACEBAR twice, insert the Zip field, and then press ENTER. So far the address looks like this:

> «Name»
> «Address1»
> «Address2»
> «City», «State» «Zip»

Now press ENTER again, type **Dear**, and then press the SPACEBAR. Insert the Greeting field, type a colon, and press ENTER twice. Complete the form letter as shown in Figure 16-4, entering the fields in the appropriate locations, and your own name in the closing. Save the letter with the name Purge Mailing List.

Viewing Records

You can see how the form letter will appear with the information from the data source even before you merge the documents. Click on the View Merge Data button. Word will replace the field codes with the actual information from the first record in the data source, as shown in Figure 16-5.

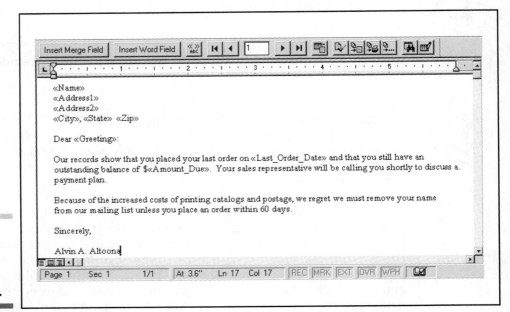

The completed sample form letter

Figure 16-4.

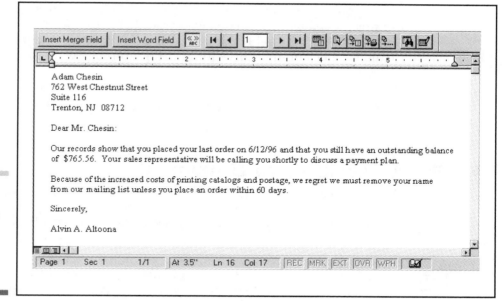

Word merges
your form
letter with the
information
from the data
source
Figure 16-5.

Use the buttons shown in the following table to change the record, or to indicate which record is being displayed.

Button	Name
◄|	First Record
◄	Previous Record
1	Go to Record
►	Next Record
►|'	Last Record

16

 If you are looking for specific information, click on the Find Record button. In the dialog box that appears, enter the information you are looking for and the field where Word can find it, and then click on OK. Word will display that record onscreen in the form document.

Before you merge, you should also check for errors. An error will occur, for example, if you use a field code for a field that does not exist. This may occur if you edit the field code after you insert it, or if you enter the codes manually. Click on the Check for Errors button to select from these choices:

♦ Simulate the merge and report errors in a new document.

♦ Complete the merge, pausing to report each error as it occurs.

♦ Complete the merge without pausing. Report errors in a new document.

Merging Form Documents

With the main document and data source complete, you can merge them at any time. Whenever you open the main document, it will automatically appear with the Mail Merge toolbar, and it will be linked with the data source.

Click on the Merge to New Document button now. Word performs the merge, creating one large document containing all of the form letters. Each of the letters will be separated by a page break. Wait until the merge letters appear, and then scroll to the start of the second letter. Notice that Word did not print a blank line for the field that contained no information.

If you click on the Merge to Printer button, Word will merge the main document with the data source records, printing a completed letter as each record is merged.

Controlling Your Merge

When you click on Merge to Printer or Merge to New Document, Word merges all of the records in the database. You can customize the merge process by clicking on the Mail Merge button to display the dialog box shown in Figure 16-6.

T ip: You can also display the Mail Merge dialog box by choosing Merge from the Mail Merge Helper.

Select where you want to merge to by choosing New Document, Printer, Electronic Mail, or Electronic Fax in the Merge To list. If you choose either Electronic Mail or Fax you can then change the Setup options. Use the Records to Be Merged option to print all of the records—the default setting—or a specific range of records. To print a range of records, enter the starting record number in the From box and the ending record number in

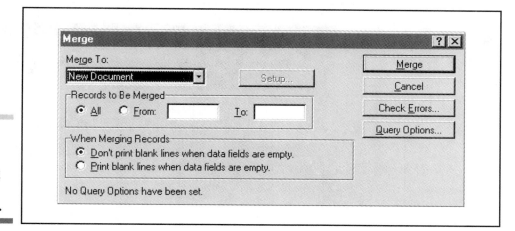

Control the
merge with
the Mail
Merge dialog
box
Figure 16-6.

the To box. For example, entering 1 and 6 would merge just the first six
records in the data source.

Your choice in When Merging Records determines whether Word will print
a blank line in an address when the only field in that line is empty.

Now close the document. Word will display a dialog box asking if you also
want to save the attached data source—select Yes.

Printing Envelopes for Form Letters

You can use Mail Merge Helper to print a series of envelopes for everyone in
your mailing list. To print envelopes, start Mail Merge Helper, click on
Create and choose Envelopes, and then select New Main Document. To use
the same data source as you used for the letters, click on Get Data, choose
Open Data Source, and then select the data source file name in the dialog
box that appears. Next, choose Setup Main Document to display the
Envelope options dialog box—the same box you learned about in Chapter 8.
Once you select the options, including envelope size, select OK to display
the Envelope Address dialog box, shown in Figure 16-7.

16

This dialog box serves as the main document for envelopes. Use the Insert
Merge Field button to insert
the merge codes for the
address, just as you did when
creating the inside address
for the letter. If you want to
include a bar code, click on
Insert Postal Bar Code to
display the options shown
here.

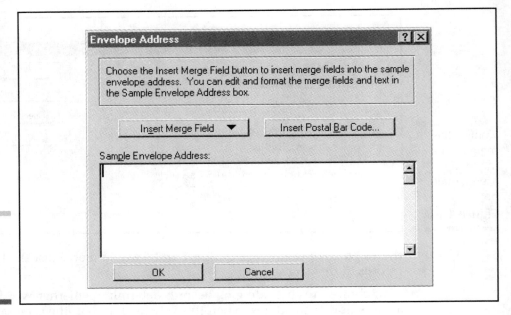

The main
document
window for
envelopes
Figure 16-7.

Pull down the Merge Field with ZIP Code list and select the name of the field
containing the ZIP code. Then pull down the Merge Field with Street Address
box and select the field with the address. Select OK twice to return to Mail
Merge Helper, and then complete the merge.

Merging to Labels

You can merge data onto mailing labels as easily as envelopes. Follow the
same procedure as you did with envelopes, but choose Mailing Labels from
the Create list. When you choose to set up the main document, you'll see
the Label Options dialog box, shown in Figure 16-8.

Choose the label form you are using from the Product Number list, choosing
between Dot Matrix and Laser to display either continuous or sheet-fed
labels. If you are using a label that is not listed in the dialog box, select one
that is similar, and then click on the Details button to see the dialog box
shown in Figure 16-9.

Enter the dimensions requested, and the number of labels across and down,
and then select OK. Select OK from the Label Options dialog box to see the
Create Labels dialog box, which has the same options as the Create
Envelopes box. Enter the field codes just as you did for envelopes and select
postal code fields.

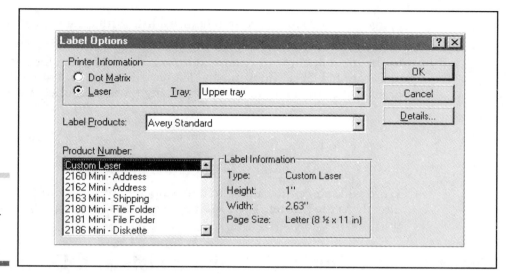

The Label
Options
dialog box for
mailing lists
Figure 16-8.

Merging Catalogs

When you create letters or envelopes, each record is separated by a page break. Labels print on special label paper. Use the Catalog option in Mail

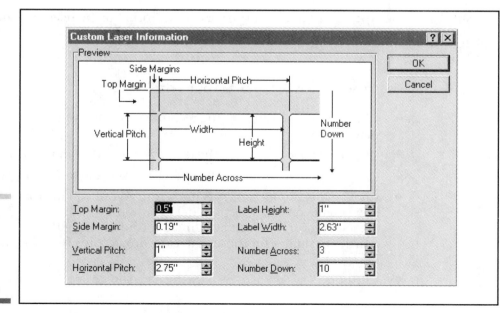

Create a
custom label
if yours is
not already
defined
Figure 16-9.

16

Merge Helper to merge your data into a list. With a catalog, Word does not insert a page break between each record.

In the main document, enter and lay out the field codes for one line of the report, or however you want the first record to appear. Press ENTER after the line (or after the final line if you are using more than one per record):

«Name»   «Last_Order_Date»   «Amount_Due»

Word will merge the catalog to a new document—you cannot merge it directly to the printer. Then add any page titles or column headings and print the document.

Working with Mailing Lists and Data Sources

Chances are your mailing list, or other database, will not remain constant. Although you can open the data source and work with it as a table, it's easier to maintain it as a data form. When you need to add, delete, or edit records in the data source, display the main document, and then click on the Edit Data Source button in the Mail Merge toolbar to display the Data Form box. (If you're not following along on your screen, look back at Figure 16-3.)

T ip: You can also display the Data Form box by selecting Edit from the Data Source section of Mail Merge Helper.

Use these options in the Data Form box:

♦ Click on *Add New* to save the record being displayed and to start a new record.

♦ Click on *Delete* to remove the displayed record from the data source.

♦ Click on *Restore* to cancel the changes you made to the displayed record.

♦ Click on *Find* to locate a specific record. Word will display a dialog box where you can select the field you want to search and the text you are looking for. You can also find a record by using the record buttons, which are similar for those when viewing records from the main document.

♦ Click on *View Source* to display the data source as a Word table.

When you select the View Source command, Word displays the data source as a table, along with the Database toolbar:

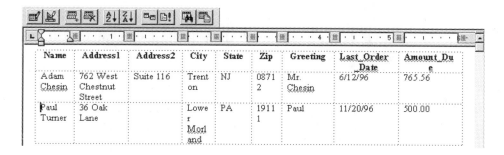

Name	Address1	Address2	City	State	Zip	Greeting	Last_Order _Date	Amount_Du e
Adam Chesin	762 West Chestnut Street	Suite 116	Trent on	NJ	0871 2	Mr. Chesin	6/12/96	765.56
Paul Turner	36 Oak Lane		Lowe r Morl and	PA	1911 1	Paul	11/20/96	500.00

The Database toolbar buttons are described in the following table:

Button	Name	Function
	Data Form	Display the Data Form dialog box
	Manage Fields	Add, remove, and rename fields
	Add New Record	Insert a new row at the end of the table
	Delete Record	Delete the record in which the insertion point is placed
	Sort Ascending	Sort the rows of the table in ascending order, using the column in which the insertion point is located
	Sort Descending	Sort the rows in descending order
	Insert Database	Insert records from another data source
	Update Fields	Update any selected Word fields in the data source

16

Button	Name	Function
	Find Record	Locate a record
	Mail Merge Main Document	Display the main document

T ip: You can use the Database toolbar to edit the information in any Word table, not just those created by Mail Merge Helper. To display the toolbar, click the right mouse button on any toolbar, and then select Database from the shortcut menu. When working with a table that is not a data source, the Mail Merge Main Document button will have no effect.

Working with Fields

When you want to change the actual fields in the data source, click on the Manage Fields button in the Database toolbar to display the options shown here.

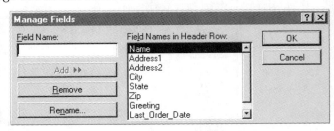

To insert a new field into the data source, type the name in the Field Name text box, then select Add. To delete a field, select it in the list box, click on Remove, then select Yes from the confirmation dialog box. To change a field's name, select it in the list box, click on Rename, type the new name in the box that appears, and then select OK.

C aution: Deleting a field also deletes all of the information for that field in the data source.

Linking a Main Document with Another Source

When you create a form letter, you have the option of editing it even before you create or select a data source. You can select the data source at a later time, or change the source if you merge it with records from another data source.

Remember: The new data source you select must include the field names used in the main document.

To select a data source, open the main document and click on the Mail Merge Helper button, or select Mail Merge from the Tools menu. Click on Get Data, and then select either Create Data Source to create a new data source for the document or Open Data Source to merge the document with an existing data source file.

Converting a Main Document

Every time you open a main document, Word displays the Mail Merge toolbar and accesses the associated data source file. If you want to later treat the document as a nonmerge document, open it, display the Mail Merge Helper, and choose Restore To Normal Word Document from the Create list.

If you want to use the document as a main document again, however, you must define its merge type and associate it with a data source. To convert an existing document into a main document, open it and select Mail Merge from the Tools menu. Click on Create, select the type of merge document, and then choose the Active Window option. Finally, click on Get Data, and then create or select the data source.

Selecting Merge Records

If you want to merge a specific record from the data source, you can display the main document, click on the View Data button, and then use the record or Find Records buttons to display the record on the screen. You can also select a specific record, or a range of records, in the Mail Merge dialog box.

When you want to merge records based on the contents—such as all clients in California—use the Query Options command to create a filter. A *filter* tells Word to use only the records that meet certain conditions for the merge operation, ignoring those that do not meet the conditions. The records not used during the merge remain in the data source—they are just ignored, not deleted.

16

To create a filter, display the Mail Merge dialog box and click on Query Options. Click on the Filter Records tab in the Query Options dialog box to display the options shown in Figure 16-10.

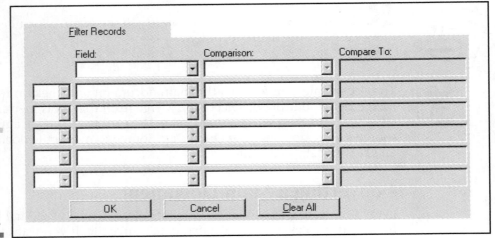

Use the Filter
Records page
to select
records for
your merge
Figure 16-10.

You use the six rows of text boxes to specify up to six conditions that a
record must meet to be used for the merge. There are three steps to setting
a condition:

1. Select a field.
2. Select a comparison operator.
3. Enter a value.

In the first row of the dialog box, pull down the
Field list and select a field that you want to use as
a condition. For example, if you want to send
letters only to clients in California, select the State
field. Next, choose an operator in the Comparison
list, shown here.

Type the value to use for the comparison in the
Compare To box. For example, to send letters to California clients, select
State as the field, choose Equal To as the comparison, and type **CA** in the
Compare To box.

Use the remaining rows of boxes to specify additional conditions. For each
condition, pull down the And/Or box and select either an AND or an OR
operation. An AND operation will select records that meet both of the
conditions; an OR operation selects those meeting one or the other or both.
So suppose you want to send letters to all clients in California who owe over
$1,000. This is an AND operation because the records must meet both
conditions—they must be in California and owe over $1,000. But suppose

you want to send letters to clients in California and Oregon. This is an OR condition because the client must meet at least one of the conditions.

When you've completed the conditions, select OK and perform the merge. To erase all of the conditions, choose Clear All.

Remember: Word saves your conditions with the main document. If you later want to merge all of the records, you must display the Query Options dialog box and choose Clear All.

Sorting Records

Before merging your main document and data source, consider whether you want to sort the records in a particular order. You may be able to take advantage of bulk-rate mail rates, for example, if you deliver the envelopes to the post office in ZIP code order. Word gives you three ways to sort the records in your mailing list.

When you are viewing the data source—click on the Edit Data Source button and then select View Source—you sort the records in two ways:

♦   Use the Sort buttons in the Database toolbar to sort records in ascending or descending order based on one field.

♦   Use the Sort command in the Table menu to sort a table on up to three fields.

You can also sort data source records for a merge operation by selecting the Sort Records tab in the Query Options dialog box. Word will display options for sorting the data source on up to three fields, much like the Sort command from the Table menu.

16

Customizing a Merge with Fields

The Mail Merge dialog box gives you several ways to control the merge process. You can also control the process by inserting merge fields into the main document itself. To insert a merge field in the main document, place the insertion point where you want the field to appear, and then click on the Insert Word Field button in the Mail Merge toolbar to see the options shown here.

Insert Word Field
A̲sk...
F̲ill-in...
I̲f...Then...Else...
Merge R̲ecord #
Merge Se̲quence #
N̲ext Record
Ne̲xt Record If...
Set B̲ookmark...
S̲kip Record If...

If you select a field with an ellipsis (...), Word will display a dialog box prompting you to select options or enter additional information to complete the field. Otherwise, the field code will appear in the document immediately.

Field codes are really for more advanced users of Word's mail merge functions. However, you may find the If...Then...Else command useful for almost any type of merge. The If...Then...Else command determines what information is inserted in the resulting form letter based on the contents of a field—for example, printing "Pay up, you deadbeat" for clients who owe over a certain amount.

When you select the field from the list, Word will display the dialog box shown in Figure 16-11.

Use the text boxes in the IF section to determine the condition for entering text. In the Insert this Text box, type the text that you want to appear when the record meets the condition. In the Otherwise Insert this Text box, type the text that you want if the record does not meet the condition, as illustrated in Figure 16-12.

When you select OK, Word will insert the field into the document and show the results of the If...Then...Else condition—the text that will appear when the letter for the current record is printed. The code looks like this:

Our records show that you placed your last order on { MERGEFIELD Last_Order_Date } and that you still have an outstanding balance of ${ MERGEFIELD Amount_Due }. Your sales representative will be calling you shortly to discuss a payment plan. {IF { MERGEFIELD Amount_Due } > 1000 "If you do not remit payment immediately, we will take legal action." "Please make every effort to remit payment in a timely manner." }

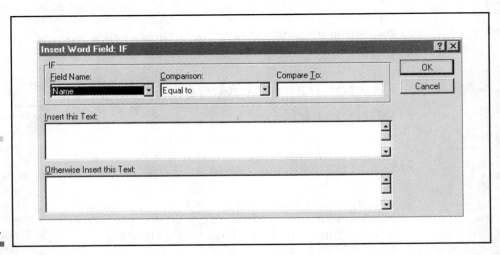

The dialog box for inserting an If...Then...Else command

Figure 16-11.

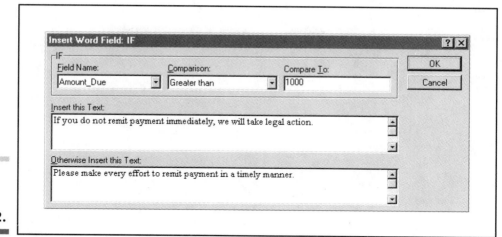

Enter the text
for both
situations
Figure 16-12.

Remember: To switch between displaying the field code and the results of the code, press ALT-F9.

When you perform the merge operation, Word will insert the appropriate text in each letter based on the contents of the field for that record.

Tables of Contents and Other Resources

It's as easy to create a long document with Word as it is a short one, even though long documents often require special sections. You can create a table of contents and index, and even tables of figures and legal citations, just by marking text or locations in your document. Word formats the table or index and inserts the page numbers for you. If you later add, delete, or edit text, you can update the table or index in seconds.

Creating a Table of Contents

A table of contents usually appears near the beginning of a document. If it includes page numbers, readers will know exactly where to find information according to subject. The table of contents also shows the overall structure of the document and its organization into topics and subtopics. Word will create a table of contents for you automatically from titles and subtitles formatted in the heading styles. You control how many heading levels are used and the format of the table.

Remember: If you plan on having a table of contents and index in the same document, create the index first to ensure that it does not include the table of contents entries.

As you type and edit your document, add titles and subtitles using heading styles. The first three heading styles are available by default in the Style list in the Formatting toolbar. You can access Heading 4 through Heading 9 from the Style dialog box or by pressing SHIFT when you pull down the Style list.

Plan your titles and subtitles to reflect the organization of the document, so they outline the flow of information. Major topic areas should begin with a title in the Heading 1 style. Subtopics relating to that subject should begin with a title in the Heading 2 style.

Depending on the length and complexity of your document, you can have further levels of subtitles in heading levels 3 through 9. Just don't overdo it; not every paragraph needs a heading. For example, this index contains only three levels:

Tip: You can automatically insert titles and subtitles in heading styles by creating an outline. Working with an outline helps you organize a document, as you'll learn in Chapter 19.

Preparing for the Table of Contents

Before you create the table of contents, you should prepare a section for it at the beginning of the document, following the title page if you have one. Normally, the pages of the table of contents itself are either unnumbered or numbered using roman numerals separately from the text. Therefore, you must set the page numbering so the first page of the document following the table starts with page number 1.

If you have a title page, replace its page break with a section break, and then insert another section break for the table of contents. If you do not have a title page, place the insertion point at the start of the document and insert a section break. To insert the break, choose the Insert menu, click on Next Page and then OK. Place the insertion point in the table of contents section and use the Page Numbers option from the Insert menu to turn on page numbering using lowercase roman numerals. Next, move the insertion point below the section break, to the first page of the actual text, and use the Format command from the Page Numbers dialog box to start numbering the section with number 1.

Generating the Table of Contents

You are now ready to generate the table of contents. Place the insertion point in the section you created for the table, and then choose Index and Tables from the Insert menu. Click on the Table of Contents tab to see the options shown in Figure 17-1. In the Formats list, select the overall look of the table—watch the Preview panel to see what it looks like. Next, select options to customize the list.

17

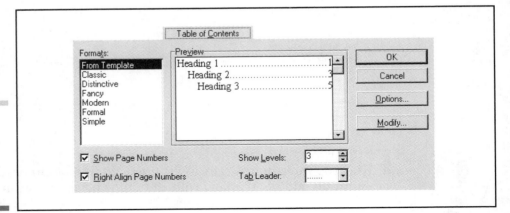

Use these
options to
generate your
table of
contents
Figure 17-1.

◆ *Show Page Numbers* determines whether page numbers appear in the
table of contents.

◆ *Right Align Page Numbers* determines whether the numbers are at the
right margin or immediately after the text of the table entry.

◆ *Show Levels* determines how many heading levels are used for the
table—the default is three. If you only use Heading 1 and Heading 2
styles in your document, set the level at 2. Increase the number for the
number of levels you want. Keep in mind that you don't need to use all
of your subtitle levels in the table.

◆ *Tab Leader* determines whether any characters print between the table
entry and the page number.

Finally, select OK to generate and display the table of contents at the
location of the insertion point.

Updating the Table of Contents

If you add, edit, or delete text so the pagination changes, you must update
the table. Click anywhere in the table, and then press F9 to see the options
shown here.

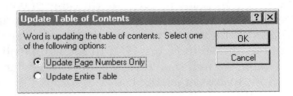

Select Update Page Numbers Only if you haven't changed any of the headings and just want the new page numbers applied to the table. If you have added, deleted, or edited any of the heading text, choose Update Entire Table.

Customizing the Format

Word formats the table of contents using the styles TOC1 through TOC9, automatically applying the TOC style to the corresponding heading. For example, it applies the TOC1 style to text formatted with Heading 1, the TOC2 style to text formatted with Heading 2, and so on.

You can change which TOC styles are applied to each heading level by selecting Options from the Table of Contents section of the Index and Tables dialog box. The dialog box in Figure 17-2 is then displayed. Enter the TOC level that you want applied to each heading level. For instance, if you want to use the TOC4 style for subtitles formatted with the Heading 3 style, enter **4** in the text box to the right of Heading 3.

Tip: If you select the Table Entry Fields check box, Word will create the table using TOC field codes that you've inserted manually, instead of the heading levels. See Chapter 23 for more information on inserting and using fields.

Modifying Styles

Each of the formats available in the Table of Contents section represents a series of TOC styles. If you choose From Template as the format, Word will

Modify the
heading styles
applied to
each level of
the table of
contents
Figure 17-2.

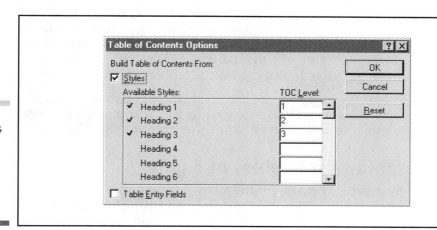

17

use the default styles of the current template. If you select another format, Word will change the default styles before generating the table.

No matter which format you select, you can modify the styles after you create the table of contents using the Styles dialog box, as explained in Chapter 12. If you select From Template as the format, you can modify the styles before you generate the table. After you select From Template as the format, click on the Modify button to display the Styles dialog box. Only the TOC styles will be listed. Click on Modify again to change any of the TOC styles. When you close the dialog boxes, the Table of Contents box will reappear so you can generate the table.

Remember: If you want to change the format of the table of contents, do so by modifying the styles, not by manually changing the formats of individual entries.

Creating a Table of Figures

If you insert a number of figures, statistical tables, or equations in your document, you should consider creating one or more tables of figures. A table of figures shows the caption of each object and the page where the object is found. You generate a separate table for each type of caption you insert—table, figure, illustration, and equation, as well as your own custom caption labels. So for example, you can have one table listing the location of figures and another table for illustrations.

Word applies the Table of Figures style to each table entry.

Start by creating a section for the table, usually at the beginning of the document, following the table of contents. Select Index and Tables from the Insert menu, and then click on the Table of Figures tab to display the options shown in Figure 17-3. Select the caption label that you want to create a table for, and then choose a format for the table. Set the other choices—making sure to modify the From Template format—and then click on OK to generate and display the table at the location of the insertion point.

Repeat the procedure for each type of caption that you want to use for the table. For example, after generating a table using figure captions, generate another for equations or some other captions that you use.

Options for Tables of Figures

By default, Word builds the table of figures from captions inserted using the Insert Caption command. If you manually typed captions and formatted them using a style, you can generate a table from these captions as well.

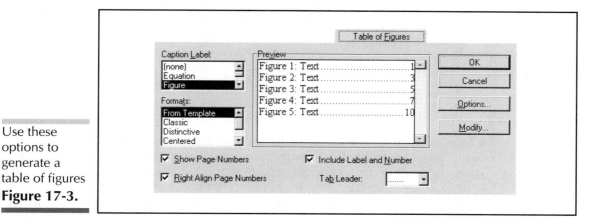

Use these
options to
generate a
table of figures
Figure 17-3.

For example, suppose you typed captions directly in the document and formatted them using the Heading 9 style. To generate a table from these captions, display the Table of Figures page of the Index and Tables dialog box, and then click on Options to see the options shown here.

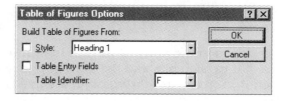

Pull down the Style list and select the style that you used to format your captions. Select OK to return to the Index and Tables dialog box, and then select OK from the Table of Figures page to generate and display the table.

Tip: Use the Table Entry Fields check box to generate a table from field codes that you've inserted manually. See Chapter 23 for more information on inserting and using fields.

Creating an Index

An index usually appears at the end of your document listing the page numbers of topics, or key words or phrases, in alphabetical order. When a topic—or main entry—can be divided into more than one subtopic, the index will contain subentries. For example, here is a section of an index containing two main entries:

—C—

Cameras, 10, 16
Computers, 3, 8, 11

Cameras are discussed on pages 10 and 16; computers on pages 3, 8, and 11. Now, both cameras and computers are rather broad topics, since there are so many types of them. Therefore, a particular reference may discuss just one type or use. Rather than referring only to the broad category, the indexer can use subentries to help readers find more specific information, as shown in this index:

—C—

Cameras
    single-lens reflex, 10
    twin-lens reflex, 16

Computers
    Apple, 8
    IBM-PC, 11
    Wang, 3

To create an index, you first have to indicate each location in the text that you want to reference, and the word or phrase to use as the main entry or subentry. You can use a word or phrase that is actually in the text, or a word or phrase that is not in the text but describes the reference. Normally, the page number of each marked location will appear in the index. You can also create a cross-reference for an entry, referring the reader to another index entry.

Marking Index Entries

To mark a specific word or phrase to use in the index, select it first or just place the insertion point at the location. Then press ALT-SHIFT-X to see the dialog box shown in Figure 17-4. If you select text first, the text will appear in the Main Entry text box. Type or edit the main entry, if it does not already contain the text you want to appear in the index. To include a subentry for the reference, enter it in the Subentry text box.

Word allows a main entry to have up to six levels of subentries. To designate a sublevel, separate it from the previous subentry with a colon, like this:

Subentry: Single-lens reflex: 35-millimeter: European

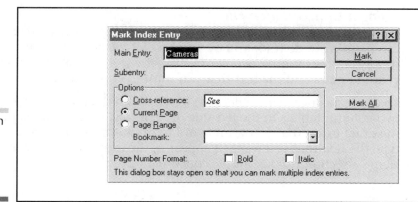

Mark the main
entry and
subentry for
the index
Figure 17-4.

Note: There are actually styles for eight levels of subentries, and you can designate all eight in the Subentry text box, but only six will appear in the index.

Next, select options for the reference. By default, the page number of the marked location will appear in the index. To create a cross-reference, click on the Cross-reference option button and then enter the citation in the text box. You can also specify a range of pages if you've already created a bookmark for that range. You'll learn more about bookmarks in Chapter 23. If you want the page number to appear in bold or italic, click on the appropriate check boxes.

Finally, click on either Mark or Mark All. Selecting Mark will mark only the location of the insertion point. If you choose Mark All, Word will search your entire document, marking each occurrence of the main entry text. Mark All is case sensitive—Word will only mark text that matches the text in the dialog box exactly. When Word marks an entry, it automatically turns on the Show/Hide option and leaves the Mark Index Entry dialog box on the screen so you can continue marking words for the index. Select the next word in the document, press ALT-SHIFT-X to insert it into the Main Entry text box, and then select Mark.

17

Caution: If you've already created a table of contents, the Mark All option may mark matching words in the table.

Using a Concordance File

Rather than scan through your entire document to mark index entries, you can have Word do it for you by using a *concordance file*. A concordance file is simply another Word document listing the words or phrases that you want Word to mark and the text that you want to appear in the index.

To create a concordance file, start a new Word document and create a two-column table. On the left side of each row, type the word or phrase—in the exact case—that you want Word to mark. On the right side of each row, type the text that you want to appear in the index for the marked word. Here's a section from a sample concordance file:

cameras	Cameras
reflex	Cameras
35-millimeter	Cameras
wide angle	Lenses
telephoto	Lenses

Generating the Index

When you've marked all of the entries for the index, move the insertion point to where you want the index to appear—usually at the end of the document. Then select Index and Tables from the Index menu and click on the Index tab to see the options shown in Figure 17-5.

Select the format for the index in the Formats list and select either Indented or Run-in from the Type section. The indented type displays subentries on separate lines underneath and indented from the main entry. Run-in places subentries on the same line as main entries. Select Right Align Page Numbers if you want the number to appear at the right margin, or deselect the option to separate the entry and page number by a comma. If you right-align page

Use these options to generate the index

Figure 17-5.

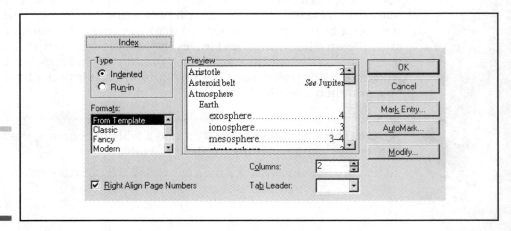

numbers, you can also choose a tab leader character to appear between the entry and number. Also, set the number of columns that you want to use for the index.

Finally, click on OK. Word will create the index and insert it in the document with a section break before and after it.

Generating the Index with a Concordance File

To generate the index when you are using a concordance file rather than manually marking the entries, display the Index and Tables dialog box, click on Automark, and then select the concordance file document from the dialog box that appears. Word will scan the document, marking each of the entries. Then display the Index and Tables dialog box again, select the formats desired, and click on OK.

Working with an Index

If you add, edit, or delete text so the pagination changes, you must update the page numbers in the index. Click anywhere in the index and press F9. Word automatically repaginates the index. If you add or delete index marks, however, you must regenerate the index. To regenerate the index, display the Index section of the Index and Tables dialog box and select OK. Word will select the entire index already in your document—no matter where your insertion point is—and ask if you want to replace the current index. Select Yes.

Each of the formats available in the Index section represents a series of styles—Index Heading, and Index 1 through Index 9. If you choose From Template as the format, Word will use the default styles of the current template. If you select another format, Word changes the default styles before creating the index.

To change the format of the index after you've created it, modify the styles. As with a table of contents, you can change the default index formats before you generate the index by choosing the From Template format and clicking on the Modify button.

Creating a Table of Authorities

17

A table of authorities is similar to an index, but it lists all of the legal citations in a document and the pages that refer to each citation. You can also subdivide the table into 16 categories, such as Cases, Statutes, Regulations, and Constitutional Provisions.

Each citation is associated with two entries, a long citation and a short citation. The long citation is the complete legal reference; the short citation is an abbreviation that you'll use for later reference. The first time you mark

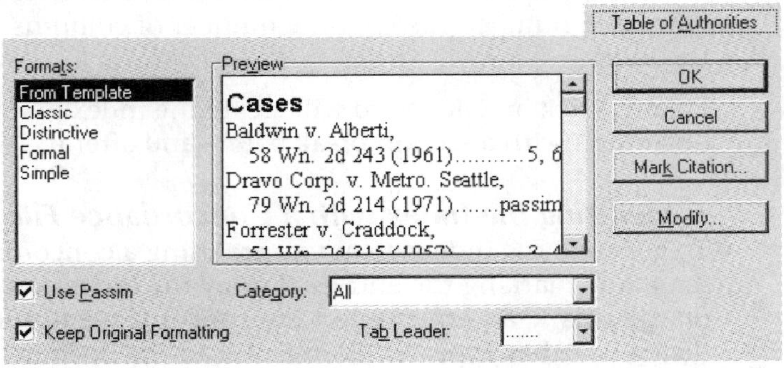

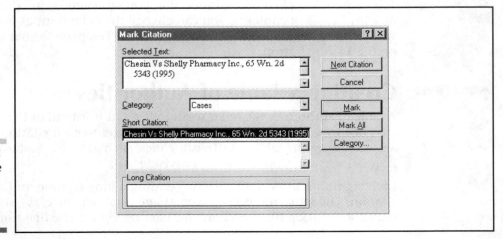

Use these
options to
mark citations
and generate a
table of
authorities
Figure 17-6.

the reference, select the long citation text, choose Index and Tables from the
Insert menu, and then click on the Table of Authorities tab to see the
options shown in Figure 17-6.

Select the format for the table and other options, and then click on Mark
Citation to see the dialog box shown in Figure 17-7. Select the category, and
then edit the short citation name. Choose Mark to mark that citation, or
choose Mark All to have Word mark all of the references to the short citation
name in your document. Use the Next Citation command to move through
the document, highlighting each citation. The Category button lets you
change the name of one or more categories. If you later want to mark a
location where you cite the reference, display this same dialog box, and then
type the short citation name or select it from the list. To generate or later
regenerate the table, display the Table of Authorities options and select OK.

Enter the short
citation for the
selected
reference
Figure 17-7.

Footnotes, Endnotes, and Annotations

18

Footnotes and endnotes are not only found in academic reports and scholarly articles. Documents of all types can benefit from notes—to cite the source of information, to provide some extra insight or explanation, or to give a personal aside. Footnotes appear at the bottom of the page on which they are referenced; endnotes appear at the end of the document, section, or chapter. Annotations are personal notes and reminders that you can print separately or, like endnotes, at the end of the document.

Typing Footnotes

Before programs such as Word came along, typing footnotes could be a laborious task because you had to judge just how much space to reserve at the bottom of the page. If you inserted or deleted text, the footnote reference could move to another page, forcing you to move the note as well, and you could only hope that there would be enough space on the new page. Well, Word takes away all of this worry. Word automatically adjusts your text so footnotes always appear on the same page as their reference numbers. You can insert or delete text—even insert and delete footnotes—and Word takes care of the rest.

To type a footnote, place the insertion point where you want the reference number or mark to appear, and then select Footnote from the Insert menu to display the dialog box shown in Figure 18-1.

Click on Footnote. To number your footnotes, leave AutoNumber, the default option, selected. If you want to use a special symbol or text, click on Custom Mark, and then enter the text in the text box; click on Symbol to select a symbol from one of the available fonts.

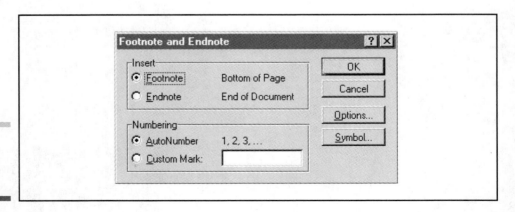

The Footnote and Endnote dialog box
Figure 18-1.

Tip: You can automatically insert symbols using the Note Options dialog box explained later in this chapter.

When you select OK, Word will insert the reference number in the text. If you are in Normal view, Word will display a separate panel at the bottom of the screen, as shown in Figure 18-2. If you are in Page Layout view, Word will move to the bottom of the page and display the footnote separator and reference number.

Remember: You use the Notes list in the toolbar to determine what appears in the footnote pane.

Type the text of the footnote, and then return to the document. In Normal view, return to the document while leaving the footnote pane displayed by pressing F6 or SHIFT-F5, or by clicking anywhere in the document pane. To return to the document and remove the footnote pane, click on Close in the Notes toolbar. In Page Layout view, press SHIFT-F5. The insertion point will appear immediately after the footnote reference number.

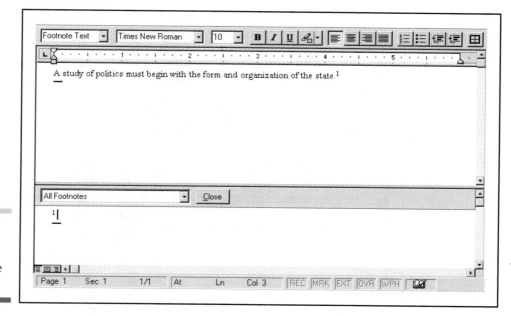

Word divides the screen, creating a footnote pane

Figure 18-2.

18

Let's see how this works by inserting several footnotes in the document Biography of Sliding Billy Watson. Open the document, change to Normal view, and then place the insertion point at the end of the second paragraph. Select Footnote from the Insert menu, click on the Footnote option button, and then click on OK to display the footnote pane.

Type **Chicago Ledger, September 18, 1921, "How He Found His Slide"**, and then press F6. Move the insertion point to the end of the first sentence in the fourth paragraph, select Footnote from the Insert menu, and then click on OK. Type **Hartford Daily Telegraph, December 21, 1911, "Sliding Watson Makes Hit at Grand"**, and then press SHIFT-F5. The footnotes and references appear as in Figure 18-3.

Your two footnotes in the document are now referenced 1 and 2. If you insert a new note in the text, Word will automatically renumber those following the insertion point. Try this now. Move the insertion point to the end of the third paragraph, select Footnote from the Insert menu, and then click on OK. The footnote that was numbered 2 is now number 3.

Type **Abel Green and Joe Laurie, Jr., *Showbiz From Vaude to Video*, Henry Holt and Company, NY, 1951**, and then click on Close.

Moving, Copying, and Deleting Footnotes

To move or copy a footnote, select its reference number in the text, not in the note pane. Then use either drag and drop or the Clipboard to move or

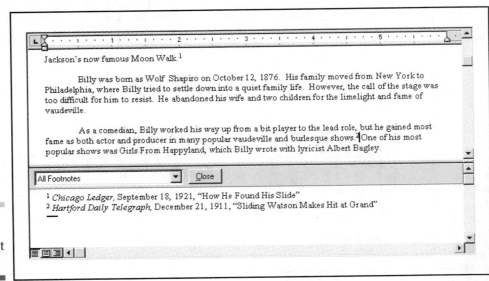

Footnotes
inserted into
your document
Figure 18-3.

copy the note to the new location. Remember, hold down CTRL while you drag and drop to make a copy of the note. Word will automatically renumber the notes. To delete a note, select its reference number and press DELETE.

Remember: Move, copy, and delete notes using the reference number in the text, not by trying to perform these actions on the note itself.

Editing Footnotes

To edit a note, you must display it. If you are in Normal view, display the note pane—if it is not already onscreen—by selecting Footnotes from the View menu, or by holding down SHIFT while you drag the split box. Then make sure that All Footnotes appears in the list box. If not, pull down the list and select All Footnotes. You can then edit and format the footnote as you would any other text.

Tip: If you are in Page Layout view, you can display the footnotes either by selecting Footnotes from the View menu or by scrolling the note into view.

Customizing Footnotes

Word gives you several ways to customize the footnotes. If you want to change the appearance of footnote reference numbers or the text, use the Styles dialog box. Modify the Footnote Reference style to change the appearance of the reference numbers in both the text and the note. By default, the number uses the default paragraph font and is a superscript. Modify the text of the note itself by changing the Footnote Text style.

To change the position or numbering method, use the All Footnotes options shown in Figure 18-4. To display these options, choose Footnotes from the Insert menu, click on the Options button in the Footnotes and Endnotes dialog box, and then click on the All Footnotes tab.

1. Pull down the Place At list to select the position on the page where your footnotes appear. The options are to place them at the bottom of the page or immediately beneath the last text on the page.

2. Pull down the Number Format list to specify the type of numbers or characters used for the reference number.

18

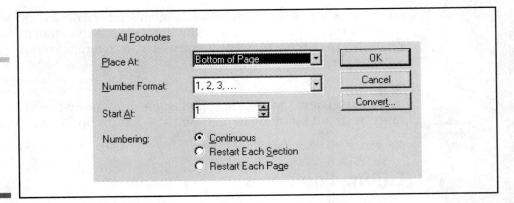

Use this page
of the Note
Options
dialog box to
change
footnote
options
Figure 18-4.

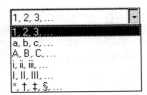

3. Enter a number in the Start At box to determine the number (or letter or symbol) of the first footnote on the page or section, depending on the setting in the Numbering section.

4. Select a Numbering method. You can choose to number footnotes continuously throughout the entire document, or to restart numbering on each page or section.

Note: You'll learn how to use the Convert option later in this chapter.

Adding Endnotes

Endnotes are references that appear at the end of the document rather than on the same page as their reference number. You insert an endnote in much the same way as a footnote, except you select Endnote from the

Footnote and Endnote dialog box. By default, endnote references use lowercase roman numerals.

If you want the endnotes to appear on their own page, enter a page break at the end of the document or section, depending on where your endnotes appear. Let's add an endnote to the document on your screen. Move the insertion point to the end of the document, and then press CTRL-ENTER to insert a hard page break. Place the insertion point after the words "Long Island" in the last paragraph and select Footnote from the Insert menu. Click on Endnote and then on OK to display the note pane. Notice that the Notes list in the toolbar is set at All Endnotes. Type the following endnote, and then press SHIFT-F5:

> According to the *New York Times* (April 7, 1926) a discharged waiter was upset over being fired for refusing to wash a patron's dog. The waiter was convicted and sentenced to a life term at Sing Sing Prison.

Finally, print a copy of the document to see how your footnotes and endnote look.

Endnote Options

Format and customize endnotes using the Endnote Reference and Endnote Text styles, and the All Endnotes options shown in Figure 18-5. To display these options, Select Options from the Footnotes and Endnotes dialog box, and then click on the All Endnotes tab. The options are similar to those for

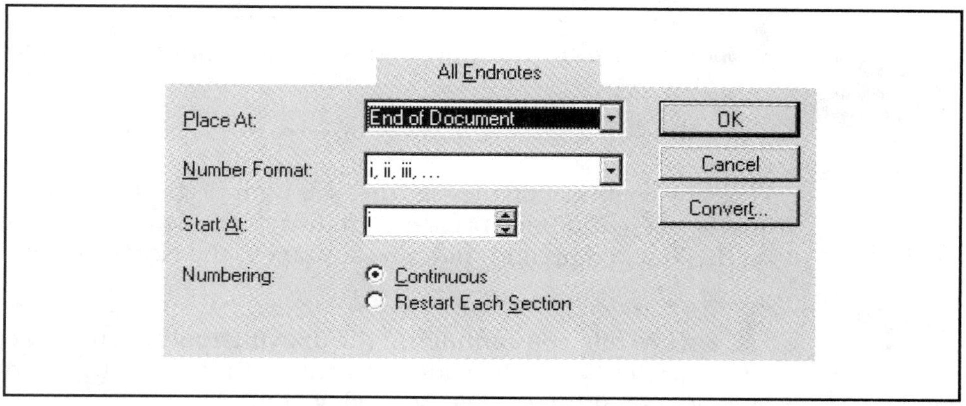

Use this page of the Note Options dialog box to change endnote options

Figure 18-5.

footnotes, except that the Place At choices are End of Document and End of Section. Since endnotes appear at the end of the document or section, there is no Restart Each Page option in the Numbering section.

Working with Notes

When you have both endnotes and footnotes in a document, you can quickly switch between them in the note pane. Pull down the Notes list and select All Footnotes or All Endnotes, depending on what you want to display.

You can also use the Notes list to modify the separator line and continuation messages. The separator line appears between the end of the text and the footnotes and endnotes. By default, the separator is a two-inch line. A Continuation Separator is a line that appears when a note must be continued onto the next page. By default, the Continuation Separator is a full line across the page. A Continuation Notice is a message that appears at the bottom of the page telling the reader that a note is continued on the next page—the default message is blank.

To modify any of these elements, you must be in Normal view. Select Footnotes from the View menu to display the Notes toolbar. To change a separator or continuation text for footnotes, pull down the Notes list and select All Footnotes; to change a separator or continuation message for endnotes, select All Endnotes. Then pull down the list again, as shown here, and select the element you want to change.

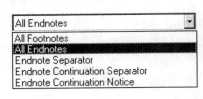

Remember: There are corresponding options for endnotes.

Type any continuation message that you want to appear. To delete the separator line, select it and press DELETE. To return to the default separator line, click on the Reset command that now appears in the Notes toolbar.

Tip: While you cannot use the drawing tools to create a custom separator line, you can create some interesting effects by inserting a series of characters using the Symbol dialog box.

Converting Note Types

If you type footnotes and then want to place them as a group at the end of your document, you can convert the footnotes to endnotes. Similarly, you can convert endnotes to footnotes if you decide you want to place them on the page of the reference number. You can convert all of your notes or just selected ones.

To convert all of your notes to the other type, choose Footnote from the Insert menu, click on Options, and then choose Convert to see the options shown here.

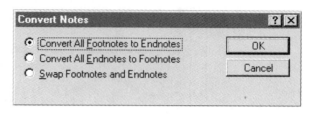

Select the appropriate option to convert all of the notes.

To convert a particular note, choose Footnotes from the View menu or switch to the note pane. Pull down the Notes list and select All Footnotes to display footnotes or All Endnotes to display the endnotes. Select the note that you want to convert and click the right mouse button to display the shortcut menu. Then select either Convert To Footnotes or Convert To Endnotes.

Inserting Annotations

Word has special features you can use if you are working on a document with other authors. You'll learn about marking revisions and selecting highlight colors in Chapter 23.

Sometimes you need to jot down a message, note, or reminder to yourself while you're working on a document. You might want to remind yourself, for example, to check a certain section of text or to format it in some way at a later date. You might also want to leave a note to someone else who will be reading or editing the document onscreen. These types of notes are called *annotations*.

Let's add an annotation to the document on the screen. Place the insertion point where you want to insert the annotation—in this case at the end of the last paragraph. Select Annotation from the Insert menu to display a pane at the bottom of the screen with the Annotation toolbar, as you can see in Figure 18-6. Word has inserted a code in the text and in the annotation pane showing the initials of the default user as well as the number of the annotation—such as [AN1] to represent the first annotation of user AN.

Type the text of your annotation: **Look up reference in Philadelphia and New York papers for January 1934**. Click on Close in the Annotation toolbar to remove the pane and to turn off the display of the annotation codes. To insert another annotation, select Annotation again from the Insert menu.

18

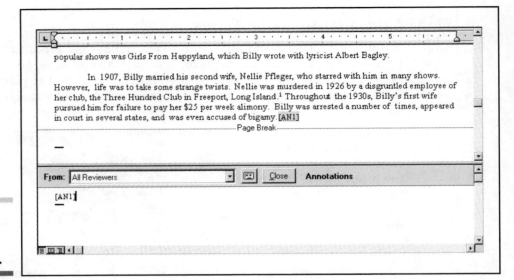

The
Annotation
pane
Figure 18-6.

Tip: If you press SHIFT-F5 after typing the annotation, Word leaves the annotation pane on the screen along with the display of the annotation codes.

Displaying and Printing Annotations

Annotations are formatted as hidden text, so they do not normally appear on the screen. If you want to see where the annotations have been inserted, select Options from the Tools menu, click on the View tab, and select the Hidden Text option from the nonprinting character section of the View page. When the annotation codes are displayed on the screen, you can display the text of an annotation in the pane by double-clicking on its code. Word will move the insertion point to the annotation text, opening the pane if it is not yet open. Once you have at least one annotation in your document, you can display the Annotation toolbar by holding down CTRL as you drag the split box.

Tip: Word will automatically display the codes when you turn on the Show/Hide command or when you display the Annotation toolbar.

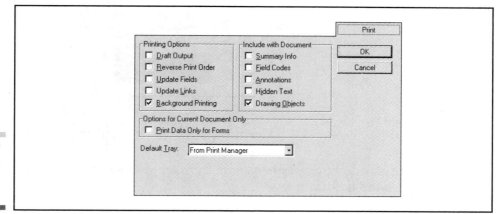

The Print page
of the Options
dialog box
Figure 18-7.

Annotations also do not normally print with your document, but you can print them in two ways. To print just the annotations with page references to where they are in the document, select Print from the File menu, pull down the Print What list, and select Annotations.

To print the annotations at the bottom of each document page, just like footnotes, select Print from the File menu and click on Options. Your screen will resemble Figure 18-7. Click on the Annotations option in the Include with Document section, select OK, and then print the document. Save and close the document.

Note: You will learn about the other printing options in Chapter 21.

Recording Voice Annotations

If your computer is equipped with hardware for recording and playing sounds, you can record an annotation instead of typing one. You, or anyone else, can later play the annotation to hear your message.

To record an annotation, click on the Insert Sound Object button in the Annotation toolbar. Windows will start the sound recorder program installed on your system. For example, here is the screen for the Sound Recorder program that comes with Windows:

18

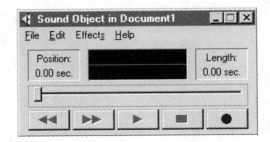

You may have another sound recorder program that was installed with your sound hardware.

Tip: To use an existing WAV-formatted file as the annotation, select Insert File from Sound Recorder's Edit menu.

[AN1] Click on the application's record button and speak into the microphone. Click on the stop button when you're finished, and then exit the application to return to Word. The sound annotation will appear as an icon of a speaker.

When you want to listen to the recorded message, display the annotation pane and double-click on the speaker icon.

Working with Outlines and Master Documents

19

Word not only helps you format long documents, but it can help you organize them as well. There's nothing like an outline to let you see your document's overall organization. By using two special Word features—outlines and master documents—you can tackle even the longest and most complicated documents with confidence.

Outline Primer

In Chapter 13 you learned how to create a numbered list and how to use a multilevel numbered list to write an outline. The numbered list command lets Word number paragraphs for you, even inserting numbers based on the indentation level. Outlining, however, goes far beyond simply numbering paragraphs. Outlining lets you integrate your outline with the document itself, so you do not need to type two documents—an outline and the complete text. You can work with one document that serves both purposes.

Outlining is easy to understand if you picture a document as having two parts—headings and body text. Headings are titles and subtitles; body text is the text of paragraphs under headings.

You can work on the document's overall organization and structure by hiding the body text and selected headings using a process called *collapsing*. This displays just the headings in an outline format. You can then edit the outline, making major changes in its organization by working with the headings alone. When you move a heading, for example, you can also move all of the text and subheadings that are under it. When you want to work with the entire document, you redisplay the body text and any collapsed subheadings in a process called *expanding*.

Outlines contain *families*. An outline family consists of a heading and all of the subheadings and text under it. For example, this is the Diagnostic Testing family in a sample outline:

```
Diagnosing Lyme Disease
        Physical Symptoms
        Rash
        Diagnostic Testing
                Titers
                Western Blot
Treating Lyme Disease
        Antibiotics
                Early Detected
                Early Disseminated
                Late Disseminated
        Patient Monitoring
        Adjunctive Therapy
```

However, if you start the family at "Diagnosing Lyme Disease", then the family contains all of the outline up to the heading "Treating Lyme Disease".

To work with an outline, you change to Outline view. In Outline view, headings and subheadings appear indented to reflect outline levels. You can still edit and format the text in Normal and Page Layout views. To switch to Outline view, select Outline from the View menu or click on the Outline View button on the left of the horizontal scroll bar.

Outline headings are associated with heading styles. In Outline view you do not have to apply the styles yourself; Word will apply them for you based on the indentation level. It will apply the Heading 1 style to the first outline level, Heading 2 to the second level, and so on. If you have already created a document using heading styles, then Word will create the outline for you instantly.

Creating an Outline

The best way to learn how to outline is to create one. Start Word and click on the Outline View button on the left of the horizontal scroll bar. Word displays the Outline toolbar and a symbol indicating an outline heading level, and it applies the Heading 1 style, as shown here.

Note: When you are in Outline view, Word removes the ruler from display and dims the Ruler option in the View menu.

Type **Diagnosing Lyme Disease** and press ENTER. Word moves the insertion point to the next line and inserts the same level indicator symbol also formatted using the Heading 1 style.

Remember: Unlike regular heading styles, which turn off when you press ENTER, outline headings remain in effect when you move to the next line.

When you want to type a heading at a lower level—indented farther to the right—press TAB or click on the Demote button in the Outline toolbar. Word moves the insertion point to the next indentation level and displays the outline like this:

⊹ **Diagnosing Lyme Disease**
▫ /

Tip: If your text is not formatted as shown here, click on the Show Formatting button in the Outline toolbar. You'll learn more about this later.

The new level is formatted using the Heading 2 style, because it is at the second outline level. Notice that the level indicator in the line above now looks like a plus sign. This indicates that the level contains sublevels or body text.

Type **Physical Symptoms** and press ENTER. Word moves the insertion point to the next line and automatically indents it to the same position as the previous line. Type **Diagnostic Testing** and press ENTER. Press TAB or click on the Demote button in the Outline toolbar to move to the third level and to apply the Heading 3 style. The level indicator immediately before changes to reflect that it now contains subheadings. Type **Titers**, press ENTER, type **Western Blot**, and press ENTER. Your outline now looks like this:

⊹ **Diagnosing Lyme Disease**
   ▫ *Physical Symptoms*
  ⊹ *Diagnostic testing*
     ▫ Titers
     ▫ Western Blot
     ▫ |

Now click on the Promote button in the Outline toolbar or press SHIFT-TAB to move the outline level one position to the left—to the next highest level and formatted in the Heading 2 style.

Tip: You can also press ALT-SHIFT-LEFT ARROW and ALT-SHIFT-RIGHT ARROW to demote and promote outline levels.

Click on the Promote button again or press SHIFT-TAB to move one more outline level one position to the left—to the next highest level and formatted in the Heading 1 style. Now complete the outline as shown in Figure 19-1.

You can insert and delete outline headings and change levels—Word will automatically adjust the levels for you. Place the insertion point at the end

19

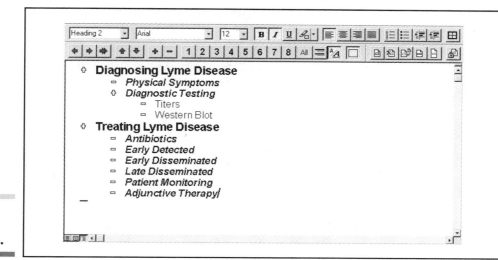

Our sample
outline
Figure 19-1.

*If you press
ENTER after
you type, Word
will insert
another outline
entry. Press
BACKSPACE to
delete the
entry and
return to the*

of the heading "Western Blot" and press ENTER. Word inserts a new level at the Heading 3 position. Since you want to insert a second-level heading, click on Promote or press SHIFT-TAB again. Type **Rash** but do not press ENTER.

You can also change an outline level by demoting and promoting. For example, place the insertion point on the heading "Early Detected" and click on the Demote button. The heading shifts to the next lowest indentation level, and the indicator of the line above changes to show that it now has subheadings:

In the same way, demote the headings "Early Disseminated" and "Late Disseminated".

Adding Body Text

So far your outline contains only headings. That's fine if the document is just an outline. By inserting body text, however, you can build your outline into a complete document. Place the insertion point at the end of the heading "Physical Symptoms" and press ENTER. Now click on the Demote to

Body Text button in the Outline toolbar. The indicator appears as a small square and Word applies the Normal style:

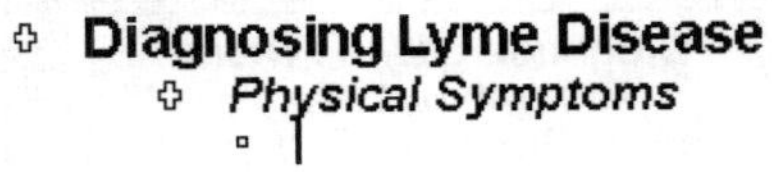

⬦ **Diagnosing Lyme Disease**
⬦ *Physical Symptoms*
▫

Type the following:

Diagnosing by physical symptoms alone is difficult because the symptoms of Lyme Disease mimic those of many other conditions. Symptoms include muscle soreness, joint swelling, fevers and sweats, and neurological problems such as forgetfulness and mood swings.

Place the insertion point at the end of the heading "Diagnostic Testing", press ENTER, and then click on Demote to Body Text. Type this:

Lyme tests may give inconsistent results, so some physicians recommend several tests by different laboratories.

Save the document with the name Diagnosing Lyme Disease. The completed outline is shown in Figure 19-2.

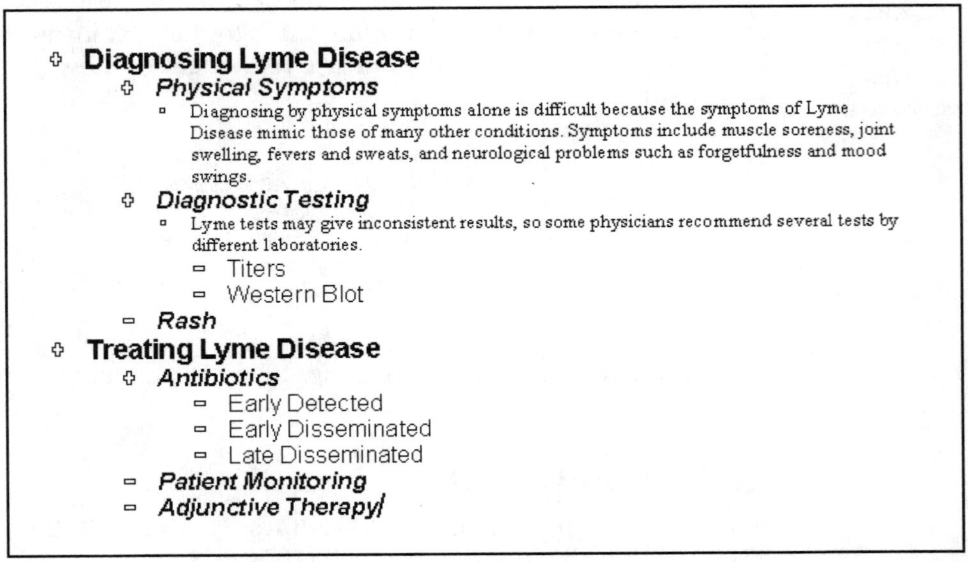

⬦ **Diagnosing Lyme Disease**
  ⬦ *Physical Symptoms*
    ▫ Diagnosing by physical symptoms alone is difficult because the symptoms of Lyme Disease mimic those of many other conditions. Symptoms include muscle soreness, joint swelling, fevers and sweats, and neurological problems such as forgetfulness and mood swings.
  ⬦ *Diagnostic Testing*
    ▫ Lyme tests may give inconsistent results, so some physicians recommend several tests by different laboratories.
      ▫ Titers
      ▫ Western Blot
  ▫ *Rash*
⬦ **Treating Lyme Disease**
  ⬦ *Antibiotics*
    ▫ Early Detected
    ▫ Early Disseminated
    ▫ Late Disseminated
  ▫ *Patient Monitoring*
  ▫ *Adjunctive Therapy*

The completed outline
Figure 19-2.

19

Outlining an Existing Document

If you've already typed a document using the heading styles, you can convert it into an outline simply by displaying it in Outline view. Word will use the existing heading styles to determine their outline levels, formatting the remaining text as body text.

To convert a document that does not contain heading styles, either format its titles and subtitles as headings in Normal or Page Layout view, or demote and promote them in Outline view. In Outline view, titles not formatted with heading styles will appear as body text.

Working with Outlines

You can edit and format text in an outline just as you can for any document. Word already applies the heading styles, but you can modify these styles and format the text any way you want. How the text appears when in Outline view depends on the Show Formatting button. When the button is pressed, your text will appear according to the applied styles and formats. When the button is not pressed, all of the text appears in one font, font size, and style, although the outline levels are still applied, as you can see here.

     ✧   Diagnosing Lyme Disease
         ✧   Physical Symptoms
             ▫   Diagnosing by physical symptoms alone is difficult because the symptoms of Lyme
                Disease mimic those of many other conditions. Symptoms include muscle soreness, joint

No matter how the button looks, the text will appear formatted when you change to Normal or Page Layout view. In fact, let's look at the document in Normal view. Click on the Normal View button next to the horizontal scroll bar or select Normal from the View menu. The outline levels are no longer indented but appear in the default paragraph formats of the heading styles, as in Figure 19-3.

Now click on the Outline View button to return to Outline view. The headings will again be formatted according to their outline levels.

Moving Outline Families

The arrangement of outlines in families makes them easier to work with. You can move sections of the outline by dragging or by clicking on these buttons in the Outline toolbar:

Move Up ⟶   ⟵ Move Down

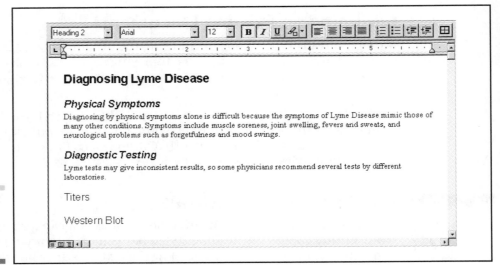

You can move just a heading, without affecting its family, or the entire family itself. To move just the heading, place the insertion point anywhere in the heading, and then click on Move Up or Move Down as desired. Moving just the heading will not affect any subheadings or subtexts in the family. To move an entire family, you must select the family. When you move a family, all of its subheadings and body text move with it.

Let's move the heading "Rash" up in the outline. Select the heading so you can practice selecting a family. To select the heading, point to the level indicator at the uppermost level of the family so the pointer is shaped as a four-directional arrow, and then click the mouse.

Click once on the Move Up button. The heading moves up one position, so it now appears to have "Western Blot" as a subheading:

Click on the Move Up button three more times to move the heading above "Diagnostic Testing".

You can also move a family by drag and drop. Click on the family level indicator, hold down the mouse button, and drag. As you drag, the mouse pointer will appear as a two-directional arrow, and Word will display a line showing the location:

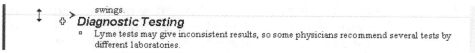

Release the mouse button when the line appears where you want to move the family.

Remember: To select consecutive families, select the first and then hold down SHIFT while you select others. You cannot select multiple families that are not consecutive.

Collapsing and Expanding Outlines

One of the advantages of working with an outline is that it lets you visualize the organization of topics and subtopics. You can see at a glance how subjects are related. When you have a long outline or a document with body text, however, headings may be too far apart to show the structure. To solve this problem, you can collapse and expand an outline.

When you collapse an outline, you select specific levels that will be displayed, hiding other levels and body text. For example, to visualize the order of just the major topics—those formatted with the Heading 1 style—you collapse the outline so only the first levels appear. To see the major topics and their immediate subtopics, you collapse the outline to the second level. Expanding an outline is just the reverse—it displays the information of the collapsed sections.

To collapse or expand a specific family, double-click on the heading level indicator or place the insertion point anywhere in the heading and use these buttons:

To expand or collapse the *entire outline* to one level, click on one of the Show buttons on the Outline toolbar:

Clicking on the 1 button, for example, will display just the level one headings, clicking on the 2 button will display level one and two headings, and so forth. Clicking on buttons 2 through 8 will either collapse or expand the outline, depending on what is already displayed. If you just collapsed the outline to level 1, for instance, clicking on 2 will expand the outline. If you just clicked on 3, however, using the 2 button will collapse the outline.

Click on the the 1 button now. This collapses the outline to its major subjects, as shown here.

♦ **Diagnosing Lyme Disease**
♦ **Treating Lyme Disease**

The shaded lines indicate that some headings or body text is not displayed. Click on the 2 button to see its effect, and then click on 3.

Word only displays body text in Outline view when the entire outline is expanded, that is, when all levels are displayed. Click on the All button now to display the entire outline—every level and all body text.

Tip: If you want some indication of the body text without displaying all of it, click on the Show First Line Only button. Word will display the first line of each body text paragraph. Click on the button again when you want to display the complete body text.

Numbering Outlines

Word's outline feature is most effective when you use it with a document. However, if you just want to print out the outline for reference, without the body text, then click on the 8 button to hide the body text. You might also want to print the outline numbered. To do this, simply add heading numbering, as explained in Chapter 15. Select Heading Numbering from the Format menu and choose the type of numbers from the dialog box. The numbers will appear in Normal, Page Layout, and Outline views. To later remove the numbers, when you want to print the document for example, display the dialog box and click on Remove.

Creating Master Documents

While outlines help you organize documents, working with a long document can be difficult. Long documents take longer to scroll through and to reformat. You may also format or edit sections of the document by mistake.

Rather than work with a long document as one object, you can create a master document. A master document is a type of outline in which outline

19

families can be stored as separate documents on your disk, called *subdocuments*. You can edit the subdocuments within the master or in its own window, and save subdocuments independently from the master.

To use a master document, either select Master Document from the View menu or click on the Master Document View button on the right of the Outline toolbar. Click on the button now. Word will display the Master Document toolbar to the right of the Outline toolbar (which it also displays if you are not already in Outline view).

You can convert the text in outline families into subdocuments—storing them individually on the disk—or insert a document already on the disk as a subdocument. To create a subdocument from existing text, select the family that you want to use for the subdocument, and then click on the Create Subdocument button. Let's do this now with the outline on the screen. Click on the level indicator next to "Diagnostic Testing" to select the family, and then click on the Create Subdocument button. The subdocument will be surrounded by a border with a subdocument icon, as shown here.

⬩ **Diagnostic Testing**
 ▫ Lyme tests may give inconsistent results, so some physicians recommend several tests by different laboratories.
  ▭ Titers
  ⬩ Western Blot
   ▫

Remember: If you select multiple families, each will become a separate subdocument.

You can edit the subdocument just as you can any other text, but you can also separate it from the master document to edit or format it in its own window. Double-click on the subdocument icon. Word opens a new document window with the subdocument, as shown in Figure 19-4. The document appears in Normal view and is followed by a section break. Place the insertion point at the end of the heading "Titers", press ENTER, and then type **There are two types of titers to test for Lyme Disease.** Save the document using the default suggested name, Diagnostic Testing. Word will automatically update the master document when you save the document in the subdocument window.

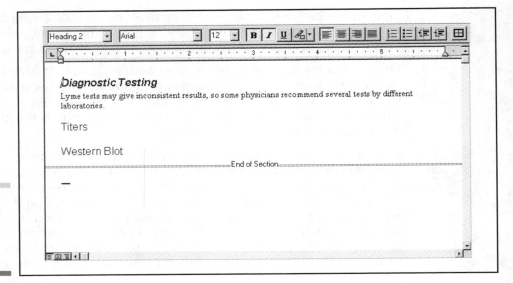

Pull down the Window menu and select Diagnosing Lyme Disease to switch back to the master document. Word has updated the master with the changes in the saved subdocument. You will also see a small padlock icon near the subdocument icon.

The padlock indicates that the subdocument in the master is locked in read-only status. You will not be able to work with the subdocument in the master until you close the separate subdocument window. So return to the subdocument window and close the document. Closing the subdocument window will remove the lock in the master.

When you save the master document, Word will also save each of the subdocuments as separate files. If you did not save and name a subdocument in its own window, Word will automatically use the first characters in the subdocument as the name without asking. You will, of course, be asked to name the master.

Save and close the document.

Working with Subdocuments

The Master Document toolbar lets you perform other operations with subdocuments.

If you have an existing document that you want to insert as a subdocument, click on the Insert Subdocument button, and then select the file name from the dialog box that appears. The document will be inserted in your master document as a subdocument, within borders and with the subdocument icon. This is different from the Insert File command that inserts only the text.

 To change a subdocument back to regular text, click on its subdocument icon, and then click on the Remove Subdocument button. The border and subdocument icon will disappear, but not the text. If you've already saved the master and subdocuments, the subdocument file will remain on the disk, but will no longer be associated with the master document.

 Tip: To delete the contents of a subdocument, click on its subdocument icon and press DELETE.

 If you want to combine two or more adjacent subdocuments into one, select them—using SHIFT as you click on the second and subsequent subdocuments—and then click on the Merge Subdocument button.

 To divide one subdocument into two separate subdocuments, place the insertion point at the beginning of the paragraph where you want to start the new document. Then click on the Split Subdocument button.

 To lock the text of a subdocument so it cannot be changed, place the insertion point in the subdocument, and then click on the Lock Document button. If you've edited the subdocument since it was last saved, Word will ask if you want to save it now. To unlock the subdocument, place the insertion point in it and click on the Lock Document button again.

You can also lock the text of the master document, but not the subdocuments. Place the insertion point in any text that is not in a subdocument and click on the Lock Document button. Word actually closes the document—so don't panic when it disappears from the screen—and then reopens it in read-only status. You can now edit and format the subdocuments but not the master.

Sharing Information Between Programs

20

Because Word is a Windows application, it takes full advantage of the Windows 95 interface. Among other things, this means that it can share information with other Windows and even some DOS programs. Sharing information lets you create compound documents. A *compound document* is one that includes information from more than one source. For example, your document may include a chart created in Excel, a picture drawn in Paint, a table created in Access, and text written in WordPerfect or some other word processing program. Rather than retyping the information, or re-creating the graph and table in Word, you combine existing files or objects in a single document.

The source may also be called the server, and the target may be referred to as the client.

Sharing information requires two types of programs—the source and the target. The *source* is the program that you use to create the information. The *target* is the program in which you will be using the data. So for example, if you want to use an Excel worksheet in Word, Excel is the source and Word is the target.

Cut and Paste:
Using the Clipboard to Share Information

One of the quickest ways to share information is through the Clipboard, using techniques similar to those you've learned for moving and copying text within a Word document. To use the Clipboard, open Word and display the document in which you want to insert the information, then open the source program and display the information that you want to use. Cut or copy the information in the source document, switch to Word, and paste the contents of the Clipboard where you want it inserted.

Tip: Depending on your Windows applications, you may also be able to drag and drop information from one application to another.

In most cases, information that you paste appears as a *static* copy. This means that there is no connection between the information and the source program. When you copy and paste cells from Excel, however, Word inserts them as a table, complete with grid lines, as shown in Figure 20-1. All of the values of the worksheet will appear, but none of the formulas and functions will be retained.

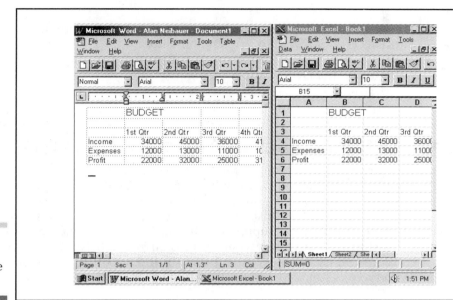

Word inserts
pasted Excel
cells as a table
Figure 20-1.

20

You can also paste information from a DOS application. When you run a
DOS program in Windows, it will appear in a special DOS window with
this toolbar:

To copy information from the DOS-application window, follow these steps:

1. Click on the Mark button in the DOS window's toolbar.
2. Drag the mouse over the text that you want to copy.

3. Click on the Copy button in the DOS window's toolbar.
4. Switch to Word and place the insertion point where you want to insert
   the text.

5. Click on Paste on Word's Standard toolbar.

Tip: You can also use the Clipboard to copy information within the DOS window. Mark and copy the text in the DOS window, place the cursor where you want to insert it, and then click on the Paste button in the DOS window's toolbar.

Opening Files in Alternate Formats

If you want to use information in a file on your disk, you may be able to open the file directly into Word. Word can automatically open documents in any Word format—previous versions of Word for Windows and for DOS, Word for the Macintosh, and Word files created with WordPad, the word processing program supplied with Windows 95. To open other formats, you must install converters when you install Word. If you have them installed, Word will try to detect the type of file and use the appropriate filter. The converters supplied with Word will open these types of files:

♦ WordPerfect for Windows and MS-DOS (versions 5.*x* and 6.0)

♦ Microsoft Excel (versions 2.*x*, 3.0, 4.0, and 5.0)

♦ RFT-DCA from IBM DisplayWrite and similar formats

♦ Microsoft Write for Windows (version 3.*x*)

♦ Microsoft Works

♦ Lotus 1-2-3 (releases 2.*x* and 3.*x*)

♦ WordStar (versions 3.3 through 7.0)

♦ Rich Text Format (RTF), which has special formatting instructions that can be recognized by other applications that can open this format

Keep in mind, however, that not every feature of every word processing program can be converted into Word's own format. Word will try to replace these formats as best it can, or delete them, so review the opened document carefully.

Upgrader: You can also open Microsoft Exchange Personal Address Books and Schedule+ Contact Lists.

If Word does not recognize the file type, it will display the dialog box you
see here.

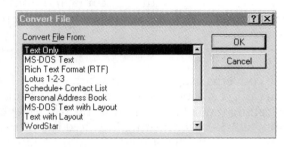

Select the file type, or one that you think is compatible, and click on OK.
Word will display an error message if it cannot open the file.

In addition to files in these formats, Word can open a document saved as a
text file. A *text file* contains characters, spaces, and codes such as carriage
returns, but no formatting information, such as for fonts and character
styles. There are two commonly used sets of characters—ANSI and MS-DOS.
The ANSI character set can be used by almost any computer, even those that
are not IBM compatible, such as Apple and UNIX systems. The MS-DOS set
includes some characters that can only be read by Windows and DOS
programs on PC-compatible computers. Word will try to detect the correct
type of text file when you open it.

You can have greater flexibility with text files, however, if you designate the
type of file yourself using the Confirm dialog box. To have this dialog box
displayed each time you open a non Word file, select Options from the Tools
menu. Click on the General tab, select the Confirm Conversion at Open
option, and then click on OK. Now when you open a text file you can select
from these choices:

♦ *Text Only* or *MS-DOS Text Only* Word opens the document exactly as it
was saved. If each line ends in a carriage return, for example, each line
will appear as a separate paragraph ending with a paragraph mark.

♦ *Text With Layout* or *MS-DOS Text With Layout* Word tries to preserve the
layout. If each line ends with a paragraph mark, for example, Word will
delete many of them so the lines wrap at the margin, forming a larger
paragraph. Blank spaces before text may be converted into indentations
and tab stops, and multiple paragraph marks may be used to determine
paragraph and line spacing.

Tip: When you open a document, Word places it in its own document window. You can use the File command from the Insert menu to open the document so it appears at the location of the insertion point in the active document.

The converters supplied with Word work with the most popular file formats. You can get additional converters for less popular formats free from Microsoft by calling (800) 360-7561, or using Text Telephone (TT/TDD) services at (800) 892-5234 for hearing-impaired users. If you have a modem, you can download converters from the MSWord Forum on CompuServe, or directly from the Microsoft Download Service at (206) 936-6735. Set your modem to no parity, 8 data bits, one stop bit, and either 1200, 2400, or 9600 baud.

Saving Files

When you save a converted document, Word will first display the dialog box you see here, asking if you want to save it as a Word document or in its original format.

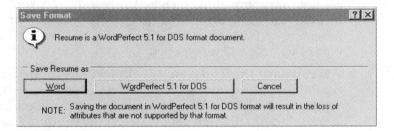

You can also use the converters to save a document in any of the formats that they can open except as Lotus 1-2-3 and Excel files. So for example, you can create a document in Word and then save it as a WordPerfect document. To save a document in a format other than Word, display the Save As dialog box, pull down the Save as Type list, and choose the format. Then name and save the file as you've already learned.

In addition to the word processing formats, you can save the document as a text file. Selecting Text Only or MS-DOS Text Only will save each paragraph as one long line. If you open the document in another word processing program, the program will use its own settings to wrap the text into paragraphs. If you select Text Only with Line Breaks or MS-DOS Text Only with Line Breaks, Word will add a paragraph mark at the end of each line. If you open the document into another word processing program, each line will be a separate paragraph.

Opening Graphics

You cannot open graphics files into Word as you do document files. To display graphics in your document, you must use the Picture command from the Insert menu. If you choose to install the graphics converters when you install Word, you can insert graphics in any of these formats:

◆ AutoCAD Format 2-D (DXF)

◆ Computer Graphics Metafile (CGM)

◆ CorelDRAW 3.0 (CDR)

◆ Encapsulated PostScript (EPS)

◆ HP Graphics Language (HPGL)

◆ Kodak Photo CD (PCD)

◆ Lotus 1-2-3 graphic (PIC)

◆ Micrografx Designer/Draw (DRW)

◆ PC Paintbrush (PCX)

◆ Tagged Image File Format (TIF)

◆ Targa (TGA)

◆ WordPerfect Graphics (WPG)

20

Tip: You can obtain additional graphics converters from Microsoft.

Linking and Embedding

When you open a file into Word, it becomes a Word document. For example, suppose you open an Excel worksheet into Word to use for a sales report, or insert it from the Clipboard using the Paste command. The worksheet will appear as a table, but there are two problems.

First, all of the functions and formulas are not in the table, and you may not be able to reproduce them using Word's table formulas. Second, if you open Excel and change the values in the worksheet, the old values will still be in the Word document. To update the values, you must delete the table from Word and open or paste the new version. If you forget to update the table, your sales report will have the incorrect values.

Three Sharing Methods

There are three ways that you can avoid one or both of the problems associated with opening another application's file in Word—Dynamic Data Exchange (DDE), embedding, and linking. Unfortunately, not every Windows application works exactly the same way when it comes to sharing information. The remainder of this chapter explains these three sharing methods using Microsoft Excel as the source. While you can apply the general concepts to most applications, some have different capabilities.

Dynamic Data Exchange

With *Dynamic Data Exchange*, the values in the document are inserted as fields linked to the worksheet file on your disk. You can use Word's capabilities to format the information, but you can update the fields using F9—just as you can update the date fields or page numbers in an index—so when you print the document the current values appear. When you first create a DDE link, and both Excel and Word are open, the link is called *hot*. This means that if you change the worksheet in Excel, the information in Word also changes, and you do not need to use the Word update command. Once you save or close the worksheet, however, the link becomes *cold*, and you must update the fields yourself. To edit the information, such as to change values and recalculate the cells, you must start Excel and open the worksheet.

Embedding

When you *embed* a worksheet in Word, you are actually placing the worksheet in the document. You cannot format or edit the information in Word because it is considered one object, not individual characters. To edit or format the information, double-click on the worksheet. Word starts Excel and moves the information from the document into the Excel window. All of the formulas and functions are retained. In a sense, then, there is a connection between the object in Word and the application that you used to create the object, Excel.

There is no connection between the information and a disk file that you may have saved with Excel. For example, suppose you create a worksheet called Sales.xls and then copy and embed a portion of the worksheet in Word. When you double-click on the object in your document, Word opens Excel, takes a copy of the object, and inserts it into the Excel window. When you change the information, the changes are recorded in the Word document, but Sales.xls is not opened or affected. Similarly, if you later start Excel and open and edit the Sales.xls worksheet, the information in the Word document will not change. There is no way to update the information to automatically match the worksheet—you must copy and embed it all over again.

Linking

When you *link* a worksheet, you are inserting a representation of it into the document. It is also an object, meaning that you cannot edit or format the information in Word but only in Excel. However, when you double-click on the object, Word starts Excel and opens the worksheet file. There is a connection between the object in Word and the disk file containing the object's information.

20

Using the Sales.xls file again as an example, when you double-click on the object, Word opens Excel and retrieves Sales.xls into the Excel window. When you edit and save the worksheet, the changes are also applied to the object in Word. Of course, you can always start Excel and open the worksheet independently from Word. You can then later update the Word document so the current version of Sales.xls is reflected in the document.

Note: While embedding and linking are two different ways to share information, they are made possible by the same resource, a process known as OLE (Object Linking and Embedding). OLE provides the programs and mechanisms for both embedding and linking. OLE is so popular that the generic term "link" usually refers to one created with OLE, not DDE.

Sharing Through the Clipboard

There are several ways that you can implement each of the sharing methods. Let's first look at using the Clipboard.

Creating a DDE Link

To create a DDE link between Excel and Word, follow these steps:

1. Start Excel and type or open the worksheet. If you type or edit the worksheet, save it.

2. Select and copy the cells that you want to insert into Word.

3. Start or change to Word and place the insertion point where you want to insert the data.

4. Select Paste Special from the Edit menu to display the following dialog box:

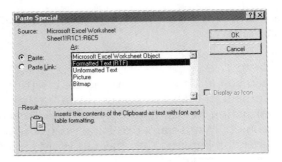

5. Select either the Formatted Text (RTF) or Unformatted Text option. Selecting Formatted Text will insert the information so it appears as a table; Unformatted Text inserts the values in the cells separated with tabs.

6. Select the Paste Link option button. If you select the Paste option instead, the information will be pasted into Word without any connection or link.

7. Click on OK.

You can now format the text and table in Word. To update the information to the current version of the saved file, select the information so the fields appear highlighted:

	BUDGET			
	1st Qtr	2nd Qtr	3rd Qtr	4th Qtr
Income	34000	45000	36000	41000
Expenses	12000	13000	11000	10000
Profit	22000	32000	25000	31000

Then press F9. You can also update the fields automatically when you print the document using the Options dialog box, as explained in Chapter 21.

Embedding Information

To embed information from a worksheet, follow the same initial steps as for a DDE link: select the information in Excel, change to Word, and choose Paste Special from the Edit menu. However, in the Paste Special dialog box, click on the Microsoft Excel Worksheet Object choice and the Paste option—not Paste Link.

If you click on the embedded object, it will appear surrounded by a border with resizing handles, not as individual fields:

20

	BUDGET			
	1st Qtr	2nd Qtr	3rd Qtr	4th Qtr
Income	34000	45000	36000	41000
Expenses	12000	13000	11000	10000
Profit	22000	32000	25000	31000

When you need to edit or format the information, double-click on it. Windows will open Excel and transmit the data from the Word document to Excel. Excel opens, however, in what is termed *in-place*—directly on the Word program window. Word's menus and toolbars are replaced with Excel's, and the worksheet appears in the Word document window, as shown in Figure 20-2. After you edit or format the information, click outside of the worksheet to return to, and update, the Word document.

Creating a Link with Object Linking and Embedding

To create a link using the resources of Object Linking and Embedding (OLE), start out using the same procedure as you do for embedding. However, in the Paste Special dialog box, select the Paste Link option, and select either the Object, Bitmap, or Picture type. Any of the three choices will create the link; they just differ in how the information is displayed. When you select the Object type, the information appears as text. When you select either

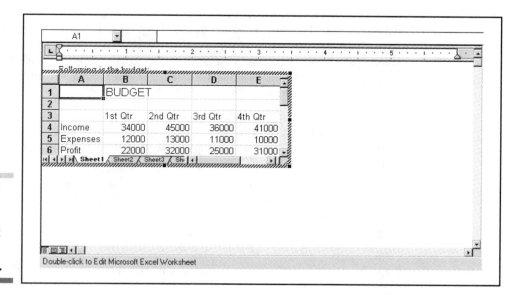

Double-click on an embedded object to edit it in place

Figure 20-2.

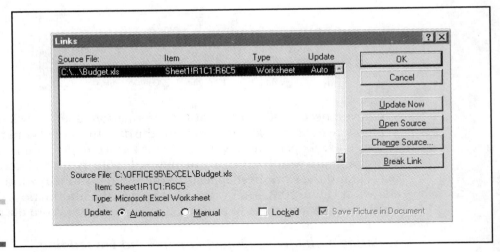

Updating links
Figure 20-3.

Picture or Bitmap, the worksheet appears as a table with grid lines—they only differ in the resolution of the graphic image.

When you double-click on a linked object, Windows starts, or switches to Excel, and then opens the linked file. Excel opens in its own window, not in-place over Word.

Not all of the options will be selectable for each type of object.

To update the linked information, select the object and press F9, or use the Links command from the Edit menu to display the dialog box shown in Figure 20-3. This box lets you update the link and change the way it is linked. Select the item that you want to update or change, and then choose an option from the dialog box. To update several links at one time, hold down CTRL when you select them.

In the Update section, choose Automatic to update the object every time you open the document, or choose Manual. With manual update, select the file in the document and press F9, or select it in this dialog box and select Update Now.

Select the Locked option when you want to prevent the object from being updated—either with F9, by using the Update Now command, or when the document is opened or printed. Deselect the check box if you later want to update the link. You can also lock an object by selecting it in the document and pressing CTRL-F11. Unlock the object with CTRL-SHIFT-F11.

Here's a summary of the other options in the dialog box:

♦ *Open Source* runs the source application used to create the linked object. It's the same as double-clicking on the object in the dialog box.

- *Change Source* lets you specify another source file. Use this option if you rename the file or move it to another disk or directory.

- *Break Link* disconnects the linkage between the object and the source file. You can also select the object in the document and press CTRL-SHIFT-F9.

- *Save Picture in Document* lets you store an entire linked graphics file in the document or just the link to it. This option is not dimmed when you select a linked graphics object.

20

Using the Insert Object Command

You can also embed and link information using the Object command from the Insert menu. To create and insert an embedded object, display the Create New page of the dialog box, shown in Figure 20-4. Notice that this is the same dialog box that you've already used to create a WordArt object, which is really an embedded object edited in-place. In the Object Type list, select the application for the object you want to insert, such as Microsoft Excel Worksheet, and then click on OK. Word will start Excel as an in-place window for you to create the worksheet.

Tip: To quickly create an embedded Excel worksheet in your document, click on the Insert Microsoft Excel Worksheet button in the Standard toolbar. Use it like the Insert Table button, to select the number of rows and columns you want. When you select the table size, Excel opens as an in-place window where you enter and format the worksheet.

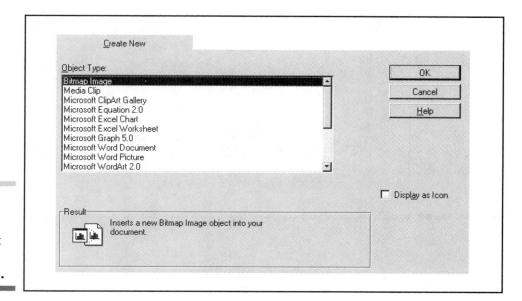

The Create
New page
of the
Insert Object
dialog box
Figure 20-4.

You can also embed a worksheet that you've already created and saved using Excel. Click on the Create from File tab of the Object dialog box to see the page shown in Figure 20-5. Use the File Name or Browse command to specify the name of the file and then select OK.

To link the file rather than embed it, select the Link to File check box.

Inserting Database Files

Files from database programs cannot normally be opened, embedded, or linked using the same methods you've learned for Excel. However, you can still import a database file or link one with Word.

Use the Database option from the Insert menu to insert a database file as a Word table—either as text or as fields using DDE. Select Get Data from the Database dialog box shown in Figure 20-6, and then choose the database file that you want to open. The Database dialog box will reappear. Use the Query Options command to select fields and to select and sort records. Use the Table AutoFormat command to format the resulting table. Then click on Inset Data to display this dialog box:

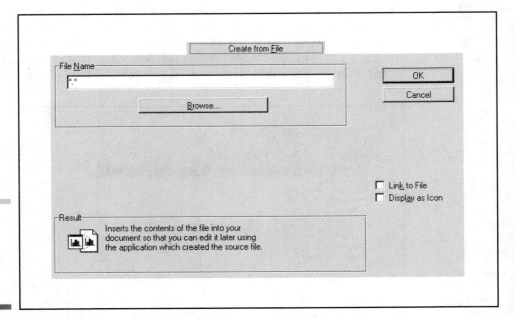

The Create from File page of the Insert Object dialog box
Figure 20-5.

20

Use the
Database
dialog box
to insert a
database as
a Word table
or as fields
using DDE
links
Figure 20-6.

Use the options to select a specific range of records. To insert the
information as DDE fields, click on the Insert Data as Field button.

If you want to use a database file as the data source for a merge operation,
choose the Open Data Source option from the Get Data command in Mail
Merge Helper. The database that you select will be linked with the form
document, so your merge will use the most up-to-date information in the
database.

PART 5

Special Word Features

Personalizing Word's Settings

21

If you don't like something about the way Word works, don't despair. Using the Options command from the Tools menu, you can customize many of Word's features to suit your own tastes and work habits. The Options command displays a dialog box with 12 pages. Each page contains a series of settings that you can use to modify what appears on the screen or how Word operates.

In previous chapters you've learned how to use several pages of this dialog box to change something about how Word works. The following table lists the options you've already read about:

Options Section	Chapter
Save	2
Spelling	10
Grammar	10
AutoFormat	3
User Info	11

This chapter looks at the other pages in the Options dialog box and examines the Save section in more detail. (You'll learn about the Revisions section in Chapter 23.)

Upgrader: The Options dialog box contains some new options, and several have been moved to different sections.

General Options

Use the following options on the General page, shown in Figure 21-1, to set some overall features of Word.

♦ *Background Repagination* means that Word automatically divides your document into pages as you type, adjusting the page breaks as you insert, delete, or format text. If you have a slower computer system, you might experience some delay when performing certain tasks as Word paginates the document. Word always paginates in Page Layout view. To turn off this feature for Normal view, deselect Background Repagination.

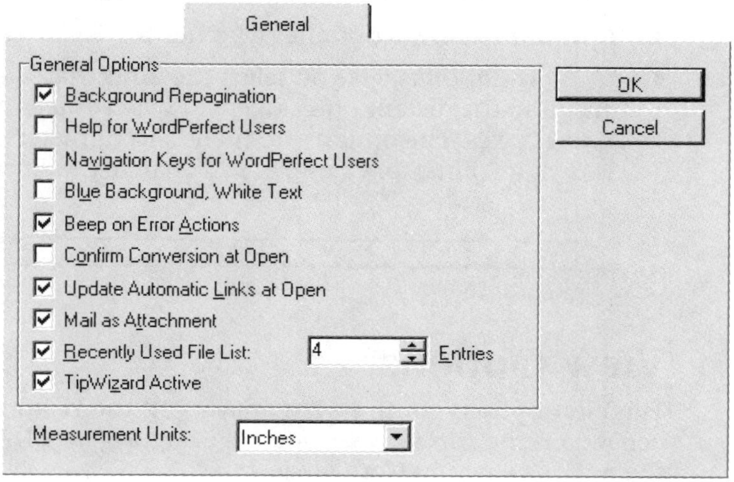

The General
options
Figure 21-1.

♦ *Help for WordPerfect Users* turns on the WordPerfect Help feature, which is also accessible from the Help menu. With this feature turned on, using a WordPerfect keyboard command will display a dialog box explaining how to perform the task in Word.

♦ *Navigation Keys for WordPerfect Users* turns on the help function for users who press WordPerfect's cursor movement keys. For example, CTRL-HOME is the WordPerfect command for Go To. With this feature turned on, pressing CTRL-HOME will show you how to use Word's Go To function from the Edit menu.

♦ *Blue Background, White Text* changes the foreground and background colors in the document window.

♦ *Beep on Error Actions* determines whether Word sounds a beep when an error condition occurs, such as trying to move the insertion point below the endmark.

♦ *Confirm Conversion at Open* will display a dialog box listing other file formats when you open a document not in Word's own format. In earlier versions of Word, this option appeared in the Open dialog box.

♦ *Update Automatic Links at Open* causes Word to retrieve the most current versions of linked objects when you open a document.

♦ *Mail as Attachment* lets you attach a document to an E-mail message from Word.

♦ *Recently Used File List* determines how many recently used files are listed at the bottom of the File menu.

♦ *TipWizard Active* determines whether the Tip Wizard is turned on or off.

♦ *Measurement Units* lets you select the units that Word displays in the ruler and the default units accepted when you enter measurements in dialog boxes. The options are Inches, Centimeters, Points, and Pica. Selecting Points, for example, will change the ruler to this:

View Options

The View options control what appears on the Word screen, and the options depend on the current view you are using. Figure 21-2, for example, shows the options when in Normal view.

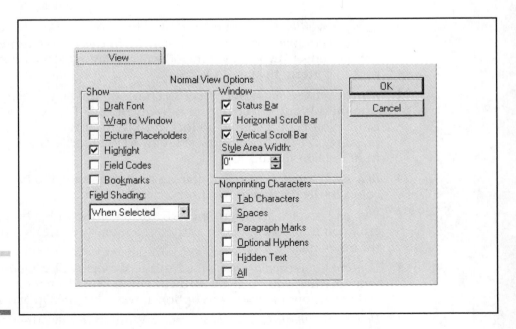

The View options

Figure 21-2.

Show Section

The options in the Show section determine whether Word displays specific objects:

♦ *Draft Font* displays all text in one font, indicating all character formats with underlines. This sometimes speeds up scrolling and other functions on slower computers.

♦ *Wrap to Window* determines whether Word displays long lines of text that would not fit in the window in Normal view by temporarily wrapping the lines at the right margin.

♦ *Picture Placeholders* determines whether Word displays actual graphics or just represents them by an empty box to speed scrolling and other features.

♦ *Highlight* controls whether color highlighting inserted using the Highlight button in the toolbar appears onscreen. You'll learn more about highlighting in Chapter 23.

♦ *Field Codes* turns on and off the display of fields.

♦ *Bookmarks* determines whether bookmark codes appear—see Chapter 23 for more information on bookmarks.

♦ *Field Shading* determines when the gray shading appears around field codes. The options are When Selected, Never, and Always.

21

In Page Layout view, the Show options do not include the Draft Font and Wrap to Window options, but do include these additional choices:

♦ *Drawings* turns on and off the display of pictures that you create using the Drawing toolbar.

♦ *Object Anchors* displays the paragraph anchors for framed objects, without selecting the Show/Hide button.

♦ *Text Boundaries* displays crop marks in the corners of the page, a dotted box around the text area of the page, and dotted boxes around text boxes.

Window Section

The Window section determines which parts of the Word screen appear, including the status bar, horizontal scroll bar, vertical scroll bar, style area in Normal view, and vertical ruler in Page Layout view. For example, if you set the magnification so you can see the full line on the screen, there is no need for the horizontal scroll bar.

Nonprinting Characters Section

The options in the Nonprinting Characters section determine which special characters appear on the screen. Selecting All turns on the Show/Hide function, which you can turn off by clicking the button in the toolbar. Choose the other options to display specific nonprinting characters.

Editing Options

The options on the Edit page, shown in Figure 21-3, let you customize some of Word's editing features.

♦ *Typing Replaces Selection* determines whether selected text is deleted when you type.

♦ *Drag-and-Drop Text Editing* turns off or on the capability to move and copy text by drag and drop.

♦ *Automatic Word Selection* controls whether whole words are selected when you select the space after the word and then drag onto the next word.

♦ *Use the INS Key for Paste* lets you press the INS key to paste text from the Clipboard.

♦ *Overtype Mode* turns on overtype, just as double-clicking on the OVR indicator in the status bar does.

♦ *Use Smart Cut and Paste* controls the feature that makes Word delete the space after a deleted word and insert a space after an inserted word.

♦ *Use Tab and Backspace Keys to Set Left Indent* lets you create a first-line indentation by inserting a tab and remove the indentation by deleting the tab.

♦ *Allow Accented Uppercase* allows the spell checker to suggest words that have accent marks above uppercase characters. Use this option if you are typing in the French language, for example. If you leave out an accent over an uppercase letter, Word will suggest adding one, if appropriate.

The Picture Editor controls what application runs when you double-click to edit a picture object drawn in Word.

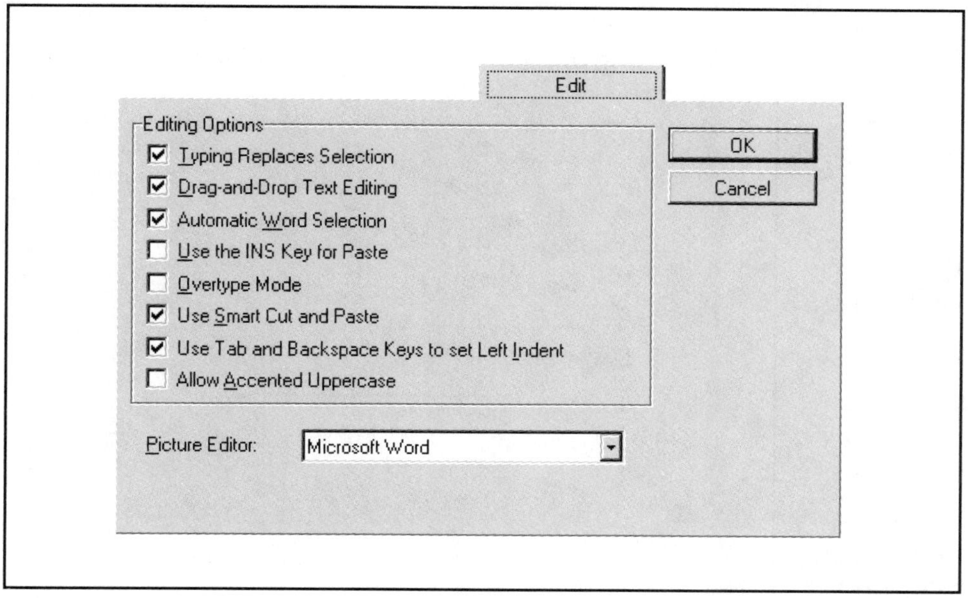

The Edit
options
Figure 21-3.

Print Options

The Print page, shown in Figure 21-4, lets you control how and what Word prints when you print your document. The Printing Options section has the following settings:

♦ *Draft Output* will switch on your printer's draft mode, if it has one. In draft mode, pictures and drawings may not print, and all text may appear in one font.

♦ *Reverse Print Order* prints your document from the last page to the first. Use this option if you have a laser printer that outputs pages face up, so the document will be in the correct order when printed.

♦ *Update Fields* automatically updates field codes before the document is printed. This includes date, index, caption numbers, and other fields whose values might have changed due to editing or formatting.

♦ *Update Links* automatically retrieves the current version of linked files.

♦ *Background Printing* allows you to continue working on a document while one is being sent to Print Manager for printing.

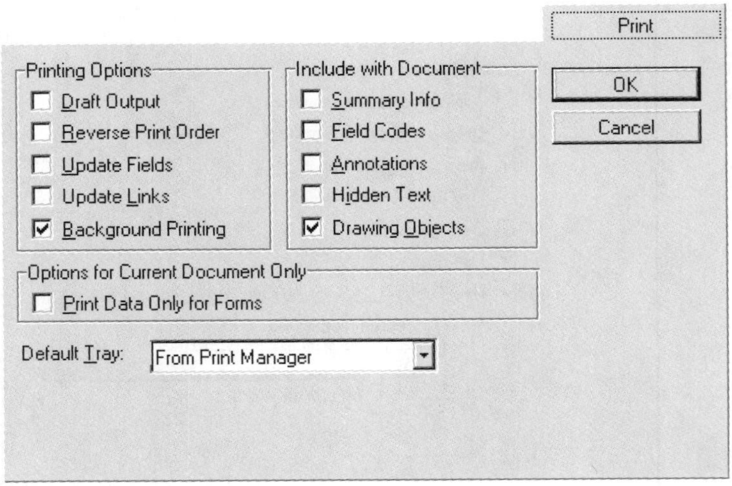

The Print
options
Figure 21-4.

The Include with Document section determines what Word prints. You can choose to print just the document or the document along with summary information, field codes, annotations, hidden text, and drawing objects. For example, if you have a document that contains field codes, you may want to select Field Codes to print a reference copy that displays the codes themselves, not just their results.

The Print Data Only for Forms option determines how forms print (forms are discussed in Chapter 23). The Default Tray option selects the printer tray for the document.

Save Options

The Save section of the Options dialog box controls how the Save and Save As commands work. You already learned about the backup and automatic save options in Chapter 2. Here's a summary of the other options:

♦ *Allow Fast Saves* lets Word speed up the saving process. When this option is turned on, Word determines how many changes you made to the document since it was last saved. If you did not make many changes, Word adds the edited material to the current version on the disk, reducing the save time but increasing the file size. Turn this option off to reduce file size, or if you have difficulty working with Word files with other applications.

♦ *Prompt for Document Properties* will display a dialog box requesting information about you and the document when you first save the document. See Chapter 22 for more information.

♦ *Prompt to Save Normal Template* determines whether Word automatically saves the Normal template when you exit the program. Turn off this option if you made changes to the template that you do not want saved.

♦ *Save Native Picture Formats Only* determines whether inserted pictures are saved only in the Windows format, or also in the format of their origin.

♦ *Embed TrueType Fonts* allows you to save the entire font for each TrueType font used in the document. Select this option if you want to print your document on another computer in which the same TrueType fonts are not installed. This option may violate the copyright of some TrueType fonts.

♦ *Save Data Only for Forms* controls what is saved when you fill in a custom form, described in detail in Chapter 23.

The File-Sharing options determine how other network users can access the current document:

♦ *Protection Password* sets the password that must be entered to open the document.

♦ *Write Reservation Password* sets the password that must be entered to allow the user to edit and save the document. If the user does not know the password, he or she can only open the document in read-only mode. In read-only mode, the user cannot alter and then resave the document under its current name.

♦ *Read-Only Recommended* informs the user that the document should be opened in read-only mode. However, the user has the option to open the document normally.

To turn on the password options, enter a password of up to 15 characters in the appropriate text boxes. Word will ask you to confirm the passwords when you exit the dialog box. If you use both passwords for a document, users must first enter the Protection Password. If they have that password, they can then enter the Write Reservation Password.

Remember: Passwords are case-sensitive.

Compatibility Options

The Compatibility page, shown in Figure 21-5, helps you control how Word converts documents created with other word processing programs. Pull down the Recommended Options For list and select the word processing format that you want to customize. The check boxes in the Options list will show what types of tasks are performed during the conversion process—a check mark means that the option is turned on. Change the setting as desired, or click on Default to return all of the settings to their default values.

Notice that many of the options begin with the word "Don't," so turning on the option actually stops Word from performing that task. For example, when you open a document created with some word processing programs, Word will insert a tab stop at the indented position for paragraphs formatted as hanging indentations. The option is "Don't add automatic tab stop for hanging indent." When the check box is not selected, the option is off, so Word *will* add the tab stop. If you choose WordPerfect 5.*x* from the list of programs, you'll see a check mark for this option—so it will be on and Word *will not* add the tab stop.

If you create all of your documents in Windows on one computer, then they will probably all be able to use the same fonts. When you open a document formatted in Arial, for instance, Word will apply the Arial font to the same text. If you open a document created with a DOS word processing program,

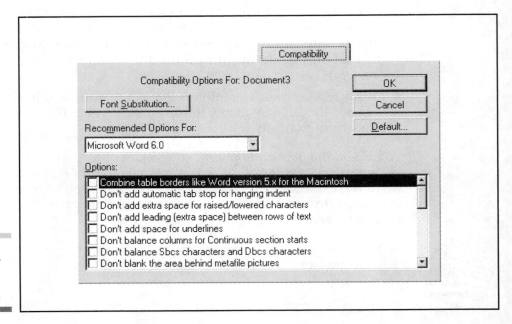

The
Compatibility
options
Figure 21-5.

or written in a different computer, then it may use fonts that you do not have available. In that case, Word will substitute compatible fonts.

You can customize which fonts are substituted in the *currently* open document by clicking on the Font Substitution button in the Compatibility section to see a dialog box similar to that in Figure 21-6. The box shown in this figure indicates that the document is using a font named "Tms Rmn" that cannot be found in your Windows system, and that the default font has been substituted for it. Near the bottom of the dialog box there's a message reporting that the default font is Times New Roman. If you want to substitute a different font, select the font in the Substituted Font list. The font substitution affects the font used to display and print the document, but the original fonts are retained. This ensures that you can still print the document using the same program and computer that you originally used to create it. Use the Convert Permanently option to actually replace the font information.

21

File Locations Options

Word assumes that documents, graphics, templates, and other types of files are stored in certain locations. The default setting for document files, for example, is the My Documents directory. When you display the Open dialog box, it will automatically display the documents in that directory—unless you've already changed the location during a previous Open operation during the current Word session.

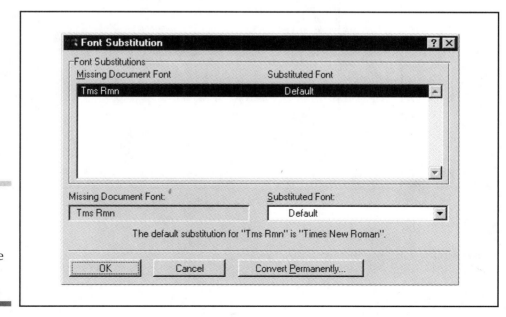

Use the Font Substitution box to substitute fonts for those not available
Figure 21-6.

If you store your files in some other location, you can change the default place that Word looks for files. Suppose, for instance, that you are working on a series of files in the Budget directory. To save time, you can set Word to look in that directory as the default.

To change the default file locations, display the File Locations page of the Options dialog box, as shown in Figure 21-7. This page lists the types of files for which you can set the default location. Click on the file type in the File Types list and then click on Modify. In the dialog box that appears, type the directory name or select it from the Look In list and then select OK.

 Note: Your default locations may differ from mine, depending on how you set up Word on your computer.

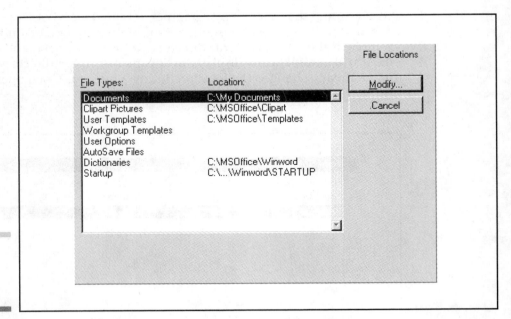

The File
Locations
options
Figure 21-7.

Document Management

22

It is easy to open documents if they are listed on the File menu, or if you know exactly where they are on your disk. But as you create folders and subfolders, it can become increasingly difficult to keep track of every document's location. Rather than spend time surfing through your disk, let Word help you locate your document.

Throughout this book, you've used the Open dialog box to open a document. However, the dialog box is much more than a convenient location to double-click on a document name—it is really the hub of a powerful document retrieval system. One reason the system is so useful is because it can locate documents based on the content as well as the file names. It also allows you to locate documents using special properties that Word assigns it and custom properties that you can create.

Document Properties

Every document is associated with a series of properties that describe the document and give you information about it. To learn how to use properties, open the Biography of Sliding Billy Watson document and select Properties from the File menu. Each page of the dialog box explains more about the document. Click on the Summary tab to see the options shown in Figure 22-1.

You can edit any of the information on the Summary page. It pays to take a few moments to fill in the boxes, because you can use the information later to find files on your disk. Word will suggest the title from the first line of the document and use the name in the User Info box for the author. Click in the

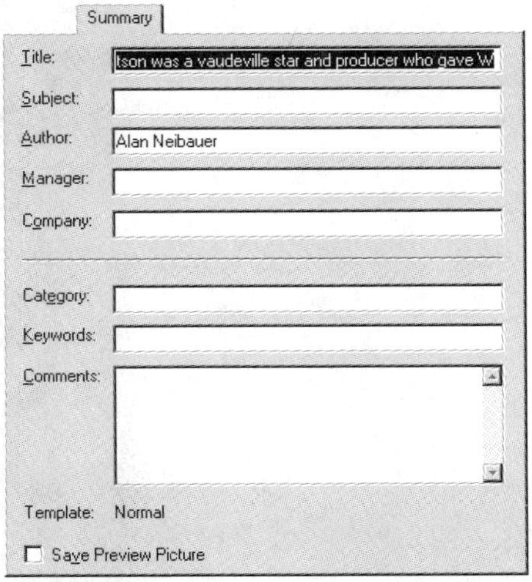

The Summary
options in the
Properties
dialog box
Figure 22-1.

Category box and type **Report**. Click in the Keywords box and type **watson vaudeville** (you don't need any punctuation between words). Click on the Save Preview Picture check box. This saves a thumbnail sketch of the document's first page to use as a preview in the Open dialog box.

Now click on the General tab to see the options shown in Figure 22-2. Of course, some of the information on your screen will be different from mine. You cannot change any of the settings on the General page, because Word maintains them for you. In addition to the name, type, and size of the document, Word shows its location on your disk and its MS-DOS name. While Windows 95 can use long file names, the MS-DOS operating system cannot. Windows automatically assigns a shorter file name to your documents so you can access them from a DOS window or on a computer not equipped with Windows 95. You will also see the date and time the document was created, last modified, and last accessed, as well as the file attributes.

Click on the Statistics tab to see even more about the document, as shown in Figure 22-3. For example, it shows when you printed the document and who saved it last. Revision Number reports how many times the document has been saved, even if you've saved it without making any changes. Total Editing Time shows the length of the editing session, or how long the file was open even if you did not edit it, but as long as you saved it. The Statistics page gives you some useful information about the length of your document.

Click on the Contents tab. The Contents page will list the document's title. If you change the title on the Summary page, it will not be updated on the

22

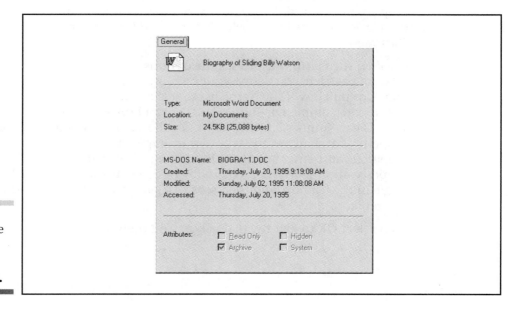

The General options in the Properties dialog box
Figure 22-2.

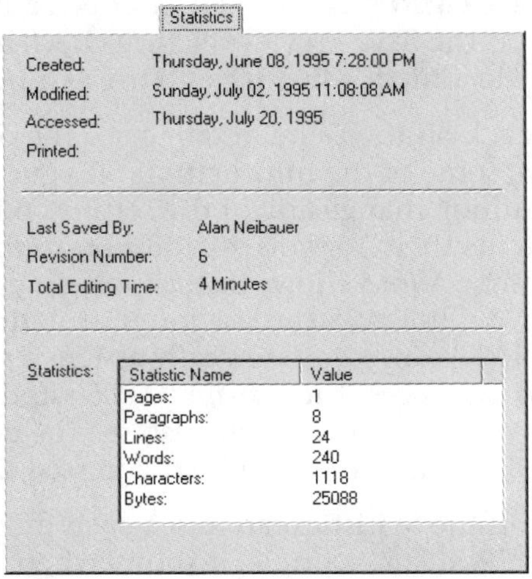

The Statistics
options in the
Properties
dialog box
Figure 22-3.

Contents page until you select OK. While this page may seem unnecessary
since the title is already listed elsewhere, the property exists for use with
Microsoft Office binders. Binders allow you to collect related documents into
a single entity and then print, save, and copy all of the documents—whether
they are from Word, Excel, Access, or PowerPoint—in one step. You can run
the Binder application by selecting it in the Programs from the Windows 95
Start menu.

Click on the Custom tab to see the options shown in Figure 22-4. The
Custom page lets you define your own properties. Type a custom property
name, or pull down the Name list to select from suggested names, such as
client, date completed, and project. Next, choose the type—the options are
Text, Date, Number, and Yes or No. In the Value box, enter a value for the
property that matches the type. For example, if you select the Number type,
then you must enter a number in the Value box. Click Add to insert the
property into the list box. To modify or delete the property, click on its
name in the list box, and then select Delete or Modify. The Modify button
will replace Add.

Now select OK to exit the dialog box, and then save and close the document.

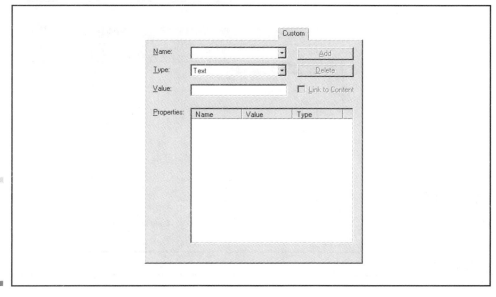

Use this page
of the dialog
box to create
custom
properties
Figure 22-4.

22

Tip: You can link a property to a bookmark. If you have a bookmark in
your document, the Link to Content check box will not be dimmed. When
you select the check box, the Value box is labeled Source. Pull down the
Source list and select the bookmark you want the property linked to. You'll
learn about bookmarks in Chapter 23.

Using the Open Dialog Box to Find Documents

Sometimes that most time-consuming task is just locating the document
that you want to edit or print. You may have saved the document on a disk
or directory other than the default, or used an extension other than DOC.
Fortunately, Word makes it easy to find documents directly from the Open
dialog box. Click on the Open button in the Standard toolbar, or select Open
from the File menu, to display the Open dialog box. Even though you've
already seen this dialog box many times, it's shown in Figure 22-5 so you
can refer to it as you read this chapter.

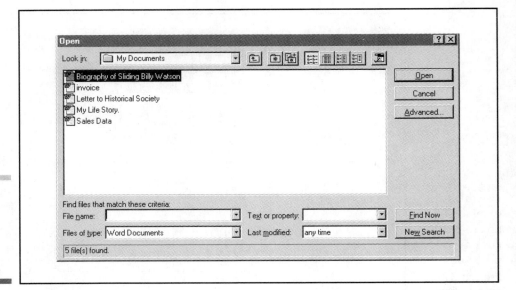

The Open dialog box is useful for document retrieval
Figure 22-5.

The Favorites Folder

One way you can find documents is to place them in a known location. Word provides a special folder called Favorites, a subdirectory under your Windows 95 directory. Because you can access this folder by clicking a button in the Open dialog box, it is a convenient place to store frequently used documents. In fact, you can insert three types of objects in the Favorites directory—a document, a shortcut to a document, and a shortcut to another folder. You can also add a folder to Favorites, but you have to do that from Windows 95, not from Word.

To save a document in the Favorites folder, click on the Favorites button when you save the document. Word will open the folder, displaying its contents in the Save As dialog box. When you later want to open the document, click on the Favorites button in the Open dialog box, and then double-click on the document name.

A shortcut is a Windows 95 feature that points to a document or directory. It is not the document or directory itself, but just a way to access the object from another location on the disk. By inserting a shortcut of a document into the Favorites directory, you can store the document where you want to but access it quickly from Favorites. Let's try this now.

If necessary, return to the My Documents directory (or wherever you save your documents), and then click on the document name Biography of

Sliding Billy Watson. Click once, do not double-click. Now click on the Add to Favorites button to display the options you see here.

Select Add Selected Item to Favorites. Word places a shortcut to the document in the Favorites folder. Now suppose you also want a way to quickly display the contents of another directory, without selecting disks, directories, and subdirectories in the Look In list. Just add a shortcut to the directory in the Favorites folder. As an example, let's add a shortcut to the My Documents directory. Even though this directory is the default, creating a shortcut to it will let you quickly return to it after looking elsewhere. Make certain that the directory you want to use for a shortcut is the one displayed in the Open dialog box—in this case My Documents. Click on Add to Favorites and select Add 'Look In' Folder to Favorites.

Now let's see how to use the Favorites folder. Click on the Favorites button. You'll see shortcuts to the Biography document and to the My Documents directory. A shortcut looks much like the regular document or folder icon, but with a tiny arrow.

22

To open the Biography document, even though it is actually located in some other directory, double-click on its shortcut icon in Favorites. If you want to quickly display the My Documents directory, double-click on its shortcut in Favorites.

Working with File Lists

Once you display the files in a specific directory, you use the other buttons in the Open toolbar to change how they are displayed. By default, the dialog box lists only the names of your files, with an icon representing the file type. This type of display is shown when the List button is selected.

Click on the Details button in the toolbar to display the name, size, and type of each document, along with the date and time each was modified, as shown here.

Name	Size	Type	Modified	
Biography of Sliding Billy Watso...	25 KB	Microsoft W...	7/30/95...	
New Wizards .doc	37 KB	Microsoft W...	7/26/95...	

By default, files are listed in ascending alphabetical order, with directories listed first. To sort another way, click on the Size, Type, or Modified column headings, or click on Name to again sort by the file name. Once you click on a heading to sort the list, clicking on it again toggles between an ascending and descending sort. For example, when the files are listed in the default ascending name order, click on Name to sort them in descending order. Click on Size once to sort in ascending order by the file size, click on it again to sort in descending order, and then yet again to return to ascending.

If you are interested in seeing information about a specific file, click on the file and then the Properties or Preview button from the toolbar. Clicking on Properties will show certain of the file's properties, based on the type of file. When you select a Word document file, for example, the window will display the properties shown in Figure 22-6, in addition to the number of paragraphs. Clicking on Preview will display the document in a preview window. If, on the Summary page of the Properties dialog box, you select to save the preview picture, you'll see a thumbnail sketch of the first page. Otherwise, you'll see the text as it appears in the document, and you can scroll the preview to read the entire document.

T ip: Selecting Properties or Preview may cause a delay as Word retrieves the information to display. Use the List or Details button instead to select the file, and then click on Properties or Preview if you need additional information.

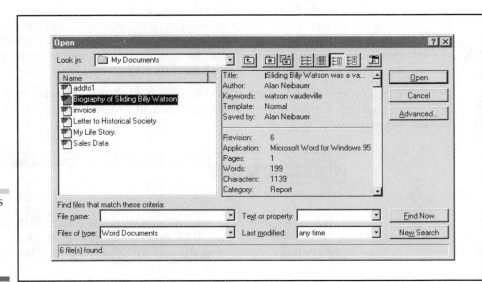

The Properties display for Word documents
Figure 22-6.

You use the Commands and Settings button to select from these options:

♦ *Open Read Only* opens the file in read-only mode, so it cannot be edited and saved under the same name.

♦ *Print* displays the Print dialog box, so you can print the selected document without opening it.

♦ *Properties* displays the Properties dialog box for the selected document.

♦ *Sorting* lets you sort the listing by name, size, type, or modified date in either ascending or descending order.

♦ *Search Subfolders* displays all of the files in the directory and all of its subdirectories, and lets you select the Group Files by Subfolder option.

♦ *Group Files by Subfolder* lists files under their directory when displaying them in Details, Properties, or Preview; when displaying a list of files, only the files themselves are shown.

♦ *Map Network Drive* lets you assign a local drive letter to a drive on another computer on the network.

♦ *Saved Searches* lets you retrieve the specifications for a file search (refer to "Advanced Searches" later in this chapter).

Searching for Documents

You know that you can change the directory listed in the Open dialog box by using the Look In list, and you can set the type of files displayed by selecting from the Files of Type list. The Files of Type list and the other text boxes at the bottom of the Open dialog box actually let you perform a search for files. The boxes represent four types of criteria specifying which files to display. You can specify one or more of the criteria to locate files. When you click in another text box, or click on Find Now, Word performs the search.

As Word searches for files that meet the criteria, the Find Now button changes to Stop. The search is complete when the Find Now button reappears. Click on Stop if the search is taking a long time and you want to stop to change the criteria or to close the dialog box.

In the Name text box, for example, type the name of the file you are looking for. You can also use the wildcards ? and *. Use a question mark to represent a single unknown character, an asterisk for multiple characters. For example, searching for **chapter*** will list all files starting with the word "chapter", such as "chapter 1", "chapter on history", and so on. Searching for **lesson?.txt** will list all text files starting with the word "lesson" and followed by one other character.

There is some interaction between the Name and Files of Type lists. If you enter a search for **lesson*.txt** in the Name box, for example, Word will automatically set Files of Type to Text Files (*.TXT), so only files with the extension TXT are listed. The same occurs for all of the extensions listed in Files of Type—DOC, DOT, RTF, TXT, SCD, PAD, ASC, ANS, WPD, and WKS. If you enter an extension other than those, it will override the Files of Type setting. So, for example, entering ***.zip** will locate all files with the extension ZIP regardless of the Files of Type setting.

To look for documents containing specific text, enter the text in the Text or Property box, such as entering **Watson** for documents that contain that word. You can also look for documents based on when they were last modified. By default, the Last Modified box is set at Any Time. Other options are Yesterday, Today, Last Week, This Week, Last Month, and This Month. Here is how you would list all of the documents that you worked on yesterday and that referred to the budget:

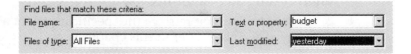

Click on New Search to reset the text boxes to display every file. Pull down the File Name and Text or Property lists to choose from settings you previously entered during the current Word session.

Tip: Microsoft Office comes with Find Fast, a program that automatically indexes the contents of your Office files to make your searches go faster. You can customize the way Find Fast works by accessing it from the Control Panel. Click on the Start button in the taskbar, point to Settings, and then click on Control Panel. See the Microsoft Office documentation for more information.

Advanced Searches

The text boxes in the Open dialog box let you search for files based on one set of criteria. The search is performed using an AND operation, meaning that all of the criteria must be met. So if you search for a DOC file with the word "Watson", Word will not list text or other files with that word.

For even more sophisticated searches, click on the Advanced button to display the dialog box shown in Figure 22-7. Through this box, you can specify any number of criteria, using both AND and OR operations, and look for files with specific text or values in their properties. You can also create and save search criteria, so once you design a search, you do not have to specify the same criteria again.

By default, the search box will be set using the same criteria for the current search set in the text boxes of the Open dialog box. You can delete these criteria and add others. To delete a criteria, select it in the list and then click on Delete. To delete all of the criteria, click in the New Search button.

To add criteria, start by choosing an option from the Property list. You can select any of the properties that you saw in the properties text box, such as author, file type, keyboards, lines, or paragraph. Next, select a condition. The options in the Condition list box depend on the property. If you choose a property that contains a number value, such as pages, the conditions will be:

22

◆ equals

◆ does not equal

Use these options to perform an advanced search

Figure 22-7.

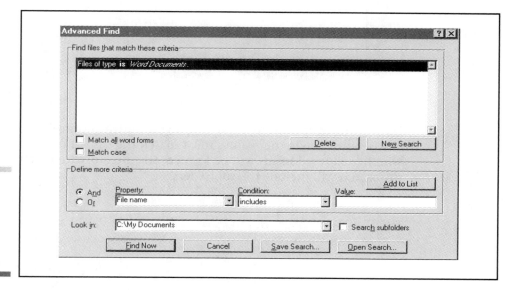

- ◆ any number between
- ◆ at most
- ◆ at least
- ◆ more than
- ◆ less than

The conditions for other properties vary. For example, when using the Creation Date or Last Modified properties, the conditions are date-oriented, such as Yesterday, Today, and This Month. For most text properties, you'll see conditions such as Includes, Begins With, and Ends With, and other properties that specify the location of the search text in the document.

Next, enter the value that you are searching for. If you are looking for a document that has the keyword "Watson", for instance, fill in the criteria like this:

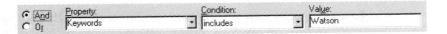

Now choose whether you want to use an AND or an OR operation, and then click on Add to List to insert the criteria in the list box. If you choose the OR operator, it will appear in the list, like this:

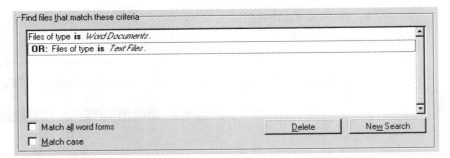

Use the other options in the dialog box to further control the search. You can determine whether values must match the case of text in the criteria, whether all word forms will be located, the directory to search, and whether the search will include the subfolders.

If you want to save the criteria to use for a search at some other time, click on Save Search, enter a name in the dialog box that appears, and then click on OK. To later recall the search criteria, click on Open Search and select the name from the list, or use the Saved Searches option in the Commands and Settings list.

Finally, click on Find Now to begin the search.

Searching in Windows

You can also search for files using the Windows taskbar. To use the Windows Find command, click on the Start button in the taskbar, point to Find, and select Files or Folders to display the dialog box shown in Figure 22-8. In addition to the options shown on the Name & Location page, use the Date Modified page to specify the date the document was last saved. You can choose to display all files, those modified between two dates, or those modified during a specific number of previous days and months. On the Advanced page, select the file type, enter text that must be in the document, and the file size.

22

When you click on Find Now, Windows will search for the files, displaying them in a window such as the one shown in Figure 22-9. Click on the column headings to sort the files. Finally, use the File command to save or recall search criteria, or use the Options menu to save the results of the search operation as well as the criteria.

The Find All
Files dialog
box
Figure 22-8.

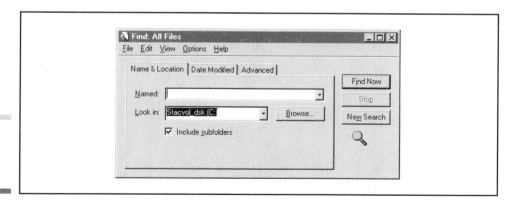

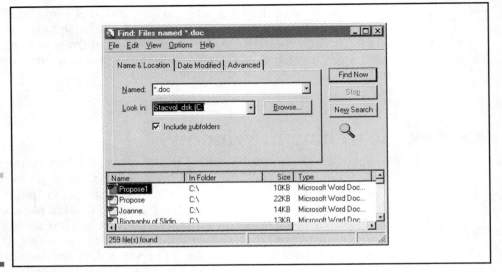

Windows
shows the
results of the
Find operation
Figure 22-9.

Advanced Word Features

23

Even with everything you've learned so far about Word, there are plenty of additional features packed into this remarkable program. In this chapter, you'll discover several ways to streamline your work. You'll learn how to use bookmarks, how to create onscreen fill-in forms, more about Word's fields, and how to revise documents that you are working on with others.

Using Bookmarks

When you are reading a book, a bookmark holds your place. To start reading where you left off, just open the book at the location of the bookmark. A bookmark in Word serves the same purpose. You set bookmarks at locations where you may want to return quickly. For example, suppose you often refer to a specific passage in a long document. If you set a bookmark at that passage, you can quickly move to it when you need to.

Word automatically sets some bookmarks for you. When you open a document, press SHIFT-F5 to return to your last editing position. If you are editing a long document, and do not have time to complete it in one session, use SHIFT-F5 to start where you left off. In fact, Word actually sets bookmarks at your last four positions. Press SHIFT-F5 to move from position to position.

Remember: Word's built-in key combinations will not work if you have Help for WordPerfect Users turned on.

You can set your own bookmarks at positions that you want to go to. To set a bookmark, place the insertion point where you want to set it—or select text at the position—and then choose Bookmark from the Edit menu to see the dialog box shown here.

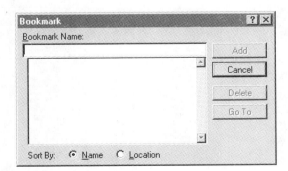

Type a name for the bookmark that will identify that position, and then click on Add.

To move to a bookmark location, select Bookmark from the Edit menu. Your bookmarks will be listed in the dialog box. Note that you can sort the bookmarks by their names or by their location in the document. Double-click on the name of the bookmark, or select it and then choose Go To. Word will move the insertion point to the bookmark position, scrolling the document if necessary. If any text was selected when you created the bookmark, the same text will be selected again. The Bookmark dialog box remains on the screen, so click on Close or move to another bookmark.

To delete a bookmark, select its name in the Bookmark dialog box and select Delete.

Creating Fill-in Forms

Forms are used just about everywhere—application forms, complaint forms, order forms. Most forms are preprinted, so you simply write in the information requested. You can also use your computer to create a form and fill it in on the screen. For instance, you can fill in a purchase order form and then E-mail or fax it to the vendor without ever having to print it out.

You create a form using special form fields where you want to insert information. There are three types of form fields, as illustrated here.

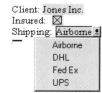

♦ A *text form field* lets you type information, such as a name and address.

♦ A *check box form field* lets you click on a box to indicate a yes or no response.

♦ A *drop-down form field* lets you select an option from a list of items.

Tip: You can also create your own help messages for each form field. For example, you can have one message appear in the status line when the field is being used and another message appear if you press F1.

Let's create a simple form. If you create a form as a document and then save it with the same name after filling it out, the next time you need to use the form, it will contain that same information; so you'd have to delete it to start over. Instead, create a form as a template so it cannot be saved under the same name. Start with these steps:

1. Select New from the File menu.
2. Click on the Blank Document icon, if it is not already selected.
3. Click on the Template option button.
4. Select OK.

Now design the form. Type **While You Were Out** and press ENTER three times. Next, use the Insert Table button in the Standard toolbar to create a table containing four rows and two columns, and then fill in the table so the document looks like this:

While You Were Out

Name:	Time:
Date:	Fax:
Phone:	Confirm Receipt:
Return Call:	

Message:

Entering Form Fields

You can enter the form fields in two ways—using a dialog box or a special toolbar. Let's look at both methods. Place the insertion point after the Name: label in the first cell and press the SPACEBAR. Select Form Field from the Insert menu to display the dialog box you see here.

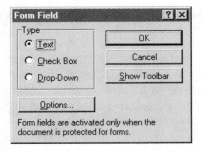

From the dialog box, you select the type of field that you want to insert and then click on OK. For now, make certain that the Text option is selected and click on OK. Word inserts the form field, indicated by the gray area:

Name:		
Date:		Time:

Now let's insert the other fields, but using the Forms toolbar. Point to one of the toolbars on the screen, click the right mouse button, and click on Forms to see the toolbar shown here.

 Tip: You can also display the toolbar by selecting Show Toolbar from the Form Field dialog box.

 Insert a space after the Date: label on the form, and then click on the Text Form Field button. In the same way, insert a space and a text form field after the Time:, Phone:, Fax:, and Message: labels.

 Place the insertion point in the blank cell in the first row, and then click on the Drop-Down Form Field button.

 Insert a space after the Return Call: label, and then click on the Check Box Form Field button. The field appears with a check box.

23

In the same way, insert a space and a check box form field after the Confirm Receipt: label.

Field Options

Before using the form, you must add items to the drop-down list in the first row. You should also customize the fields. For example, you can limit the number of characters in a text form field to keep the text in one line of the table or to specify a certain type of information, such as a date, time, or number. You can also set the size of the check box, and whether it is checked by default.

Customizing Text Form Fields

 Click in the shaded form field next to the Name: label, and then click on the Form Field Options button in the Forms toolbar. You can also double-click on the form field. You'll see options for text form fields, as shown in Figure 23-1.

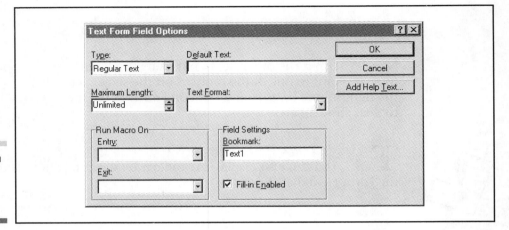

The Text Form
Field Options
dialog box
Figure 23-1.

Tip: You can set options as you create the fields by selecting Options from the Form Field dialog box.

Select Maximum Length and enter **35**. This will prevent you from typing more than one line of text. Next, pull down the Text Format list and select Title Case to ensure that the first letter of each word in the name will be uppercase. The other choices are Uppercase, Lowercase, and First Capital.

The other options let you further control the way form fields appear and operate.

♦ In the *Default Text* box you can specify information you want to appear in the field by default.

♦ The *Run Macro On* section lets you run a macro when you enter or exit the field.

♦ The *Bookmark* box lets you name the field for use in macros or calculation fields.

♦ *Fill-in Enabled* determines whether you can enter information into the field or must accept the default value.

Now select OK to return to the form.

By default, text form fields accept any type of input. You can specify another type, however, if you want to limit the input to a date, time, or number. Double-click on the form field next to the Date: label to display the Text Form Field Options dialog box again. Pull down the Type list to see the options shown here.

Tip: You use the Calculation type to compute a value based on other fields or table cells.

Select Current Date. Pull down the Date Format list to see a selection of date and time formats. The name of the Format list and the choices in it depend on the type of entry. With date and time types, you can select a date or time format; with number and calculation types, you can select a numeric format; with the text type, you select capitalization. Select the format M/d/yy and then click on OK.

Now set the field next to the Time: label so it is the Current Time type with the format h:mm AM/PM, and set the maximum length of the Phone and Fax fields to 14 characters.

Tip: With the Current Date and Current Time fields, Word inserts the information for you. If you want to be able to enter the date or time, set the form type to the Date or Time type.

Customizing Check Box Fields

Now set options for the check box fields. Double-click on the field next to the Return Call: label to display the dialog box shown in Figure 23-2. You can set the size of the box and its default status. Click on Checked in the Default Value section so the box is selected automatically, and then click on OK.

23

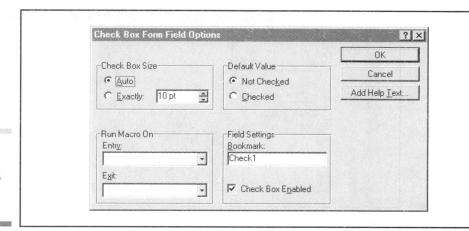

The Check Box Form Field Options dialog box
Figure 23-2.

Customizing the Drop-Down List Box

A drop-down form field must contain items from which to select. You designate the items using the Drop-Down Form Field Options dialog box for the form field. To try this, double-click on the field in the blank cell in the top row to display the dialog box shown in Figure 23-3. To add an item to the list, you type it in the Drop-Down Item text box, then click on Add. Type **Called**, and then click on Add to insert the item into the list. Type **Visited** and click on Add. In the same way, insert the items **Faxed** and **E-mailed** to the list.

You can delete items from the list and change their position. To delete an item, select it in the list and click on Remove. To change the position of an item, click on it and then click on either the up or down arrows.

Click on OK. The first item in the list will appear by default in the field.

Tip: If you do not want the form fields to be shaded, display the Forms toolbar and click on the Shading button.

Protecting the Form

In order to use the form, you must first protect it. Protecting the form ensures that you can only enter information into fields, select check boxes, or select an item in a drop-down list. You will not be able to edit any of the other text on the form.

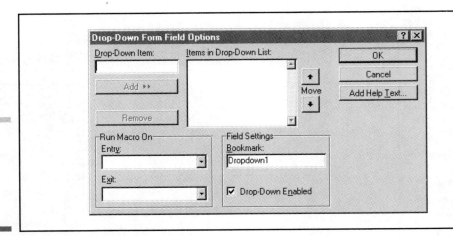

The Drop-Down Form Field Options dialog box
Figure 23-3.

To protect the form, click on the Protect Form button in the Forms toolbar. You can also select Protect Document in the Tools menu to display the dialog box shown here, and then click on the Forms option.

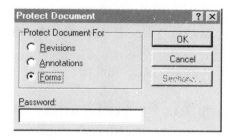

This box also lets you assign a password to prevent others from unprotecting the form. If you later want to edit the form, you must first unprotect it— select UnProtect Document from the Tools menu or click on the Protect Form button in the toolbar.

Once you protect the form, save it with the name While You Were Out and then close the document. Close the Forms toolbar.

Using the Form

23

When you want to use the form, you start a new document using the form's template. Let's do that now. Select New from the File menu, and then double-click on the template named While You Were Out. The form appears onscreen with the current date and time already in the appropriate fields.

Since the form is protected, you can only place the insertion point in form fields or other unprotected sections. The insertion point is automatically on the first form field—Name—so type **sally hellerman** using all lowercase letters. Press TAB to move to the next form field. Because you set the format of the Name field to Title Case, Word capitalizes the first letter of each word in the name. Pull down the list box following the word "Called" to display the drop-down list. Click on Visited to enter it into the field. To use the keyboard, move to the field, press F4 or ALT-DOWN ARROW to display the list, and press DOWN ARROW to select the item.

Remember: In a form, move forward from field to field by pressing TAB or the DOWN ARROW key. Move backward through fields by pressing SHIFT-TAB or the UP ARROW key. You can also click on a form field with the mouse.

Press TAB once to reach the Phone field—skipping over Date and Time, which are already filled in for you—and type **555-1234**. Click on the Return Call check box to deselect it, and then click on the Confirm Receipt check box. To select or clear a check box with the keyboard, move to the field and press the SPACEBAR or the X key. Next, click on the form field next to the Message: label and type **Delivered the check to the cashier.**

Print a copy of the completed form, close the document without saving it, and then start a new document.

Options for Printing and Saving Forms

When you print a form, all of the prompts (such as Name:), the table grid lines, and check boxes print with it. This is ideal when you're printing the form on blank paper. But what if you've designed the template to print on a preprinted form that already includes the prompts, lines, and check boxes?

To print just the information you filled in, but in the exact position where it appears on the form on the screen, select Options from the Tools menu, display the Print page of the Options dialog box, and select Print Data Only For Forms. When you print the form, only the information in form fields will print, including the X marks in check boxes.

You can also use the Options menu to save just the information, not the design of the form itself. Select Options from the Tools menu, display the Save page of the Options dialog box, and then select Save Data Only For Forms. When you save the form, the content of the fields will be saved as a text file in this format:

"Sally Hellerman","Visited","06/17/96","10:52 AM","555-1234","",0,1,
"Delivered the check to the cashier"

Information in text form fields will be in quotation marks, and selected check boxes are indicated by the number 1, deselected boxes with the number 0. Saving just the text of the fields reduces the size of the file, and the text files can be used with merge documents or other applications to perform statistical analysis using the form data.

Other Word Fields

You've learned about a number of Word's fields throughout this book, but they only touch the surface of this powerful feature. Word has many other fields that let you automate your work, perform math, and otherwise manipulate information. A thorough review of Word's fields could easily fill an entire book, but as an example, this section covers several that you may find useful.

There are two ways that you can insert a field. If you know the name of the field, and how it works, press CTRL-F9 while in your document to display a set of braces—{ }. The insertion point is in the braces, so type the field. Try it now. Press CTRL-F9 and type **Author.** Now press F9 to update the field—your screen should now display the author's name from the Properties dialog box, without the braces.

If you do not know the name of the field, you can select it from a dialog box. Move the insertion point under your name, and then select Field from the Insert menu to display the dialog box shown in Figure 23-4. When the All option is selected in the Categories list, every Word field will be listed in the Field Names list. To display specific types of fields, select a category.

Scroll the Field Names list and select the File Size field. The Options button becomes selectable—no longer dimmed—indicating that you can set some additional features for this command, called *switches*. Click on Options to display the dialog box shown in Figure 23-5. The options and the number of pages depend on the field. In this case, the dialog box contains two pages, General Switches and Field Specific Switches. Use the General Switches page to select the number format of any field containing numeric information. As you select an item, a description of it appears in the box at the bottom. Click on the Field Specific Switches tab to see its page, shown in Figure 23-6. For the File Size field there are two switches—\k displays the size in kilobytes, and \m displays the size in megabytes. Click on \k and then on Add to Field. The switch appears in the Field Codes box to show the format of the field.

23

Now click on OK to close the Field Options dialog box. Click on OK again to close the Field box and to display the results of the field—the size of the file in kilobytes.

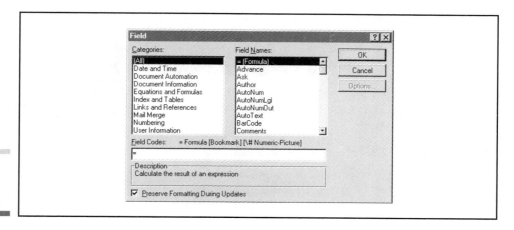

The Field
dialog box
Figure 23-4.

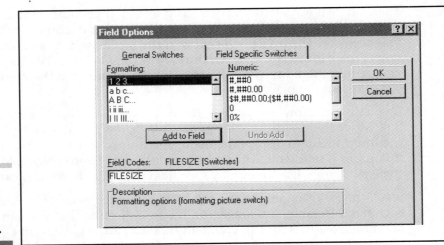

The Field
Options
dialog box
Figure 23-5.

 Remember: To switch between the display of field codes and their results, press ALT-F9, or use the Field Codes option on the View page of the Options dialog box.

Now on your own, practice using some of the other form fields. For example, insert your address into a document with the UserAddress field, or your name with the UserName field. You'll find that you can insert all of the document properties using fields from the Date and Time category and the Document Information category in the Field dialog box.

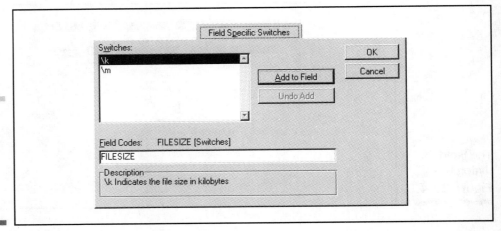

The Field
Specific
Switches page
of the Field
Options
dialog box
Figure 23-6.

Marking and Using Revisions

If you work on a document with other authors, it can become difficult to keep track of the changes. How can you tell, for example, which of your text other authors deleted, or what text they added? By using the revisions feature, you can change a document while showing what changes have been made. If someone deletes text, for example, it is not actually removed from the document, just marked to show that someone wants to delete it and which author is suggesting the change. Likewise, inserted text is marked to show someone wants to add text.

Inserted and deleted text will appear in one of eight colors to indicate which of up to eight authors made the change. Word will mark deleted text with a strikeout and inserted text with underlines. It also inserts a vertical line—called the *revision line*—next to the text to make it stand out.

Note: In Normal view, the revision line always appears in the left margin. In Page Layout view, the line appears in the left margin unless Mirror Margins has been selected in the Page Setup dialog box.

Open the Letter to Historical Society document, and let's make some changes. Double-click on the characters MRK in the status bar, or select Revisions from the Tools menu to display this dialog box:

23

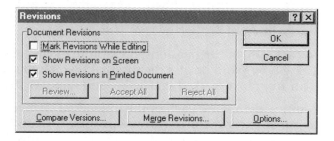

Click on Mark Revisions While Editing, and then click on OK.

Now edit the document as you would normally. Double-click on the word "burlesque" in the first sentence and press DELETE. Word strikes through the word and changes its color rather than actually deleting it, and it adds a revision line at the left margin.

Now type the word **vaudeville** and insert a space. Word displays it underlined and in color. Delete the word "three" in that same paragraph and type four in its place, followed by a space. Again, the changes are marked as revisions.

Remember: To turn off revision marking, display the Revisions dialog box and clear the Mark Revisions While Editing check box.

Working with Revisions

After you make your revisions to the document, you control how they appear by selecting options from the Revisions dialog box. To display the dialog box, double-click on MRK in the status bar, or select Revisions from the Tools menu. For example, if you find the revision marks distracting as you proofread the document, deselect Show Revisions On Screen. Onscreen, Word will appear to delete the text that you delete, and display inserted text in the standard color. However, the deleted text and revision markings will reappear when you select the option again.

When you print the document, the revision lines, strikethrough, and underlining will also print. To print the document as it will appear if you accept the revisions, deselect the Show Revisions In Printed Document option.

Reviewing Revisions

After you've made revisions to the document, you can accept them, remove them from the document, or review the individual changes. To accept all of the revisions, click on the Accept All button in the Revisions dialog box. Word will erase the text marked as deleted, remove the revision lines, and restore inserted text to the standard color.

To cancel all of the revisions, click on the Reject All button in the Revisions dialog box. Word deletes the inserted text, removes the strikethrough and color from text marked as deleted, and removes the revision lines.

You can also review each of the individual changes, with the option to accept or reject each. To review changes, click on the Review command button in the Revisions dialog box to display this dialog box:

Use the Find buttons to move through the document, from revision to revision, selecting each in turn. As each is selected, the name of the author who made the change, and the date and time it was made, will be displayed in the Description panel, and you can either accept or reject it. Instead of selecting Find for each change, you can select the Find Next After Accept/Reject option. Word will then move automatically to the next revision after you accept or reject the previous one. The dialog box also lets you hide the revision marks and undo your last accept or reject choice.

Now use the Revisions dialog box to accept all of the changes to the document. Save and then close the document.

Working with Multiple Documents

Sometimes several authors work on their own copies of the same document. Rather than use revision marks, each actually deletes and inserts text. The Compare Versions option in the Revisions dialog box automatically compares two versions of the same document, inserting revision marks where the text differs. To use this feature, open one of the documents, display the Revisions dialog box, and click on Compare Versions. In the dialog box that appears, select the document you want to compare it with and then choose OK. After Word inserts the revision marks, use the Revisions dialog box to accept, reject, or review the changes.

If each author made his or her changes by marking revisions, combine all of the marks with the Merge Revisions option. It works the same as Compare Versions but incorporates the revision marks from both versions.

23

Customizing Revision Marks

You can change the way Word marks revisions using the Revisions page of the Options dialog box, shown in Figure 23-7. In the Inserted Text section,

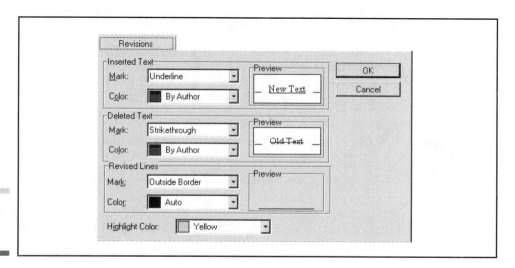

The Revisions options
Figure 23-7.

choose the way you want the inserted text marked—the options are None, Bold, Italic, Underline, and Double Underline. You can also choose the color to use. When the color is set at By Author, Word uses a different color for each person making changes. You can also select a specific color to use for all revisions.

In the Deleted Text section, select the mark to use—either Hidden or Strikethrough—and select the color. In the Revised Lines section, select the color and position for revision lines—the position choices are None, Left Border, Right Border, and Outside Border.

The Highlight Color option lets you set the highlight color, a new Word feature discussed next.

Highlighting

Almost everyone has certainly seen those highlighting pens with brightly colored transparent ink, such as yellow and pink. You use a highlighting pen to mark a section of text that you want to bring to someone's attention. Word comes with its own highlighting pen that lets you mark sections of text in color.

Highlighting is most effective when your document will be read or reviewed on the screen, since the bright colors make it easy to see important sections of text. The colors will also print if you have a color printer. If your printer does not produce color, Word will replace the colors with varying shades of gray—the lighter the color, the lighter the shade.

 Look at the Highlight button in the Formatting toolbar. The picture on the button shows the highlighting pen with a small square indicating the current highlight color. If the square is white, then highlighting is turned off. You can highlight text either before or after you select it.

If you select the text first, just click on the Highlight button to apply the color. To use a different color for selected text, pull down the Highlight list and click on the color that you want to apply. The color you select from the list will become the new default color, indicated in the square on the button.

 Note: Following the None option in the list, the colors are yellow, green, cyan, and magenta.

You can also select text and apply a highlighting color at the same time. When no text is selected, click on the Highlight button, or pull down the list and select another color. (When you select a color, it automatically turns on the highlighting feature.) The mouse pointer will appear as an I-beam with the highlighter pen. Now select the text to apply the color to. The Highlight button will remain pressed down, so you can immediately apply the same color to other text. To stop highlighting, click on the button again.

To remove highlighting from text, select the text and then choose None from the drop-down list, or select None and then drag over the text. You can also remove highlighting by applying the same color. For example, if you've highlighted a word in yellow, and yellow is still shown as the default color, select the word and click on the Highlight button.

Although only four colors, and None, are available in the Highlight list, you can select other colors from the Revisions page of the Options dialog box. The color shown in the dialog box will be the current default color shown on the Highlight button. Pull down the list to select from None and eight colors—the same four that are available in the Highlight list along with black, red, blue, and white. The selected color will now appear in the Highlight button, but the button will not be turned on.

Using a highlighting color the same color as the text will make it unreadable. Choosing the white highlight color is not exactly the same as choosing None. When you highlight in white, you are actually "painting" a white highlight around the text, although you will not see it on the white screen. The White color is useful if you're using the blue background option from the General page of the Options dialog box, or highlighting text or graphics on a color background.

23

Tip: To hide highlighting, clear the Highlight option on the View page of the Options dialog box.

Creating Cross-References

Another way to call attention to text is to create a cross-reference to it. A cross-reference refers the reader to the location of a heading, bookmark, footnote, endnote, equation, figure, or table. For example, you can refer the reader to a section titled "Computers" using the reference "Please see the section Computers on page 23." Or if you make changes to a paragraph on page 20, you can insert a bookmark in that paragraph and use a cross-reference such as "See my additions on page 20."

To create a cross-reference, place the insertion point where you want the cross-reference to appear in the document. Type any text that you want to appear with the reference, such as "Please refer to ", and then select Cross-reference from the Insert menu to see a dialog box like the one shown in Figure 23-8.

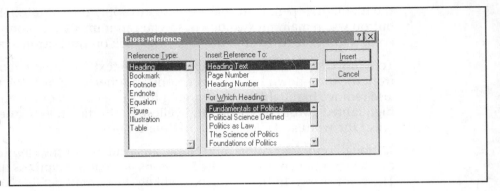

Inserting a
cross-reference
Figure 23-8.

Select the type of item you want to reference in the Reference Type list. Word will change the contents of the Insert Reference To and the For Which lists based on your choice.

For example, when you cross-reference a heading, the Insert Reference To list will appear as shown in Figure 23-8, and all of your headings—text formatted using heading styles—will be listed in the For Which Heading list. If you choose to reference a Bookmark type, the Insert Reference To list will contain the options Bookmark Text, Page Number, and Paragraph Number. Your bookmarks will now be listed in the For Which Bookmark list.

Next, select what you want to reference in the Insert Reference To list. If you want to insert the heading in the reference, for instance, select Heading Text. Finally, select the specific heading in the For Which Heading list, and then click on Insert and then on Close. To insert a reference to a heading and its page number, repeat the procedure but select Page Number in the Insert Reference To list.

Cross-references are fields. If editing your text causes the page numbers or text of a reference item to change, select the entire document and press F9 to update the references.

Creating Macros and Customizing Word

24

The commands that Word provides are powerful, but imagine creating your own Word commands and features. You can create your own toolbars, menus, and shortcut key combinations to perform the tasks that you use most often. For example, do you frequently print envelopes or create WordArt objects? Just add buttons for these features to the toolbar so you can perform them with a click of the mouse. You can even create custom commands by recording your actions in a macro.

Creating a Macro

A *macro* is a stored collection of keystrokes and mouse actions that perform a task. For instance, suppose you regularly create a shadow box around text using the Borders and Shading dialog box. Each time you create the box, you must display the dialog box, click on the Shadow preset, and then choose the line and shading options. If you store that series of actions in a macro, you can repeat all of them by running the macro, rather than performing the individual steps. You can even assign the macro to a button on the toolbar, to a shortcut key combination, or to one of Word's menus. When you want to create the shadow box, just click on the toolbar button, press the key combination, or select the option from the menu.

You create a macro by recording the keystrokes and mouse selections as you perform the task. To create a macro that prints the current page, for example, you actually print a page of a document, recording the actions that you perform. You can then run the macro later to print whatever page the insertion point is located on.

As an example, let's record a macro that updates all of the fields in a document and then prints only the current page. Start by double-clicking on the dimmed characters REC in the status bar, or select Macro from the Tools menu, and then select Record. You'll see the dialog box shown in Figure 24-1. Word will suggest Macro1 as the name of the first macro that you record, Macro2 for the second, and so forth. You can accept the suggested name, but it will be easier to run the macro if you give it a name that explains the function it performs. Macro names must start with a letter and cannot contain punctuation marks or spaces. Now type **UpdatesAndPrintsPage**—using capitalization to indicate words— in the Record Macro Name text box.

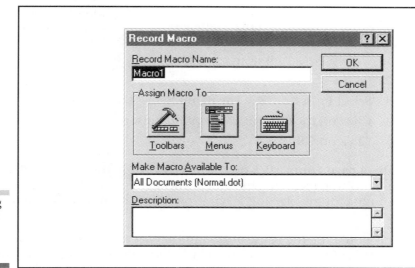

Word's dialog
box to record
macros
Figure 24-1.

Macros are saved in templates. The setting in the Make Macro Available To box determines which template the macro will be stored in. When set at All Documents (Normal.dot), the macro will be available for use with every document. If you are using another template, you can store the macro there by choosing that template in the Make Macro Available To list.

You can also enter a description of the macro to help you identify it later, and you can use the Assign Macro To options to run the macro by using a keystroke combination, clicking on a toolbar button, or selecting it from a menu. You'll learn more about these options later. For now, select OK so you can record the macro.

24

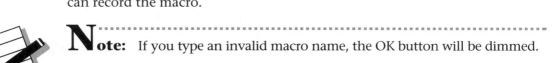

Note: If you type an invalid macro name, the OK button will be dimmed.

The macro toolbar appears, and the mouse pointer includes an icon of a cassette tape when it is in the text area, as shown here.

 When recording a macro, select text and move the insertion point with the keyboard—you can use the mouse only to select menus and

dialog box options. Now make sure that your printer is turned on
and ready to print, and then follow these steps to record the macro:

1. Choose Select All from the Edit menu.
2. Press F9.
3. Select Print from the File menu to display the Print dialog box.
4. Click on the Current Page option button.
5. Click on OK.

 After a page prints, click on the Stop button in the Macro toolbar. You
can also stop recording by double-clicking on the REC indicator in the
status bar or by selecting Macro from the Tools menu and then choosing
Stop Recording.

 You would use the Pause button in the Macro toolbar to temporarily stop
recording so you can perform a task that you do not want as part of the
macro. Click on the Pause button again to continue recording.

Running a Macro

Whenever you want to perform the recorded function, you run the macro. If
you've saved the macro in the Normal template, you can run it when any
document is on the screen, not just the document that was displayed when
you recorded the macro.

Let's run the macro now. Open the Letter to Historical Society document.
Because the macro is designed to run the current page, let's divide the letter
into two pages to ensure that the macro works. Place the insertion point
after the third paragraph and press CTRL-ENTER.

Now select Macro from the Tools menu to display the dialog box shown in
Figure 24-2. If the Macros Available In list is set to All Active Templates,
you'll see all of the macros available in the Normal template, and any
that are attached or global templates. Double-click on the macro name
UpdatesAndPrintsPage, or select it and click on Run. Word runs the macro,
repeating its commands to update any fields in the document and then
prints the current page.

Now close the document without saving the changes.

Using Word's Sample Macros

Word includes complete sample macros in five templates. For example, one
template contains a macro called ArrangeWindows. If you have several

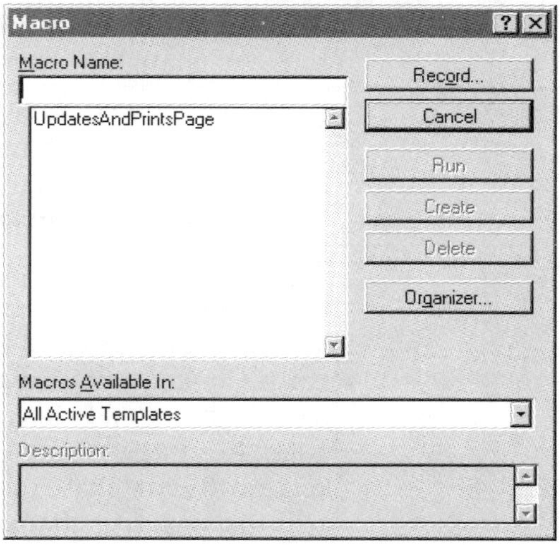

Run and
delete macros
in this dialog
box
Figure 24-2.

documents open on the screen, you can run the macro to tile the windows horizontally, vertically, or cascaded.

You access the macros by attaching the template or by making the template global, as you learned to do in Chapter 11. The templates are in the Winword\Macros subdirectory. Select Templates from the File menu. Then to attach a template, click on Attach and select the template that you want to use. To make a template global, click on Add and select the template. When you display the Macro dialog box, select All Active Templates in the Macros Available In list. The dialog box will then list all of the available macros. Table 24-1 summarizes the macros available in the templates.

24

Customizing Word's Interface

There are three main ways to communicate with Word—with the keyboard, the toolbars, and the menus. Word's default settings provide most of the functions that users typically perform. If you plan on using a macro, style, or other Word function frequently, however, you can assign it to a shortcut key, create an icon for it on a toolbar, or add it to one of the pull-down menus.

To assign an existing item, such as a style or macro that you've already recorded, start the process by selecting Customize from the Tools menu to

Template	Macro Description
Convert7	Convert one or more files between Word and other formats; change conversion options
Layout7	Arrange windows; increase and decrease right and left paragraph indentation; print an overscore above selected text; print a table of all characters in a selected font; display and manage the format of sections
Macros7	Turn automatic backup on and off; exit all open documents; find and replace symbols; create a table showing samples of all installed fonts; insert a footnote; run a Concentration-type game; edit headings and footers in Normal view; create an organization chart using headings; view and change Word's settings in the registration database (use with caution); save selected text to a disk file; change printing parameters (use with caution); display complete document statistics; run a puzzle game
Present7	Create a PowerPoint presentation from a Word outline
Tables7	Export table contents into a Microsoft Access database; create table formulas; automatically number table rows and columns

Word Provides Some Useful and Some Fun Macros in Templates
Table 24-1.

see the options shown in Figure 24-3. The box has three pages, one for each of the three elements that you can customize.

To assign the macro as you record it, click on the Toolbars, Menus, or Keyboard button on the Assign Macro To page of the Record Macro dialog box before you start. The Customize dialog box will appear with the appropriate page displayed, and the options will be ready for you to assign the macro.

T ip: To assign a shortcut key combination to a style as you create it, select the style in the Style dialog box, click on Modify, and then on Shortcut Key.

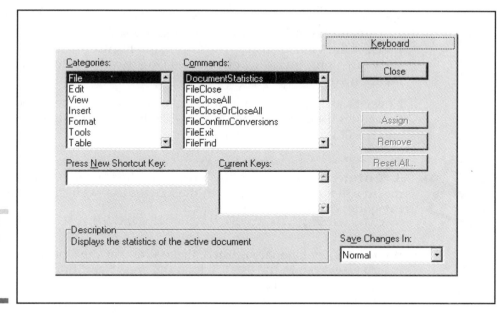

The Keyboard
options in the
Customize
dialog box
Figure 24-3.

Creating Custom Shortcut Keys

A shortcut key combination is a quick way to run a macro, apply a style, or perform some Word command when you do not want to take your hands off the keyboard. Just picture how easy it would be, for example, to update the fields in a document and print the current page by pressing ALT-1 (for 1 page) or some other combination.

To assign an item to a key combination, display the Keyboard page of the Customize dialog box. (That page will automatically be displayed if you select the Keyboard button when recording a macro.)

The Categories list contains all of the categories of Word functions, as well as the choices Macros, Fonts, AutoText, Styles, and Common Symbols. This means that you can use a key combination to perform a Word command, run a macro, switch to a new font, insert an AutoText entry, apply a style, or insert a special symbol. When you select a category, the items that make up the category appear in the Commands list box. So to assign an item to the keyboard, you first select the category of the function you want to perform, and then you select the specific function.

24

For example, suppose you want to press a key combination to display the Header and Footer area. This is a standard Word feature in the View menu, so select the View category. The Command list will then show all of the View functions, including one named GoToHeaderFooter that performs the function you want to perform.

Now let's assign the UpdatesAndPrintsPage macro to the keyboard. Scroll the Categories list and select Macros. The Command list will be labeled Macros, and it will list the available macros.

Note: If you are assigning a macro to the keyboard as you create it, that macro will already be selected in the Macros list—you cannot change categories or choose another macro.

If you have several macros listed, make sure that the UpdatesAndPrintsPage macro is selected in the list. Click on the Press New Shortcut Key text box and press ALT-1—the key combination that you want to assign. You can use any combination of the CTRL, SHIFT, and ALT keys along with one letter or number. (You cannot use SHIFT by itself with a letter or number because these combinations are reserved for punctuation marks and uppercase letters.) The combination you type will appear in the text box, and Word will display a message, like the one you see here, showing whether the combination is already assigned.

Press New Shortcut Key:
Alt+1

Currently Assigned To:
[unassigned]

Caution: You can continue even if the key combination is already being used. However, this reassigns the combination to the new task. For example, if you assign your own macro to CTRL-1, pressing those keys will no longer format text as single-spaced, which is the original Word default for CTRL-1.

You can add one more letter or number to the combination by pressing its key. Word separates it with a comma, such as Alt+1,L to indicate that you must press and release the first combination—ALT-1—and then press the other character—L.

When you've entered the combination you want, click on the Assign button and then Close. Now when you press ALT-1, Word runs the macro.

Tip: If you are creating a macro, and you've selected the Keyboard button in the Record Macro dialog box, start recording the keystrokes when you close the Customize dialog box.

Customizing Toolbars

It is just as easy to add a macro, style, font, AutoText entry, or other Word command to a toolbar. You then perform the command by clicking on the toolbar button. You assign an item to a toolbar using similar techniques as you learned for key combinations; however, the toolbar that you want to add the button to must be displayed before you begin. If you want to add a button to the Borders toolbar, for example, make certain it is already displayed on the screen.

Let's customize two toolbars. First, add a button to the Formatting toolbar to create a superscript with a click of the mouse. Follow these steps:

1. If the Formatting toolbar is not displayed on your screen, display it now using the Toolbars command from the View menu.

2. Select Customize from the Tools menu and click on the Toolbars tab to display the options shown in Figure 24-4.

3. Select Format in the Categories list to see a series of buttons that perform format functions:

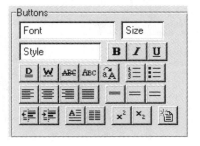

24

4. Click on the Superscript button, and its function will appear in the Description panel.

5. Drag the icon of the Superscript button up to the Formatting toolbar beside the Underline button and release the mouse button.

6. Close the Customize dialog box.

As you can see here, the Superscript button is now part of the Formatting toolbar, so when you want to type a superscript, just click on the button.

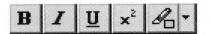

Tip: You can display the Customize dialog box by selecting Customize from the Toolbars dialog box (select Toolbars from the View menu) or from the shortcut menu displayed when you right-click on a toolbar.

You can also add toolbar buttons for macros, styles, AutoText entries, and fonts. However, with these items you can choose to insert a button that contains text or an icon. As an example, let's add a button to run the UpdatesAndPrintsPage macro.

Select Customize from the Tools menu to display the Toolbars options. Scroll to the bottom of the Categories list to display the options Macros, Fonts, AutoText, and Styles. Click on Macros to list your macros, instead of displaying a series of buttons. Drag UpdatesAndPrintsPage next to the Print button in the Standard toolbar. When you release the mouse button, a blank button will appear and Word will display the dialog box shown in Figure 24-5.

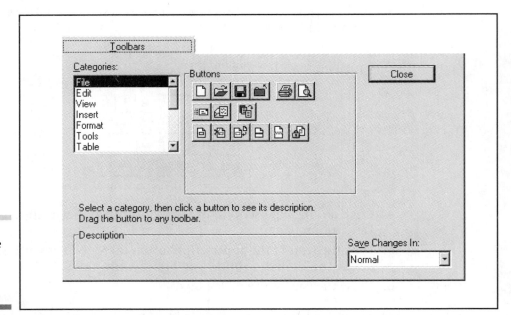

The Toolbars options in the Customize dialog box
Figure 24-4.

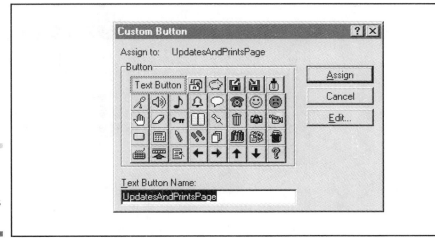

You can create a button that contains text or an icon. To enter text on the face of the button, select Text Button—the default setting—and then enter the text in the Text Button Name box. For now, click on an icon that you think represents the function, then click on Assign and close the Customize dialog box. When you point to the button in the toolbar, the ToolTip will show the name of the macro that it runs.

Editing Icons

If you do not like any of the icons shown, you can create your own or edit one of those suggested by Word. When the Custom Button dialog box is displayed, select Text Button if you want to start with a blank button face, or click on an existing button that you want to modify. Next, click on Edit to display the Button Editor shown in Figure 24-6.

The Picture section is a grid, with each square representing another dot of color—called a pixel—in the icon. The squares with the gray diagonal lines will appear as the gray background around the icon. In the Colors section, select the color of the pixel you want to insert, and then click on the square in the grid. To erase a dot, click on it again when using the same color, or click on Erase and then on the square. To erase the entire icon, click on Clear. Use the arrows in the Move section to shift the entire drawing up, down, left, or right one column or row at a time. The arrows will not move individual pixels. As you draw the icon, a sample of it in its actual size will appear in the Preview pane. When you're done, click on OK and then close the Customize dialog box.

24

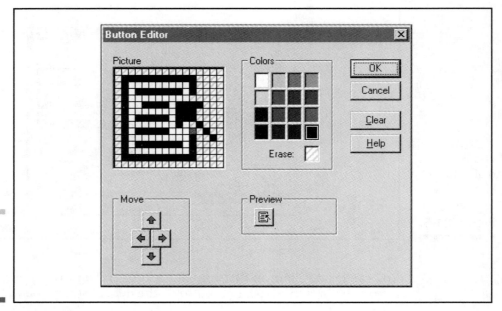

Fine-Tuning Your Toolbars

To delete a button from a toolbar, make certain that the bar is displayed. Point to the button, hold down ALT, and then drag the button into the document window. When you release the mouse, the button will be deleted, and the others will shift over to fill in the empty space. Do that now to delete the buttons that you just added.

To move the button to another toolbar, or to another position on the same toolbar, hold down ALT and drag the button to the new position. Hold down CTRL as well if you want to make a copy of the button.

When the Toolbars page of the Customize dialog box is displayed, you do not have to hold down ALT to delete or move a button. You can also edit a button by pointing to it and clicking the right mouse button to display the shortcut menu shown here.

Copy Button Image
Paste Button Image
Reset Button Image

Choose Button Image...
Edit Button Image...

Select Choose Button Image if you want to select another icon for the button. Select Edit Button Image to display the Button Editor.

Tip: You can use the shortcut menu to copy the icon into your document as a Word picture object. Select Copy Button Image, close the Customize dialog box, and then select Paste from the Standard toolbar to paste the icon.

If you delete a default toolbar function accidentally, select Toolbars from the View menu or from the shortcut menu displayed when you right-click on a toolbar, click on the toolbar you want to restore, select Reset, and then click on OK.

To create an entirely new toolbar, select New from the Toolbars dialog box, type a name for the toolbar, and then select OK.

Customizing a Menu

As an alternative to assigning a key combination or toolbar button, you can add another Word feature, macro, style, font, or AutoText entry to a pull-down menu. You can even create new menus on the menu bar. To customize a menu, click on the Menus tab of the Customize dialog box to see the options shown in Figure 24-7.

24

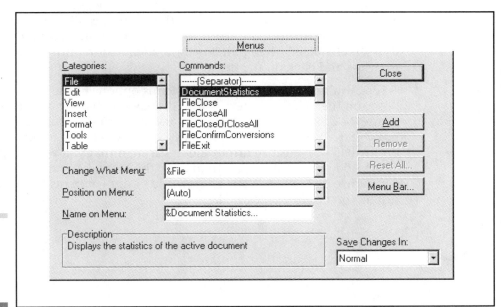

The Menus options in the Customize dialog box
Figure 24-7.

Select the category of the item you want to add to the menu and then the specific item from the list box. Then specify the menu, the position on the menu, and the text:

1. In the Change What Menu list, select the menu you'd like to add the item to.

2. In the Position on Menu list, select a position. The default setting, (Auto), will place the macro at the end of the menu. You can also select At Top, At Bottom, or the existing menu item that you'd like the new item to follow.

3. In the Name on Menu box, type the text that you want to appear on the menu. Enter an ampersand before the letter you want underlined (the hot key), as in **&Print Current Page**.

4. Select Add. (The button will be labelled Add Below if you've selected an existing item in the Position on Menu list that you want the new item to follow.)

Repeat the steps for each item you want to add to the menu, adding the (Separator) item in the Commands list to insert a line separating items. Finally, close the dialog box.

If you select a command or item already in the menu, the Remove button will no longer be dimmed. Click on Remove to delete the item. You can also delete a menu item, however, when the Customize dialog box is not displayed. Press ALT-CTRL-HYPHEN to change the mouse pointer to a large hyphen character. Then pull down the menu containing the item you want to delete and click on the item.

To create a new menu, display the Menus options in the Customize dialog box, and then click on Menu Bar to display the dialog box that you see in Figure 24-8. Type the name for the new menu in the Name on Menu Bar text box. Next, select a position in the list—you can choose to place it first or last on the bar—or select a current menu bar item that you want to precede it. Select Add or Add After, and then close the Menu bar, and then the Customize dialog box. You can now add your own items to the new menu, just as you've already learned.

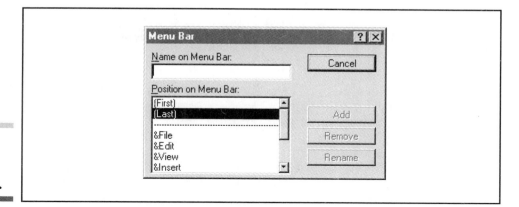

Creating a
new menu
bar item
Figure 24-8.

Tip: To delete an entire menu, display the Menu Bar dialog box, click on the menu name in the Position on Menu Bar list, and click on Remove. Select Reset All to return all of Word's menus to their default values.

24

Index

M

Q

R

S

Z

Your Choice...

This book is available *with* and *without* an interactive CD-ROM tutorial from Personal Training Systems

If your edition of *Microsoft Word for Windows 95 Made Easy* came packaged *with* a CD-ROM, you'll find three interactive tutorials covering:

♦ Beginning Word

♦ Intermediate Word

♦ Advanced Word

♦ Charts and Databases

In addition, you'll receive:

♦ An online quick reference document

♦ An online extra practice document

If you purchased the version *without* the CD-ROM, and you would like to receive it now, please call Personal Training Systems at 1-800-832-2499 (or 415-462-2100 outside the U.S.), Monday through Friday, 7:30-5:30 (Pacific Standard Time) to order a copy. The cost is $10 for the disk, plus $5.95 shipping and handling.

For CD-ROM technical support, call 1-800-832-2499 (or 415-462-2100 outside the U.S.), Monday through Friday, 7:30-5:30 (Pacific Standard Time). If you need help loading your CD-ROM, or if you have questions about how to use the tutorials, Personal Training Systems will be happy to help you.

System Requirements for CD-ROM:

♦ 486 or higher computer, 8 MB RAM (16 recommended)

♦ 640 × 480 Super VGA with 256 colors

♦ Double-speed CD-ROM drive

♦ 8-bit Windows-compatible sound card (16-bit recommended)

♦ 2 MB free hard disk space

♦ Printer

♦ Mouse

♦ Windows 95 software

♦ Word for Windows 95 software

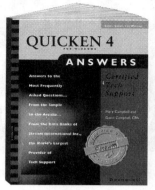
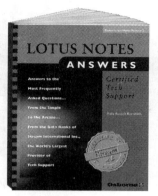

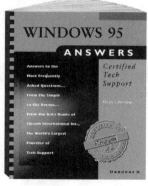

MY TOUGHEST CRITICS RIDE TRICYCLES, PLAY PATTY-CAKE, AND REFUSE TO EAT THEIR PEAS.

Hi, I'm Eric Brown. As executive editor for *NewMedia* magazine, it's my job to evaluate new multimedia technology.

As a parent, it's my job to help my kids discover the joy of learning.

The critics and their mother

That's why I've selected and reviewed the best 100 fun educational titles on the market in my new book **That's Edutainment!**

That's Edutainment! explores the new thinking behind the latest edutainment software and offers tips on building lifelong learning skills. It even includes a CD-ROM packed with try-before-you-buy software and demos.

It's not easy to get applause

from media-savvy kids like Cecilia and Isabela-- not to mention their mom

ISBN: 0-07-882083-9,
400 pages, $29.95, U.S.A.
Includes one CD-ROM

Cynthia--but **That's Edutainment!** has earned the respect from critics who really count.

That's Edutainment! A Parent's Guide to Educational Software is available now at book and computer stores.

Or call toll-free 1-800-822-8158 and use your VISA, American Express, Discover, or MasterCard.

Draw on Our Expertise

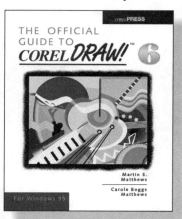